Minority Groups and Judicial Discourse in International Law

International Studies in Human Rights

Volume 102

Minority Groups and Judicial Discourse in International Law

A Comparative Perspective

By

Gaetano Pentassuglia

MARTINUS NIJHOFF PUBLISHERS

LEIDEN • BOSTON
2009

This book is printed on acid-free paper.

Library of Congress Cataloging-in-Publication Data

Pentassuglia, Gaetano.
Minority groups and judicial discourse in international law : a comparative perspective / by Gaetano Pentassuglia.
p. cm. — (International studies in human rights ; v. 102)
Includes bibliographical references and index.
ISBN 978-90-04-17672-0 (hardback : alk. paper)
1. Minorities—Legal status, laws, etc. 2. Discrimination—Law and legislation. 3. International courts. I. Title.

K3242.P455 2009
341.4'853—dc22

2009015086

ISSN 0924-4751
ISBN 978 90 04 176720

PRINTED IN THE NETHERLANDS

For my little Virginia

'Già, è tutto qui: ancora'

(Leonardo Sciascia,
Alfabeto pirandelliano,
Milano 1989, pp. 63–64)

Contents

PART II

Acknowledgments

I am extremely grateful to the University of Liverpool Research Development Fund for awarding me a one year grant (2005–2006) to support the writing of this book. Particular gratitude is due to Tawhida Ahmed for her meticulous research assistance with the vast body of international and domestic cases. I am indebted to many other people for their useful feedback and suggestions over the past five years. I would especially like to thank the participants in international symposia where earlier parts of this work were presented, including the minority rights panel session of the Inaugural Conference of the European Society of International Law (Florence, Italy 13–15 May, 2004), and the Workshop on 'Human Rights and Global Law' at Palermo University, Italy on 3–7 June, 2008. My thanks also go to Bill Bowring for his comments and encouragement in the final stage of this work. The usual disclaimer applies. Once again, I owe an immense debt of gratitude to Sofia, my partner, for helping me organise the text, and above all for supporting this process with so much grace, patience and understanding. I remain grateful to Wilma de Weert, Lindy Melman and Bea Timmer at Martinus Nijhoff Publishers for their impeccable technical assistance.

Gaetano Pentassuglia

Table of Cases

Permanent Court of International Justice (PCIJ)

Denmark v. Norway, Ser. A./B., No. 53, 1933

Interpretation of the Convention Between Greece and Bulgaria Respecting Reciprocal Emigration, Signed at Neuilly-Sur-Seine on November 27th, 1919 (Question of the 'Communities'), Advisory Opinion of 17 January, 1930, Ser. B., No. 17, 1930

Minority Schools in Albania, Advisory Opinion of 23 January, 1935, Ser. A./B., No. 64, 1935

Question Concerning the Acquisition of Polish Nationality, Advisory Opinion of 15 September, 1923, Ser. B., No. 7, 1923

Questions Relating to Settlers of German Origin in Poland, Advisory Opinion of 2 March, 1923, Ser. B., No. 6, 1925

Rights of Minorities in Upper Silesia (Minority Schools), Judgment of 26 April, 1928, Ser. A., No. 15, 1928

Treatment of Polish Nationals and Other Persons of Polish Origin or Speech in the Danzig Territory, Advisory Opinion of 4 February, 1932, Ser. A./B., No. 44, 1933

International Court of Justice (ICJ)

Accordance with International Law of the Unilateral Declaration of Independence by the Provisional Institution of Self-Government of Kosovo, Order of 17 October 2008

Case concerning the Application of the Convention on the Prevention and Punishment of the Crime of Genocide (Bosnia and Herzegovina v. Serbia and Montenegro), Judgment of 26 February 2007

La Grand (Germany v. United States), Reports 2001, 466

Land, Island and Maritime Frontier Dispute (El Salvador/Honduras: Nicaragua intervening), Reports 1992, 351

South West Africa (Second Phase), Reports 1966, 6

Territorial Dispute (Libyan Arab Jamahiriya v. Chad), Reports 1994, 6

Western Sahara, Advisory Opinion, Reports 1975, 12

Human Rights Committee (HRC)

Althammer v. Austria, Comm. No. 998/2001, Views of 8 August 2003

Anni Äärelä and Jouni Näkkäläjärvi v. Finland, Comm. No. 779/97, Views of 24 October 2001, CCPR/C/73/D/779/1997

Antonina Ignatane v. Latvia, Comm. No. 884/1999, Views of 25 July 2001, CCPR/C/72/D/884/1999 (1999)

Apirana Mahuika et al. v. New Zealand, Comm. No. 547/1993, Views of 27 October 2000, U.N. Doc. CCPR/C/70/D/541/1993

Ballantyne et al. v. Canada, Communications Nos. 359/1989, 385/1989, Views of 31 March 1993

Bernard Ominayak, Chief of the Lubicon Lake Band v. Canada, Comm. No. 167/1984, Views of 26 March 1990, (1990) II Annual Report 1

Broeks v. The Netherlands, Comm. 172/1984, Views of 9 April 1987, (1987) Annual Report 139

Coeriel and Aurik v. the Netherlands, Comm. 453/1991, UN Doc E/CN4/Sub.2/AC.5/2006/4

Dante Piandiang and Ors v. The Philippines, Comm. No. 869/1999, Views of 19 October 2000

Dominique Guesdon v. France, Comm. No. 219/1986, Views of 25 July 1990, (1990) II Annual Report 61

George Howard v. Canada, Comm. No. 879/1999, Views of 26 July 2005, CCPR/C/84/D/879/1999

Hopu and Bessert v. France, Comm. No. 549/1993, Views of 29 July 1997, (1997) II Annual Report 70

I. Länsman v. Finland, Comm. No. 511/1992, Views of 26 October 1994, (1995) II Annual Report 66

Jarle Jonassen and Members of the Riast/Hylling Reindeer Herding District v. Norway, Comm. No. 942/2000, Views of 25 October 2002, UN Doc. CCPR/C/76/D/942/2000 (2000)

J. G. A. Diergaardt et al. v. Namibia, Comm. No. 760/1997, Views of 25 July 2000, CCPR/C/69/D/760/1996

J. I. Länsman v. Finland, Comm. No. 671/1995, Views of 30 October 1996, (1997) II Annual Report 191

Jouni Länsman, Eino Länsman and the Muotkatunturi Herdsmen's Committee, Comm. No. 1023/2001, Views of 17 March 2005, CCPR/C/83/D/1023/2001

Kitok v. Sweden, Comm. No. 197/1985, Views of 27 July 1988, (1988) Annual Report 221

Marie-Hèlene Gillot et al. v. France, Comm. 932/2000, Views of 15 July 2002, U.N. Doc. CCPR/C/75/D/932/2000 (2000)

Marshall et al. v. Canada, Comm. No. 205/1986, Views of 4 November 1991, (1992) Annual Report 201
Mikmaq Tribal Society v. Canada, Comm. No. 78/1980, Views of 29 July 1984, UN Doc. A/39/40
Sandra Lovelace v. Canada, Comm. No. 24/1977, Views of 30 July 1981, (1981) Annual Report 166; (1983) Annual Report 248
Sergei Malakhovsky and Alexander Pikul v. Belarus, Comm. No. 1207/2003, Views of 26 July 2005, CCPR/C/84/D/1207/2003 (2005)
Singh Bhinder v. Canada, Comm. No. 208/86, Views of 9 November 1989, (1990) Annual Report 50
Sister Immaculate Joseph et al. v. Sri Lanka, Comm. No. 1249/2004, Views of 21 October 2005, CCPR/C/85/D/1249/2004 (2005)
Tadeusz Kleczkowski (Tadeuš Klečkowski) v. Lithuania, Comm. No. 1032/2001, submitted on 3 October 2001
Unn and Ben Leirvåg et al. v. Norway, Comm. No. 1155/2003, Views of 3 November 2004
Waldman v. Canada, Comm. No. 694/1996, Views of 3 November 1999, UN Doc. CCPR/C/67/D/694/1996 (1996)

Committee on the Elimination of Racial Discrimination (CERD)

A. Koptova v. Slovakia, Comm. No. 13/1998, Opinion of 1 November 2000, CERD/ C/57/D/13/1998
L.R. et al. v. Slovak Republic, Comm. No. 31/2003, Opinion of 7 March 2005
The Documentation Advisory Centre on Racial Discrimination v. Denmark, Comm. No. 28/2003, Opinion of 3 December 2002, CERD/C/63/D/28/2003
The Jewish Community of Oslo et al. v. Norway, Comm. No. 30/2003, Opinion of 15 August 2005, CERD/C/67/D/30/2003

European Commission of Human Rights (EurCommHR)

Buckley v. United Kingdom, Report of 11 January 1995, 19 EHRR CD 20
Case Relating to Certain Aspects of the Laws on the Use of Languages in Education in Belgium, Report of 25 June 1965
East African Asians v. United Kingdom, (1973) 3 EHRR
G and E v. Norway, Applications Nos. 9278/81 and 9415/81, DR, vol. 35, 35

European Court of Human Rights (EurCrtHR)

Affaire Sampanis et Autres c. Grèce, Application No. 32526/05, Judgment of 5 June 2008 (final on 5 September 2008)
Ağtas v. Turkey, Application No. 33240/96, Judgment of 2 February 2006
Airey v. Ireland, Application No. 6289/73, 9 October 1979, Series A, No. 32
Anguelova v. Bulgaria, Application No. 38361/97, Judgment of 13 June 2002
Artun and Others v. Turkey, Application No. 33239/96, Judgment of 2 February 2006
Association Ekin v. France, Application No. 39288/98, Judgment of 17 July 2001
Bekos and Koutropoulos v. Greece, Application No. 15250/02, Judgment of 13 December 2005
Buckley v. United Kingdom, Judgment of 25 September 1996, Reports 1996–IV
Canea Catholic Church v. Greece, Judgment of 16 December 1997, Reports 1997–VIII
Case of Oršuš and Others v. Croatia, Application No. 15766/03, Judgment of 17 July 2008
Case of Oršuš and Others v. Croatia, Application No. 15766/03, Request for Referral to the Grand Chamber on Behalf of the Applicants, 13 October 2008
Case Relating to Certain Aspects of the Laws on the Use of Languages in Education in Belgium, Judgment of 23 July 1968, Series A, No. 6
Chapman v. United Kingdom, Application No. 27238/95, Judgment of 18 January 2001
Connors v. the United Kingdom, Application No. 66746/01, Judgment of 27 May 2004
Cyprus v. Turkey, Application No. 25781/94, Judgment of 10 May 2001
DH and others v. The Czech Republic, Application No. 57325/00, Judgment of 7 February 2006 [C] and Judgment of 13 November 2007 [GC]
Dicle for the Democratic Party (DEP) v. Turkey, Application No. 25141/94, Judgment of 10 December 2002
Doğan and others v. Turkey, Applications Nos. 8803–8811/02, 8813/02 and 8815–8819/02, Judgment of 29 June 2004
Dudgeon v. UK, (1982) 4 EHRR 149
East African Asians v. United Kingdom, (1973) 3 EHRR
E.K. v. Turkey, Application No. 28496/95, Judgment of 7 February 2002
Evans v. UK, (2006) 43 EHRR 41
Freedom and Democracy Party (ÖZDEP) v. Turkey, Judgment of 8 December 1999, Reports 1999–VIII
Gorzelik and others v. Poland, Application No. 44158/9820, Judgment of 20 December 2001 [C] and Judgment of 17 February 2004 [GC]

Hasan and Chaush v. Bulgaria, Application No. 30985/96, Judgment of 26 October 2000
Hingitaq 53 and others v. Denmark, Application No. 18584/04, Admissibility Decision of 12 January 2006
Hoogendijk v. The Netherlands, Application No. 5864/00, Judgment of 6 January 2005
Hugh Jordan v. UK, Application No. 24746/94, Judgment of 4 May 2001
Loizidou v. Turkey, Application No. 15318/89, Judgment of 18 December 1996
Loizidou v. Turkey (Preliminary Objections) (1995) 20 EHRR 99
Jeļena Grišankova and Oļegs Grišankovs v. Latvia, Application No. 36117/02, Admissibility Decision of 13 February 2003
Jewish Liturgical Ass'n Cha'are Shalom ve Tsedek v. France, Application No. 27417/95, Judgment of 27 June 2000
Johtti Sapmelaccat Ry and others v. Finland, Application No. 42969/98, Admissibility Decision of 18 January 2005
Kelly v. United Kingdom, Application No. 30054/96, Judgment of 4 May 2001
Kuharec alias *Kuhareca v. Latvia*, Application No. 71557/01, Judgment of 7 December 2004
Kuharec alias *Kuhareca v. Latvia*, Application No. 71557/01, Admissibility Decision of 7 December 2004
Leyla Sahin v. Turkey, Application No. 44774/98, Judgment of 10 November 2005
Mamatkulov and Askarov v. Turkey, Applications Nos. 46827/99 and 46951/99, Judgment of 4 February 2005
Masson & Van Zon v. The Netherlands, (1995) 22 EHRR 491
Mathieu-Mohin and Clerfayt v. Belgium, Judgment of 2 March 1987, Series A, No. 113
Mentzen alias *Mencena v. Latvia*, Application No. 71074/01, Judgment of 7 December 2004
Mentzen alias *Mencena v. Latvia*, Application No. 71074/01, Admissibility Decision of 7 December 2004
Metropolitan Church of Bessarabia and others v. Moldova, Application No. 45701/99, Judgment of 13 December 2001
Moldovan v. Romania, (2007) 44 EHRR
Muonio Saami Village v. Sweden, Application No. 28222/95, Judgment of 9 January 2001
Nachova and others v. Bulgaria, Applications Nos. 43577/98 and 43579/98, Judgment of 6 July 2005
Noack v. Germany, Application No. 46346/99, Admissibility Decision of 25 May 2000
Otto-Preminger-Institut v. Austria, Judgment of 20 September 1994, Series A, No. 295

Ouranio Toxo and Others v. Greece, Application No. 74989/01, Judgment of 20 October 2005
Podkolzina v. Latvia, Application No. 46726/99, Judgment of 9 April 2002
Polish Orthodox Autocephalic Church v. Poland, Application No. 31994/03
Refah Partisi (The Welfare Party) and others v. Turkey, Applications Nos. 41340/98, 41342/98, 41343/98 and 41344/98, Judgment of 31 July 2001 [C] and Judgment of 13 February 2003 [GC]
Rolf Gustafsson v. Sweden, Reports 1997–IV
Selmouni v. France, Application No. 25803/94, Judgment of 28 July 1999
Serif v. Greece, Application No. 38178/97, Judgment of 14 December 1999
Sidiropoulos and others v. Greece, Judgment of 10 July 1998, Reports 1998–IV
Slivenko v. Latvia, Application No. 48321/99, Judgment of 9 October 2003
Socialist Party and others v. Turkey, Judgment of 25 May 1998, Reports 1998–III
Stankov and the United Macedonian Association Ilinden v. Bulgaria, Applications Nos. 29221/95 and 292225/95, Judgment of 2 October 2001
The Gypsy Council and others v. the United Kingdom, Application No. 66336/01, Admissibility Decision of 14 May 2002
The Liberal Party, Mrs R. and Mr P. v. United Kingdom, Application No. 8765/79, 21 DR 211
The United Macedonian Organisation Ilinden and others v. Bulgaria, Application No. 59491/00, Judgment of 16 February 2006
Thlimmenos v. Greece, Application No. 34369/97, Judgment of 6 April 2000
Timishev v. Russia, Applications Nos. 55762/00 and 55974/00, Judgment of 13 December 2005
United Communist Party of Turkey and others v. Turkey, Judgment of 30 January 1998, Reports 1998–I
Unsal Ozturk v. Turkey, Application No. 29365/95, Judgment of 4 October 2005
Velikova v. Bulgaria, Application No. 41488/98, Judgment of 18 May 2000
Yazar, Karatas, Aksoy and the People's Labour Party (HEP) v. Turkey, Applications Nos. 22723/93, 22734/93 and 22725/93, Judgment of 9 April 2002
Young, James and Webster v. United Kingdom, Judgment of 13 August 1981, Series A, No. 44
Ždanoka v. Latvia, Application No. 58278/00, (2007) 45 EHRR 17

European Court of Justice (ECJ)

Bilka-Kaufhaus GmbH v. Karin Weber von Hartz, Case 170/84, [1986] ECR 1607
Carlos Garcia Avello v. Belgium, Case 148/02, Judgment of 2 October 2003, [2003] ECR I-11613
Centrum voor gelijkheid van kansen en voor racismebestrijding v. Firma Feryn NV, Case C-54/07, 10.07.08

Criminal Proceedings against Otto Bickel and Ulrich Franz, Case 274/96 [1998] ECR I-7637

Criminal Proceedings against Robert Heinrich Maria Mutsch, Case 137/84 [1985] ECR 2681

Enderby v. Frenchay Health Authority, Case C-127/92 [1993] ECR I-5535

Groener v. Minister for Education, Case 379/87 [1989] ECR 3967

Gruber v. Silhouette International Schmied GmbH & Co KG, Case C-249/97 [1999] ECR I-5295

Korkmaz v. Commission, Case T-2/40, Order of 30 March 2006

Kurdistan Workers' Party (PKK) and Kurdistan National Congress (KNK) v. Council, Case T 229/02, Order of 15 February 2005

Nolte v. Landesversicherungsanstalt Hannover, Case C-317/93 [1995] ECR I-4625

O'Flynn v. Adjudication Officer, Case C-237/94 [1996] ECR I-2617

Roman Angonese v. Cassa di Risparmio di Bolzano SpA, Case 281/98 [2000] All ER (EC) 577

R v. Secretary of State for Employment, ex parte Seymour-Smith, Case C-167/97 [1999] ECR I-623

Spain v. UK, Case 145/04, Opinion of 6 April 2006

Inter-American Commission of Human Rights (IACommHR)

Garifuna Community of Cayos Cochinos and its members v. Honduras, Report No. 39/07, Petition 1118–03, Admissibility, 24 July 2007

Garifuna Community of 'Triunfo de la Cruz' and its members v. Honduras, Report No. 29/06, Petition 906–03, Admissibility, 14 March, 2006

Guahibo, Case No. 1690 (Colombia)

Kelyenmagategma Indigenous Community of the Enxet People v. Paraguay, Annual Report 2004

Mary and Carrie Dann v. United States, Report No. 75/02, Case 11.1140, December 27, 2002

The Kichwa Peoples of the Sarayaku Community and its Members v. Ecuador, Report No. 64/04, Petition 167/03, Admissibility, October 13, 2004

Maya Indigenous Communities of the Toledo District v. Belize, Report No. 96/03, Case 12.053, October 24, 2003

Petition to the Inter-American Commission on Human Rights Seeking Relief from Violations Resulting from Global Warming Caused by Acts and Omissions of the United States, Submitted by Sheila Watt-Cloutier with the Support of the Inuit Circumpolar Conference, on Behalf of All Inuit of the Arctic Regions of the United States and Canada, 7 December 2005

Report on the situation of human rights of a segment of the Nicaraguan population of Miskito origin, OEA/Ser.L./V.II.62, doc.10 rev.3, 29 November 1983

Yanomami v. Brazil, Resolution No. 12/85, Case No. 7615, March 5, 1985

Inter-American Court of Human Rights (IACrtHR)

Aloeboetoe and others v. Suriname, Judgment of 10 September 1993 (Reparations), Series C No. 15

Bámaca Vèlasquez v. Guatemala, Judgment of 25 November 2000, Series C No. 70

Juridical Condition and Rights of Undocumented Migrants, AO OC-18/03, Series A No. 18

Kankuamo Indigenous Peoples v. Colombia (Provisional measures), Order of 5 July 2004, Series E (2004)

Mayagna (Sumo) Awas Tingni Community v. Nicaragua, Judgment of 31 August 2001, Series C No. 79

Mayagna (Sumo) Awas Tingni Community v. Nicaragua, Monitoring Compliance with Judgment, Order of 7 May 2008

Masacre de Plan de Sánchez v. Guatemala, Judgment of 19 November 2004 (Reparations), Series C No. 116

Moiwana Village v. Suriname, Judgment of 15 June 2005, Series C No. 124

Moiwana Village v. Suriname, Interpretation of the Judgment on the Preliminary Objections, Merits and Reparations, Judgment of 8 February 2006, Series C No. 145

The Right to Information on Consular Assistance within the Framework of the Guarantees of Due Process, AO OC-16/99, Series A No. 16

The Saramaka People v. Suriname, Judgment of 28 November 2007, Series C No. 172

The Saramaka People v. Suriname, Interpretation of the Judgment on Preliminary Objections, Merits, Reparations, and Costs, Judgment of 12 August 2008, Series C No. 185

Sarayaku Indigenous communities v. Ecuador (Provisional measures), Order of 6 July 2004, Series E (2004)

Sawhoyamaxa Indigenous Community v. Paraguay, Judgment of 29 March 2006, Series C No 146

Sawhoyamaxa Indigenous Community v. Paraguay, Monitoring Compliance with Judgment, Order of 2 February 2008

Sawhoyamaxa Indigenous Community v. Paraguay, Monitoring Compliance with Judgment, Order of 8 February 2008

Velásquez Rodríguez v. Honduras, Judgment of 29 July 1988, Series C No. 4

Yakye Axa Indigenous Community v. Paraguay, Judgment of 17 June 2005, Series C No. 125

Yakye Axa Indigenous Community v. Paraguay, Interpretation of the Judgment of Merits, Reparations and Costs, Judgment of 6 February 2006, Series C No. 142

Yakye Axa Indigenous Community v. Paraguay, Monitoring Compliance with Judgment, Order of 8 February 2008
Yatama v. Nicaragua, Judgment of 23 June 2005, Series C No. 127

African Commission on Human and Peoples' Rights (AfrCommHPR)

Advisory Opinion of the African Commission on Human and Peoples' Rights on The United Nations Declaration on the Rights of Indigenous Peoples, May 2007
Anuak Justice Council v. Ethiopia, Comm. 299/2005, 20th activity report
Cemiride (on Behalf of the Endorois Community) v. Kenya, Comm. No. 276/2003
Katangese Peoples' Congress v. Zaire, Comm. No. 75/92 (1995)
Legal Resources Foundation v. Zambia, Comm. No. 211/98 (2001)
Malawi African Association and Others v. Mauritania, Comm. Nos. 54/91, 61/91, 98/93/, 164/97 à 196/97 and 210/98 (2000)
The Social and Economic Rights Action Center for Economic and Social Rights v. Nigeria, Comm. No. 155/96, 2001

International Criminal Tribunal for Rwanda (ICTR)

Kayishema and Ruzindana, (ICTR-95-I-T), Judgment and Sentence, 21 May 1999
Prosecutor v. Akayesu, (ICTR-96-4-T), Judgment, 2 September 1998

International Criminal Tribunal for Yugoslavia (ICTY)

Prosecutor v. Brađanin, Case No. IT-99-36-T, Judgment, 1 September 2004
Prosecutor v. Krstić, Case No. IT-98-33-T, Judgment, 2 August 2001

National Courts

Australia

Gerhardy v. Brown, 159 CLR 70 (1985)
Mabo v. Queensland, No. 2, 175 CLR 1 (1992)
R. v. Murell and Bummaree, Forbes C.J., Supreme Court of New South Wales, 5 February, 1836

Belize

Aurelio Cal et al. v. The Attorney General of Belize and the Minister of Natural Resources and Environment, Claims Nos. 171 and 172 of 2007, Judgment of 18 October 2007

Bosnia and Herzegovina

Case 5/98, *Constitutional Court of Bosnia and Herzegovina*, Partial Decision of 1 July 2000

Bulgaria

The Status of the Movement of Rights and Freedom (MRF), Constitutional Court of Bulgaria, Decision of 22 April, 1992

Canada

Arsenault-Cameron v. Prince Edward Island & Ors, [2000] S.C.R. 3
Andrews v. Law Society of British Columbia, [1989] S.C.R. 143
Canada AG v. Lavell, [1974] S.C.R. 1349
Delgamuukw v. British Columbia, [1997] S.C.R. 1010
Ford v. Quèbec, [1988] S.C.R. 712
Haida Nation v. British Columbia (Minister of Forests), [2004] SCC 73
Mikisew Cree First Nation v. Canada, [2005] S.C.R. 388
Multani v. Commission scolaire Marguerite-Bourgeoys, [2006] SCC 6
Reference Re Secession of Quebec, [1998] S.C.R. 2
R v. Bernard, [2005] S.C.R. 220
R. v. Drybones, [1970] S.C.R. 282
R v. Gray, [2006] S.C.R. 686
R v. Marshall, [2005] S.C.R. 220
R v. Sappier, [2006] S.C.R. 686
R. v. Sparrow, [1990] S.C.R. 1075
R. v. Van der Peet, [1996] S.C.R. 507
Taku River Tlingit First Nation v. British Columbia (Project Assessment Director), [2004] SCC 74

Germany

BVerfG, Judgment of the Maastricht Treaty of October 12, 1993
Ludin, 2 BVerfG 1436/02, Judgment of September 24, 2003

Hong Kong

Lau Wong Fat v. Attorney General, [1997] HKCA 199

India

A.M. Patroni v. E.C. Kesavan, A.I.R. 1965 Kerala
Consumer Education & Research Centre v. Union of India, A.I.R. 1995 S.C. 922
Danial Latifi and Anr v. Union of India, A.I.R. 2001 S.C. 3958, Judgment of 28 September 2001
Madhu Kishwar and ors v. State of Bihar and ors, 1991 (2) SCALE 148 [794]
Mohammed Ahmed Khan v. Shah Bano Begum, A.I.R. 1985 945, Judgment of 23 April 1985
Mohini Jain v. Karnataka, A.I.R. 1993 S.C. 2178
Narmada Bachao Andolan v. Union of India, [2000] 10 S.C.C. 664
Olga Tellis v. Bombay Municipal Corporation, [1985] 3 S.C.C. 545
S.P. Gupta v. Union of India, A.I.R. 1982 S.C. 149

Ireland

Connors v. Molly Heffernan's Public House, DEC-S/2001/003, 1 June 2001
O'Brien v. Killarney Ryan Hotel, DEC-S/2001/008, 20 August 2001

Japan

Kayano et al. v. Hokkaido Expropriation Committee, Judgment of the Sapporo District Court, Civil Division No. 3, 27 March 1997, in (1999) 38 ILM 397

Malaysia

Adong Kuwait v. Kerajaan Negeri Johor, [1997] 1 MLJ 418
Sagong Tasi and Ors v. Negeri Kerajaan Selangor and Ors, [2002] 2 CLJ 543
T.M.A. Pai Foundation and ors v. State of Karnataka and ors, WP (Civil) No. 317/1993 (31 Oct. 2002)

New Zealand

King-Ansell v. Police, [1979] 2 N.Z.L.R. 531

Romania

Dec. No. 114 of 20 July 1999, Constitutional Court of Romania

South Africa

Alexkor Ltd and the Government of South Africa v. The Richtersveld Community and Others, CCT 19/03 (2003), Judgment of 14 October 2003
Government of South Africa v. Grootboom, (11) BCLR 1169
Khosa v. Minister of Social Development, 2006 (4) SA 505 (CC)

Minister of Health v. Treatment Action Campaign, (2) 2002 (5) SA 721 (CC)
Nonkululeko Letta Bhe, the Women's Legal Centre Trust et al. v. Magistrate Khayelitsha, the President of the Republic of South Africa, the Minister for Justice and Constitutional Development et al., CCT 49/03; *Charlotte Shibi v. Mantabeni Freddy Sithole, the Minister for Justice and Constitutional Development et al.*, CCT 69/03; *South African Human Rights Commission and Women's Legal Centre Trust v. the President of the Republic of South Africa, the Minister for Justice and Constitutional Development et al.*, CCT 50/03, Constitutional Court of South Africa, Judgment of 15 October 2004
Occupiers of 51 Olivia Road v. City of Johannesburg, Case No. CCT 24/07 Interim Order, 30 August 2007.
Soobramoney v. Minister of Health, 1998 (1) SA 176 (CC)
State v. Makwanyane, CCT/3/94, [1995] 1 LRC 269
The Richtersveld Community and Others v. Alexkor Limited and the Government of the Republic of South Africa, Case No. 488/2001, Judgment of 24 March 2003

Tanzania

Ephrahim v. Pastory, (1992) 87 ILR 106

United Kingdom

CRE v. Dutton, [1989] QB 783
Ghaidan v. Godin-Mendoza, [2004] UKHL 30; [2004] 2 A.C. 557
Mandla (Sewa Singh) v. Dowell Lee, [1983] AC 548

United States

Employment Division v. Smith, 494 U.S. 872 (1990)
Lyng v. Northwest Indian Cemetery Protective Association, 485 U.S. 439 (1988)
Morton v. Mancari, 417 U.S. 535 (1974)
Santa Clara Pueblo v. Martinez, 98 U.S. 167 (1978)
United States v. Carolene Products Co., 304 U.S. 144 (1938)
Wisconsin v. Yoder, 406 U.S. 205 (1972)

Zimbabwe

Magaya v. Magaya, [1999] 3 LRC 35

Other Cases

European Community Arbitration Commission, Opinion No. 2, 11 January 1992, (1992) 31 ILM 1497

Island of Palmas Case, Netherlands, USA, 1928, 2 Reports of International Awards 829

Report of Commission of Rapporteurs on the Aaland Islands Question, League of Nations Doc. B7 21/68/106 (1921)

Report of International Commission of Jurists on Legal Aspects of the Aaland Question, League of Nations Official Journal, Spec. Supp., No. 3, 3 (1920)

Chapter 1

Introduction

Whether it's the Iraqi Kurds, the Tutsi of Rwanda, the Bosnian Muslims of Srebrenica, the Ogoni of Nigeria, the Albanians of Kosovo, or the ethnic tribes of western Darfur, the international community has been constantly reminded, in most dramatic ways, of the vital importance to protect minority groups and to react decisively to stop atrocities being committed against them. While patterns of gross human rights violations against such groups do not account for the far more numerous cases that do not reach that threshold, they indirectly amplify the theme of minority protection, bringing to the fore successes and failures of states to respond to their plight by way of effective protective regimes as well as forms of monitoring and enforcement. Indeed, contemporary debates over humanitarian interventionism in conflict situations affecting the very existence of ethno-cultural communities could be said to somewhat echo the international system's deeper oscillations between commitment and disengagement, advances and retreats in relation to the international legal protection of those communities.

There is a tremendous body of literature providing in-depth analysis of the respective international instruments and thus no attempt will be made here to engage in a similar exercise.[1] Suffice it to say that the oscillations in question

---

1 Aside from an extremely wide range of classical works, literature from the past few years has continued to expand: see e.g. L. Rodríguez-Piñero, *Indigenous Peoples, Postcolonialism, and International Law* (Oxford, 2005); J. Gilbert, *Indigenous Peoples' Land Rights under International Law: From Victims to Actors* (Ardsley, 2006); S. Wheatley, *Democracy, Minorities and International Law*, (Cambridge, 2005); A. Xanthaki, *Indigenous Rights and United Nations Standards: Self-Determination, Culture and Land* (Cambridge, 2007); G. Pentassuglia (ed.), 'Reforming the UN Human Rights Machinery: What Does the Future Hold for the Protection of Minorities and Indigenous Peoples?' (2007) 14 *International Journal on Minority and Group Rights*, Special Issue; H. O'Nions, *Minority Rights Protection in International Law: The Roma of Europe* (Ashgate, 2007); M. Weller (ed.), *The Rights of Minorities: A Commentary on the European Framework Convention for the Protection of National Minorities* (Oxford,

can be captured in four movements[2] in past and recent history, which speak to the complexities of minority protection within the human rights canon.

Minority protection: a story in movements

The first movement features minority instruments without an established international framework of human rights. As is widely known, the post-World War I League of Nations system was designed to accommodate nationals who belonged to 'racial, religious or linguistic minorities' living within the newly emerged or enlarged states resulting from the redrawing of boundaries which had been caused by the disintegration of three multinational empires, i.e. Austria-Hungary, Prussia and the Ottoman Empire. The system consisted of special treaty- and declaration-based obligations undertaken by the affected states, whose external 'guarantee' was vested in the League of Nations. The Council of the League was made competent to address cases of actual or potential infractions of minority obligations brought to its attention by council members, while the Permanent Court of International Justice (PCIJ) was empowered to deliver impartial decisions over differences of opinion on questions of law or fact arising out of the relevant regimes. Although they did produce a measure of protection, the League of Nations norms came under attack as they were not intended to be for general application nor did they entitle the groups concerned to initiate proceedings before the Council or to appear before it or other competent bodies for oral hearings.

The exploitation of the 'minority card' by Nazi Germany for the purpose of revising the 1919 Versailles settlement further contributed to the eventual demise of the League of Nations experiment along with the League of Nations itself. More importantly, it set the stage for the post-1945 hostility towards minority guarantees. And so we come to the second movement – one that turns to international human rights as a substitute for minority rights. Whereas the League of Nations system introduced the concept of international minority rights by building, not on an established human rights framework, but on earlier occasional protection for religious minorities,[3] the post-World

2005); F. Lenzerini (ed.), *Reparations for Indigenous Peoples: International and Comparative Perspectives* (Oxford, 2008).

2 We use 'movement' in the sense of 'trend' or 'progress' in the field: *Oxford Advanced Learner's Dictionary of Current English* (Oxford, 2005), p. 999.

3 G. Gilbert, 'Religio-Nationalist Minorities and the Development of Minority Rights Law' (1999) 25 *Review of International Studies*, p. 389 et seq. Significant indicators of the approach of the time include rejection of proposals for equality clauses to be included in the Covenant of the League of Nations and, outside this system, a rather timid concern for 'indigenous

War II scene did establish such framework, yet it viewed it as an antidote to the perceived flaws and political inconvenience of the post-War minority arrangements.

In other words, the universal human rights that were affirmed in the United Nations Charter, and spelled out in the Universal Declaration of Human Rights, as well as main regional instruments in Europe and the Americas, were regarded as instrumental in, *inter alia*, disallowing minority identity claims and their concomitant collective dimension. The human rights approach of the time was meant to remove 'ethnic particularism'[4] from the code of rights available to everyone. The effects of this identity-blind notion of human rights were never entirely consequential, though. For one thing, at a time when the West objected to recommendations for generalising the legally binding regime on minorities of the 1920s, it was precisely the West that came to offer most of the 'best practices' on how effectively to protect minorities domestically, in (at least implied) connection with notions of democracy and human rights.[5] On the other hand, the authoritarian regimes of the Cold War East, such as Hungary and the Soviet Union, resisted the Western approach to international human rights by putting forward proposals for international minority standards as early as during the Paris Peace Conference of 1946 and the drafting of the Universal Declaration of Human Rights.[6] This might perhaps indicate that one can paradoxically have a democratic state grudgingly concede on substance rather than principles and an undemocratic state pro-actively concede on principles rather than actual protection.

What is clear is that, the second movement was never complete, caught as it was between universalistic ideals and the pressing need to attend to group issues on the ground. It is no coincidence that, as the newly founded United Nations proclaimed its individualistic faith in respect for human rights and fundamental freedoms for all, states showed resolve to learn from the terrible collective experience of the Holocaust by adopting the Genocide Convention in 1948. This step arguably contributed to opening up a much wider discursive space about minority groups and rights in general. If the first movement had exposed minority rights without international human rights, and the second movement had called for human rights without minority rights, the third

---

workers' in the context of colonialism: G. Pentassuglia, *Minorities in International Law: An Introductory Study* (Strasbourg, 2002), pp. 84–85; L. Rodríguez-Piñero, *Indigenous Peoples, supra* note 1, chapter 1.

4 I. Claude, *National Minorities: An International Problem* (Harvard, 1955), p. 211.

5 W. Kymlicka, *Multicultural Odysseys: Navigating the New International Politics of Diversity* (Oxford, 2007).

6 This legacy arguably continued with Yugoslavia's proposal for a UN minority declaration in the late 1970s.

movement was to be defined precisely by minority related standard-setting as a way of integrating minority provisions into the international framework of human rights, beyond cases of gross abuse.

In actual fact, the minority question has been on the United Nations agenda since its very inception. The story has been told many times and is very well documented. Although neither the UN Charter nor the Universal Declaration of Human Rights contains provisions on minority groups, both of them do refer to the principle of non-discrimination. The Sub-Commission which was established in 1946 as a subsidiary body to the Commission on Human Rights did include 'protection of minorities' alongside 'prevention of discrimination' in its title. General Assembly resolution 217 A (III), which was passed together with the resolution containing the Universal Declaration, referred the question to the Economic and Social Council (ECOSOC) for a thorough study of the problems of minority groups to be produced by the Sub-Commission. The latter's work during the 1950s and 1960s proved pivotal to the drafting of the would-be Article 27 of the International Covenant on Civil and Political Rights (ICCPR) in 1966. A minority rights provision finally made it into the most classical general human rights treaty ever adopted, recognising the right of persons belonging to 'ethnic, religious or linguistic minorities' to enjoy their own culture, to profess and practice their own religion, or to use their own language. Considerable progress was of course made with the end of the Cold War. Partly (though by no means exclusively) as a result of new minority related disputes that emerged in Central and Eastern Europe, the General Assembly adopted a Declaration on the Rights of Persons Belonging to National or Ethnic, Religious and Linguistic Minorities (UNDM) in 1992, further expanding the scope of the UN protection of minority rights. Unsurprisingly, UN standards were then reinforced by a plethora of instruments at the European level, including the 1995 Council of Europe's Framework Convention for the Protection of National Minorities.

Parallel to this, the protection of indigenous communities has progressively brought to the fore specific questions pertaining to the treatment of their distinctive identity. As early as 1957, the International Labour Organisation (ILO) adopted Convention 107 on Indigenous and Tribal Populations, to which not only Latin American countries, but also a number of African and Asian countries adhered. But it was in fact in the 1970s that the situation of indigenous groups gained momentum at the international level, as a result of a comprehensive study on the problem of discrimination against 'indigenous populations' prepared by the then UN Special Rapporteur Martinez Cobo. This extremely well-documented report established itself as a powerful source of information on the plight of those groups and inspired subsequent developments in this context. The process culminated in the adoption in 1989 of ILO Convention 169 Concerning Indigenous and Tribal Peoples in Independent

Countries. By thoroughly revising the largely assimilationist orientation of Convention 107, the 1989 treaty came to embrace greater protection for indigenous values and systems. The United Nations work on indigenous issues has been relentless over the years, principally marked by the activities of a Working Group on Indigenous Populations, two 'international decades for indigenous peoples' (1995–2004; 2005–2015), and tremendous pressure from indigenous groups themselves. In 1997, a Draft Declaration on the Rights of Indigenous Peoples was adopted within the Inter-American system. More importantly, a Declaration on the Rights of Indigenous Peoples (UNDIP) was passed by the UN General Assembly in 2007, setting out a general framework for protection as part and parcel of the human rights canon.

The third movement, just as the previous two, has not gone unchallenged. The developments that have occurred over the past several decades – as important as they certainly are – have always gone hand-in-hand with opposition, from at least sectors of the international community, to either robust minority rights regimes or the very notion of minority rights.[7] There are at least two ways of looking at this process. One is to expose the reluctance by states to uphold standards that can meet the core of minority demands and thus provide advanced forms of protection under positive international law. With the exception of standards focused on indigenous communities, the strictly individualistic approach underpinning minority provisions, coupled with the notable lack of direct entitlements to territorial or non-territorial autonomy or solid language and education rights,[8] raise questions over the nature and effectiveness of the connection between minority rights and international human rights regimes. The minimum standards set forth in the UNDM cannot per se yield any legally binding obligations, and proposals for building upon that text to draft a universal treaty on minority rights have not been followed through so far.[9] Even when advanced forms of protection are adopted, they are typically met with varying degrees of criticism, leaving their ramifications partly unclear. While the assimilationist ILO Convention 107 was accepted by some countries in Africa and Asia, no state in these continents (i.e. aside from Latin America) has ratified ILO Convention 189 so far (the only exception at present being Nepal). The Working Group on Indigenous Populations was set-up within the UN Sub-Commission in 1982. More than

[7] The French and Turkish refusal to recognise the existence of minorities within their borders has become textbook examples of this most extreme form of hostility.

[8] G. Pentassuglia, *Minorities in International Law, supra* note 3; P. Thornberry, *International Law and The Rights of Minorities* (Oxford, 1991).

[9] The (then) Sub-Commission on the Promotion and Protection of Human Rights issued recommendations to that effect: e.g. UN Docs 2000/16, para. 9; 2001/19, para. 7; see also UN Doc. E/CN.4/2002/91/Add.1.

ten years later, a Draft Declaration on the Rights of Indigenous Peoples was produced. But, it was not until June of 2006 that the Human Rights Council – which has now replaced the Commission on Human Rights – approved the Declaration and passed it on to the General Assembly for adoption. The United States, New Zealand, Australia and Canada voted against the 2007 text, and another eleven countries abstained.

The other way of appreciating tensions within the third movement is to highlight the scope of the supervisory procedures that have been established under minority instruments, or are associated with them. Here two aspects stand out. First, none of the comprehensive minority rights instruments that have been adopted as from the late 1980s makes provision for a judicial body to monitor its implementation. Attempts to make minority rights the subject of jurisprudential analysis under specialised instruments have fallen on deaf ears, notably in Europe. The most classical example of this is the refusal to endorse a proposal from the Council of Europe's Parliamentary Assembly in 1993 to adopt a protocol on minority rights to the European Court of Human Rights (EurCrtHR), or even to allow the EurCrHR to deliver advisory opinions on matters relating to the Framework Convention for the Protection of National Minorities.[10] Second, a variety of monitoring structures have been set up, yet the terms of their mandate are generally weak or vaguely worded. Most of these structures constituted a response to security and human rights concerns in the 1980s and 1990s. The relative easing of tensions and emergencies generated by the collapse of the Soviet Union and Yugoslavia as well as ethnic conflicts in other parts of the world, has not only provided an opportunity for re-considering the impact of these mandates, it has also re-created, at least in part, long-standing idiosyncrasies towards the minority question as a whole.

The UN debate

The UN framework has been typically at the centre of debates over monitoring and implementation of specific minority provisions. In addition to the Working Group on Indigenous Populations, the Sub-Commission established a Working Group on Minorities in 1995. Both of them undoubtedly secured a channel for groups' representatives to voice their grievances and to bring them to the attention of their own governments, and made a contribution to the monitoring and development of standards, the most evident example of which was the adoption by the WGIP of the Draft Declaration on the Rights of Indigenous Peoples in 1993. Nevertheless, neither working group could hear

10 Council of Europe Parliamentary Assembly Recommendation 1492 (2001), para. 12(x).

individual complaints, nor could they act as an early warning mechanism, let alone rapidly react to crisis situations. In an external review of the first ten years of WGM work undertaken in 2004, it was noted that the ad hoc nature of WGM proceedings and the fact that the WGM could not decide or make recommendations on individual cases or disputes had made it difficult for it to generate a sustained focus on both standard-interpretation, particularly in terms of their implementation at the domestic level, and constructive dialogue between minority groups and governments.[11] No such review was ever conducted of the WGIP's work but questions started to be raised in the late 1990s over its continuing effectiveness.

The UN response to this increasing sense of malaise was the creation of a new set of structures. In 2000, a Permanent Forum on Indigenous Issues (PFII) was established as a subsidiary body to the ECOSOC. In 2001, a Special Rapporteur on the Situation of Human Rights and Fundamental Freedoms of Indigenous People (SRIP) was appointed by the Commission. In 2005, an Independent Expert on Minority Issues (IEMI) was appointed by the High Commissioner for Human Rights at the request of the Commission. Like their predecessors, though, these mechanisms reveal structural limitations from a legal or security perspective. The IEMI does not act – contrary to earlier suggestions – as a special representative of the Secretary-General, but her mandate contains little detail on specific activities. The SRIP is allowed *inter alia* to receive communications from indigenous organisations, other NGOs or UN procedures regarding alleged violations of the human rights of indigenous groups, and may even respond through 'allegation letters' or 'urgent appeals', yet the outcome of this process does not involve any decisions or substantive conclusions on individual cases nor is it linked to any early warning procedure. The PFII does not have a specific human rights mandate, though its general remit makes it arguably the most comprehensive body dealing with the situation of indigenous communities within the United Nations system. In the final analysis, these structures pursue fundamentally promotional objectives on the basis of research analyses and thematic recommendations rather than finding legal obligations in relation to a particular group or a particular country.

The recent reform of the UN human rights machinery has provided an additional dimension to this process. Under General Assembly Resolution 60/251, the Human Rights Council had been tasked with reviewing all mandates, mechanisms, functions and responsibilities of the Commission on Human Rights. At the end of the review process, the Council was required to

[11] T. Hadden, 'The Role of the Working Group on Minorities', 26 January 2004, UN Doc. E/CN.4/Sub.2/AC.5/2004/WP.3.

establish a system of universal periodic review, and to 'maintain a system of special procedures, expert advice and a complaint procedure'. The potential implications for the minority structures were manifold, involving the continuing existence of the WGM and WGIP and the impact of the reform of special procedures on the work of the IEMI and the SRIP. While the latter's mandates have been eventually renewed subject to review at the end of the additional period, the WGM and WGIP have been both replaced by a Forum on Minority Issues (FMI) and an Expert Mechanism on the Rights of Indigenous Peoples (EMRIP), respectively.[12] The move did not come as a surprise. In February 2007, the Secretary-General had submitted to the Council a report containing a review of the performance and effectiveness of the WGM and IEMI.[13] The report noted that the Council was mandated to be a forum for dialogue on thematic issues and therefore recommended that it consider 'how it can maintain and improve existing mechanisms, including a forum on minority issues offering opportunities for the meaningful participation of civil society and a special procedure of the Council'. In March 2007, the SRIP of the time, Mr. Rodolfo Stavenhagen, had presented a report to the Council in which he emphasised the accomplishments of the WGIP and appealed for the incorporation of indigenous human rights issues into a 'new expert body'.[14]

While the actual impact of these new bodies remains to be seen, the terms of their mandates speak volumes of the reluctance of states to endorse forms of supervision that can match the ambitions reflected in UN minority instruments. The FMI will largely operate along the lines of the WGM, with emphasis being placed on thematic contributions and identification of 'best practices' regarding the implementation of the UNDM. Ironically, though, its mandate seems to be, if anything, more rather than less restrictive than that of its predecessor. Whereas the WGM used to meet annually for five working days (further reduced to three working days in 2005), the FMI will meet annually for only two working days. Whereas the WGM delivered its own recommendations as an autonomous structure, the FMI's recommendations will only be part of the IEMI's annual reports to be submitted to the Human Rights Council for consideration. Whereas the WGM was open to minority organisations and other NGOs with or without consultative status with the ECOSOC, the FMI's mandate emphasises admission of those NGOs which have such status and makes access of other NGOs dependent on a measure of consultation with the states concerned. Both the FMI and EMRIP are subsidiary structures to the Human Rights Council. This EMRIP's mandate

[12] HRC Res. 6/15, 2007; HRC Res. 6/36, 2007.

[13] A/HRC/4/109.

[14] A/HRC/4/32, paras. 82–83.

could not have been any clearer on this: the body is only allowed to produce 'studies and research-based advice' in the manner and form requested or approved by the Council; it may not adopt resolutions or decisions.

Much more detail should be added on the contours and operational practice of all these supervisory structures – a discussion which would go far beyond the limited purpose of the present introduction.[15] Enough has been said, though, to give an indication of the kind of tensions that exist within the third movement in terms of bridging the gap between proclaimed principles as part of the international human rights framework and their actualisation within domestic systems.

What is more important to note at this juncture is that, while such tensions are very real, they provide us with an accurate account of neither the role of these mechanisms nor wider developments that are relevant to the legal protection of minority groups. As regards the first aspect, two elements should be noted. In spite of the dilemmas and controversies surrounding the minority rights regime, there seems to be renewed emphasis on minority issues from a political or policy perspective. The 2000 General Assembly Millennium Declaration,[16] the 2004 *Report of the High-level Panel on Threats, Challenges and Change*[17] and the 2005 Outcome Document of the World Summit of Heads of State and Government[18] all recognise protection of minority groups as a major factor for securing social and political stability, accommodating diversity and enhancing democracy and respect for human rights. The adoption of the controversial UN Declaration on the Rights of Indigenous Peoples by the Human Rights Council first, and subsequently by the General Assembly further suggests political resolve of some kind. Remarkably, the 2005 Plan of Action, presented in May 2005 by the High Commissioner for Human Rights as a response to a specific request from the Secretary-General in his report *In Larger Freedom: Towards Development, Security and Human Rights for All*,[19] reaffirms the importance of non-discrimination and the protection of vulnerable groups, and takes the lead in affirming that any meaningful conception of democracy based on human rights standards must safeguard

[15] For a summary of recent activities, see generally A. Eide & R. Letschert, 'Institutional Developments in the United Nations and at the Regional Level', in G. Pentassuglia (ed.), 'Reforming the UN Human Rights Machinery: What Does the Future Hold for the Protection of Minorities and Indigenous Peoples?', *supra* note 1, p. 299 et seq.; G. Pentassuglia, 'International Law and Institutions', in R. Green (ed.), *The State of the World's Minorities 2006* (London, 2006), p. 27 et seq.

[16] General Assembly Resolution 55/2.

[17] A/59/565.

[18] General Assembly Resolution 60/1.

[19] A/59/2005.

'the rights, interests and "voice" of minorities'; 'real democracy is absent'– it is stated – if these rights and other basic freedoms are denied.

Thus, the most veritable mantra ever since the UN started intensifying work on minority groups in the post-Cold War era has been re-stated, namely the need to protect such groups as a fundamental way of responding to human rights and conflict prevention concerns. Against this backdrop, the role of the UN supervisory structures mentioned above – and indeed that of similar mechanisms that have been created over the past several years at the regional, notably European level[20] – should not be solely defined by an assessment of their individual mandates. Aside from their formal (non-judicial or juridical) competencies or internal weaknesses, they have come to represent an essential catalyst for a *global discourse*, involving international organisations, minority representatives, NGOs and academics, about the ramifications of international standards and their impact on domestic systems in terms of human rights and security.

In other words, these structures do not stand in isolation to each other; they should be taken cumulatively as being part of wider networks of state and non-state actors that are committed to the internal diffusion of minority standards. The European supervisory framework offers important examples of 'bottom-up' and 'top-down' pressure affecting governmental power. Not only EU- or Council of Europe-sponsored minority rights conditionality policies but also lower key mechanisms of supervision are making a contribution to somewhat reshaping the relationship between the state and ethno-cultural communities in order to bring out change in policy and legislation.[21] At the United Nations level, the panoply of old and new structures of monitoring, while admittedly less direct and intrusive than some of the European mechanisms, have nevertheless helped 'normalise'[22] minority standards within the human rights framework, crucially in synergy with other UN bodies.[23] They have reinforced the notion that the protection of minority groups is a legitimate concern of the international community.[24]

---

[20] A. Eide & R. Letschert, 'Institutional Developments in the United Nations and at the Regional Level', *supra* note 15, pp. 309–317.

[21] G. Pentassuglia, 'On the Models of Minority Rights Supervision in Europe and How They Affect a Changing Concept of Sovereignty' (2001/2) 1 *European Yearbook of Minority Issues*, p. 29 et seq. at pp. 53–55; at the universal level, some form of conditionality has been applied through international financial institutions: see e.g. World Bank Directive 4.10 (revising earlier Directive 4.20), which makes World Bank loans dependent on respect for indigenous communities' land and way of life.

[22] W. Kymlicka, *Multicultural Odysseys, supra* note 5, p. 42.

[23] G. Pentassuglia (ed.), 'Reforming the UN Human Rights Machinery: What Does the Future Hold for the Protection of Minorities and Indigenous Peoples?', *supra* note 1.

[24] P. Hilpold, 'UN Standard-Setting in the Field of Minority Rights', *ibid.*, p. 181 et seq.

The emerging fourth movement

There is, though, a second, more strictly legal dimension to this discussion. If the third movement marks the era of standard-setting and discursive practice associated with the gradual acknowledgement of minority rights within the post-1945 international human rights framework, a fourth movement seems to be emerging which is relatively insulated from whatever uncertainties or limitations may have been generated by earlier – and still ongoing – international efforts. It consists of a rapidly expanding body of international jurisprudence on minority issues, particularly under general human rights treaties, and its direct or indirect relation to developing case law at the domestic level. While the basic architecture of the third movement remains in place, this bourgeoning fourth movement speaks to the capacity of jurisprudential assessments to address minority claims within the human rights canon. While it assumes the *acquis* of the third movement, it partly transcends it in ways that deepen the understanding of international human rights law relative to minority groups.

The aim of the book is to explore this flourishing movement. Seen retrospectively, international jurisprudence is not new to the field. The PCIJ and – to a lesser extent – the International Court of Justice (ICJ), did engage with questions relating to minority groups and identity claims in what are still regarded as landmark cases in international law.[25] In many ways, that jurisprudence, particularly the PCIJ's, reminded states of the possibility of imbuing (then inchoate) human rights notions with an acute sense of awareness of minority issues – an awareness that was effectively sidelined by contingent political developments in the 1930s and the removal of (ethno-cultural) difference from the sphere of human rights protection recognised after the Second World War, either in principle or through national practices.[26] And yet, we may argue that this legacy has never been completely lost. Not only has it continued to frame discussions of minority groups as part of the gradual renewal in interest in the subject within the third movement, it can be importantly located within

[25] P. De Azcárate, *League of Nations and National Minorities: An Experiment* (New York, 1972); K. Knop, *Diversity and Self-Determination in International Law* (Cambridge, 2002), Chapter 4; A. N. Mandelstam, *La Protection Internationale des Minoritès* (Paris, 1931), Chapter VII, Section IV; S. RS Bedi, *The Development of Human Rights Law by the Judges of the International Court of Justice* (Oxford/Portland Oregon, 2007); T. Koivurova, 'The International Court of Justice and Peoples' (2007) 9 *International Community Law Review*, p. 157 et seq.

[26] H. Arendt, 'The Perplexities of the Rights of Man', in P. Baehr (ed.), *The Portable Hannah Arendt* (London, 2000), p. 31 et seq.

a wider context of contemporary jurisprudential analyses that appear historically to vindicate, at least partially, those earlier attempts. As we will see in the following chapters, from the UN Human Rights Committee (HRC) to the EurCrtHR, from the European Court of Justice (ECJ) to the Inter-American Court of Human Rights (IACrtHR) and the Inter-American Commission of Human Rights (IACommHR), from the Committee on the Elimination of Racial Discrimination (CERD) to the African Commission on Human and People's Rights (AfrCommHPR), from international criminal tribunals to *ad hoc* bodies, international jurisprudence on minority issues shows, in different ways and within different settings, signs of unprecedented rejuvenation.

A number of internal and external factors may help briefly explain why this is the case. The minority question has come under intense scrutiny over the past twenty years or so at the domestic level. Books on multiculturalism and multinationalism keep filling the shelves of university libraries all over the world, providing platforms for discussion within academia and civil society.[27] Heated political debates have raised issues of cultural identity, democratic participation and social cohesion – the 'headscarf question' being only the most recent source of contention.[28] From western to eastern Europe, from Latin America to parts of Africa and Asia, from New Zealand and Australia to Canada and the United States, domestic courts have increasingly engaged with the complexities of minority group issues, and some aspects have inevitably permeated the docket of international bodies.

But there is more to that. International instruments on minority rights – i.e. those which took centre stage during the third movement – are boosting minority communities' and NGOs' confidence in the capacity of judicial discourse to absorb and expound some of the elements underpinning them. Despite the pervasiveness and commendable activism of 'global policy networks',[29] the third movement has left the contours of the international legal protection of minority groups partly unresolved. For one thing, the often elusive language of minority standards still needs to be explained, particularly (though by no means exclusively) in terms of the relationship between soft

27 See e.g. S. Choudhry (ed.), *Constitutional Design for Divided Societies: Integration or Accommodation?* (Oxford, 2008).

28 See the decision of the EurCrtHR in *Leyla Sahin v. Turkey*, Application No. 44774/98, Judgment of 10 November 2005; Dissenting Opinion of Judge Tulkens. For a broader theoretical perspective on diversity and citizenship, see S. Benhabib, *The Rights of Others: Aliens, Residents and Citizens* (Cambridge, 2004).

29 This expression is used by Kofi Annan in United Nations, *We the Peoples: The Role of the United Nations in the 21st Century* (New York, 2000).

law standards and international human rights treaties. At the same time, the demand for more effective legal regimes of protection is leading groups, NGOs and experts to re-consider the minority question within the wider international human rights canon. Large sectors of that canon which have been traditionally unfamiliar with ethno-cultural diversity are, to an ever greater extent, being brought in to articulate basic principles and guarantees pertaining to minority groups. As a result, a distinctive form of *judicial discourse* is fast emerging that appears to be contributing to a relatively more solid 'legalisation' of minority issues, regardless of the treaty or regime in question.

Enhanced assessments of the international legal treatment of minority groups have combined with increased access to international forums generated by post-Cold War dynamics. Europe is a case in point. The steadfast increase in the number of states party to the ECHR resulting from the eastward expansion of the ECHR system, the adoption of general instruments protecting European minorities, and even the adoption of a protocol to the ECHR setting forth a general prohibition of discrimination,[30] seem to be lying behind a growing ECHR case load regarding ethno-cultural communities. As such communities become increasingly vocal before international (and domestic) bodies, the question arises of how these bodies are addressing their concerns, and to what extent their jurisprudential reasoning impinges on their fundamental demands.

As we step outside the area of ethno-cultural diversity, one can hardly miss the (implicit) connection between the said emerging jurisprudence and the ongoing process of 'globalisation of law' driven by a variety of international courts and court-like bodies in fields as diverse as international trade, international law of the sea, international criminal justice, and of course international human rights.[31] The adjudicatory procedure before the Appellate Body of the World Trade Organisation – open to state and non-state actors – is frequently referred to, and quite rightly so, as reflecting a dramatic expansion of the judicial function on the international plane.[32] More importantly, human rights stand at the forefront of this expansion in ways that suggest greater interaction between international and domestic judicial levels. National courts increasingly appeal to one another's case law on human rights matters

[30] Protocol No. 12 to the Convention for the Protection of Human Rights and Fundamental Freedoms, E.T.S. 177, Nov. 4, 2000.

[31] Commentators have gone as far as to call for a World Court of Human Rights: M. Nowak, 'The Need for a World Court of Human Rights' (2007) 7 *Human Rights Law Review*, p. 251 et seq.

[32] B. Zangl, 'The Rule of Law: Internationalization and Privatization: 4. Is There an Emerging International Rule of Law?' (2005) 13 *European Review*, p. 73 et seq.

and frequently resort to international human rights law as the standard against which legislation and governmental action are examined. Established international courts, too, such as the EurCrtHR and the ECJ, often refer to each other's decisions and make use of domestic jurisprudence as a source of authority.[33]

Unsurprisingly, judicial activism in international law is being mainly considered from a systemic point of view. The establishment of new international courts have raised concerns of judicial proliferation and the extent to which they might pose a threat to the unity of international law. The 'unity versus fragmentation' debate is a well-rehearsed one, involving either inquiries into the possibility of divergent interpretations of international norms and the impact of the judicial function on general international law, or procedural views of the extent to which these various courts can and should be co-ordinated.[34] Another major theme is that of judicial cross-citation across international and national lines, as the sign of an inchoate global community of courts that enables communication between different legal orders otherwise constrained or denied by the state's legislative and administrative apparatus.[35]

The systemic approach of course helps better appreciate the greater influence of jurisprudence in the international and comparative legal space by providing strong benchmarks for a general assessment of the evolving scope and nature of the international legal order. While we assume these broader, more structural concerns or dynamics, an analysis of their implications falls clearly beyond the purview of the present inquiry. Rather, the following chapters will attempt to provide an account of the actual role of international jurisprudence in one particular area of human rights protection. The question being posed by this type of investigation is relatively straightforward: What do courts and court-like bodies say when they talk about minority groups? The book discusses the dimensions of judicial discourse as such, regardless of its real or potential repercussions on a systemic level in the above-mentioned sense.

---

[33] C. McCrudden, 'A Common Law of Human Rights? Transnational Judicial Conversations on Constitutional Rights', in K. O'Donovan & G. R. Rubin (eds.), *Human Rights and Legal History: Essays in Honour of Brian Simpson* (Oxford, 2000), p. 29 et seq.; L. R. Helfer & A.-M. Slaughter, 'Toward a Theory of Effective Supranational Adjudication' (1997) 107 *The Yale Law Journal*, p. 273 et seq.; A-M. Slaughter, 'Judicial Globalization' (2000) 40 *Virginia Journal of International Law*, p. 1103 et seq.

[34] B. Conforti, 'The Role of the Judge in International Law' (2007) 1 *European Journal of Legal Studies*, p. 1 et seq.; P.-M. Dupuy, 'The Unity of Application of International Law at the Global Level and the Responsibility of Judges', *ibid.*

[35] A.-M. Slaughter, *A New World Order* (Princeton, 2004), pp. 79–81.

Having in mind geographical areas as diverse as Western and Eastern Europe, Latin America, Africa and Asia, we will assess the arguments that are reflected in that discourse to articulate minority issues and what they tell us about the (judicially-generated) role of international human rights law in addressing ethno-cultural diversity. Despite the quite conspicuous literature on international minority rights, very little scholarly attention has been directed to the general impact of international jurisprudence on minority claims. There are at least three reasons for this. First, the field has been traditionally explored either from the perspective of international diplomacy and political theory[36] or from the standpoint of the specific international *instruments* and *organisations* that are intended to generate protection and monitoring under international law.[37] This is hardly surprising. Most of these works, including most of the present author's earlier writings, document and examine major institutional or standard-setting components of the third movement, particularly in relation to the scope and ramifications of the specialised mechanisms that emerged in the early 1990s, and the dilemmas they still pose. While a measure of jurisprudential analysis generally accompanies this type of assessments, what takes centre stage is the fundamentally institutional dimension of the process associated with the rebirth of minority rights in the post-Cold War era.[38] Second, those (few) works that do attempt to highlight the distinctive role of jurisprudence tend to do so mainly with a view to compiling and classifying the case law rather than discussing judicial discourse per se.[39] Third, where theoretical perspectives are offered on international jurisprudence in relation to minority groups, they usually lack an across-the-board comparative

---

[36] W. Kymlicka, *Multicultural Odysseys, supra* note 5; T. H. Malloy, *National Minority Rights in Europe* (Oxford, 2005).

[37] L. Thio, *Managing Babel: The International Legal Protection of Minorities in the Twentieth Century* (Leiden/Boston, 2005); R. M. Letschert, *The Impact of Minority Rights Mechanisms* (The Hague, 2005); P. Thornberry & M. A. Martin Estébanez, *Minority Rights in Europe: A Review of the Work and Standards of the Council of Europe* (Strasbourg, 2004); A. Verstichel, A. Alen, B. De Witte, & P. Lemmens (eds.), *The Framework Convention for the Protection of National Minorities: a Useful Pan-European Instrument?* (Antwerpen/Groningen/Oxford, 2008).

[38] This is most evident in the context of debates over EU policies regarding minority protection: Toggenburg (ed.), *Minority Protection and the Enlarged European Union: The Way Forward* (Budapest, 2004).

[39] A. Moucheboeuf, *Minority Rights Jurisprudence* (Strasbourg, 2006); B. Bowring, 'European Minority Protection: The Past and Future of a "Major Historical Achievement"' (2008) 15 *International Journal on Minority and Group Rights*, pp. 413–421; Marc Weller (ed.), *Universal Minority Rights: A Commentary on the Jurisprudence of International Courts and Treaty Bodies* (Oxford, 2007).

dimension, as they concentrate on either one particular setting[40] or one particular type of group.[41]

This is obviously not to underestimate the importance of the existing international and comparative law literature that has started to expose the jurisprudential dimension in ways that had not been done before. But, if anything, the tendencies just mentioned give an indication of the need for a general reflection on the international jurisprudence on minority issues. The following chapters attempt to do so in three senses. First, they seek to expose adjudication as a means of advancing the interpretation and application of minority related human rights standards. They engage in a case-based analysis of a range of substantive and procedural matters, spanning from way of life, property, and the implications of the principle of equality, to issues of evidence and standard of proof. A number of crucial questions are directly or indirectly raised: What contribution is international human rights law making to the protection of minority groups through judicial discourse? Or more precisely: What sort of contribution is judicial discourse making to the protection of such groups through universal and regional human rights norms? How does it read the question of ethno-cultural diversity within the scope of its interpretive practice? What are the implications of such discourse for domestic legislation affecting minority groups? Is there some kind of typology of judicial discourse that could be proposed in the context of international human rights affecting ethno-cultural communities? Should adjudication be limited to making sure that the political decision-making process is open to all actors, including minority voices, or should it engage with the substance of minority claims? Are procedural and substantive approaches to adjudication of minority claims necessarily incompatible with one another?

---

[40] A. M. de Zayas, 'The International Judicial Protection of Peoples and Minorities', in C. Brölmann, R. Lefeber & M. Zieck (eds.), *Peoples and Minorities in International Law* (Leiden/Boston, 1993), p. 253 et seq.; J. Ringelheim, *Diversité Culturelle et Droits de l'Homme: L'Émergence de la Problématique des Minorités dans le Droit de la Convention Européenne des Droits de l'Homme* (Bruxelles, 2006); G. Gilbert, 'The Burgeoning Minority Rights Jurisprudence of the European Court of Human Rights' (2002) 24 *Human Rights Quarterly*, p. 736 et seq.; J. Marko (Guest Editor), 'Minority Rights in an Expanding EU' (2003) 25 *Journal of European Integration*, p. 175 et seq.; R. Murray & S. Wheatley, 'Groups and the African Charter on Human and Peoples' Rights' (2003) 25 *Human Rights Quarterly*, p. 213 et seq.

[41] B. Kingsbury, 'Reconciling Five Competing Conceptual Structures of Indigenous Peoples' Claims in International and Comparative Law' (2001) 34 *New York University Journal of International Law and Politics*, p. 189 et seq.; E. Benvenisti, 'National Courts and the International Law on Minority Rights' (1997) 2 *Austrian Review of International and European Law*, p. 1 et seq.; M. Scheinin, 'The Right to Enjoy a Distinct Culture: Indigenous and Competing Uses of Land', in T. S. Orlin, A. Rosas & M. Scheinin (eds.), *The Jurisprudence of Human Rights Law: A Comparative Interpretive Approach* (Turku/Åbo, 2000), p. 159 et seq.

Second, the investigation is comparative in that it does not focus on minority issues as adjudicated by one particular forum, but discusses simultaneously the extent to which a set of similar themes has been addressed by international supervisory bodies. The comparative dimension internal to genuinely international human rights case law will be reinforced by bringing into focus a sample of those national legal systems where minority issues are a subject of substantial litigation and express judicial articulation (e.g. on issues of indigenous property, equality, women's rights), or where socio-economic rights matters are addressed before domestic courts which traditionally mirror debates over the capacity of courts to consider minority claims as part of human (or constitutional) rights protection.

Although this approach to different jurisdictions does not do away with the obvious systemic differences that exist between them, both internationally and domestically, the practical interaction between different levels of international jurisprudence and between different levels of international and domestic judicial practice will to some extent echo aspects of the above-mentioned generalist literature on cross-judicial conversations or cross-citation. As indicated earlier, the following chapters do not discuss the extent or nature of inter-judicial dialogue per se, nor do they engage systematically with the theoretical literature on constitutional review in ways that make minority issues merely incidental to an assessment of processes of global 'judicialization' or supposedly global legal pluralism.[42] More modestly, they assume the fact of a plurality of human rights regimes and look at them by comparing specific lines of jurisprudential reasoning and their implications for minority groups.

This brings us to the third of the three senses mentioned above: while still informed by varying degrees of doctrinal analysis, and aside from the aspects just referred to, the inquiry is mainly concerned with conceptual issues. It does not seek to examine the entire body of jurisprudence, but it does seek to be illustrative of the actual and potential role of judicial discourse in the field. Here again questions are raised and some answers attempted: What broad structures of thinking does judicial discourse imply in terms of protecting minority cultures? To what extent do they facilitate the recognition of minority identity, the (re-)consideration of minority claims, or greater access of those claims to procedural techniques of litigation? How diversified is the judicial approach when it comes to articulating the minority question as a

[42] For a discussion from the perspective of legal pluralism, see e.g. P. S. Barman, 'Global Legal Pluralism', (2007) 80 *Southern California Law Review*, p. 1155 et seq.; F. Viola, 'The Rule of Law in Legal Pluralism', in T. Gizbert-Studnicki & J. Stelmach (eds), *Law and Legal Cultures in the 21st Century: Diversity and Unity* (Warszawa, 2007), p. 105 et seq.

distinctive human rights issue? In short, the next chapters do not provide a systematic review of regimes, instruments or mechanisms regarding minority groups, a full empirical account of matters relating to national compliance with international decisions, let alone a general theory of judicial review under international human rights law. They assume contemporary achievements and failures in the field and concentrate on the emerging fourth movement by exploring the more general, 'preliminary' question of how courts and court-like bodies construe minority issues for purposes of human rights protection.

Saramaka *as an illustration of judicial discourse*

We propose to consider judicial discourse through the prism of four basic jurisprudential dimensions, which will be referred to as recognition, elaboration, mediation, and access to justice. Conceptually, they expose different moments of judicial intervention that revolve around the legal acknowledgment of group existence or identity, the adjustment of human rights norms to accommodate the group's perspectives, the establishment of processes designed to address the complexities resulting from competing claims, and the expansion of procedural avenues within litigation.

The Saramaka People v. Suriname – one of the decisions of the IACrtHR that will be frequently mentioned throughout the book[43] – helps provide a somewhat preliminary and sketchy illustration of some of the aspects involved. It originated from a petition lodged with the IACommHR by representatives of the Saramaka people – an ethno-cultural community living in the Upper Suriname River region. Following on from recommendations made to Suriname by the IACommHR in 2006, the case was subsequently submitted by the latter to the jurisdiction of the IACrtHR. The dispute essentially turned on whether the state had failed both to recognise the right to property of the members of the Saramaka people over the territory that they had traditionally used and occupied, and to allow effective judicial protection of such right, under the American Convention on Human Rights (ACHR).[44] The case provided an opportunity for an articulated account of the position of the Saramakas as a group, and its relation to the ACHR in terms of substantive rights, the procedural management of competing claims, and litigation itself.

---

[43] Judgment of 28 November 2007, Series C No. 172. See also *The Saramaka People v. Suriname, Interpretation of the Judgment on Preliminary Objections, Merits, Reparations, and Costs*, Judgment of 12 August 2008, Series C No. 185.

[44] Articles 3, 21 and 25 in conjunction with Articles 1(1) and 2.

The Saramaka people are amongst the descendents of African slaves who were forcibly taken to Suriname during the colonisation period in the 17th century.[45] While the state disputed whether they could be regarded as a tribal community under international human rights law, the IACrtHR found that they have a distinctive identity associated with their traditional land and must be considered similar, for factual and legal purposes, to indigenous communities despite their not being indigenous to the region.[46] In practice, the IACrtHR relied upon expert evidence to articulate the legal existence of the Saramaka people as a group qualifying for protection within the context of its 'indigenous jurisprudence'. The point was further reinforced by the notion that the existence of individual members of the Saramaka people who live outside the traditional territory and do not follow Saramaka traditions and laws does not affect the distinctiveness of the Saramakas as a group whose members enjoy protection under the ACHR.[47] The IACrtHR also discussed the conceptual ramifications of the right to property under Article 21 ACHR in relation to indigenous (including tribal) communities. For one thing, it construed that right in such as way as to include the natural resources that lie on and within the land; on the other hand, it explained that the natural resources in question are (only) those which are traditionally used by the group and thus essential for their physical and cultural survival.[48] If the dimension of recognition is reflected in the articulation of the group's existence, the dimension of elaboration turns on the re-conceptualisation of the right to property in order to clarify the relationship between indigenous land and natural resources as being instrumental in protecting indigenous integrity. The IACrtHR does so by both firmly locating those resources within the (indigenous) property construct and by elaborating on the extent to which the link between land and resources may generate a view of (indigenous) territory which is protected under 21 ACHR.

There are at least two elements in the decision that underpin the dimension of mediation – the third dimension mentioned earlier. By 'mediation' we mean an attempt to strike a balance between competing claims in ways that

[45] Judgment of 28 November 2007, paras. 78–86.

[46] *Ibid.*, paras. 78–86.

[47] *Ibid.*, para. 164.

[48] *Ibid.*, paras. 120–123. The IACrtHR explained, though, that development activities relating to natural resources that are *not* necessary for the group's survival may be equally limited under Article 21 ACHR to the extent they affect the use of natural resources which *are*, *ibid.*, paras. 125–128. For a somewhat similar reasoning turning on the indirect impact of development activities on indigenous lands and resources, see also the Individual Observation concerning Indigenous and Tribal Peoples Convention, 1989 (No. 169), Guatemala, 2007, para. 5.

preserve the substance of rights while opening up a negotiating space between the group and the state over the details of an emerging regime. In *Saramaka*, the IACrtHR recognised that property rights, including those that accrue to indigenous communities, are not absolute and that restrictions may thus be legitimate even if they come in the form of logging and mining concessions for the exploration and extraction of natural resources that are found on the land. At the same time, the IACrtHR acknowledged the complexities involved in indigenous land claims, particularly in relation to natural resources, and set out the *additional* requirements of effective participation, benefit-sharing and environmental and social impact assessment as preconditions for the state to be able to justify any such restrictions. It is precisely those pre-conditions that permeate the IACrtHR's discourse in an effort to explain the scope of each of them,[49] and their implications for future and existing logging and gold-mining concessions affecting the Saramaka territory. Indeed, these procedural benchmarks add up to a more general procedure developed by the IACrtHR in the event of a real or apparent friction between indigenous communal property and individual private property.[50] The second mediating element turns on the domestic recognition of the juridical personality of the Saramaka people. Faced with a dispute between the state and the Saramaka representatives over who was actually entitled to act on behalf of the community, the IACrtHR pointed to juridical personality, to be established in consultation with the group, as one mechanism that could transcend state-group (and, by implication, inter-communal) controversies over representation by securing rights protection for the benefit of the people as a whole.[51]

This second aspect is in fact related to the fourth dimension of our proposed typology. Juridical personality is not seen as simply an optional measure aimed at improving the relationship between the state and the group, but rather as a 'natural consequence' of the enjoyment of certain rights under the ACHR in a communal manner.[52] From this perspective, recognising juridical personality opens the courtroom's gates to greater and effective group protection in conjunction with the access to justice guarantees in Articles 3 and 25 ACHR.[53] Several other aspects of the decision can be read through the lens of an expansion of opportunities for group representatives to participate in, and benefit from the proceedings. First, the IACrtHR held that the Association of Saramaka Authorities as well as the twelve Saramaka captains who

[49] Particularly on consultation and consent as components of 'effective participation', *ibid.*, paras. 133–137.

[50] *Ibid.*, para. 164.

[51] *Ibid.*, paras. 170–171, 174.

[52] *Ibid.*, para. 172.

[53] *Ibid.*, paras. 174–175.

had petitioned the IACommHR on behalf of the community did not need to obtain prior authorisation from the leader of that community for the petition to be regarded admissible.[54] Second, it importantly recognised *locus standi in iudicio* for the Saramaka alleged victims and their representatives in relation to pleadings, motions and evidence,[55] and based this expansion on a connection between participation in proceedings and access to justice under international human rights law. Third, it understood 'injured party' under Article 63(1) ACHR to include all members of the Saramaka people – though not individually named – as being entitled to 'collective forms of reparations'.[56] Such reparations included a variety of legislative and administrative measures, as well as financial redress, such as funding for social and cultural projects of relevance to the community.[57]

In short, recognising the Saramakas as a community, elaborating on the rights to which they are entitled and how such rights become affected by their position as a group, setting out a framework for managing frictions between Saramaka and non-Saramaka claims, and expanding the avenues available to the Saramakas for making their claims before international and domestic bodies and obtaining redress that duly accounts for the distinctiveness of the group, all capture to varying degrees of intensity core aspects of the four dimensions of recognition, elaboration, mediation, and access to justice that the book will explore. They all speak to the capacity of judicial discourse to address ethno-cultural claims within the human rights canon from different angles, that is, the acknowledgment of group identity, the re-assessment of rights, process rather than result, and access to the judicial space. It goes without saying that while *Saramaka* encompassed central elements of all of the above dimensions, the significance of many other cases may be appreciated in terms of one or more, not all such dimensions.[58] What we aim to achieve is a comparative perspective on a set of themes that conceptually define the content and scope of those jurisprudential assessments.

---

[54] *Ibid.*, paras. 19–24.

[55] *Ibid.*, paras. 25–29. As is known, individuals and groups as such may not petition the IACrtHR.

[56] *Ibid.*, paras. 188–189.

[57] *Ibid.*, paras. 190–202.

[58] Conversely, *Saramaka* does not cover all aspects of those dimensions that are discussed in the book.

A note on terminology and structure

Having shifted the focus from the law-making and institutional developments of the third movement, particularly from the late 1980s onwards, to the specificities of the fourth movement, that is, of a legal discourse construed around emerging multiple dimensions of minority related jurisprudence, it is necessary to clarify our understanding of some of the key terms that have already been used in this introduction, namely 'minority protection', 'minority rights' and 'judicial discourse'.

In the context of the book, we use 'minority protection' (and, by implication, minority 'issues', 'claims' or 'question') as an umbrella term that encompasses a flexible range of matters relating to 'minority groups', i.e. *non-dominant ethno-cultural communities, including indigenous groups*, falling within the scope of either *general human rights treaties* or *specialised instruments.* They may also surface in connection with international or domestic jurisprudence that is not built around specific notions of minority protection but that nevertheless reflects wider narratives and arguments which are of relevance to minority groups. 'Minority rights' (and by implication, minority 'provisions' or 'instruments'), though partly overlapping with this wider notion of minority protection, signifies a separate umbrella category which designates *exclusively* those rights that have been set forth over the years in a limited number of declarations or treaties regarding such groups. While controversies persist over definitional terms and their implications, 'minorities' and 'indigenous peoples' have, admittedly, come to represent distinctive tracks in terms of international legal protection.[59] This book recognises the distinctiveness of these tracks and conforms to traditional terminology in the context of relevant international instruments or jurisprudence, particularly in respect of those additional layers of protection that are specific to indigenous communities. However, it does so in ways that do not affect a wider conceptualisation of indigenous protection as part of 'minority protection' for the purpose of the analysis, which is to discuss overarching themes of (jurisprudential) discourse rather than a particular legal regime.

[59] See e.g. G. Pentassuglia (ed.), 'Reforming the UN Human Rights Machinery: What Does the Future Hold for the Protection of Minorities and Indigenous Peoples?', *supra* note 1, especially the contributions by Peter Hilpold and Jérémie Gilbert; id., *Minorities in International Law, supra* note 3, Chapter III; M. Scheinin, 'What are Indigenous Peoples?', in N. Ghanea & A. Xanthaki (eds.), *Minorities, Peoples and Self-Determination* (Leiden/Boston), p. 3 et seq. On the *sui generis* international legal status of Roma, see e.g. I. Pogány, 'Minority Rights and the Roma of Central and Eastern Europe' (2006) 6 *Human Rights Law Review*, p. 1 et seq.

Moreover, the international legal differences between the minority and indigenous tracks should not distract us from an increasing sense of (partial) overlap between the respective legal standards. For one thing, indigenous communities do qualify, first and foremost, as minorities under traditional international instruments. Indeed, they have constantly used such instruments to frame at least some of their claims, irrespective of any additional measure of protection they are entitled to under the indigenous track. At the same time, the indigenous concept appears to interact with the core notion of 'minority' within the African and Asian settings.[60] As may be inferred from the above clarification, the perspectives offered in the following chapters do not focus on groups other than traditional ethno-cultural ones, including immigrant communities. Whether migrant communities constitute minorities in international law remains highly contentious in Europe, while the basic notion of minority as traditional community has been reaffirmed.[61] General human rights provisions are obviously applicable to all individuals, regardless of group classifications under specialised instruments, and the significance of the following assessment to the interests and needs of immigrant communities very much depends on the issue, instrument or legal setting concerned.

The term 'judicial discourse' requires a brief explanation of what we mean by 'judicial' and 'discourse', respectively. Admittedly, not all of the cases that will be used in the course of this discussion have been decided by international courts or tribunals in a narrow sense. As indicated earlier, those organs which are usually referred to as quasi-judicial bodies, such as the HRC or the IACommHR, are an important part of the jurisprudential debate that follows. It is commonly accepted that such bodies – while they are not, strictly speaking, judicial organs – have come to perform functions that are of a fundamentally judicial nature.[62] It is thus entirely appropriate to regard the minority related

60 See e.g. W. Kymlicka, *Multicultural Odysseys*, *supra* note 5, pp. 266–291.

61 See e.g. A. von Bogdandy, 'The European Union as Situation, Executive, and Promoter of the International Law of Cultural Diversity' (2008) 19 *European Journal of International Law*, p. 246. For a clear distinction between traditional groups and immigrant communities, see also Resolution P6_TA(2005)0228 on 'Protection of minorities and anti-discrimination policies in an enlarged Europe' adopted by the European Parliament in 2005.

62 A. Amor, 'Le Comité de Droits de l'Homme des Nations-Unies: Aux Confins d'une Juridiction Internationale des Droits l'Homme?', in N. Ando (ed.), *Towards Implementing Universal Human Rights: Festschrift for the Twenty-Fifth Anniversary of the Human Rights Committee* (Leiden/Boston, 2004) p. 53.; H. J. Steiner, 'Individual Claims in a World of Massive Violations: What Role for the Human Rights Committee?', in P. Alston & J. Crawford (eds.), *The Future of UN Human Rights Treaty Monitoring* (Cambridge, 2000); J. M. Pasqualucci, 'The Evolution of International Indigenous Rights in the Inter-American Human Rights System' (2006) 6 *Human Rights Law Review*, p. 281 et seq.; M. Evans & R. Murray, *The African Charter on Human and Peoples' Rights: The System in Practice 1986–2006* (Cambridge, 2008).

jurisprudence of court-like bodies established within particular human rights regimes as having judicial significance. Overall, a selection of leading cases from international, regional and national jurisdictions covers a period from the 1920s to 2008, with a special emphasis on recent decisions. At the same time, the characterisation of this jurisprudence as a discourse mirrors the conceptual line of inquiry mentioned above. Armstrong, Farrell and Lambert write:

> [A]s a discourse, human rights law provides the vocabulary, concepts and terms of debate over the relationship between the state and individuals. In this sense, it does much more than regulate this relationship. It actually constitutes it.... [t]his is very much a debate between states, but non-state actors (especially, human rights international non-governmental organisations...) are also powerful voices in this discourse. Courts and tribunals, at the national, regional and international levels, are equally important agents in interpreting and applying (and thereby also 're-reading') legal norms of human rights.[63]

Whatever one's view of a constructivist approach to international law in general, and international human rights law in particular,[64] there can be little doubt that human rights debates help expound principles and policies as an inevitable supplement to the characteristically meagre articulation of standards in treaties and declarations. From this perspective, we understand judicial discourse precisely as one (by no means the only) component of a wider human rights discourse that cuts across global and regional structures and actors. This does not in any way overlook the significance of minority related international jurisprudence in terms of a more traditional assessment of rules and principles of positive international law. Rather, we seek to provide a view of such jurisprudence that accounts for its argumentative value, its capacity to intervene, and partly shape, human rights debates relating to the international legal protection of minority groups.

In Part I, the four proposed dimensions of recognition (Chapter 2), elaboration (Chapter 3), mediation (Chapter 4) and access to justice (Chapter 5) are explored through a wide range of cases from several jurisdictions. Recognition is considered in relation to both international jurisprudence and the specific role of domestic courts. Elaboration signifies an expansive role of jurisprudence in accommodating minority interests and needs within the framework of general international human rights law. Mediation emerges in two main areas of contention – majority-minority relations and inter-minority dissent – with particular reference to the position of minority women. Finally, access

---

[63] D. Armstrong, T. Farrell & H. Lambert, *International Law and International Relations* (Cambridge, 2007), pp. 155–156.

[64] For discussion, *ibid.*, Chapters 3 and 5; C. Reus-Smit (ed.), *The Politics of International Law* (Cambridge, 2004); M. Koskenniemi, *The Gentle Civilizer of Nations: The Rise and Fall of International Law 1870–1960* (Cambridge, 2001), Chapter 6.

to justice is viewed through a number of aspects affecting the availability of litigation to minority groups.

Part II relates the cased-based framework provided by the four dimensions of international jurisprudence concerning minority groups to wider theories of judicial review and legal interpretation in plural societies, as well as normative justifications of international human and minority rights (Chapter 6). Participation-oriented approaches to decision-making processes constrain the role of judicial review. Contemporary models of deliberative democracy reproduce and amplify this claim in the context of cultural or minority disputes. Overall, procedural accounts of judicial review assume that human and minority rights norms can be automatically applied or that any interpretation of those norms must result from solely deliberative (non-judicial) processes. On the other hand, human rights norms are often indeterminate and need to be given substance through contextual considerations. Procedural and substantive elements of minority related international jurisprudence are thus re-assessed in the light of this debate as a way to offer a deeper account of its significance within the international human rights canon. From a different perspective, these same elements feed into a debate over the relationship between classical universalistic notions of international human rights and justice-based arguments underpinning distinctive minority claims.

The book ends with some brief thoughts about the complexities and promise of the fourth movement within the international law framework of minority protection.

Part I

Chapter 2

Recognition

Throughout history, and in ethnic terms, population groups – whatever their specific legal status – have been variably considered for purposes of international and domestic law.[1] Judicial discourse has often attempted to address, with varying degrees of consistency and intensity, a range of issues posed by the existence of ethno-cultural communities in the midst of international and domestic legal complexities.

In this sense, the question of whether and to what extent judicial discourse can make a contribution to the recognition of minority groups in law includes yet partly transcends the long-standing debate about how to define such groups in international law. 'Recognition' will thus be used broadly to signify, not only the judicial acknowledgement of the existence of a minority group on the basis of an implicitly or explicitly assumed set of definitional criteria, but also the valuing of group identity for legal purposes.

At least four aspects of recognition so understood can be identified, and will be discussed in this chapter. First, recognition can involve minority groups in the sense of international law whose very existence is either opposed by the government or has been in fact deprived of legal consequences at the domestic level. Second, recognition can affect minority groups which do not entirely fit into existing international law definitions and categories or reflect specific social realities that are even removed from the traditional international law canon. Third, recognition can target, not the group as such, but the structures through which the group can manifest and preserve its identity. Fourth, recognition may occur on a purely domestic level, and may or may not be based on international law parameters.

---

1 See e.g. I. Brownlie, 'The Rights of Peoples in Modern International Law', in J. Crawford (ed.), *The Rights of Peoples* (Oxford, 1988), p. 1 et seq.; N. Berman, 'The International Law of Nationalism: Group Identity and Legal History', in D. Wippman (ed.), *International Law and Ethnic Conflict* (Ithaca/London, 1998), p. 25 et seq.

As the following will show, these multiple aspects, taken separately or together, expose narratives which revolve around minority identity per se, as well as most elementary concerns for physical integrity and non-discrimination.

Spaces of group identity

One important strand of judicial discourse associated with the existence of ethno-cultural groups can be found in the recent jurisprudence of the international criminal tribunals for Rwanda (ICTR) and the former Yugoslavia (ICTY). The reasoning informing the case law suggests three ramifications of a more general discourse about the 'national, ethnical, racial or religious' groups enjoying protection under the Genocide Convention of 1948.

These tribunals' perspectives on the community at issue well illustrate, directly or indirectly, the impact of judicial narratives on the most elementary components of minority protection. In *Prosecutor v. Akayesu*,[2] the ICTR was confronted with the difficulty of characterising the Hutu and Tutsi as being two separate groups for the purposes of that convention, given their broadly similar ethno-cultural peculiarities. While recognising Rwanda's Tutsi as an ethnic group on the basis of local factors, the ICTR also argued more generally that, all 'permanent and stable' groups fell within the protective scope of the Genocide Convention. In effect, it upheld a markedly objective approach to determining the existence and identity of a group, which rejected a narrow understanding of that group as a national, ethnical, racial or religious one. This line has proved problematic in later ICTR decisions, though it appears to have been echoed in the Report of the International Commission of Inquiry on Darfur of January 2005:

> What matters from a legal point of view is the fact that the interpretative expansion of one of the elements of the notion of genocide (the concept of protected group)...is in line with the object and scope of the rules on genocide (to protect from deliberate annihilation essentially stable and permanent human groups, which can be differentiated on one of the grounds contemplated by the Convention and the corresponding customary rules).[3]

All ethno-cultural groups covered by the Genocide Convention are essentially stable and permanent communities, but the question arises as to whether the objective criterion of stability and permanency can make any group qualify for

[2] ICTR-96-4-T, Judgment of 2 September 1998, paras. 428–429.

[3] International Commission of Inquiry in Darfur, Report to the Secretary-General Pursuant to Security Council Resolution 1564 of 18 September 2004, 25 January 2005, para. 501.

protection against genocide under the 1948 regime. A second narrative was upheld by other ICRT Trial Chambers and the ICTY. In *Prosecutor v. Krstić*,[4] the ICTY leaned towards what might be called the minority approach:

> [T]he Genocide Convention does not protect all types of human groups. Its application is confined to national, ethnical, racial or religious groups.
>
> > National, ethnical, racial or religious group are not clearly defined in the Convention or elsewhere. In contrast, the preparatory work on the Convention and the work conducted by international bodies in relation to the protection of minorities show that the concepts of protected groups and national minorities partially overlap and are on occasion synonymous. European instruments on human rights use the term "national minorities"…, while universal instruments more commonly make reference to "ethnic, religious or linguistic minorities"…; the two expressions appear to embrace the same goals…In a study conducted for the Sub-Commission on Prevention of Discrimination and Protection of Minorities in 1979, F. Capotorti commented that "the Sub-Commission on Prevention of Discrimination and Protection of Minorities decided, in 1950, to replace the word 'racial' by the word 'ethnic' in all references to minority groups described by their ethnic origin"…The International Convention on the Elimination of All Forms of Racial Discrimination…defines racial discrimination as "any distinction, exclusion, restriction or preference based on race, colour, descent, or national or ethnic origin"…The preparatory work on the Genocide Convention also reflects that the term "ethnical" was added at a later stage in order to better define the type of groups protected by the Convention and ensure that the term "national" would not be understood as encompassing purely political groups…
>
> The preparatory work of the Convention shows that setting out such a list was designed more to describe a single phenomenon, roughly corresponding to what was recognised, before the second word war, as "national minorities", rather than to refer to several distinct prototypes of human groups. To attempt to differentiate each of the named groups on the basis of scientifically objective criteria would thus be inconsistent with the object and purpose of the Convention.

In essence, *Krstić* exemplifies an understanding of 'national, ethnic, racial or religious' groups which, far from embracing an open-ended notion linked to the requirement of stability and permanency of the community in question, is more strictly defined by the conceptual and legal bounds of minority protection. As a result, the combination of objective and subjective criteria traditionally used to identify 'national minorities' is implicitly assumed to guide the conceptualisation of ethno-cultural groups under the Genocide Convention.

[4] Case No. IT-98-33-T, Judgment, 2 August 2001, paras. 554–556.

A third narrative builds upon the minority approach (objective/subjective) to partly modify the subjective test typically attached to that approach. For example, in *Kayishema and Ruzindana*,[5] the ICTR recognised that an ethnic group in the sense of the Genocide Convention could be identified not only by means of its objective features (common language, culture, etc.) but also on the basis of the group's self-identification or others' perception of the group, including the perpetrators of the crime. The criterion of self-identification has come to gain prominence in relation to minority communities, most notably indigenous ones, though it has been tied up with the establishment of objective links with the group. The criterion of *others'* identification of the group, while suggested in early definitions of 'national minority' has never been part of any genuine understanding of minority groups under international law.[6]

The ICTR's approach is hardly surprising. The Holocaust was committed against what essentially amounted to a 'minority by force' (the Jewish community), not a 'minority by will' (the only target group for purposes of minority protection). This accentuation (and re-assessment) of the subjective test was upheld by the ICTR in *Prosecutor v. Brađanin*,[7] and even the International Commission of Inquiry on Sudan. This latter body argued that, although the tribes that had been the object of attacks and killings (mainly the Fur, Massalit and Zaghawa) did not appear to differentiate themselves from the ethnic group to which persons and militias who had attacked them belonged, they could nevertheless be regarded as separate ethnic groups, because they 'perceive[ed] each other and themselves as constituting distinct groups'.[8] The issue may be raised whether a discursive move from the 'stable and permanent' thesis to a robust subjective test, including perpetrators' and victim's perceptions, can be justified. *Brađanin* upheld the minority approach and the modification of the subjective test to include primarily 'minorities by force'. Yet, the ICTR went on to say that:

> The correct determination of the relevant protected group has to be made on a case-by-case basis, consulting both objective and subjective criteria…This is so because subjective criteria alone may not be sufficient to determine the group

---

5 ICTR-95-I-T, Judgment and Sentence of 21 May 1999, para. 98.

6 CERD General Recommendation VIII (1990), UN A/45/18; G. Pentassuglia, *Minorities in International Law: An Introductory Study* (Strasbourg, 2002), pp. 56–57; J. Gilbert, 'Indigenous Rights in the Making: The United Nations Declaration on the Rights of Indigenous Peoples, in G. Pentassuglia (ed.), 'Reforming the UN Human Rights Machinery: What Does the Future Hold for the Protection of Minorities and Indigenous Peoples?' (2007) 14 *International Journal on Minority and Group Rights*, Special Issue, pp. 216–218.

7 Case No. IT-99-36-T, Judgment of 1 September 2004.

8 International Commission of Inquiry in Darfur, Report to the Secretary-General Pursuant to Security Council Resolution 1564 of 18 September 2004, 25 January 2005, para. 509.

> targeted for destruction and protected by the Genocide Convention, for the reason that the acts identified in subparagraphs (a) to (e) of Article 4(2) must be in fact directed against "members of the group".[9]

Here again, the themes of discourse somewhat echo those underlying the legal identification of minority groups. The perpetrators of genocide may deny that the group is a 'national, ethnical, racial or religious' one; conversely, a purely political group may perceive itself as being precisely that sort of group. The role of judicial discourse becomes then one of recognising the paramount objective of the Genocide Convention while at the same time avoiding the excesses of under- or over-inclusive approaches to determining the existence of a protected group. Physical destruction driven by racist assumptions about the position of a group as a 'national, ethnical, racial or religious' does not lead up to the conclusion that group identities, whether in the context of the Genocide Convention or otherwise, can be reduced to ephemeral perceptions. In the *Case concerning the Application of the Convention on the Prevention and Punishment of the Crime of Genocide (Bosnia and Herzegovina v. Serbia and Montenegro)*,[10] the ICJ made the point that a positive and objective identification of the group is required, as opposed to a purely negative understanding built around the perpetrators' perspectives. At the same time, it did make room for a 'combined subjective-objective approach', in line with international jurisprudence.

In fact, judicial discourse has been implicated in recognising and/or qualifying group identity in multiple ways. The European Union framework provides an example of wider narratives about supranational and national (and sub-national) communities. In *Spain v. UK* brought under Article 227 EC Treaty,[11] the issue was raised of whether people who do not possess the nationality of a member state may be allowed to vote in European Parliament elections. In his Opinion, Advocate General Tizzano argued that the expression 'peoples of the States brought together in the Community' in Articles 189 and 190 EC Treaty embraced a civic, not ethnic, notion of 'people'. He made a distinction between the concept of 'nation' in the sense of 'the totality of individuals linked by the fact of sharing traditions, culture, ethnicity, religion and so on, regardless of whether they belong to the same organised state (and therefore regardless of their status as citizens thereof)'[12] and the concept of 'people' understood as in principle comprising of a 'community of individuals politically organised within a specific territorial area and linked by the legal

[9] Case No. IT-99-36-T, Judgment of 1 September 2004, para. 684.

[10] ICJ, Judgment of 26 February 2007, para. 191.

[11] Case 145/04, Opinion of Advocate General Tizzano, 6 April 2006.

[12] *Ibid.*, para. 79.

bond of citizenship'.[13] He went on to note that the general overlap between 'people' and 'citizens' does not preclude a member state from granting voting rights to non-EU citizens, as long as the extension is kept within the limits and conditions set out by Community law (i.e. reasonableness, proportionality and non-discrimination).

The deeper assumptions of this line are relatively straightforward: EU supra-nationalism is meant to define the European legal space as the reflection of a functional demos, not to champion an exclusionary ethnos defined by the national identity of EU member states. Nations, ethno-cultural minority groups, EU and non-EU citizens alike are all allowed to benefit, to a greater or lesser extent, from the network of rights, prerogatives, and powers generated by the general affinities and decision-making processes which make up the European Union as an institutional framework. This discourse can be usefully contrasted with the sub-text of the widely-known 1993 'Maastricht decision' of the German Federal Constitutional Court.[14] The Court concluded that German ratification of the Maastricht Treaty was compatible with the *Grundgesetz*. Still, it did express more general concerns about the potential undemocratic character of the evolving process of European integration, given the lack of a legitimising European polity or nation essentially understood in the same, ethno-cultural, 'Volkish' sense that they understood the German polity or German national identity.[15]

The Court's line on this particular aspect of the decision can be summarised as follows: i) states derive democratic legitimation from spiritually, socially and politically coherent demoi, and such legitimation needs to be preserved as they adhere to wider inter-state alliances; ii) there is no European demos that can match the national (German) demos defined – as suggested by Joseph Weiler – by 'the conflation of State, Volk/Nation and Citizenship';[16] iii) European integration must therefore be kept under the strict leash of parliamentary control. Whereas Advocate General Tizzano's argument in *Spain v. UK* transcended ethnos, the *Bundesverfassungsgericht's* appeared to (re-)affirm it in ways which in fact do not do justice, not only to the complexities of the EU's democratic deficit, but also to the measure of cultural diversity which is allowed to exist and flourish within German society.[17]

---

[13] *Ibid.*, para. 80.

[14] BVerfG, Judgment of the Maastricht Treaty of October 12, 1993.

[15] The Court similarly spoke of the democratic people (*demos*) as a 'political community of fate' (*ethnos*) in an earlier decision which ruled against a law passed by the assembly of Schleswig-Holstein allowing foreigners to vote in local and district elections, BVerfG, 83, II, Nr. 3, p. 37 (31 October, 1990).

[16] J. H. H. Weiler, 'The State "über alles": Demos, Telos and the German Maastricht Decision' (1995) 6 *The Jean Monnet Working Papers*, p. 1 et seq.

[17] *Ibid.*, p. 14.

More importantly for present purposes, judicial discourse, in this context as in the genocide jurisprudence, stands out as a major (though far from uncontroversial) assessor of national and sub-national group identities and the extent to which they enter the relevant legal space. For example, the debate about multiculturalism and German national identity has been reignited by judicial pronouncements on the issue of wearing the Islamic headscarf in public institutions, such as schools. In the case of *Ludin*,[18] involving the rejection by a state school of a Muslim woman's application for a position as a teacher on the grounds that she would wear the head scarf in the classroom, the Constitutional Court held that the school's rejection was unconstitutional because it infringed on freedom of conscience and the value of religious diversity attached to it. At the same time, it conceded that wearing the head scarf in a public school may pose a 'danger' to social cohesion and pedagogical needs. It has been argued that, the strong defence of religious diversity by the Court was qualified by its implicit acceptance of (the supremacy of) Christian culture as a broad notion informing religious tolerance and non-discrimination, and ultimately German identity itself.[19] This 'jurisprudence of fear', as it has been dubbed,[20] echoes the 'fear of otherness' reflected in the Maastricht decision at the supranational level.

The above-mentioned case law under the Genocide Convention indicates the conceptual challenge that judicial discourse may have to face when determining the situation of certain groups of persons within a particular legal context. In fact, by taking up this interpretative task, that discourse defines the space of group recognition along relatively less conventional lines. In its Advisory Opinion on *Question Concerning the Acquisition of Polish Nationality*,[21] the PCIJ was confronted with the argument made by Poland that, under the Minorities Treaty of 1919, persons of German origin were not *ipso facto* a minority, since acquisition of minority status had been made a function of acquisition of citizenship, and this latter matter was first to be determined under Polish law. The problem with the Polish thesis was clearly (albeit indirectly) captured by the PCJI when referring to what was expected of the newly created or newly enlarged states which were signatories of the Minorities Treaties in general, and the Polish Treaty in particular:

> One of the first problems which presented itself in connection with the protection of the minorities was that of preventing these States from refusing their nationality, on racial, religious or linguistic grounds, to certain categories of persons,

[18] 2 BVerfG 1436/02, Judgment of September 24, 2003.

[19] O. Gerstenberg, 'Germany: Freedom of Conscience in Public Schools' (2005) 3 *International Journal of Constitutional Law*, p. 94 et seq.

[20] *Ibid.*, p. 106.

[21] Advisory Opinion of 15 September, 1923, Ser. B., No. 7, 1923.

> in spite of the link which effectively attached them to the territory allocated to one or other of these States.[22]

Rejecting the Polish contention that the citizenship status of persons of German origin was merely a domestic issue and therefore did not fall within the guarantee of the League of Nations as provided for under the 1919 Treaty, the PCIJ concluded that Article 4 of that treaty did set out a right to Polish nationality to the benefit of persons of non-Polish origin, whose implementation was indeed placed under international supervision. The wider rationale for this argument was that, the 1919 Treaty did not exclusively contemplate minorities of Polish nationals or of inhabitants of Polish territory, thereby enabling the League's protection to cover clauses which only used the latter, broader expression.[23] In essence, this line aimed to prevent Poland from 'depri[ving] the Minorities Treaty of a great part of its value',[24] given the obvious treaty-based link between territory, citizenship and minority status.

In short, the PCIJ sought to identify an interpretive space that allowed consideration (and recognition) of a group whose minority status, far from being unquestioned, had become exposed to the vagaries (and abuse) of domestic law. This elaborate approach was probably not necessary. Lord Finlay, in his concurring opinion, rightly pointed out that, as the majority itself had implied, persons of German origin fell within the scope of Article 4 of the 1919 Treaty. As a result, they were to be regarded as Polish nationals *ipso facto*, constituting the German minority by reference to the whole body of Polish *ressortissants*. He emphasised the distinction made in the treaty between elementary rights such as those of life and liberty which were guaranteed to all inhabitants, and those more specific rights (i.e. minority rights) which were limited to Polish nationals belonging to 'racial, religious or linguistic minorities'. In fact, the PCJI generally upheld this line in *Minority Schools in Albania*,[25] when explaining the aims of the system of minority protection established under the aegis of the League of Nations. In an earlier Advisory Opinion, regarding *Treatment of Polish Nationals and Other Persons of Polish Origin or Speech in the Danzig Territory*,[26] the PCJI employed a more specific terminology that shed light on the logic and limits of the 'all inhabitants approach' resorted to nine years before in *Polish Nationality*:

> It will be seen that so far as the treatment of minorities is concerned, a distinction is drawn in the Treaty [i.e. the 1919 Treaty] between minorities in the broad

[22] *Ibid*., p. 15.
[23] *Ibid*., pp. 16–17.
[24] *Ibid*., p. 17.
[25] Advisory Opinion of 23 January, 1935, Ser. A./B., No. 64, 1935, p. 17.
[26] Advisory Opinion of 4 February, 1932, Ser. A./B., No. 44, 1933, p. 39.

> sense and minorities in the narrow sense. Article 2 refers to "all inhabitants", which also included minorities consisting of non-citizens of the State. This interpretation is in conformity with the practice of the Council and with the Court's Advisory Opinion No. 7 on the question concerning the acquisition of Polish nationality. The members of minorities who are not citizens of the State enjoy protection – guaranteed by the League of Nations – of life and liberty and the free exercise of their religion, while minorities in the narrow sense, that is, minorities the members of which are citizens of the State, enjoy – under the same guarantee – amongst other rights, equality of rights in civil and political matters, and in matters relating to primary instruction.

The 1932 decision broadly confirmed the connection between 'minorities' (in the narrow sense) and minority rights. The link between citizenship and territory, which had been espoused in *Polish Nationality*, and the resulting distinction between general rights and rights accrued to members of specific minority groups, were not regarded to be unreasonable or unjust.[27] In this sense, *Treatment of Polish Nationals* echoes Lord Finlay's points in *Polish Nationality* regarding the core notion of minority and the rights to be related to that notion 'in the immense majority of cases'.[28] At the same time, the 1923 and 1932 advisory opinions taken together, also reveal something of a creative tension in the PCIJ's endeavour to accommodate certain territorially concentrated yet domestically unrecognised groups (persons of German origin in Poland) and foreigners defined by a certain ethnicity or nationality (Polish citizens, whether or not belonging to minorities in Poland, and other persons of Polish origin or speech in the Free City of Danzig), within the remit of specific treaties. Judicial interpretation of such treaties ultimately becomes a vehicle for *sui generis* recognition of minority status (German minority) or acknowledgement of general group related issues that could invite even greater protection by the state (minorities in the wide sense).

While based on the framework established by those treaties, the PCIJ's reading proved essential to exploring the relationship between factual existence and legal relevance (and recognition) of the groups concerned. Its Advisory Opinion on *Interpretation of the Convention Between Greece and Bulgaria Respecting Reciprocal Emigration, Signed at Neuilly-Sur-Seine on November 27th, 1919 (Question of the 'Communities')*[29] – or the *Greco-Bulgarian 'Communities'*

[27] *Ibid.*, p. 40.

[28] *Question Concerning the Acquisition of Polish Nationality*, Advisory Opinion of 15 September, 1923, Ser. B., No. 7, 1923, pp. 25–26. In other words, for Lord Finlay the point was not merely academic – it did have very practical implications, as the question of 'unfair treatment of minorities' was typically bound to arise in relation to identity matters, and could only rarely emerge in the generic form of denial of life and liberty to 'a mass of inhabitants, whether Polish nationals or not'.

[29] Advisory Opinion of 17 January, 1930, Ser. B., No. 17, 1930.

case – illustrates this point further. The PCJI explained that, the convention in question applied only to persons who formed minorities in either Greece or Bulgaria, and was intended to allow 'as wide a measure of reciprocal emigration as possible'[30] in order to stabilise and pacify the region. On the other hand, that convention did not contain a definition of the term 'community' used in some of its provisions. The PCJI noted that '[t]he existence of communities is a question of fact; it is not a question of law'.[31] Despite the insistence on factual existence, though, the communities relevant to the convention were not self-evident, as the very question put to the PCIJ on this issue clearly implied. The PCIJ built upon factual elements to produce legal effects, most notably the recognition of communities:

> By tradition, which plays so important a part in Eastern countries, the "community" is a group of persons living in a given country or locality, having a race, religion, language and traditions of their own and united by this identity of race, religion, language and traditions in a sentiment of solidarity, with a view to preserving their traditions, maintaining their form of worship, ensuring the instruction and upbringing of their children in accordance with the spirit and traditions of their race and rendering mutual assistance to each other.
>
> Nowhere is evidence to be found that the Greco-Bulgarian Convention of November 27th, 1919, regarding emigration intended, by some special stipulation, to depart in any of its provisions and particularly in Article 6, paragraph 2, from this general traditional conception.[32]

Admittedly, the socio-historical approach underlying this traditional conception can also reflect rigid notions of nationalism and the nation-state. In recent years, states like Greece, Bulgaria, Poland or Turkey have denied the existence or authenticity of minority group identities being asserted before the EurCrtHR. They have done so by arguing either that the claims could not be proved on points of history and in fact constituted a threat to the 'real' (i.e. sociologically and historically validated) national identities they embodied[33] or that the legal existence of the group (i.e. the recognition of its identity as a purely legal construct) was incompatible with the constitution as the guarantor of national unity.[34]

---

[30] *Ibid.*, p. 20.

[31] *Ibid.*, p. 22.

[32] *Ibid.*, p. 21.

[33] *Sidiropoulos and Others v. Greece*, Judgment of 10 July 1998, Reports 1998–IV; *Stankov and the United Macedonian Association Ilinden v. Bulgaria*, Applications Nos. 29221/95 and 292225/95, Judgment of 2 October 2001; *Gorzelik and others v. Poland*, Application No. 44158/9820, Judgment of 20 December 2001 [C] and Judgment of 17 February 2004 [GC].

[34] See the several cases involving pro-Kurdish organisations in Turkey, *infra*, Chapter 3.

For its part, the PCJI put that traditional conception (aside from its real or potential nationalist overtones) to the service of a context-sensitive assessment of facts. In other words, by exposing a traditional narrative of 'community', the PCJI did not create the groups as legal artefacts; rather, it made them legally relevant within the context of that treaty:

> The question whether, in deciding on the application of the Convention, a particular community does or does not conform to the conception described above is a question of fact which it rests with the Mixed Commission to consider having regard to all the circumstances.[35]

Here again, interpretation is instrumental in the recognition of group identities, transforming specific social realities into essential benchmarks for legal discourse.

In fact, jurisprudential analysis can produce some form of recognition of identity, not only at the level of treaty law (as in most of the above examples), but also in terms of general international law. In the case of *Western Sahara*, the ICJ was asked to determine if Western Sahara was *terra nullius* at the time of its colonisation by Spain and, if not, what the legal ties between Western Sahara and Morocco and the Mauritanian entity were.[36] Although the opinion was located within the context of self-determination for Western Saharan territory, the ICJ still managed to account for the social complexities arising from that territory. Discussing classical international law – far from precise and clearly in the hands of European colonizers – the ICJ held that Western Sahara was not *terra nullius* because it was 'inhabited by peoples which, if nomadic, were socially and politically organized in tribes and under chiefs competent to represent them'.[37] The recognition of indigenous identity set clear(er) limits to the use of the doctrine of *terra nullius* to justify occupation of territory under international law.

The upholding of a narrow reading of that classical doctrine, allowing occupation of territories which were genuinely uninhabited, opened up a discursive space that established the international legal significance of indigenous tribes in a non-European setting. Judicial recognition of factual existence in *Western Sahara* came in marked contrast with the much earlier indifference to the reality of the Inuit communities of Greenland in *Legal Status of Eastern Greeland* before the PCIJ.[38] In the latter case, the PCIJ was only concerned with

[35] *Interpretation of the Convention Between Greece and Bulgaria Respecting Reciprocal Emigration, Signed at Neuilly-Sur-Seine on November 27th, 1919 (Question of the 'Communities')*, Advisory Opinion of 17 January, 1930, Ser. B., No. 17, 1930, p. 22.

[36] Advisory Opinion, Reports 1975, p. 12.

[37] *Ibid.*, p. 39.

[38] *Denmark v. Norway*, PCJI Ser. A./B., No. 53, 1933.

the degree of 'effective occupation' of that part of Greenland by the disputing parties. It did not consider the status of the native inhabitants. Morocco's thesis in *Western Sahara* was partly grounded on *Eastern Greenland*, in which the Inuit remained excluded from the international legal discourse of sovereignty and *terra nullius*. The ICJ did not uphold Morocco's approach,[39] and even inspired a racial discrimination-based understanding of the *terra nullius* doctrine in *Mabo v. Queensland* before the High Court of Australia.[40]

While referring to the indigenous communities of Western Sahara as 'independent tribes', the ICJ declined, though, to argue that they had sovereignty over the territories in the sense of nineteen-century international law. As a matter of fact, indigenous 'independence' has mostly defined an area of autonomy that is only loosely associated with sovereignty. In *R. v. Murell and Bummaree, Forbes C.J.*,[41] Justice Burton argued that the Australian aborigines 'were entitled to be recognized as free and independent', but were in fact not in a position to be so, because they had no sovereignty. In *Santa Clara Pueblo v. Martinez*,[42] the US Supreme Court, quoting from earlier US jurisprudence, regarded Indian tribes as '"distinct, independent political communities, retaining their original natural rights" in matters of local self-government'.[43] The ICJ in *Western Sahara* did acknowledge that Spain had entered into agreements with the local tribes, but did not elaborate on the international legal status of such agreements. The outer limit of the ICJ approach is arguably to be found in the lack of recognition of the indigenous tribes of Western Sahara as international legal subjects. But the indigenous experience was nevertheless brought into the realm of international law in two fundamental ways. First, the fact of indigenous existence and way of life neutralised the *terra nullius* argument. Second, ties of legal nature were recognised between the indigenous tribes and both Morocco and the Mauritanian entity as a non-state entity of the time.

While Morocco's claim to Western Sahara blended the political notion of state sovereignty with religious bonds and ties of allegiance to the Sultan,

---

39 It should be pointed out that, aside from the question of *terra nullius*, the ICJ effectively refrained from considering the indigenous dimension in the *Territorial Dispute* case (Libyan Arab Jamahiriya v. Chad), Reports 1994, p. 6; and *Land, Island and Maritime Frontier Dispute* (El Salvador/Honduras: Nicaragua intervening), Reports 1992, p. 351. For a critique, see M. Riesman, 'Protecting Indigenous Rights in International Adjudication', (1995) 89 *American Journal of International Law*, p. 350 et seq.

40 No. 2, 175 CLR 1 (1992); see also *Alexkor Ltd and the Government of South Africa v. The Richtersveld Community and Others*, Constitutional Court of South Africa, CCT 19/03 (2003), Judgment of 14 October 2003 [role of indigenous law in establishing indigenous title].

41 Supreme Court of New South Wales, 5 February, 1836.

42 98 U.S. 1670 (1978).

43 *Ibid.*, p. 1675.

Mauritania's was based on the argument that the Mauritanian entity, which included the tribes of Western Sahara, in fact signified a coherent and distinctive community defined by ethno-cultural elements, notably a common language, way of life and religion, which was governed by Saharan law.[44] In short, the claim presented the entity as a configuration 'of tribes, confederations and emirates jointly exercising co-sovereignty over the Shinguitti country',[45] by following in the footsteps of nineteen-century and early twentieth-century claims to national autonomy or self-determination. Interestingly, Spain contested such claim by arguing that the people of Western Sahara had an identity of their own, which was different from that of other neighbouring countries such as Shinguitti.

The ICJ concluded that, the Mauritanian entity did not have international legal personality due to the lack of common institutions that could avail themselves of obligations incumbent upon the entity's constituent tribes, confederations and emirates. As a result, no ties of sovereignty between Western Sahara and the Mauritanian entity could be established. On the other hand, the ICJ did recognise the 'special characteristics of the Saharan region and peoples'[46] and find 'other ties of a legal character'[47] between the Bilad Shinguitti and the tribes of Western Sahara:

> [T]he nomadism of the great majority of the peoples of Western Sahara at the time of its colonization gave rise to certain ties of a legal character between the tribes of the territory and those of neighbouring regions of the Bilad Shinguitti. The migration routes of almost all the nomadic tribes of Western Sahara... crossed what were to become the colonial frontiers and traversed, *inter alia*, substantial areas of what is today the territory of the Islamic Republic of Mauritania. The tribes, in their migration, had grazing pastures, cultivated lands, and wells or water-holes in both territories, and their burial grounds in one or other territory. These basic elements of the nomads' way of life... were in some measure the subject of tribal rights, and their use was in general regulated by customs. Furthermore, the relations between all the tribes of the region in such matters as inter-tribal clashes and the settlement of disputes were also governed by a body of inter-tribal custom. Before the time of Western Sahara's colonization by Spain, those legal ties neither had nor could have any other source than the usages of the tribes themselves or Koranic law. Accordingly, although the Bilad Shinguitti has not been shown to have existed as a legal entity, the nomadic peoples of the Shinguitti country should, in the view of the Court, be considered as having in the relevant period possessed rights, including some rights relating to the lands through which they migrated. These rights... constituted legal ties between the territory of Western Sahara and the "Mauritanian entity", this expression being

[44] Advisory Opinion, ICJ Reports 1975, para. 131.
[45] *Ibid.*, para. 138.
[46] *Ibid.*, para. 148.
[47] *Ibid.*, para. 151.

> taken to denote the various tribes living in the territories of the Bilad Shinguitti which are now comprised within the Islamic Republic of Mauritania. They were ties which knew no frontier between the territories and were vital to the very maintenance of life in the region.[48]

This rather flexible understanding of 'legal ties' was obviously, albeit implicitly, informed by a sense of identity ascribed to a larger community. As Judge Dillard explained in his separate opinion, the legality of those ties were to be understood, not by reference to the post-Reformation Western-oriented idea of obligation owed vertically towards those in power, but by valuing the fact that, 'the tribes criss-crossing the Western Sahara felt themselves to be part of a larger whole, while also claiming rights in the territory focused on the intermittent possession of water-holes, burial grounds and grazing pastures'.[49] In this sense, the ICJ unearthed group identities and made them part of the general international legal discourse, just as the PCIJ embraced a traditional conception of community in the *Greco-Bulgarian 'Communities'* case to make that conception work in the context of a particular treaty. Neither of these courts (certainly not the ICJ, which had been asked to interpret the international law in force at the time of Spanish colonization) could have relied upon any established (or long-established) notions of minority rights. Yet, both of them engaged with ethno-cultural identity to generate international recognition of the minority groups involved as either beneficiaries of protection or legally relevant non-state actors.

Whereas *Western Sahara* identified group identity or way of life mainly in connection with traditional pasture (and other land) rights, the case of *J. G. A. Diergaardt et al. v. Namibia*[50] before the HRC problematised the connection between that identity and the use of lands as the base for the group's economic activities. The complaint involved the Rehoboth Baster Community, a group of some 35,000 people – descendents of indigenous Khoi and Afrikaans settlers – who have been occupying an area of 14,216 square kilometres south of Windhoek (Namibia) since 1872. They had long enjoyed self-government under both German colonial rule and South Africa's mandate for South West Africa, but such autonomy had not been recognised by the government of Namibia following independence. The authors argued that the community had suffered severe encroachments on its rights as a minority group, particularly by way of confiscation of the lands they held in collective property and which constituted the basis of their economic and cultural livelihood. For one thing, the HRC acknowledged that, in the course of history the community

[48] *Ibid.*, para. 152.

[49] *Ibid.*, Separate Opinion of Judge Dillard, p. 126.

[50] Comm. No. 760/1997, Views of 25 July 2000, CCPR/C/69/D/760/1996.

had come to develop its own society, culture, language and economy. At the same time, they rejected the notion that the existence of the community as comprising of mainly cattle raising farmers could justify a cultural claim under Article 27 ICCPR:

> As to the related issue of the use of land, the authors have claimed a violation of article 27 in that a part of the lands traditionally used by members of the Rehoboth community for the grazing of cattle no longer is in the de facto exclusive use of the members of the community. Cattle raising is said to be an essential element in the culture of the community. As the earlier case law by the Committee illustrates, the right of members of a minority to enjoy their culture under article 27 includes protection to a particular way of life associated with the use of land resources through economic activities, such as hunting and fishing, especially in the case of indigenous peoples... However, in the present case the Committee is unable to find that the authors can rely on article 27 to support their claim for exclusive use of the pastoral lands in question. This conclusion is based on the Committee's assessment of the relationship between the authors' way of life and the lands covered by their claims. Although the link of the Rehoboth community to the lands in question dates back some 125 years, it is not the result of a relationship that would have given rise to a distinctive culture. Furthermore, although the Rehoboth community bears distinctive properties as to the historical forms of self-government, the authors have failed to demonstrate how these factors would be based on their way of raising cattle. The Committee therefore finds that there has been no violation of article 27 of the Covenant in the present case.[51]

One may wonder whether the HRC's reading of the land-based claim as being of a fundamentally economic rather than cultural nature[52] was also meant to imply unwillingness to recognise the community as an 'ethnic, religious or linguistic minority' under the ICCPR. Clearly, the insistence by the HRC on the need to establish a visible and genuine connection between the cultural and economic components of the claim,[53] set a limit to the extent to which minority community identity and existence can be inferred from pasture and other land rights – the same rights that were regarded as the main signposts

---

[51] *Ibid.*, para. 10.6.

[52] *Ibid.*, concurring individual opinion of Messrs Elizabeth Evatt and Cecilia Medina Quiroga.

[53] *Kitok v. Sweden*, Comm. No. 197/1985, Views of 27 July 1988, (1988) Annual Report 221, para. 9.2. From different jurisdictions, see further the Canadian Supreme Court in *R. v. Van der Peet*, [1996] 2 S.C.R. 507, p. 549; *R v. Sappier; R v. Gray*, [2006] 2 S.C.R. 686 [distinctive 'activities' relevant to aboriginal culture]; the IACrtHR in *The Saramaka People v. Suriname*, Judgment of 28 November 2007, Series C No. 172, paras. 80–86, 118–123 [land tenure and identity]; Advisory Opinion of the African Commission on Human and Peoples' Rights on *The United Nations Declaration on the Rights of Indigenous Peoples*, May 2007, para. 43 [multifaceted notion of culture].

of group identity in *Western Sahara*. On the other hand, the HRC did uphold elements of the group's identity by both recognising the Rehoboth Baster Community's autonomy and culture in general, and accepting the authors' additional argument relating to the use of their mother tongue in connection with Article 26 ICCPR.[54] Going beyond the broader narratives of *Western Sahara*, *Diergaardt* illustrates how recognition of a minority group can be made (at least implicitly) a function of a potentially controversial relationship between spheres of community action and spheres of ethno-cultural identity.

The interface of land use and culture has been further elaborated upon by the IACrtHR in *Sawhoyamaxa Indigenous Community v. Paraguay*,[55] where indigenous communities' lands were presented as being the manifestation of multiple dimensions of identity, including 'spiritual or ceremonial boundaries; settlements and sporadic cultivations; seasonal or nomadic hunting, fishing or gathering; the use of natural resources connected with [indigenous] customs; and any other characteristic of [indigenous] culture'.[56] This broad, and broadly contextual approach to the group's 'constitutive' relationship to its traditional lands[57] arguably suggests a greater role for judicially-generated recognition of the group as such. Interestingly, in *Moiwana Village v. Suriname*[58] and *Saramaka*,[59] the IACrtHR developed a discourse about an 'all-encompassing relationship' between the Maroon communities in question and their land that somewhat equated them to indigenous peoples. Both groups are not indigenous to the region, yet they possess core social, cultural and economic characteristics which make them different from the rest of the population. Here again, land serves as the principal marker of the group's factual existence and legal exposure. As the IACrtHR put it, '[l]and is more than merely a source of subsistence for them; it is also a necessary source for the continuation of [their] life and cultural identity'.[60]

---

[54] Comm. No. 760/1997, Views of 25 July 2000, CCPR/C/69/D/760/1996, paras. 3.4–3.5, 10.10.

[55] Judgment of 29 March 2006, Series C No. 146.

[56] *Ibid.*, para. 131.

[57] In this sense, it goes beyond the specific connection between economic activity and minority culture upheld by the HRC in *Kitok*, *supra* note 53.

[58] Judgment of 15 June 2005, Series C No. 124, para. 133.

[59] Judgment of 28 November 2007, Series C No. 172, paras. 78–84.

[60] *Ibid.*, para. 82; see also para. 164; in *Aurelio Cal et al. v. The Attorney General of Belize and the Minister of Natural Resources and Environment* (Claims Nos. 171 and 172 of 2007, Judgment of 18 October 2007), involving Maya communities of Belize, the Constitutional Court stated that land 'nurtures and sustains... their very way of life and existence', *ibid.*, para. 102. For a similar approach to 'non-native' communities by the IACommHR, see *Garifuna Community of Cayos Cochinos and its members v. Honduras*, Report No. 39/07, Petition 1118-03, Admissibility, 24 July 2007.

Judicial discourse can become implicated in the recognition of minority identity in ways that do not necessarily expose the existence of minority groups per se, but rather focus on real or potential requirements set out by the state as conditions for domestic recognition. For example, the IACrtHR's jurisprudence on indigenous property rights[61] rests on the fundamental notion that a traditional – material and(/or) spiritual – relationship with the land does represent a key factual indicator of indigenous identity worthy of protection under international law, regardless of any registered property title under domestic law. Spiritual (i.e. non-material) elements are typically related to the fact of prior dispossession the group has suffered.[62] The rationale for this construction is essentially the rejection of state-sponsored strategies that use internal requirements to undermine, and eventually remove, the very basis of the community experience.[63]

States' claims can affect the legal status of groups and group structures themselves. In the *Greco-Bulgarian 'Communities'* case, the PCIJ dismissed the argument – implied by Bulgaria – that the existence of a minority community within the meaning of the convention in question depended on whether or not that community had been recognised as a juridical person under domestic law. It held that, while internal recognition could affect the forms of possession of property held by the community, no 'special legal recognition by the local legislation' was required for a community to qualify for the purposes of the convention.[64] The emphasis on factual existence mentioned above was meant to distinguish between the convention's recognition (linked by the PCIJ to factual criteria) and Bulgaria's or Greece's potentially more restrictive practices regarding the conferment of legal personality on minority institutions.

This legal scenario is far from being a relic of the past. A somewhat similar question was raised in the mid-1990s in *Canea Catholic Church v. Greece*,[65] before the EurCrtHR. The applicant church had been prevented from protecting its properties as a result of a failure by Greece to recognise the church's legal personality. The Court deemed this to be in breach of Article 6 (1) ECHR,

---

[61] See *infra*, Chapter 3.

[62] *Mayagna (Sumo) Awas Tingni Community v. Nicaragua*, Judgment of 31 August 2001, Series C No. 79; *Moiwana Village v. Suriname*, Judgment of 15 June 2005, Series C No. 124; *Sawhoyamaxa Indigenous Community v. Paraguay*, Judgment of 29 March 2006, Series C No. 146.

[63] For examples of restrictive national tests for establishing title, see J. Gilbert, *Indigenous Peoples' Land Rights under International Law: From Victims to Actors* (Ardsley, 2006), Chapter 2, especially pp. 72–73.

[64] *Interpretation of the Convention Between Greece and Bulgaria Respecting Reciprocal Emigration, Signed at Neuilly-Sur-Seine on November 27th, 1919 (Question of the 'Communities')*, Advisory Opinion of 17 January, 1930, Ser. B., No. 17, 1930, p. 22.

[65] Judgment of 16 December 1997, Reports 1997–VIII.

taken alone or in conjunction with Article 14 (based on comparisons with the treatment of the Greek Orthodox Church and the Jewish community).[66] In *Yakye Axa Indigenous Community v. Paraguay*,[67] Paraguay had conditioned the availability to the applicant indigenous group of the administrative procedure for the restitution of ancestral lands on the group being recognised as a juridical person by the state. The IACrtHR importantly rejected Paraguay's argument by explaining that the protection of indigenous land rights did not stem from any prior domestic recognition of the legal status of the group, though juridical personality made those pre-existing rights operational. Indeed, in *Saramaka* the IACrtHR reversed Paraguay's point in *Yakye Axa* by holding that juridical personality is not a *prius* but, if anything, derives from community existence as a special measure enabling the members of the group to enjoy certain rights collectively.[68]

This type of cases has a sub-text attached to it, namely the state's attempt to deny or considerably limit the legal spaces of recognition for the group. In *Metropolitan Church of Bessarabia and others v. Moldova*,[69] the EurCrtHR found that, the refusal by Moldovan authorities to register the church of a *de facto* minority religious community was in breach of the right to freedom of religion in Article 9.[70] In *Sister Immaculate Joseph et al. v. Sri Lanka*,[71] the HRC held that the rejection of the Order's incorporation was an infringement on the authors' rights in Articles 18 (freedom of religion) and 26 (right to equality). One major effect resulting from the failure to incorporate the Order – which represented a long-standing Catholic minority community in Sri Lanka – was its inability to hold property and thus to establish places of worship and charitable and humanitarian institutions.[72] In *Sergei Malakhovsky and Alexander Pikul v. Belarus*,[73] the HRC similarly found that the failure by the state to register the Krishna group as a religious association run counter to Article 18.

Unsurprisingly, all these cases reflected opposition from the government to the religious group gaining legal recognition internally. Moldova perceived

[66] A similar issue has been raised more recently in *Polish Orthodox Autocephalic Church v. Poland* [App. 31994/03], in which the applicant Church alleges discrimination in relation to acquisition of property compared to the Catholic Church.

[67] Judgment of 17 June 2005, Series C No. 125.

[68] Judgment of 28 November 2007, Series C No. 172, para. 172.

[69] Application No. 45701/99, Judgment of 13 December 2001.

[70] On other cases involving denial of registration to associations asserting minority interests, see further, Chapter 3.

[71] Comm. No. 1249/2004, Views of 21 October 2005, CCPR/C/85/D/1249/2004 (2005).

[72] *Ibid.*, para. 3.3.

[73] Comm. No. 1207/2003, Views of 26 July 2005, CCPR/C/84/D/1207/2003 (2005).

the applicant church as being in dispute with the Patriarchate of Moscow, while Belarus argued that the authors sought to monopolise representation of Vishnuism in the country. Sri Lanka, for its part, was concerned that the Order's incorporation could 'impair the very existence of Buddhism or the *Buddha Sasana*'.[74] It is no coincidence that most of the religious bodies that had been incorporated had Buddhist orientation,[75] raising an obvious issue of (in)equality of treatment between different religious communities. In such instances, not only did judicial discourse defend the very existence of religious pluralism,[76] it did create an opportunity for the group to be admitted and protected as such within the domestic legal space.

Incidentally, it should be pointed out that, denial of group existence can also occur 'from within', i.e. as an attempt at distorting, and ultimately dispensing with, that same cultural pluralism that has been recognised in principle. For example, in *Serif v. Greece*[77] and *Hasan and Chaush v. Bulgaria*,[78] the EurCrtHR found a violation of Article 9 ECHR in that the respondent state had invalidated appointments of Muslim religious leaders by the community and replaced them with individuals appointed according to its own procedures. The underlying theme was not religious freedoms per se, but rather the actual extent to which the state allowed minority communities to exist and flourish alongside the majority culture. In *Serif*, the applicant argued that his conviction by the Greek authorities following his appointment as *mufti* was 'just one aspect of the policy of repression applied by the Greek State *vis-à-vis* the Turkish-Muslim minority of western Thrace'.[79] Besides reaffirming pluralism as a value inherent to the ECHR, the EurCrtHR responded to the state's determination of the group's internal hierarchy by strictly separating state-controlled and unified religious leaderships (prohibited by the ECHR)[80] from respect for the institutional set up freely chosen by the members of the community. Judicial recognition of the group's internal organisation and functioning – in short, protection of its own structures – can thus prove a substitute for a discourse that openly revolves around the substantive articulation of minority identity.

74 Comm. No. 1249/2004, Views of 21 October 2005, CCPR/C/85/D/1249/2004 (2005), paras. 2.3, 7.3.

75 *Ibid.*, para. 3.1.

76 A different issue may arise as to the modalities of such pluralism: see e.g. the case decided by the EurCrtHR in *Jewish Liturgical Ass'n Cha'are Shalom ve Tsedek v. France*, Application No. 27417/95, Judgment of 27 June 2000; see *infra*, Chapter 4.

77 Application No. 38178/97, Judgment of 14 December 1999.

78 Application No. 30985/96, Judgment of 26 October 2000.

79 Application No. 38178/97, Judgment of 14 December 1999, para. 48.

80 *Ibid.*, para. 52.

Domestic courts and international law

As briefly alluded to in the previous section, domestic courts can also have a role to play in conceptualising, recognising and/or qualifying spaces of identity on a national or sub-national level. They can be involved not only in developing broad narratives of the kind reflected in the German Constitutional Court's Maastricht decision, but also in establishing the very existence of a minority group from a legal perspective. To better illustrate and discuss this point, four examples are offered from the jurisprudence of the UK, Ireland, India and Japan.

In *Mandla (Sewa Singh) v. Dowell Lee*,[81] involving an orthodox Sikh boy who had been refused admission to a private school unless he removed his turban and cut off his hair, the question arose as to whether Sikhs constituted a racial group for purposes of the Race Relations Act 1976. The judge answered in the negative, but the boy argued that the term 'ethnic' used in that Act was intended to broadly cover a cultural, linguistic or religious community. While the Court of Appeal confirmed the judge of first instance's position, the House of Lords allowed the appeal by holding that Sikhs did constitute an 'ethnic group'. Lord Fraser set out criteria for identifying an ethnic group, distinguishing essential from non-essential (though helpful) characteristics of a distinct community:

> The conditions which appear to me to be essential are these: (1) a long shared history, of which the group is conscious as distinguishing it from other groups, and the memory of which it keeps alive (2) a cultural tradition of its own, including family and social customs and manners, often but not necessarily associated with religious observance. In addition to those two essential characteristics the following characteristics are, in my opinion, relevant: (3) either a common geographical origin, or descent from a small number of common ancestors (4) a common language, not necessarily peculiar to the group (5) a common literature peculiar to the group (6) a common religion different from that of neighbouring groups or from the general community surrounding it (7) being a minority or being an oppressed or a dominant group within a larger community…

The so-called Mandla conditions have been applied ever since by British courts, including the case of *CRE v. Dutton*,[82] where members of the Roma community were found to be an ethnic group because they met the essential requirements and even some of the non-essential ones. Interestingly, most of these elements – or a combination of those – can be found *grosso modo* in international definitions of 'minorities' and 'indigenous peoples'.[83] A conscious

---

[81] [1983] AC 548.

[82] [1989] QB 783.

[83] On definitional matters and their respective controversies, see *supra*, Chapter 1, note 59.

and active ethno-cultural identity is clearly a key group feature, although the secondary role of a common language in Lord Fraser's test probably understates the link between ethnicity and mother tongue as the main medium of cultural preservation. On the other hand, such test blurs (at least in principle) the distinction between minority and majority groups, or dominant and non-dominant ones, as long as they all present certain ethnic peculiarities. More than that, Lord Fraser, quoting approvingly from the decision of the New Zealand Court of Appeal in *King-Ansell v. Police*,[84] provides an understanding of an ethnic group that is based on both the group's self-perception and the perception of those outside the group. In this respect, the test and international definitions tend to diverge. That an ethnic group may well be discriminated against while being in the majority within a country is beyond dispute, as the classical case of pre-democratic South Africa illustrates. Whether the same is possible where the group is a structurally dominant one within the larger community is arguably more open to doubt. More importantly, international law, as mentioned earlier, recognises the identity of minority groups without the interposition of others' prior acceptance.

The British case seems to suggest that the complex relationship of objective and subjective factors in establishing minority identity may be read by domestic courts in ways that help determine the scope of internal legal categories. For example, the Equality Tribunal of Ireland has interpreted the definition of 'Travellers' for purposes of Section 2 of the Equal Status Act 2000 so as to include both those who identify themselves as Travellers but do not live a nomadic life (as long as they satisfy a link to a nomadic lifestyle in the past),[85] and even those who do not identify themselves as Travellers but are the descendents of members of the Traveller community.[86] Definitional references to others' recognition are in practice downplayed, while protection is also offered to those who do not meet a specific subjective requirement. In

[84] [1979] 2 N.Z.L.R. 531.

[85] In *Chapman v. United Kingdom* (Judgment of 25 September 1996, Reports 1996-IV), the EurCrtHR recognised that the Roma/Gypsies no longer live a wholly nomadic existence.

[86] *Connors v. Molly Heffernan's Public House* (DEC-S/2001/003), 1 June 2001; *O'Brien v. Killarney Ryan Hotel* (DEC-S/2001/008, 20 August 2001); to some extent, the protective approach to equality rights in *O'Brien* transcends long-established international standards on self-identification as a major precondition for minority status: see e.g. *Rights of Minorities in Upper Silesia (Minority Schools)*, Judgment of 26 April, 1928, Ser. A, No. 15, 1928; CERD has clarified that self-identification shall be used under the ICERD while determining group membership, if no justification exists to the contrary: CERD General Recommendation VIII (1990), UN A/45/18. Interestingly, in *DH and others v. The Czech Republic* (Application No. 57325/00, Judgment of 13 November 2007), the EurCrtHR (Grand Chamber) held that 'no waiver of the right not to be subjected to racial discrimination can be accepted', para. 204.

short, Irish case law is having an important impact on interpreting Traveller identity within a particular legal context.

Similar considerations can be made in relation to the understanding of minority groups which has been upheld in Indian jurisprudence in order to account for the several linguistic and religious groups to be protected under the Constitution. Absent a specific definition of what constitutes a minority under Indian law, the Supreme Court's understanding of it has come to reflect international criteria relating to the numerical size and cultural features of the group, while departing from them with regard to the unit to be used to determine the very existence of the group. Given the specific constellation of languages across state lines in India, particularly the creation of state units based on linguistic dominance within a particular region, the court has interpreted the minority provisions of the Constitution to acknowledge minority status at the level of the state rather than the country as a whole.[87]

In *Kayano et al. v. Hokkaido Expropriation Committee*,[88] turning on the impact of a governmental decision to construct a dam in the south-western part of Hokkaido on the identity of the Ainu people – the original inhabitants of the Nibutani region –, the Sapporo District Court made a major contribution to (re-)assessing the legal status of the Ainu as a group. They noted that the government of Japan had recognised the Ainu people as a minority under Article 27 ICCPR in a report submitted to the HRC pursuant to Article 40 of that treaty in 1991. It would be too simplistic, though, to argue that the court simply fell back on what the government appeared to have conceded within an international forum six years before. In fact, they did recognise that the matter raised before it, revolving around the identity of an ethno-cultural community, was something of a new frontier for the domestic system, since it had not been previously discussed before Japanese courts.[89] That set the stage for a ground-breaking decision on the legal recognition of the Ainu under Japanese law. The intriguing aspect of this part of the court's reasoning is the conflation of 'minorities' and 'indigenous peoples' as legal categories. For one thing, the court upholds the minority status of the Ainu. At the same time, it does call for increased protection of them as an indigenous group:

---

[87] See e.g. *A.M. Patroni v. E.C. Kesavan*, A.I.R. 1965 Kerala; *T.M.A. Pai Foundation and ors v. State of Karnataka and ors*, WP (Civil) No. 317/1993 (31 Oct. 2002), paras. 73,76, 79. Compare with the HRC's decision in *Ballantyne et al. v. Canada*, Communication Nos. 359/1989, 385/1989, Views of 31 March 1993.

[88] Judgment of the Sapporo District Court, Civil Division No. 3, 27 March 1997, in (1999) 38 ILM, 397.

[89] *Ibid.*, p. 417.

> If one minority group lived in an area prior to being ruled over by a majority group and preserved its distinct ethnic culture even after being ruled over by the majority group, while another came to live in an area ruled over by a majority after consenting to the majority rule, it must be recognised that it is only natural that the distinct ethnic culture of the former group requires greater consideration.[90]

The court's approach was informed by the 'growing international movement' towards respect for 'indigenous peoples' culture, lifestyle, traditional ceremonies, [and] cultural practices', and even resulted in setting out a definition of 'indigenous people' broadly taken from international standards.[91] What follows from this premise is essentially an account of the several failed attempts by non-Ainu Japanese persons ('*wa-jin*') to assimilate the Ainu people into Japanese society throughout history.[92] The conclusions are clearly stated:

> [W]e can see that for the most part the Ainu people have inhabited Hokkaido from before the extension of our country's rule. They formed their own culture and had an identity. And even after their governance was assumed by our country, even after suffering enormous social and economic devastation wrought by policies adopted by the majority, they remain a social group that has not lost this unique culture and identity. Accordingly, the definition provided above of an "indigenous people" should certain apply.[93]

In the court's argument the indigenousness of the group was not associated with specific claims, such as protection of land rights. In essence, it upheld the narrative of Ainu's pre-existence and rejection of assimilation to recognise them as an indigenous minority group.

Besides confirming the role of judicial discourse in determining spaces of group identity through a delicate weighing up of legal principles and respect for facts, those examples also expose, albeit indirectly, the active or passive role that international law can play before domestic courts in matters of group existence. The gist of the Sapporo District Court's line was based on the notion that international law (*in casu*, Article 27 ICCPR and developments in the area of indigenous rights) required Japan to respect Ainu identity, although such notion was cast in the language of a connection between international law and the Japanese Constitution. Writing the decision in 1997, the court recognised the Ainu as an indigenous minority at a time when the HRC was expounding the role of Article 27 ICCPR *vis-à-vis* indigenous communities. In other words, the reading of the Ainu people' status under Japanese law was largely driven by external criteria defined by international law.

---

90 *Ibid.*, p. 419.
91 *Ibid.*, pp. 419–420.
92 *Ibid.*, pp. 420–423.
93 *Ibid.*, p. 422.

By contrast, the Mandla conditions set out by Lord Fraser in the House of Lords reflected a specific national experience and were not (at least not openly) inspired by international standards. The point here is that domestic law may meet particular needs (*in casu*, defining 'racial group', 'ethnic origins' or 'Traveller identity', regardless of minority status, or identifying regional minority groups, for purposes of a piece of legislation on non-discrimination or specific constitutional provisions), but may not, or should not do so in a way that group recognition is essentially left to an assessment by the majority. Unsurprisingly, *Mandla (Sewa Singh)* raised the issue of whether Parliament had intended to recognise membership of an ethnic group in the context of the Race Relation Act 1976. Lord Fraser construed 'ethnic' in a broad cultural and historic sense, yet he sought justification for this in the legislature's intention. He broke new ground in advancing the scope of the 1976 Act, yet he anchored (ethnic) group recognition to *internal* criteria on an institutional and societal level, i.e. approval from Parliamentary majority and acceptance of the group by others. Only the content and objectives of the domestic measures in question can tell whether or not this type of argument is justifiable.[94]

From the perspective of international law, national definitions of minority groups may prove under-inclusive, leaving specific groups at the margins of political and legal recognition. The outright denial of minority existence, produced by traditional nation-state policies in countries like France or Turkey, often gives way to a more subtle approach, which was broadly captured by General Recommendation XXIV adopted by CERD in 1999:

> [A] number of States parties [to the International Convention on the Elimination of All Forms of Racial Discrimination – ICERD] recognize the presence on their territory of some national or ethnic groups or indigenous peoples, while disregarding others. Certain criteria should be uniformly applied to all groups, in particular the number of persons concerned, and their being of a race, colour, descent or national or ethnic origin different from the majority or from other groups within the population.
>
> ...
>
> Some State parties fail to collect data on the ethnic or national origin of their citizens or other persons living on their territory, but decide at their own discretion which groups constitute ethnic groups or indigenous peoples that are to be recognized and treated as such. The Committee believes that there is an

94 For an example along potentially restrictive lines, see E. Benvenisti, 'National Courts and the International Law on Minority Rights' (1997) 2 *Austrian Review of International and European Law*, pp. 17–18.

> international standard concerning the specific rights of people belonging to such groups, together with generally recognized norms concerning equal rights for all and non-discrimination.

Where this approach intersects – as it frequently does – the recognition of minority groups in the sense of international law, domestic courts can and should be doubly vigilant in making sure that international standards are accounted for. In this sense, *Kayano* used international law to transform a previously idiosyncratic domestic law.

But what if domestic courts do not do that? While it is true that domestic courts can protect (and recognise) minority groups against the hostility or abuses of majority power, it is also true that they can uphold the executive's exclusively domestic (and potentially discriminatory) perspectives on whether or not certain communities enjoy minority status. In terms of judicial discourse, the question arises as to the role of international jurisprudence in reviewing national (and often judicially backed up) criteria for recognition.

In *Polish Nationality*, the PCIJ rejected the Polish argument that it was for Poland to first recognise its own 'racial, religious or linguistic minorities' under domestic law, and then place those groups under international protection. In fact, the PCIJ construed the 1919 Treaty in a way that prioritised internationally set criteria over domestic requirements that were meant to bypass the former. The underlying point made in the judgment was that, the 1919 Treaty and the wider system to which it was connected and of which it was the most visible component, ascribed to themselves the right to identify the groups within Poland which were entitled to protection under international law. Polish law was required to conform to that understanding, not to modify or qualify it in any way. The case did not revolve around judicially generated notions of ethno-cultural minority groups, yet it signified a powerful call by the PCIJ for the autonomy of international law (and, for that matter, international judicial discourse) vis-à-vis any self-serving approach to minority recognition by state authorities.

The *Greco-Bulgarian 'Communities'* case largely followed in the footsteps of *Polish Nationality* in that it reaffirmed the supremacy of international law over restrictive understandings of 'community' set by the parties' domestic legislation. Again, it was the PCIJ's reading of the Greco-Bulgarian Convention of 1919 which came to set the benchmark against which domestic practices were to be measured. A preliminary screening of relevant groups through the test of internal legal personality was dismissed by the PCIJ as being incompatible with the objective of that convention and the general body of international measures designed to protect minority communities in the region.

Admittedly, both of these cases, amongst others, highlighted the role of the PCIJ as the judicial arm of a rather elaborate system that the Versailles

Conference and the League of Nations devised for a limited number of states, and sought to enforce. Institutionally, the top-down approach was clear, and unsurprisingly, it did not go unchallenged. In a more conventional jurisprudential setting, international jurisprudence may prove more lenient towards domestic views. In *Gorzelik and others v. Poland*,[95] the Grand Chamber stressed that Polish authorities had consistently recognised the existence of a Silesian ethnic minority and the right of Silesians to associate with one another. In fact, the Katowice Court of Appeal and the Supreme Court[96] had provided their own understanding of 'national or ethnic minorities' under Article 35 of the Constitution. The Court of Appeal argued that in order for a group to constitute a national minority, this group must be linked to a majority outside Poland and/or reflect the existence of a nation accepted by others. Arguably, both this characterisation of 'national minority' and the distinction between 'national' and 'ethnic' minorities are in effect at odds with international law criteria, thereby resulting in real or potential arbitrary classifications. Nevertheless, the EurCrtHR did not challenge the domestic courts' line of reasoning.[97]

In *Hingitaq 53 and others v. Denmark*,[98] members of the Inughuit in the north-west of Greenland claimed that they had been deprived, on a continuing basis, of their traditional homeland as a result of the establishment of US military bases in 1951 and 1953. As emphasised by the Supreme Court of Denmark, the main argument made by the applicants was that the Inughuit – or Thule Tribe – constituted a distinctive indigenous or tribal people within the meaning of ILO Convention No. 169 concerning Indigenous and Tribal Peoples in Independent Countries of 1989. In a previous decision by the High Court of Eastern Denmark, it was acknowledged that the tribe could be regarded as a tribal people as this concept was defined by Article 1 (1)(a) of that convention. While upholding the High Court's judgment, the Supreme Court dismissed the notion that the Thule Tribe represented either an indigenous people or a tribal people within that meaning. The tribe's

---

[95] Application No. 44158/9820, Judgment of 20 December 2001 [C] and Judgment of 17 February 2004 [GC].

[96] *Ibid.*, Judgment of 20 December 2001, paras. 19, 23.

[97] In January 2005, the Polish Parliament passed The Act on National and Ethnic Minorities as well as Regional Language, which provides a definition of national and ethnic minority. For a commentary on this controversial piece of legislation, see A. Malicka & K. Zabielska, 'Legal Status of National Minorities in Poland: The Act on National and Ethnic Minorities as well as Regional Language' (2005/6) 5 *European Yearbook of Minority Issues*, p. 471 et seq., at pp. 475–477; compare also G. Pentassuglia, *Minorities in International Law*, *supra* note 6, pp. 58–60.

[98] Application No. 18584/04, Admissibility Decision of 12 January 2006.

language characteristics and self-identification as an indigenous group (a prominent criterion under ILO Convention 169) were deemed insufficient to establish the existence of the tribe as an indigenous group separate from the indigenous people of Greenland taken as a whole.

It may be argued that the international law criteria were applied restrictively to the Thule Tribe, and it may also be questioned the notion that, even assuming the complete homogeneity of the Inuit as an indigenous people, severe interferences with one of its main groups' traditional way of life, based on hunting and fishing, could automatically imply that they were not entitled to protection under ILO Convention 169 or other international instruments. For its part, the EurCrtHR only considered whether the compensation offered to the tribe as a result of acts of expropriation was appropriate to meet the interests of the persons concerned, but essentially deferred to domestic law in respect of the key factual and legal background to the case. An assessment of the tribe's land claim (rejected *ratione temporis*) would have required the EurCrtHR to discuss the status of the tribe under domestic and international law.

In *Sidiropoulos and Others v. Greece*,[99] the EurCrtHR's intervention proved more intrusive, though. The case turned essentially on whether the applicants' association – called 'Home of Macedonian Civilisation' and aimed, according to its memorandum, at promoting the culture of the Florina region, in northern Greece – was in fact seeking recognition of the existence of a 'Macedonian' minority in Greece and even concealing separatist intentions for the Greek province of Macedonia. The Florina Court of First Instance had openly regarded the idea that there existed a Macedonian minority in Greece as contrary to the country's national interest and contrary to law.[100] The Salonika Court of Appeal went at great length to explain the historical role of Greek civilisation in the region, dismissing the notion that there was any such thing as 'Greek Macedonians' forming a separate ethnic group. This court also referred to the exchanges of populations that took place either voluntary or following bilateral agreements, such as the one between Greece and Bulgaria in 1926.

The applicants strongly opposed the view that domestic law, and domestic courts, were the only vehicle for recognition, similarly to what Poland had claimed before the PCIJ in *Polish Nationality* several decades earlier. They argued that 'the existence of minorities and different cultures in a country was a historical fact that a "democratic society" had to tolerate and even protect

[99] Judgment of 10 July 1998, Reports 1998–IV.
[100] *Ibid.*, p. 4.

and support according to the principles of international law'.[101] Like in the cases of the Silesians of Poland,[102] the Macedonians of Bulgaria[103] and the Kurds of Turkey,[104] the EurCrtHR did not directly address the status of the group under international law. Still, it did hold that the aims of the association, as set out in its memorandum, – that is, to preserve and develop the traditions and folk culture of the Florina region – were 'perfectly clear and legitimate', as the inhabitants of a region are entitled to promote the region's special traits, for historical and economic reasons. It went on to say that even if the real objective of the association were to 'assert a minority consciousness',[105] the (then) CSCE 1990 Copenhagen Document on the Human Dimension and the Charter of Paris for a New Europe – both signed by Greece – allowed them to associate themselves to protect their cultural and spiritual heritage. Despite the cautiousness of this line, the EurCrtHR did not accept the Greek courts' purely national approach to the group's status. Echoing *Kayano* before the Sapporo District Court, international standards were ultimately upheld in the face of previous attempts to deny recognition to minority groups. As the next chapter will illustrate, the EurCrHR's discourse in most of the above cases, while avoiding a stance on the group's status, has created a space for asserting and debating group identities within a democratic setting, as a way of compensating for the states' idiosyncrasies towards ethno-cultural diversity.[106]

The examples mentioned so far show a spectrum of possibilities for international judicial discourse to relate to domestic perspectives on minority groups. Although the existence of an internal mechanism to seek minority status may

---

[101] *Ibid.*, para. 41.

[102] *Gorzelik and others v. Poland*, Application No. 44158/9820, Judgment of 20 December 2001 [C] and Judgment of 17 February 2004 [GC].

[103] *Stankov and the United Macedonian Association Ilinden v. Bulgaria*, Applications Nos. 29221/95 and 292225/95, Judgment of 2 October 2001.

[104] See e.g. *United Communist Party of Turkey and others v. Turkey*, Judgment of 30 January 1998, Reports 1998–I; *Socialist Party and others v. Turkey, Ibid.*, 1998–III, Judgment of 25 May 1998; *Freedom and Democracy Party (ÖZDEP) v. Turkey, Ibid.*, 1999–VIII, Judgment of 8 December 1999; *Yazar, Karatas, Aksoy and the People's Labour Party (HEP) v. Turkey*, Applications 22723/93, 22734/93 and 22725/93, Judgment of 9 April 2002.

[105] Judgment of 10 July 1998, Reports 1998–IV, para. 44.

[106] But this may also prove of particular importance with regard to problematic claims being made by the group itself: see e.g. W. Kymlicka, *Multicultural Odysseys: Navigating the New International Politics of Diversity* (Oxford, 2007), pp. 284–285; in *Diergaardt* (Comm. No. 760/1997, Views of 25 July 2000, CCPR/C/69/D/760/1996), the HRC in practice opened up a similar discursive space while still protecting elements of the group's identity. As a slight variation on this approach, the EurCrtHR has characterized the Roma community 'une minorité défavorisée et vulnerable qui a un caractère particulier': *Affaire Sampanis et Autres c. Grèce*, Application No. 32526/05, Judgment of 5 June 2008 (final on 5 September 2008), para. 72 (in French).

benefit the people concerned,[107] no specific acts of domestic recognition are required for a minority group to enjoy protection under international law. The well-known case of *Sandra Lovelace v. Canada*[108] before the HRC illustrates the point at the level of individual group membership. The case turned on whether the complainant's loss of her Indian (Maliseet) status under the Canadian Indian Act (as a result of her previous marriage with a non-Indian) violated the ICCPR. The HRC concluded that, while Sandra Lovelace was no longer recognised as an Indian under Canadian legislation, she was still entitled to recognition as an indigenous member of a minority group in the sense of Article 27 ICCPR. Here, international law made up for the lack of recognition resulting from the workings of domestic law.[109]

Conversely, the lack of an internal mechanism for minority status may in practice turn out to reinforce state discretion over the treatment of all or certain of the groups concerned – in *Gorzelik*, Poland strongly denied that the community of Silesians was a national minority. The capacity of international judicial discourse to avoid under-inclusive approaches to minority protection under domestic law is most often a function of the (judicially upheld) independence of international law vis-à-vis domestic practices. *Polish Nationality* reflects a model of scrutiny that contrasts with the more hesitant approach of *Gorzelik*. The EurCrtHR has consistently established the autonomy of the ECHR in respect of national judicial and non-judicial readings of the ECHR's terms, though so far it has not used this discourse to insulate 'national minority' under Article 14 ECHR from the uncertainties, if not hostilities, of domestic law. The lack of specific minority provisions in the relevant instrument, as in the case of the ECHR, does not necessarily stand in the way of the assertiveness of international law. As hinted at in the previous section and discussed later in the book, the IACommHR's and IACrtHR's jurisprudence on indigenous communities provides an interesting indication of how such autonomy can have a major impact on the interpretation of both evidence and facts, as well as the substance of the claim itself.

---

107 For a similar argument under the Inter-American system, see *The Saramaka People v. Suriname*, Judgment of 28 November 2007, Series C No. 172, para. 172.

108 Comm. No. 24/1977, Views of 30 July 1981, (1981) Annual Report 166; (1983) Annual Report 248.

109 Kymlicka argues that the distinction between status and non-status Indians in Canadian public policy 'is in many respects an artificial distinction': W. Kymlicka, *Multicultural Odysseys*, *supra* note, 106, p. 158, fn. 21.

Chapter 3

Elaboration

The extent to which general human rights categories are being used to the benefit of minority groups represents an important way of looking at the actual or potential role of judicial discourse in relation to minority protection. In this sense, judicial protection can be conceptualised on two basic levels.

First, judicial discourse points to indirect protection against interference in those elementary spaces of freedom that are vital to the articulation of minority demands and assertion of minority identity. The central theme is not the distinctiveness of minority groups per se, but rather the areas of freedom within which their own identity happens to emerge and flourish. This will be illustrated in the following section by a comparative assessment of the jurisprudence of the EurCrtHR regarding freedom of association and expression. Second, judicial discourse can provide direct yet implicit protection of certain aspects of minority identity taken separately. In the remainder of the chapter, areas such as private and family life, property or non-discrimination will exemplify this line.

While the first approach is confined to essentially widening the scope of general human rights vis-à-vis minority members, the second one tends to deepen the ramifications of those rights in order to accommodate the identity of minority groups. Both narratives reflect, in different ways, the role of judicial discourse in re-assessing general human rights law within the context of minority protection.

Indirect protection: spaces of freedom or the 'hands off approach'

As is widely known, the ECHR does not contain any specific minority rights provisions. This has been reaffirmed by the Strasbourg bodies on several occasions in earlier times. Nevertheless, in recent years there has been a significant increase in the number of cases brought up before the EurCrtHR regarding minority groups, seemingly inspired by a number of important changes in the landscape of minority protection in Europe and beyond.[1]

The Court has come to set a benchmark for minority identity in the context of freedom of expression and freedom of association, in Articles 10 and 11 ECHR. In *Young, James and Webster v. United Kingdom*,[2] the EurCrtHR had already referred in general to the criteria of 'pluralism, tolerance and broad-mindedness' as hallmarks of a democratic society which implied the 'fair and proper treatment of minorities' as a necessary limit on the views of the majority. However, in a group of recent cases – all involving Turkish political parties with a pro-Kurdish agenda – the EurCrtHR recognised in particular that seeking solutions for the benefit of a distinctive ethno-cultural group, ranging from ways of enhancing dialogue between the latter and the rest of the population to endorsing a federal system within existing state borders to the conferral of minority language rights, could not in itself justify the dissolution of the political party that publicly advocated or embraced those solutions.

The EurCrtHR has gone further by stating that a call for autonomy or even secession of part of the country's territory by a group of freely associated persons or a political party, with its derivative demands for fundamental constitutional and territorial changes, cannot automatically justify a prohibition of its assemblies, let alone its compulsory dismantling or even the termination of the mandates of MPs belonging to that party.[3]

However, the EurCrtHR has clarified that the body in question must reject the use or propagation of violence and firmly endorse democratic principles for it to enjoy protection under the ECHR. In *Dicle for the Democratic Party (DEP) v. Turkey*,[4] it appeared to accept that some potential for violence seemingly conveyed by a public political speech can be tolerated provided that the ensuing threat is very limited, and therefore that the penalty of dissolving an entire political party remains in itself disproportionate under Article 11. A similar line, *mutatis mutandis*, has been taken by the EurCrtHR in another set of cases, such as *E.K. v. Turkey*,[5] *Association Ekin v. France*,[6] and *Unsal*

[1] See *supra*, Chapter 1.

[2] Judgment of 13 August 1981, Series A, No. 44.

[3] Leading cases include *United Communist Party of Turkey and others v. Turkey*, Reports 1998–I, Judgment of 30 January 1998; *Socialist Party and others v. Turkey*, Judgment of 25 May 1998, *ibid.*, 1998–III; *Freedom and Democracy Party (ÖZDEP) v. Turkey*, Judgment of 8 December 1999, *ibid.*, 1999–VIII; *Yazar, Karatas, Aksoy and the People's Labour Party (HEP) v. Turkey*, Applications Nos. 22723/93, 22734/93 and 22725/93, Judgment of 9 April 2002.

[4] Application No. 25141/94, Judgment of 10 December 2002, para. 64.

[5] Application No. 28496/95, Judgment of 7 February 2002.

[6] Application No. 39288/98, Judgment of 17 July 2001.

Ozturk v. Turkey,[7] in which the applicants complained of a breach of Article 10 ECHR by contesting measures taken against them as a result of the publication of material which was aimed at disseminating ideas relating to the situation and/or claims of a minority group.

Other cases have gone beyond the issue of supporting minority demands politically by raising – explicitly or implicitly – the specific question of whether the manifestation or assertion of minority identity through the proclaimed objectives of an association, particular public meetings or simply the general activities of the group concerned should be protected by the ECHR. While *Sidiropoulos and others v. Greece*[8] linked the assertion of minority identity to the registration of an association, *Stankov and the United Macedonian Association Ilinden v. Bulgaria*[9] interestingly acknowledged a further space of freedom for a minority group in that it led to a finding of a violation of Article 11 in banning *Ilinden* – an unregistered association claiming the recognition of a 'Macedonian minority' in Bulgaria – from holding public meetings to commemorate certain historical events. The case of *Ilinden* was brought up again in *The United Macedonian Organisation Ilinden and others v. Bulgaria.*[10] In this case, like in *Sidiropoulos*, the EurCrtHR held that denial of registration was in itself disproportionate and thus in breach of Article 11.

In the case of *Gorzelik*,[11] though, the EurCrtHR accepted Poland's speculative allegation that the applicant association of Silesians, by seeking registration as an organization of the 'Silesian national minority', had tried to circumvent Polish electoral law conferring special benefits on registered associations of national minorities. By contrast, in the *Sidiropoulos* case, involving applicants who claimed to have a Macedonian ethnic origin and 'national consciousness', the EurCrtHR rejected the suspicions and doubts voiced by the respondent government regarding the true (separatist) intentions of the association's founders as justifying an interference with freedom of association in Article 11.[12] The emphasis here was on actions taking priority over declarations or suppositions, regardless of the existence of the group at issue, while the Grand Chamber in *Gorzelik* more ambiguously included the intentions 'impliedly declared' in the association's programme to justify pre-emptive state measures.

---

[7] Application No. 29365/95, Judgment of 4 October 2005.

[8] Judgment of 10 July 1998, Reports 1998–IV.

[9] Applications Nos. 29221/95 and 292225/95, Judgment of 2 October 2001.

[10] Application No. 59491/00, Judgment of 16 February 2006.

[11] Application No. 44158/9820, Judgment of 20 December 2001 [C] and Judgment of 17 February 2004 [GC].

[12] See also *United Macedonian Organisation Ilinden and Others v. Bulgaria*, Application No. 59491/00, Judgment of 16 February 2006, para. 77 [alleged propagation of violence by Ilinden].

Gorzelik arguably diluted the demanding evidentiary test established in the above cases to review the state party's margin of appreciation.

Taken as a whole, this jurisprudence clearly indicates increasing endorsement by the EurCrtHR of important areas of pluralism, grounded on the prohibition of arbitrary interference in the expression of minority demands and assertion of minority identity. In *Gorzelik* itself, the Grand Chamber recognised the instrumental value of Article 11 in helping a minority group to preserve and uphold its rights:

> [A]ssociations formed for other purposes, including those... seeking an ethnic identity or asserting a minority consciousness, are also important to the proper functioning of democracy. For pluralism is also built on the genuine recognition of, and respect for, diversity and the dynamics of cultural traditions, ethnic and cultural identities, religious beliefs, artistic, literary and socio-economic ideas and concepts.[13]

Such discourse exemplifies the judicial widening of general human rights protection without engaging with the substance of minority issues as such. In other words, those issues do not form a distinctive basis for the relevant right; rather, it is the right that, on its own terms, is made more effective by reaching out to minority groups. The theme of pluralism has been extended to the sphere of religion, as is illustrated by a number of cases in which state authorities were found to have disproportionately interfered with the activities of a minority religious community by either refusing to register the church of that community or determining its internal hierarchy. For example, in *Metropolitan Church of Bessarabia and others v. Moldova*,[14] the EurCrtHR held that the lack of recognition of the applicant church by Moldovan authorities – construed as a response to a perceived dispute between the Patriarchates of Bucharest and Moscow as well as underlying political factors – interfered with the actual organisation and functioning of this church to such an extent as to amount to a denial of the right to freedom of religion in Article 9 ECHR.

The parameter of non-arbitrary interference resembles the equally – at least primarily – negative rationale of Article 27 ICCPR, which provides that persons belonging to ethnic, religious or linguistic minorities 'shall not be denied' the right to enjoy their own culture, to profess and practice their own religion, or to use their own language. The hands off approach reflected in the criterion of non-denial is measured against the backdrop of a marked inter-

---

[13] Application No. 44158/9820, Judgment of 17 February 2004, para. 92. The case of *Timishev v. Russia* confirms that democratic society is 'built on the principles of pluralism and respect for different cultures', Applications 55762/00 and 55974/00, Judgment of 13 December 2005, para. 58.

[14] Application No. 45701/99, Judgment of 13 December 2001.

action between individual rights and aspects of group protection. Irrespective of any positive action attached to Article 27, this element is tentatively echoed by the reference in the provision to the communal exercise of rights. In a typical Article 27 dispute the respondent state generally positions itself as an intermediate actor between either the group and its complaining members – as a result of legislative or other measures adopted for the benefit of the community as a whole but wholly or partially impugned by the applicant(s) – or the group and its members, on the one hand, and private parties, on the other – as a result of legislative or other measures benefiting these latter that allegedly affect the exercise of Article 27 rights. In other words, 'non-denial' by the state is essentially defined by whether certain steps taken by such state still permit or cumulatively erode the enjoyment of a collectively construed minority identity, or – alternatively – may be justified by the aim of preserving this identity while producing individual restrictions on Article 27 rights themselves.

Such a community dimension is lacking in the ECHR cases mentioned above. In these cases, the spaces of freedom upheld by the EurCrtHR benefit a minority group as they are construed as 'necessary in a democratic society' rather than necessary for the protection of minority identity, very much in line with the theme of protection against abuse of majority rule underpinning *Young* with regard to the very different issue of membership in labour unions. Instead of the triangular relation which de facto underlies most Article 27 disputes as indicated earlier, those cases reflect a classic binary relation in which individual applicants challenge state measures which directly target their basic liberties. In other words, there is no determination of the specific minority position and claims of the relevant groups – whether it's the Turkish Kurds, the Greek Macedonians or the Polish Silesians – let alone their multiple ramifications. The principle of non-arbitrary interference on which those cases are based, while instrumentally impacting on minority groups, stops short of upholding any distinctive identity rights. The whole minority question is bound to remain in the background.

In this sense, it might be argued that, judicial discourse takes here a procedural twist in that fundamental freedoms are used, not to address minority claims, but to reinforce the legal framework within which those claims must be allowed.[15] Somewhat echoing the ECHR jurisprudence, in *Malawi African Association and Others v. Mauritania*,[16] involving Black Mauritanians who had been arrested because they had distributed a document providing evidence of racial discrimination to which Black ethnic groups from southern Mauritania

[15] For this procedural approach, see *infra*, Chapter 6.

[16] Comm. Nos. 54/91, 61/91, 98/93/, 164/97 à 196/97 and 210/98 (2000).

had been subjected and called for the opening of a dialogue with the government, the AfrCommHPRs found a violation of the rights to freedom of expression and assembly recognised in the African Charter on Human and Peoples' Rights (ACHPR), regardless of any particular minority claims. A similar theme is reflected in the decision of the Bulgarian Constitutional Court in the case concerning *The Status of the Movement of Rights and Freedom (MRF)*.[17] According to the petitioners, 99 percent of MRF membership belonged to the Turkish minority in Bulgaria. They demanded that MRF be outlawed on the grounds that Article 11(4) of the Constitution prohibits political parties along ethnic, racial or religious lines. The Constitutional Court interpreted the Article 11 prohibition as a ban on parties that excluded potential members on ethno-cultural grounds, and which therefore did not apply to MRF, whose founding document did not contain any such exclusionary rules. More than that, it recognised that past abuses suffered by the Turkish minority justified the emergence of a political organisation campaigning for the rights of this group.[18] In practice, the constitutional reading offered in the 1992 decision did not protect the distinctiveness of the Turkish community per se, but rather widened the right to political participation of MRF as a way of allowing minority claims to enter, and be part of the political process.

The protection is ultimately indirect in nature. Here judicial discourse is meant to create a space for open debate and mutual tolerance. In *Ouranio Toxo and Others v. Greece*,[19] arising from a mob attack on a political party defending the interests of the Macedonian community in Greece, the EurCrtHR held that the Greek authorities had somewhat fomented an atmosphere of confrontation instead of facilitating inter-communal tolerance, and found a breach of Article 11. The same spirit of tolerance and respect underlies *Sidiropoulos*, alongside *Stankov*, the several cases involving the Kurds of south-east Turkey, and even *Gorzelik*. Group claims must be allowed in a democratic society, even when they (peacefully) advocate secession or radical constitutional changes in order to accommodate those claims.

This may also partly explain the silence of the EurCrtHR on the fundamental issue of the legal status of the group within the country.[20] The assumption is that freedom of expression and freedom of association will instrumentally lead to some kind of 'reflexive reconstitution of collective identities',[21] allow-

[17] Constitutional Court of Bulgaria, Decision of 22 April, 1992.

[18] The court noted that MRF in effect constituted a political 'movement' rather than a political party *stricto sensu*.

[19] Application No. 74989/01, Judgment of 20 October 2005.

[20] See *supra*, Chapter 2.

[21] S. Benhabib, *The Claims of Culture: Equality and Diversity in the Global Era* (Princeton, 2002), pp. 70–71.

ing democratic dissent and contestation to nurture a fluid process of constant (re-)negotiation of cultural differences within the public sphere.[22] That such space is of the utmost importance can be further demonstrated by contrasting this jurisprudence with the earlier and more conservative *Otto-Preminger-Institut v. Austria*,[23] in which the EurCrtHR concluded that censoring a satiric movie over the Christian faith in Innsbruck was compatible with the ECHR, especially because the vast majority of the people of Tyrol professed that faith. Little or no room was made for non-dominant views within the horizon of the ECHR's democratic society. It is precisely such views that were protected by the HRC in *Unn and Ben Leirvåg et al. v. Norway*,[24] where the authors, adhering to a humanist non-religious life stance, complained about the lack of full exemption for their children from the instruction of 'Christian Knowledge and Religious and Ethical Education' – a new compulsory subject introduced in the Norwegian school system in 1997. The HRC concluded that both the teaching of that subject per se, and the system of only partial exemption did not secure religious pluralism and was thus in violation of Article 18(4) ICCPR. Although the authors withdrew a complaint under Article 27, they did emphasise the firm opposition to the 1997 reform by all religious and life stance minority groups. The fact that the overwhelming majority of the population were members of the Evangelical Lutheran Church as the official and constitutionally protected state religion, did not justify (unlike *Otto-Preminger-Institut*) the restrictions imposed on different and non-dominant narratives and worldviews within the public school system, whether or not associated with a specific minority group.

While representing an important way of (re-)conceptualising the role of general human rights in relation to minority groups, the inherent limits of this approach are reflected in the difficulties of securing a more positive balancing act of state and minority interests as such. The state's margin of appreciation allowed by the EurCrtHR tends to broaden as more open and complex findings may become involved. In *Gorzelik*, which originated from a controversy over the existence and status of the Silesians as a national minority, the EurCrtHR embraced a doubtful interpretation of Polish electoral law by Polish domestic courts, and held that there had been no breach of freedom of association per se; rather, the Silesians were not allowed to call themselves a nation or a national minority. While importantly affirming the significance of democratic pluralism to identity claims, the case exposes the boundaries of such pluralism, rather than its positive ramifications, as broadly exemplified

---

22 See *infra*, Chapter 6.

23 Judgment of 20 September 1994, Series A, No. 295.

24 Comm. No. 1155/2003, Views of 3 November 2004.

by *United Communist Party of Turkey and others v. Turkey, Stankov*, and *Sidiropoulos*. The EurCrtHR rejected the applicants' claim by stressing that groups of individuals should be prepared to limit some of their freedoms for the sake of the stability of the country as a whole, defined by the protection of its electoral system. But what if it is the state that is not prepared to do so *vis-à-vis* a minority group? In *I. Länsman v. Finland*,[25] the HRC stated that the freedom of a state to pursue its own interests (*in casu*, development or economic activity by enterprises) should not be assessed by reference to a margin of appreciation ascribed to it, as contended by the respondent (which had recalled the EurCrtHR's approach under the ECHR), but by reference to whether the exercise of that freedom amounted to a denial of Article 27 rights.

Direct protection: diffusing general human rights

Unlike the HRC, the EurCrtHR does not have an explicit ethno-cultural parameter on which to rely within the scope of the ECHR. This might provide a justification for the language of indirect protection that characterises the above jurisprudence, in which the factual repercussions for the group's ability to articulate identity claims in the public sphere are different to a direct and sustained legal assessment of any such claims from the perspective of minority protection. As noted earlier, though, judicial discourse can also re-conceptualise general human rights categories when dealing with issues that specifically concern the identity of minority groups. Despite the lack of minority provisions in the relevant instruments, such discourse appears in effect capable of adjusting general human rights in order to uphold, directly albeit implicitly, elements of ethno-cultural diversity. In other words, the indirect approach discussed in the previous section stands alongside a more pro-active line that engages, to a greater or lesser extent, with the very substance of minority claims. The following provides illustrations of this in a variety of jurisprudential settings.

Private and family life

Jurisprudential discourse about Article 8 ECHR has led to an interesting re-conceptualisation of its scope in relation to specific minority issues. Human rights claims made by members of minority groups inevitably raise the question of how far the distinctive situation of the group is relevant.

[25] Comm. No. 511/1992, Views of 26 October 1994, (1995) II Annual Report 66.

The issue of whether an individual defined by his or her ethno-cultural origin – and *a fortiori* a member of a minority group – may enjoy protection of his or her personal name as written in accordance with the language of origin, not the language of the state in which such individual resides, provides an indication of this. In *Kuharec* alias *Kuhareca v. Latvia*,[26] the applicant – a 'non-citizen' of Latvia of Russian ethnic origin – claimed that Latvian spelling of her surname in her passport as Kuhareca instead of Kuharec (according to Russian spelling), used by Latvian authorities in keeping with Latvian legislation, run counter to her rights under Article 8 (1).

This type of case requires an assessment of national legislation regarding recognition of civil status names vis-à-vis names of individuals with a distinctive ethnic origin. This is especially the case when members of minority groups are involved, in view of the right to use, and to official recognition of, minority name(s) and surname as established under international human rights instruments.[27] Interestingly, in *Coeriel and Aurik v. the Netherlands*,[28] the HRC found a breach of the right to privacy in Article 17 ICCPR as a result of a refusal by the state party to change the authors' surnames into Hindu names. The case was not submitted by a minority member, but nevertheless the HRC broadly held that requests for a change of name can only be refused on reasonable grounds under the circumstances,[29] and that compulsory change of surname for all foreigners is clearly an interference with Article 17 ICCPR. In *Kuharec*, the EurCrtHR did not find a breach of Article 8 ECHR because under national legislation the Latvian government allowed both Latvian and non-Latvian spellings of names, and accepted to use the original spellings in passports alongside Latvian ones, upon request from the individuals concerned. In short, the system, although a draconian one compared to other European countries, was *not* deemed to entail forced nationalisation of non-Latvian names. Although the EurCrtHR upheld Latvia's official language as a way of protecting the rights of others (i.e. its speakers), it did not reaffirm the aim of unifying the nation and strengthening national identity as emphatically

[26] Application No. 71557/01, Admissibility Decision of 7 December 2004; see also *Mentzen* alias *Mencena v. Latvia*, Application No. 71074/01, Admissibility Decision of 7 December 2004.

[27] *See, e.g.*, Article 11 (1) of the Framework Convention for the Protection of National Minorities and Article 7 (2) of Recommendation 1201 (1993) on an additional protocol on the rights of minorities to the European Convention on Human Rights, adopted by the Parliamentary Assembly of the Council of Europe on 1 February 1993.

[28] Comm. 453/1991, UN Doc E/CN4/Sub.2/AC.5/2006/4.

[29] Refusal to change children's surname to include the father's name was deemed in breach of EC law in *Carlos Garcia Avello v. Belgium*, Case 148/02, Judgment of 2 October 2003, on the basis of Articles 12 (non-discrimination on grounds of nationality) and 17 (rights of citizens) EC Treaty. The Advocate General's Opinion challenged Belgium's argument on the grounds of non-discrimination and respect for cultural diversity, *ibid.*, para. 72.

invoked by the government, and even suggested that in other cases the Latvian system of transcription of non-Latvian names could be at odds with the ECHR. This line can be partly open to question,[30] yet it unquestionably raises the important dimension of involuntary change of one's name resulting from state-sponsored social engineering.

The link between the issue of name (mis)spelling and the wider effect of depriving minority members of a fundamental trait of their individual and ultimately collective identity has historically represented a major component of patterns of abuse against minority groups.[31] In another case before the HRC, this time struck out of the list, a Lithuanian citizen of Polish origin complained, *inter alia*, of a breach of his Article 27 rights as a result of Lithuanian legislation imposing the use of Lithuanian instead of mother tongue spelling for personal names.[32] As a member of the Polish community in Lithuania, the author claimed that Article 27 protected against the assimilation pressure that ethnic Poles were facing to change their names into Lithuanian ones, as a means of safeguarding an essential element of their culture and identity. In these cases, the distinctiveness of minority identity provides, implicitly or explicitly, an overarching theme of discourse that exposes the convergences and possibilities of the interpretive process.

A central aspect of this discourse in the context of Article 8 ECHR concerns the overall way of life of a minority group. In *G and E v. Norway*,[33] Sami members of Norway claimed that the decision of the Norwegian government to erect a hydroelectric plant in the Alta Valley would affect their traditional activities in that area, including reindeer herding, hunting and fishing. Although the case was declared inadmissible due to the specific nature of the claims, the (then) European Commission on Human Rights (EurCommHR) importantly understood Article 8 (1) in the sense of entitling in principle a minority group to claim 'the right to respect for the particular life style it may lead as being "private life", "family life" or "home"'. In *Buckley v. United Kingdom*,[34] a case concerning a Roma/Gypsy woman who claimed to be able

[30] The EurCrtHR did not explain how strict requirements for the spelling of foreign names affected the protection of Latvian speakers (through their national language), nor did it refer to the specific group dimension involved.

[31] Consider, for example, the case of the members of the German-speaking community in South Tyrol whose family names were 'Italianised' under the Mussolini regime, and then reinstated under the Paris Agreement between Italy and Austria of 5 September 1946. For an account of this case in general, see G. Pentassuglia, *Minorities in International Law: An Introductory Study* (Strasbourg, 2002), pp. 183, 232–233.

[32] *Tadeusz Kleczkowski (Tadeuš Klečkowski) v. Lithuania*, Comm. No. 1032/2001, submitted on 3 October 2001.

[33] Applications Nos. 9278/81 and 9415/81, DR, vol. 35, 35.

[34] Report of 11 January 1995, (1995) 19 EHRR CD 20, para. 64.

to park her caravan on her land notwithstanding the absence of planning permission, the EurCommHR consistently held that 'the traditional lifestyle of a minority may attract the guarantees of Article 8'. It found a violation of Article 8, but the EurCrtHR[35] reversed the decision, highlighting solely the applicant's right to a home, not a particular way of life. In a series of recent similar cases involving Roma/Gypsy individuals, the new Court (sitting as a Grand Chamber) established following the reforms introduced by Protocol No. 11, recalled the *Buckley* jurisprudence, particularly in regard to a wide margin of appreciation enjoyed in principle by national authorities in the choice and implementation of planning policies, and concluded that the relevant facts did not disclose any violation of Article 8. Conceptually, though, the EurCrtHR appeared to engage with the theme of minority identity as being implicitly relevant to a broader construction of that provision.

In *Chapman v. United Kingdom*,[36] the EurCrtHR, joining the EurCommHR's view in *Buckley*, indeed acknowledged that the applicant's traditional lifestyle, as part of their long-standing cultural identity, attracted the protection of private life, family life and home under Article 8, and that the contested measures affecting it constituted an interference subject to the parameters set forth in paragraph 2 of this provision.[37] Also, it referred to 'an emerging international consensus' within the Council of Europe 'recognising the special needs of minorities and an obligation to protect their security, identity and lifestyle', and identified a positive duty under Article 8 'to facilitate the Gypsy way of life'.[38] Nevertheless, the EurCrtHR[39] did not bring the above 'emerging consensus' to bear upon the case, and dismissed the notion that Article 8 imposed upon the respondent state a duty to make available to the Roma/Gypsy community an adequate number of suitably equipped caravan sites.

A strong dissent of seven judges stressed the need to give practical effect to the rights guaranteed by the ECHR, especially in the light of current developments in the field of minority protection within the Council of Europe. In essence, they argued for a narrower margin of appreciation on the part of national authorities on planning matters in the context of the measures interfering with the applicants' lifestyle. Indeed, they considered that such measures did not reflect any compelling justifications that could make them 'necessary in a democratic society' in the sense of Article 8 (2), and insisted on Article 8 as prescribing a positive duty to ensure that Roma/Gypsies be

[35] Judgment of 25 September 1996, Reports 1996-IV.

[36] Application No. 27238/95, Judgment of 18 January 2001, para. 73.

[37] See also the earlier *Noack v. Germany*, Application No. 46346/99, Admissibility Decision of 25 May 2000 (available in French).

[38] Application No. 27238/95, Judgment of 18 January 2001, paras. 93, 96.

[39] *Ibid.*, para. 94.

afforded a practical and effective opportunity to enjoy their rights to home, private and family life. This line inevitably re-read Article 8 on the basis of a connection between effectiveness of rights and new content.[40]

Overall, the important conceptual move reflected in *Chapman* on minority identity is limited by a dialogic acceptance and rejection of the minority perspective in framing the central issue for determination. The EurCrtHR's majority eventually shifted the focus from an identity-based understanding of Article 8 to the identity-blind construction of the right to a home embraced in *Buckley*. By contrast, the EurCommHR (and partly the dissent in *Chapman*) had discussed the home issue by attempting to inject substantive considerations regarding the specific way of life of the applicant into the reading of Article 8.

The protection of the particular way of life of a minority group has been recognised by the HRC within the context of a number of individual communications involving Article 27 ICCPR. In the case of *Bernard Ominayak, Chief of the Lubicon Lake Band v. Canada*,[41] regarding claims that industrial exploitation of resources threatened the band's way of life, the HRC defined such way of life by the social and economic activities that are distinctive to the culture of the group, and found that the relevant developments had encroached on it, in breach of Article 27. The HRC has consistently held this broad view of minority way of life, also explaining that the latter qualifies for protection even though the traditional means of livelihood have been adapted to modern technology.[42] As hinted at earlier, the HRC has stressed that state discretion with regard to economic or other activities – benefiting either private parties or the group itself – is limited by respect for the way of life of persons belonging to minority groups as required by Article 27, although the HRC appears to give states a certain leeway on these matters before a breach of Article 27 can be actually established.

In *Wisconsin v. Yoder*,[43] the US Supreme Court went as far as to limit state authority in that it struck down a state compulsory school attendance law that severely threatened the way of life of the Amish community by exposing Amish children to modern secondary public education that was incompatible with the values and lifestyle mandated by the Amish religion. Interestingly, the minority way of life theme is being used to modify the understanding of basic human rights categories, such as the right to life and human treatment.

---

[40] *Ibid.*, Joint Dissenting Opinion of Judges Pastor Ridruejo, Bonello, Tulkens, Strážnická, Lorenzen, Fischbach and Casadevall, paras. 3, 9; on the relationship between identity concerns and the effectiveness of general rights, see *infra*, Chapter 6.

[41] Comm. No. 167/1984, Views of 26 March 1990, Annual Report, vol. II, 1990, 1.

[42] *Ibid.*, para. 9.3.

[43] 406 U.S. 205 (1972).

In *Kayano*,[44] involving the impact of a governmental decision on the identity of the Ainu people, the Sapporo District Court conceptualised Article 13 of the Japanese Constitution regarding the right to life and liberty to include 'the right to enjoy the distinct ethnic culture of the Ainu people, which is the minority to which the plaintiffs belong'.[45] The basis for this argument was that there was no other way to provide meaningful protection of that right but to assume that human, and indeed cultural, diversity did fall within its own purview. In effect, the court embraced the substance of Article 27 ICCPR (to which it had referred as a distinct source of obligation) to redefine the right to life as encompassing the right to a particular (minority) way of life. A similar understanding of the right is presented in a recent decision of the Supreme Court of Belize regarding claims by some Mayan villagers of Southern Belize to their traditional lands. For this Court, 'life' and identity converge, whereby the latter informs a meaningful conception of the former – without protection of the rights of the Maya communities to their land, 'the enjoyment of their right to life and their very lifestyle and well-being would be seriously compromised and be in jeopardy'.[46]

The IACrtHR[47] and IACommHR[48] have come to recognise a link between the right to life and ethno-cultural identity in a string of cases, all involving claims to physical and cultural access to traditional lands by indigenous groups. As explained by Judge Ramirez in *Yatama v. Nicaragua*,[49] the IACrtHR in *Yakye Axa* understood the right to life both in the traditional sense (i.e. as a protection against arbitrary taking of life by the state) *and* – similarly to the conception upheld by the Sapporo District Court in *Kayano* – as an entitlement to a 'worthy life', that is, to live under conditions that are – as further explained in *Sawhoyamaxa* – 'minimally compatible with the dignity of the human person' and the cultural identity associated with it. In *Moiwana*,[50] the IACrtHR also found that the fact that the Moiwana community members

---

[44] Judgment of the Sapporo District Court, Civil Division No. 3, 27 March 1997, in (1999) 38 ILM, p. 397.

[45] *Ibid.*, p. 419.

[46] *Aurelio Cal et al. v. The Attorney General of Belize and the Minister of Natural Resources and Environment*, Claims Nos. 171 and 172 of 2007, Judgment of 18 October 2007, para. 117.

[47] See e.g. *Yakye Axa Indigenous Community v. Paraguay*, Judgment of 17 June 2005, Series C No. 125, para. 167; *Sawhoyamaxa Indigenous Community v. Paraguay*, Judgment of 29 March 2006, Series C No. 146, para. 153.

[48] See e.g. *Maya Indigenous Communities of the Toledo District v. Belize*, Report No. 96/03, Case 12.053, October 24, 2003, paras. 153–154.

[49] Judgment of 23 June 2005, Series C No. 127, Concurring Opinion of Judge Ramirez, paras. 23–24.

[50] Judgment of 15 June 2005, Series C No. 124, paras. 98–103.

could neither bury their loved ones in accordance with fundamental norms of N'djuka culture, nor enjoy their own traditional way of life as being inextricably linked to their land, was in breach of the right to physical and moral integrity in Article 5 (1) ACHR. In *The Social and Economic Rights Action Center for Economic and Social Rights v. Nigeria*,[51] involving the impact of oil development activities on the Ogoni people living in the area of the Niger delta, the AfrCommHPRs found *inter alia* a breach of the right to life in Article 4 ACHPR in connection with the pollution and environmental degradation of the Ogoniland that threatened the survival of the Ogonis and their traditional livelihood.[52]

The conceptual theme of these cases is pretty straightforward: the general human right at issue is informed by the specific interests and needs of minority groups, thereby enabling that right to work for the benefit of the group and its members. Article 8 ECHR provides a similar case through the arguably more congenial notion of 'private and family life'. In *Johtti Sapmelaccat Ry and others v. Finland*,[53] members of the Sami people of Finland complained that:

> Their right to respect for their private and family life had been violated since the Sami people, as a national minority and an indigenous people, were entitled to request that their special way of life was respected. That way of life, which included fishing as part of the Sami tradition, had to be regarded as "private and family life" protected by Article 8.

The EurCrtHR implicitly accepted this construction, thought it found no violation of the provision in the instant case. In the case of *Connors v. United Kingdom*,[54] concerning a summary eviction from a local authority Roma/Gypsy caravan site, the EurCrtHR emphasised Roma/Gypsy needs and way of life and found a breach of Article 8, though unlike *Chapman*, there had been no prior breach of planning law by the applicants.

Whereas the HRC's reading of minority way of life in Article 27 ICCPR is premised on the established, public dimension of group identity, 'private and family life' in Article 8 ECHR would appear to preclude a proactive consideration of those articulated components of minority identity, such as social or economic activities, that transcend the situation of specific individuals or

[51] Comm. No. 155/96, 2001, para. 67.

[52] All these cases somewhat mirror similar attempts to inject socio-economic considerations into the reading of the right to life: see e.g. the judgment of the Indian Supreme Court in *Olga Tellis v. Bombay Municipal Corporation*, [1985] 3 S.C.C. 545; S. Joseph, J. Schultz & M. Castan, *The International Covenant on Civil and Political Rights: Cases, Materials, and Commentary* (Oxford, 2004), pp. 184–187.

[53] Application No. 42969/98, Admissibility Decision of 18 January 2005.

[54] Application No. 66746/01, 27 May 2004, ECHR, paras. 83–84.

families. In *Slivenko v. Latvia*,[55] the EurCrtHR narrowed 'family life' to the core family, although earlier case law seems to allow a somewhat broader concept that includes near relatives, or values wider yet specific aspects of integration in the event of individuals' displacement.[56] In short, that notion seems *prima facie* exclusive rather than inclusive in scope from the standpoint of the relationship of the affected people to larger communities and the essential elements of their ethno-cultural identities. This need not be always the case, though. For example, in *Cyprus v. Turkey*,[57] the EurCrtHR made room for wider considerations by finding that adverse circumstances affecting the Greek-Cypriot population in the Karpas region, including, *inter alia*, insufficient number of priests for religious services and difficulties regarding secondary education for children, were so highly intrusive and invasive as to amount to a violation of their Article 8 right to respect for private and family life. This right may also be conceptualised to encompass the cultural values of families, including values based on the ancestral histories of minority groups. In *G and E*, the Sami applicants claimed that the flooding of a 2.8-kilomentre area of their ancestral hunting grounds by a hydroelectric project would be in breach of Article 8 ECHR. A similar argument was considered, *mutatis mutandis*, in the *Kayano* decision on the Nibutami dam, though the Sapporo District Court framed the issue in terms of the right to enjoy Ainu culture. The EurCommHR more openly based the re-conceptualisation of Article 8 ECHR on a connection between family livelihood and minority identity. And indeed, Article 17 ICCPR – somewhat the counterpart to Article 8 ECHR – was interpreted broadly by the HRC in the case of *Hopu and Bessert v. France*.[58]

The claim brought by native Tahitians against a French government decision to allow construction of a hotel complex in an ancient Polynesian grave site could not be considered under Article 27 due to the well-known reservation by France to this provision. Nevertheless, it was decided on the basis of Articles 17 and 23, most notably by understanding 'family' in connection with the community's social and cultural practices as well as traditions, and the relationship of the authors to their ancestors as an essential element of their

---

[55] Application No. 48321/99, Judgment of 9 October 2003, paras. 94–95.

[56] *Ibid.*, paras. 94–95, and the Partly Concurring and Partly Dissenting Opinion of Judge Klover, Section I. For a recent case involving a breach of Article 8 in connection with the internal displacement of the Kurdish population in south-east Turkey, see *Doðan and Others* v. *Turkey*, Applications Nos. 8803–8811/02, 8813/02 and 8815–8819/02, Judgment of 29 June 2004, para. 159; see also *Artun and Others v. Turkey*, Application No. 33239/96, Judgment of 2 February 2006; *Ağtas v. Turkey*, Application No. 33240/96, Judgment of 2 February 2006.

[57] Application No. 25781/94, Judgment of 10 May 2001, paras. 295–296.

[58] Comm. No. 549/1993, Views of 29 July 1997, [1997] II Annual Report, 70.

identities, although no direct kinship between them and the persons buried there had been established. The burial grounds, the HRC held, 'play[ed] an important role in the authors' history, culture and life'. Conceptually, this raises the issue of attending to cultural differences or perspectives in interpreting legal terms. Four dissenting HRC members stated that 'even when the term "family" is extended... [it] does not include all members of one's ethnic or cultural group' nor does it necessarily include one's ancestors.[59]

To be sure, this is precisely the way the IACommHR understood 'family' in the case of *Aloeboetoe and others v. Suriname*;[60] it argued that the villagers of the Saramaka community, to which the victims belonged, 'constitute[d] a family in the broad sense of the term'. While the IACrtHR did not accept the IACommHR's argument that reparation should be made to the group as a whole because of the murder of one of its members, it did acknowledge that the family structure and customary law of the Maroons, of which the Saramakas are a part, had to be taken into account in determining the victim's successors to whom compensation would be paid. In the more recent *Moiwana*, involving the N'djuka Maroon village of Moiwana, the IACrtHR construed a breach of the right to human treatment in Article 5 ACHR around aspects of family and communal life, such as the impossibility for the community members to bury their deceased ones in keeping with their customs, to obtain justice for the victims, and to reunite with their homeland.[61] Echoing *Aloeboetoe*, the IACrtHR awarded individual reparations in conjunction with reparation of moral damages for the community.[62] In *Bámaca Vèlasquez v. Guatemala*,[63] the IACrtHR considered the impact of the right of the victim's relatives to the mortal remains of the latter on the Maya culture. In *Maya Indigenous Communities of the Toledo District v. Belize*,[64] the IACommHR confirmed the deep-seated interplay of family relations, religious practices and land:

> The concept of family and religion within the context of indigenous communities, including the Maya people, is intimately connected with their traditional land, where ancestral burial grounds, places of religious significance and kinship patterns are linked with the occupation and use of their physical territories.[65]

[59] *Ibid.*, paras. 4–5.

[60] Judgment of 10 September 1993 (Reparations), Series C No. 15.

[61] Judgment of 15 June 2005, Series C No. 124, paras. 94–103.

[62] *Ibid.*, para. 194. On these aspects, see *infra*, Chapter 5.

[63] Judgment of 25 November 2000, Series C No. 70.

[64] Report No. 96/03, Case 12.053, October 24, 2003.

[65] *Ibid.*, para. 154.

Property

Both the IACommHR and the IACrtHR have engaged in a remarkable re-conceptualisation of property rights in relation to indigenous communities. In fact, during the 1980s and most of the 1990s indigenous issues had been raised before those bodies, though the question of property *stricto sensu* had hardly appeared in their jurisprudential discourse.

In its 1983 *Report on the situation of human rights of a segment of the Nicaraguan population of Miskito origin,*[66] the IACommHR considered a range of complaints that had been lodged with it on behalf of the Miskito Indians inhabiting the Atlantic Coast of Nicaragua. Although most such complaints turned on the physical integrity of the Miskitos, one of them did allege a violation of the right to property set forth in Article 21 ACHR as a result of the denial by the Sandinista government of an 'inherent right of the Indian people to possess, use and enjoy their ancestral lands, as well as its resources and riches'.[67] The IACommHR held that it was not in a position to decide 'on the strict legal validity of the claim', yet it acknowledged the seriousness of the problem of ancestral lands and land tenure systems deeply affected by colonial and post-colonial legacies, and recommended the government to study a 'just solution' to it.[68] In *Yanomami v. Brazil,*[69] the IACommHR could not address the complaint under the ACHR, as Brazil had not ratified it, but it nevertheless found a violation of broadly construed general rights recognised in the American Declaration of the Rights and Duties of Man (ADRDM) and recommended that the government set and demarcate the boundaries of the Yanomami park – the traditional area of the Yanomami Indians.

Conceptually, these cases, while not directly referring to property rights, reflected an emerging understanding of indigenous identity as defined by indigenous land. Within the wider Inter-American system, this cultural link was indirectly reinforced by a sustained review of the situation of human rights and indigenous groups in OAS member states by the IACommHR, friendly settlements that had been prompted by claims to ancestral lands of which such groups had been deprived, and the recognition by the IACrtHR of certain practices rooted in the communities' customary laws.[70]

---

[66] OEA/Ser.L./V.II.62, doc.10 rev.3, 29 November 1983.

[67] *Ibid.*, Part II, F.1.

[68] *Ibid.*, Part II, F.6, Resolution on the Friendly Settlement Procedure regarding the Human Rights Situation of a Segment of the Nicaraguan population of Miskito origin, OEA/Ser. L/V/II.62, May 16, 1984.

[69] Resolution No. 12/85, Case No. 7615, March 5, 1985.

[70] OEA/Ser.L/V/II.108, 20 October 2000.

The case of *Mayagna (Sumo) Awas Tingni Community v. Nicaragua*[71] somewhat accomplished a turn towards openly locating indigenous land issues within the scope of Article 21 ACHR. The IACommHR asked the IACrtHR to pronounce on *inter alia* Nicaragua's failure to demarcate the communal lands of the Awas Tingni Community, to adopt effective measures to ensure their property rights, and to obtain their consent to logging operations on their lands. Unlike a situation where the specific property rights of the community, while neglected in practice, are recognised under domestic law, this case was clearly one in which 'the Community has no real property title deed to the lands it claims.'[72] As explained by one of the expert witnesses:

> Problems arise when the State decide to issue deed titles to those lands or to grant concessions or to allow the clearing of those lands, to authorize the use of those lands for other purposes determined by various economic interests. That is when many indigenous peoples realize that juridically speaking they are not the authentic owners of the territories which they have occupied traditionally.[73]

The IACommHR argued that property rights should be upheld on the basis of an inextricable connection between indigenous customary law land tenure systems and indigenous communities' way of life, regardless of whether the group had formal title to the lands under domestic law. By contrast, Nicaragua essentially centred its line of defence on proper registering and titling of the territory as a precondition for recognition of property, notwithstanding protection of indigenous land rights in the Constitution and national legislation. It is here that the IACrtHR established its own identity-based conceptualisation of property under the ACHR. The interpretation of Article 21 ACHR was built around the notion that terms of an international human rights treaty should be regarded as autonomous to national law concepts, and their interpretation should be adapted to present-day conditions and be such that the scope of rights is not restrictive. On this reading, 'property' is presented as being at the intersection of material and cultural attachments:

> Among indigenous peoples there is a communitarian tradition regarding a communal form of collective property of the land, in the sense that ownership of the land is not centred on an individual but rather on the group and the community. Indigenous peoples, by the fact of their very existence, have the right to live freely in their own territory; the close ties of indigenous people with the land

[71] Judgment of 31 August 2001, Series C No. 79.

[72] *Ibid.*, para. 103, lit. g. See, by contrast, *Garifuna Community of 'Triunfo de la Cruz' and its members v. Honduras*, Report No. 29/06, Petition 906–03, Admissibility, 14 March, 2006, para. 3.

[73] Judgment of 31 August, 2001, Series C No. 79, para. 83, lit. d [expert opinion by Rodolfo Stavenhagen Gruenbaum], p. 26.

> must be recognized and understood as the fundamental basis of their cultures, their spiritual life, their integrity, and their economic survival. For indigenous communities, relations to the land are not merely a matter of possession and production but a material and spiritual element which they must fully enjoy, even to preserve their cultural legacy and transmit it to future generations.[74]

From the perspective of the ACHR, possession of the land is thus made sufficient to obtain international legal recognition and protection of the property of indigenous communities lacking real title to it. The theme of domestic versus international law is indirectly taken up by Judge Montiel Argüello's dissenting opinion, which insisted on the existence of a national mechanism for titling indigenous groups' lands. This point may in fact be viewed as being either procedural or substantive. Procedurally, the IACrtHR defined indigenous property rights through the state's duty to delimit, demarcate and title the lands in question, thereby requiring an effective domestic procedure to realise those rights. Since the dissent did not refer to the concept of indigenous property within the scope of Article 21 ACHR, the title to property argument might be read in the sense of emphasising that Nicaragua had complied with that procedural duty, despite the fact that the internal system could be further improved. Substantively, though, the national law thesis might be justified on the basis that no property claim may be protected under the ACHR unless such claim is rooted in a right or title *that already exists* under domestic law. Like Nicaragua in *Mayagna*, Turkey made this argument before the EurCrtHR in *Doĝan and others v. Turkey*, which originated from forced evictions of the applicants from their houses and village in south-east Turkey by security forces as a result of violent clashes between the latter and sectors of the Kurdish community living in the region. In this case, the EurCrtHR rejected Turkey's claim and embraced an autonomous notion of 'possessions' that included the overall economic activities of the villagers deriving from their traditional land tenure system as a community, despite the absence of title deeds under Turkish law.[75]

It is clear that the IACrtHR's judgment does assume the independent interpretive role of the ACHR and, by implication, other international human rights standards, vis-à-vis the actual set up of domestic property regimes. In *Yakye Axa* and *Sawhoyamaxa*,[76] involving claims to ancestral lands by the community, the IACrtHR even conceded that, in the event of a conflict between indigenous communal property and individual private property, the

[74] *Ibid.*, para. 149.

[75] Applications Nos. 8803–8811/02, 8813/02 and 8815–8819/02, Judgment of 29 June 2004, paras. 137–139.

[76] Judgment of 17 June 2005, Series C No. 125; Judgment of 29 March 2006, Series C No. 146.

former may prevail over the latter in order the protect indigenous identity as part of the 'democratic and pluralistic society' upheld by the ACHR, so long as that conflict is decided on a case-by-case basis and is in conformity with Article 21 (2) ACHR. The mere fact that the reclaimed lands are in private hands and are being productively used does not provide an 'objective and fundamental' reason to reject an indigenous claim. Judge Salgado Pesantes in *Mayagna* alluded, by contrast, to limitations on indigenous property rights in the name of social interest under Article 21 (1) ACHR.[77]

That frictions may indeed arise between domestic property law and international standards can be illustrated by *Jarle Jonassen and Members of the Riast/Hylling Reindeer Herding District v. Norway*,[78] in which the authors – Sami reindeer herders of Norway – challenged Norwegian Supreme Court rulings that denied them the right to reindeer herding on privately owned lands of the Riast/Hylling district. In essence, they argued that it was virtually impossible for them to acquire grazing rights under Norwegian property law as compared with non-Sami people, and that a 1997 Supreme Court decision heavily relied upon a late nineteenth century Supreme Court case law that discriminated against the Sami by favouring landlords' rights to private property. The case raised issues under Articles 2, 26 and 27 ICCPR, but the HRC declared the communication inadmissible in respect of all parts of their claim. A minority led by Mr Henkin disagreed with this conclusion and favoured an assessment of Norwegian property law in the context of Article 27 ICCPR. Although the authors claimed special use rights rather than property rights, they reaffirmed the connection between land and identity that underlies *Mayagna* and other cases, while bringing to the fore, albeit indirectly, the role of international human rights law in assessing restrictive domestic (property) regimes.

As Judge Ramírez noted in *Mayagna*, 'use and enjoyment of his property' in Article 21 ACHR, instead of 'private property' from an earlier draft of this article, can be taken to imply rejection of a single model of property and to allow for accommodation of all subjects protected by the ACHR 'according to [their] culture, interests, aspirations, customs, characteristics and beliefs'.[79] The re-conceptualisation of property based on the co-existence of indigenous and non-indigenous models was reaffirmed in *Yakye Axa* and, more recently, *Sawhoyamaxa* and *Saramaka*.[80] The latter case crucially reinforces

[77] Judgment of 31 August 2001, Series C No. 79, Concurring Opinion of Judge Hernán Salgado Pesantes, para. 5.

[78] Comm. No. 942/2000, Views of 25 October 2002, UN Doc. CCPR/C/76/D/942/2000 (2000).

[79] Judgment of 31 August 2001, Series C No. 79, Concurring Opinion of Judge Sergio García Ramírez, para. 11.

[80] Judgment of 17 June 2005, Series C No. 125, paras. 135, 137, 154; Judgment of 29 March 2006, Series C No. 146, paras. 118–128; Judgment of 28 November 2007, Series C No. 172, paras. 87–96.

the articulation of property rights by regarding the natural resources that lie on and within the land as being an integral part of the notion of indigenous property to the extent that they are necessary for the sustainability of the group's way of life.[81]

In *Moiwana*, the IACrtHR applied the *Mayagna* jurisprudence to a displaced tribal community which, like the Mayagna Awas Tingni community of Nicaragua, lacked official title to the land despite their historical occupancy.[82] The attachment of indigenous groups to their traditional lands has taken on a two-pronged – 'external' and 'internal' – relational meaning. For one thing, factual possession has been externally singled out as an autonomous criterion for establishing indigenous property rights under the ACHR, as opposed to notions of legal title and recognition under domestic law. At the same time, indigenous possession itself has been internally (re-)defined to include not only a strict physical relationship with the land but also a variety of spiritual and cultural bonds that have been maintained despite the loss of the land for reasons outside the group's will. The indigenous model of property thus lies at the intersection of this critical understanding of possession and title, on the one hand, and material and spiritual basis of identity on the other.

In short, the re-assessment of property matters within the Inter-American system is being defined by a distinctive injection of human rights considerations. *Mary and Carrie Dann v. United States*[83] provides further illustration of this. The petitioners were members of an Indian band belonging to the Western Shoshone indigenous people in the state of Nevada. They had long refused to accept the permit system for grazing rights on traditional Western Shoshone lands (including their own). They argued that by limiting the occupation and use of those lands, the United States had violated their property rights under Article XXIII ADRDM. Whereas the respondent state had presented the case as simply one concerning land title and land use under US law, the IACommHR by referring to 'evolving rules and principles of human rights law in the Americas and in the international community more broadly, as reflected in treaties, custom and other sources of international law,'[84] framed the dispute on the basis of 'distinct human rights considerations relating to the ownership, use and occupation by indigenous communities of their traditional lands.'[85] In other words, it was the interplay of identity and land that informed the narrative of indigenous property as a human rights

81 See further on this point, *supra*, Chapter 1, note 48.

82 Judgment of 15 June 2005, Series C No. 124, para. 133. The IACommHR took a similar line in *Garifuna Community of Cayos Cochinos and its members v. Honduras*, Report No. 39/07, Petition 1118-03, Admissibility, 24 July 2007.

83 Report No. 75/02, Case 11.1140, December 27, 2002.

84 *Ibid.*, para. 124.

85 *Ibid.*

issue in the IACommHR's perspective, as opposed to an identity-blind (and human rights-free) construct revolving around merely technical notions or procedures of national law.

On a more general level, these competing approaches are somewhat reminiscent of the clash of interpretations surfaced in *Buckley* under the ECHR, regarding the question of whether the protection of the way of life of Roma individuals outweighed under Article 8 ECHR considerations regarding compliance with UK planning regulations. In that case 'private and family life' was understood by the EurCommHR in a way that allowed for accommodation of Roma identity, but the EurCrtHR failed to embrace identity aspects and considered the case as raising an issue of respect for the applicant's right to a home in conjunction with domestic planning laws. While still obviously retaining a human rights perspective, the EurCrtHR's reading was far from endorsing 'distinct human rights considerations' in the sense of *Mary and Carrie Dann*.

Overall, the broad reading of the right to property within the Inter-American system rests on a cross-fertilisation interpretive process, whereby the scope of Articles 21 ACHR and XXIII ADRDM is being expanded by considering relevant precepts or aspects of indigenous protection under international human rights law. By regarding the ACHR as having an 'autonomous meaning' (compared to domestic law) and being a 'living instrument' (i.e. in accordance with present-day conditions and the wider legal system), the IACrtHR in *Mayagna* essentially reaffirmed the teleological line endorsed by the EurCrtHR on several occasions when interpreting the ECHR.[86] It is a systemic (re-)assessment of the Inter-American instruments that has proved key to valuing the issue of indigenous property within their own purview. In its Advisory Opinion on *The Right to Information on Consular Assistance within the Framework of the Guarantees of Due Process*, the IACrtHR elaborated upon the ICJ jurisprudence in *South West Africa (Second Phase)* by holding that 'the interpretation of a treaty must take into account not only the agreements and instruments related to the treaty...but also the system of which it is part'.[87] The *Yakye Axa* decision reaffirmed the understanding of the interpretive context adopted by the IACrtHR in that advisory opinion:

> The *corpus iuris* of international human rights law comprises a set of international instruments of varied content and juridical effects (treaties, conventions, resolutions, and declarations). Its dynamic evolution has had a positive impact on international law in affirming and building up the latter's faculty for regulat-

[86] See *infra*, Chapter 6.

[87] AO OC-16/99, Series A No. 16, para. 113. For the *South West Africa* case, see below in the chapter.

> ing relations between States and the human beings within their jurisdictions. This Court, therefore, must adopt the proper approach to consider this question [in casu, the right to due process of law] in the context of the evolution of the fundamental rights of the human person in contemporary international law.[88]

More specifically, in both *Yakye Axa* and *Sawhoyamaxa*, ILO Convention 169 was regarded as a major part of the wider international human rights system affecting the reading of Article 21 ACHR. In *Saramaka*, the concept of property and its ramifications in relation to natural resources were re-assessed in the light of the right to self-determination in common Article 1 of the UN Covenants, Article 27 ICCPR, regional and domestic jurisprudence, as well as the IACrtHR's earlier jurisprudence.[89] The IACommHR consistently upheld an equally broad argument in cases such as *Maya*, *Mary and Carrie Dann* and *The Kichwa Peoples of the Sarayaku Community and its Members v. Ecuador*.[90] In *Mary and Carrie Dann*, the United States argued that the ACHR, the Draft American Declaration on the Rights of Indigenous People, and ILO Convention 169, were all irrelevant to the case because the state was not a party to the first and third instruments, and the second one was merely 'soft law'. A similar point was made by Ecuador in *The Kichwa Peoples* case, in relation to ILO Convention 169. In both cases, the IACommHR dismissed the argument by linking the ADRDM to the wider (treaty- and customary law-based) canon of international indigenous rights in general, and indigenous land rights in particular, and even regarded the ACHR as an 'authoritative expression of the fundamental principles set forth in the American Declaration.'[91] In *Hingitaq 53* before the EurCrtHR, members of the Thule tribe of Greenland implicitly relied upon the substance of Articles 14 and 16 ILO Convention 169 (previously invoked before the domestic courts) to frame their claim of a breach of property rights under Article 1 of Protocol 1 ECHR, though the EurCrtHR found that it had no jurisdiction *ratione temporis* in respect of the contested 1950s interferences with the Thule tribe's homeland.

Similarly to *Mayagna*, *Maya* focused primarily on claims to indigenous property made by the Maya communities of Belize as a response to non-indigenous settlements and large scale logging and oil development activities on their traditional lands. The petitioners had invoked aboriginal title

---

[88] Judgment of 17 June 2005, Series C No. 125, paras. 126–128.

[89] Judgment of 28 November 2007, Series C No. 172, paras. 92–96, 120–122, fn. 122. Conceptually speaking, *Saramaka* arguably goes beyond the cautious approach of both ILO Convention 169 and the UNDIP on the question of indigenous ownership of natural (sub-surface) resources: see *infra*, Chapter 7.

[90] Report No. 64/04, Petition 167/03, Admissibility, October 13, 2004.

[91] *Ibid.*, para. 97; the IACrtHR has primarily – though by no means exclusively – relied on treaties and declarations ratified or supported by the state concerned.

especially on the basis of *Mabo* before the High Court of Australia,[92] but the IACommHR noted that it was unclear as to whether the Maya had any such title under constitutional or common law. At the same time, it applied and expanded on *Mayagna* by holding that the property right of the Maya people under international law (based on multiple universal and regional standards, as indicated in *Mary and Carrie Dann*, that feed into the reading of Article XXIII ADRDM) was not dependent on particular concepts of property under common law. Conversely, in *Aurelio Cal et al.*, the Supreme Court of Belize built upon the *Maya* decision to affirm that Maya customary land tenure constitutes a form of property that is protected directly by the Constitution.[93]

The elaboration on indigenous property within the Inter-American system and its domestic fallout also testify to the contribution being made by judicial discourse to conceptualising the distinctive and complex nature of indigenous property rights. In *Mayagna*, the IACrtHR held that 'article 21 of the Convention protects the right to property in a sense which includes, among others, the rights of members of the indigenous communities within the framework of communal property'.[94] In his concurring opinion, Judge Ramirez noted 'an intimate and inextricable link between individual and collective rights, a linkage that is a condition *sine qua non* for genuine protection of persons belonging to indigenous ethnic groups'.[95] The actual degree to which indigenous claims find a place in international law very much depends on the multiple processes that are designed to address them. This is exemplified by the not necessarily identical logics of ILO Convention 169, the UNDIP, and the Draft American Declaration the Rights of Indigenous People. In *Maya*, the IACommHR recognised indigenous rights as rights 'that can only be properly ensured through their guarantee to an indigenous community as a whole. The right to property has been recognized as one of the rights having such a collective aspect'.[96]

---

[92] No. 2, 175 CLR 1 (1992).

[93] Claims Nos. 171 and 172 of 2007, Judgment of 18 October 2007, paras. 99–100, 102.

[94] Judgment of 31 August, 2001, Series C No. 79, para. 148; the point was subsequently confirmed in *Yakye Axa Indigenous Community v. Paraguay*, Judgment of 17 June 2005, Series C No. 125, para. 147; *Moiwana Village v. Suriname*, Judgment of 15 June 2005, Series C No. 124, paras. 129–133; *Sawhoyamaxa Indigenous Community v. Paraguay*, Judgment of 29 March 2006, Series C No. 146, paras. 117, 134–136.

[95] Judgment of 31 August 2001, Series C No. 79, Concurring Opinion of Judge Sergio García Ramírez, para. 14.

[96] Report No. 96/03, Case 12.053, October 24, 2003, para. 112. In *Aurelio Cal et al.*, the Supreme Court of Belize found a collective title to the land that included 'the derivative individual rights and interests of Village members' in accordance with Maya customary practices: Claims Nos. 171 and 172 of 2007, Judgment of 18 October 2007, para. 136(b).

In a similar case, *The Social and Economic Rights Action Center*,[97] the AfrCommHPRs found a breach of the Ogonis' right to freely dispose of their wealth and natural resources under Article 21 ACHPR, in addition to a violation of the individual right to property under Article 14. For one thing, the discourse about Article 21 ACHPR, which focussed on the destruction of the Ogoniland and a lack of Ogoni participation in decisions affecting that land, did resemble the narrative that underpins indigenous land rights decisions. On the other hand, the AfrCommHPRs also found a breach of the right to protection against forced evictions as part of the individual right to adequate housing, which was presented as a right to be enjoyed by the Ogonis collectively.[98] In *Hingitaq 53*, where, as noted above, the applicants' property claims under Article 1 of Protocol 1 ECHR had been implicitly construed in connection with ILO Convention 169 land rights, the EurCrtHR held that the Supreme Court of Denmark had struck a fair balance 'between the general interest of the community and the need to protect the individual's fundamental rights.'[99]

Education, language, participation

Traditional themes, such as education, language and political participation, offer further illustrations of the role of judicial discourse in articulating, and progressively embracing, aspects of minority identity within the general human rights canon.

As is widely known, in the landmark *Case Relating to Certain Aspects of the Laws on the Use of Languages in Education in Belgium*,[100] the EurCrtHR held that there was no right to receive instruction in a special way, or in a special language, under Article 2 of Protocol 1 ECHR, taken alone or in conjunction with Article 14. In the recent case of *Jeļena Grišankova and Oļegs Grišankovs v. Latvia*,[101] the applicants – a mother and her son, both Latvian citizens of Russian ethnic origin – complained about the Education Law passed by Latvian Parliament in 1998 providing for, in particular, a shift to public secondary education (from the 10th grade onwards) in Latvian as the only language of instruction as from 1 September 2004. They claimed a denial of

97 Comm. No. 155/96, 2001.

98 Especially the right to housing and the right to food – both of them not explicitly mentioned in the ACHPR – were found on the basis of a combination of individual and collective rights set forth in the instrument.

99 Application No. 18584/04, Admissibility Decision of 12 January 2006, Section A.

100 Judgment of 23 July 1968, Series A, No. 6.

101 Application No. 36117/02, Admissibility Decision of 13 February 2003, (available in French).

the right to education in Article 2 of Protocol 1. The second applicant referred to the forthcoming obligatory change from Russian – the teaching language in his own school in Riga, through which he had completed his studies at the primary level – to Latvian as destined to put Russian-speaking pupils at a severe disadvantage compared to native Latvians, thereby amounting in fact to a denial of the right to education in Article 2 of Protocol 1. With regard to education rights, the first applicant also argued that, as a result of this provision, compelling her son to pursue secondary school education in a language other than his own run counter to her religious and philosophical convictions in the sense of the second sentence of Article 2 of Protocol 1. The EurCrtHR declared the application inadmissible because of a failure to exhaust local remedies, but left open the substantive question of whether the claim as such could disclose a breach of the ECHR.

In effect, in the earlier *Cyprus* case, the EurCrtHR, without reversing the *Belgian Linguistics* case approach to mother tongue education, took an unprecedented flexible line when addressing the educational situation of children of Greek-Cypriots living in northern Cyprus. On the one hand, it noted that, the presence of Turkish- and English-speaking secondary schools in the north satisfied the 'primary' obligation set out by Article 2 of Protocol 1, which 'does not specify the language in which education must be conducted in order that the right to education be respected'.[102] On the other hand, it stressed that the authorities in the north must have been aware of 'the wish of Greek-Cypriot parents that the schooling of their children be completed through the medium of the Greek language', coming to the conclusion that 'having assumed responsibility for the provision of Greek-language primary schooling, the failure of the "TRNC" authorities to make continuing provision for it at the secondary-school level must be considered in effect to be a denial of the substance of the right at issue'.[103] The EurCrtHR's reasoning was arguably affected by the particular situation of northern Cyprus, and especially the fact that the Turkish-Cypriot authorities (TRNC) were responsible for Greek-language primary education and had abolished provision for Greek-language secondary education. There can be little doubt, though, that the EurCrtHR did engage in a discourse that was intended to accommodate the position of a (de facto) minority group within the scope of the ECHR. This seems to suggest a deeper re-assessment of the right to education in a way that enables a finding of *implicit* exceptions to the no-mother tongue education rule under the ECHR, at least when the claimed mother tongue education adds to mother tongue schooling levels for which the state is responsible, represents a way

[102] Application No. 25781/94, Judgment of 10 May 2001, para. 277.
[103] *Ibid.*, para. 278.

of restoring the education previously available under domestic law, and is rooted in a clear wish of the community in question. On this approach, as Geoff Gilbert rightly points out, mother tongue education can be upheld 'wherever there exits a slow decline in inter-communal relations between the state and the minority'.[104]

These elements might have arguably been established in *Jeļena Grišankova*, as is further suggested by rather sharp criticisms even of later amendments to the Education Law believed to disproportionately curtail, while not completely abolishing, public minority education in Latvia.[105] In *Belgian Linguistics* the EurCrtHR, while denying the existence of the right to mother tongue education under Article 2 of Protocol 1, did imply the existence of a linguistic component in such provision. It affirmed that 'the right to education would be meaningless if it did not imply, in favour of its beneficiaries, the right to be educated in the national language or in one of the national languages, as the case may be'.[106] In *Cyprus*, the substance of the right is defined by a combination of objective needs (i.e. to continue receiving mother tongue education in secondary schools) and legitimate aspirations (i.e. to preserve one's own ethno-cultural identity).[107] As the EurCrtHR makes the right 'practical and effective',[108] it inevitably suggests a broader reading of that right – a combination somewhat reminiscent of the dissent in *Chapman*.[109] Indeed, *Cyprus* might conceptually be taken to indicate that, while mother tongue education cannot be claimed as a matter of right, the linguistic component implicitly attached to Article 2 of Protocol 1 does not always exclude protection of education in a non-dominant language.

A minority related discursive space may also develop around classical human rights categories such as freedom of expression and participation rights. For example, in *J. G. A. Diergaardt et al. v. Namibia*,[110] the issue of whether Article 19 (2) ICCPR would allow for linguistic preferences in the public sphere, particularly in the sense of allowing minority groups to use their mother tongue in such sphere, was discussed by individual HRC members. The joint dissent led by Mr Bhagwati argued that 'the authors could not legitimately contend that they should be allowed to use their mother tongue

---

104 G. Gilbert, 'The Burgeoning Minority Rights Jurisprudence of the European Court of Human Rights' (2002) 24 *Human Rights Quarterly*, p. 762.

105 See e.g., Minority Issues in Latvia, Nos. 71 (16 August 2003), 79 (23 January 2004), 80 (21 February 2004), accessible at <www.minelres/lv/count/latvia.htm#MinIssuesLatvia>.

106 Judgment of 23 July 1968, para. 3.

107 Application No. 25781/94, Judgment of 10 May 2001, para. 478.

108 *Airey v. Ireland*, Application No. 6289/73, 9 October 1979, Series A, No. 32, para. 24.

109 See *supra*, note 40.

110 Comm. No. 760/1997, Views of 25 July 2000, CCPR/C/69/D/760/1996.

in administration or in the Courts or in public life, and the insistence of the State party that only the official language shall be used cannot be regarded as violation of their right under Article 19, paragraph 2'.[111]

This approach confirms the HRC's earlier view in the case of *Dominique Guesdon v. France*,[112] that the fact that the author – a French-speaking Breton – had not been able to speak his mother tongue [i.e. Breton] before French courts 'raised no issues' under Article 19 (2). It also appears reminiscent of a statement made by the HRC in *Ballantyne et al. v. Canada*, apparently suggesting that, a state does not violate Article 19 (2) when prohibiting linguistic freedom in the spheres of *public* life, in line with its official language(s) policy.[113] In essence, the HRC appeared to distinguish between linguistic freedom in the private sphere (allowed under that provision) and language rights involving a direct relation with any branch of government. In *Ford v. Quebec*,[114] the Canadian Supreme Court confined the latter dimension to specific constitutional rights as opposed to general human rights entitlements such as freedom of expression, though those rights may not always override an official monolingual policy.[115] In *Diergaardt*, the joint concurring opinion led by Mrs Evatt maintained instead that the Article 19 issue reflected an additional aspect of the case, and that the refusal by the civil servants in question to use the authors' mother tongue when replying to written or oral communications from the authors, even if they had the personal capacity to do so, amounted to an unjustified restriction on Article 19 (2). Here again, similarly to the nuanced approach to mother tongue education in *Cyprus*, minority concerns appeared to militate in favour of a minority-friendly understanding of the right at issue. In essence, the joint concurring opinion suggested active knowledge of the relevant language by the public officials involved as a test for determining whether or not the lack of mother tongue communication with public bodies has restricted the freedom to receive and impart information of minority members.

In *Podkolzina v. Latvia*,[116] the applicant attempted to re-open the debate as to whether Article 3 of Protocol 1 ECHR (electoral rights) can be read in a way to establish a 'public' linguistic component. In *Mathieu-Mohin and Clerfayt v. Belgium*,[117] in line with even earlier jurisprudence, the EurCrtHR

---

111 *Ibid.*, para. 2.

112 Comm. No. 219/1986, Views of 25 July 1990, (1990) II Annual Report 61.

113 Communications Nos. 359/1989, 385/1989, Views of 31 March 1993, para. 11.4.

114 [1988] S.C.R. 712, para. 43.

115 See e.g. T. H. Malloy, *National Minority Rights in Europe* (Oxford, 2005), pp. 193–195 [language protection in Macedonia].

116 Application No. 46726/99, Judgment of 9 April 2002.

117 Judgment of 2 March 1987, Series A, No. 113.

dismissed the existence of such a component when assessing the position of the French-speakers elected in *Halle-Vilvoorde*, despite the language requirements under Belgian law that de facto precluded their membership in the Dutch regional council dealing with their constituencies. Ingrîda Podkolzina had registered as a candidate for the national elections of 1998 and supplied a certificate attesting to her upper level knowledge of Latvian, as required by the legislation on parliamentary elections. She was subsequently removed from the list of candidates due to her inadequate command of Latvian, as a result of a separate language examination undertaken by a civil servant of the State Language Centre. She argued, *inter alia*, that, as a member of the Russian-speaking minority in Latvia, she did not need to be proficient in Latvian to discharge the parliamentary mandate that she received from her Russian-speaking electors or to communicate with them.

By appealing to the margin of appreciation doctrine in language matters involving national Parliaments, the EurCrtHR did not really address the point made by the applicant, that in certain circumstances mother tongue communication might be a means of securing the effectiveness of Article 3 of Protocol 1 (apparently confirmed, to some extent, by the abolishment of Latvian language requirements to stand for parliamentary and local elections passed by Latvian Parliament in 2002 following this case). Nevertheless, the decision was construed around the additional claim that the language skills in question had been inappropriately tested by the authorities. Indeed, the EurCrtHR questioned the legal basis for a re-assessment of the applicant's language knowledge and found that, in any event, the full discretion left to a single civil servant in this process 'was incompatible with the requirements of procedural fairness and legal certainty'.[118] While the court's response turned on procedural rather than substantive issues, it also made implicitly room for a re-consideration of participation rights that takes due account of minority concerns. In other words, limitations on state language requirements simultaneously impact on the degree of effective participation of minority groups in public life. The same point had been made one year earlier by the HRC in *Antonina Ignatane v. Latvia*,[119] where a breach of Article 25 ICCPR was found under almost identical circumstances, though Ingrîda Podkolzina also made the mother tongue communication claim and both applicants had claimed that the 'third-level knowledge' or high level of proficiency of Latvian required of prospective candidates in parliamentary and local elections, respectively, was

118 Application No. 46726/99, Judgment of 9 April 2002, para. 36. For a similar type of review in the context of procedures to disqualify potential candidates, see e.g. *Ždanoka v. Latvia*, Application No. 58278/00, (2007) 45 EHRR, para. 115(e).

119 Comm. No. 884/1999, Views of 25 July 2001, CCPR/C/72/D/884/1999 (1999).

manifestly disproportionate to the aim pursued – an assumption implicitly accepted by the 2002 legislation mentioned above.

Aside from issues of language use, the position of minority groups can affect the reading of participation rights on a more specific level. In *Diergaardt*, the HRC did not resort to group considerations in dealing with the Article 25 claim made by the authors, but Mr Scheinin in his concurring opinion noted that there might be situations where special arrangements, going beyond the individual right to vote in general elections, are called for to secure effective participation rights of members of minority groups, particularly indigenous groups, under that provision. In *Yatama*,[120] the IACrtHR implicitly upheld the thrust of this proposition by offering a nuanced understanding of the right to political participation in Article 23 ACHR. Based on a decision of the Supreme Electoral Council of Nicaragua, representatives of a local indigenous political party had been refused to stand as candidates in the municipal elections that took place in 2000 in the Autonomous Regions of the Northern and Southern Atlantic Coast of the country. Under a new electoral law adopted in 2000, the party had not met the requirement that candidates be registered in eighty per cent of the relevant municipalities. The IACrtHR found such requirement to be unduly restrictive on the Atlantic Coast's indigenous groups as they lacked the resources, structures and interest to enter a higher number of candidates which included non-indigenous areas. One major point made by the IACommHR before the IACrtHR was that, contrary to general and Inter-American international law, Nicaragua had failed to secure effective participation of these persons and, under the electoral law, it had obliged indigenous groups and organisations (just as non-indigenous movements) to establish themselves as political parties in order for them to participate in the electoral process, notwithstanding their very different customary practices and values.

Importantly, the IACrtHR combined the distinctiveness of indigenous and ethnic minority groups,[121] the constitutional recognition of indigenous identity,[122] and several regional and universal instruments elaborating on the notion of representative democracy and political participation,[123] to conclude that the requirement of presenting indigenous candidates only through political parties, as in the instant case, infringed on uniquely indigenous conceptions and methods of association and organisation (as opposed to other understandings of political activity and structures), and was therefore in breach of Article 23

[120] Judgment of 23 June 2005, Series C No. 127.
[121] *Ibid.*, para. 202.
[122] *Ibid.*, para. 205.
[123] *Ibid.*, paras. 192, 207–208.

read against the general principle of non-discrimination in Article 24.[124] In short, participation rights, especially passive electoral rights,[125] were re-read to include other (non-party-based) forms of participation that accounted for indigenous modalities of political representation, to the extent compatible with human rights law.

Non-discrimination

In *South West Africa*, Judge Tanaka delivered a dissenting opinion in which he addressed *inter alia* the theme of non-discrimination in relation to ethnic groups within a multicultural setting. Comparing the logic of the minorities treaties and that of apartheid or separate development, he identified two strands of protection reflected in those treaties. One was non-discrimination, that is a prohibition 'to exclude members of a minority group from participating in rights, interests and opportunities which a majority population group can enjoy'.[126]

The other was a guarantee for members of minority groups per se, which such members could freely choose to accept or refuse. Far from allowing a choice for group protection on ethno-cultural grounds, the policy of apartheid in South Africa amounted to an imposed and comprehensive form of group differentiation along purely racial lines, and was thus not justified.[127] Here the assumption is that no group-based treatment can be imposed and all individuals must be protected against discrimination – the point about segregation indirectly intersects the complex relationship between minority protection and the anti-discrimination approach as gradually developed in twentieth century international law.

Confronted with the issue of apartheid in South Africa, Judge Tanaka's language of non-discrimination understandably highlighted integration rather than identity. Although discrimination on account of ethnicity is, or can be a form of racial discrimination,[128] racism is defined by others' prejudice

---

124 *Ibid.*, paras. 218–219.

125 On rights of voters, *ibid.*, para. 227.

126 (Second Phase), ICJ Reports 1966, p. 307.

127 See also the IACrtHR's Advisory Opinion on the *Juridical Condition and Rights of Undocumented Migrants*, AO OC-18/03, Series A, No. 18, para. 84 [distinction and discrimination].

128 *Timishev v. Russia*, EurCrtHR, Application Nos. 55762/00 and 55974/00, Judgment of 13 December 2005; *DH et others v. The Czech Republic*, id., Application No. 57325/00, Judgment of 13 November 2007 [GC], para. 176; *Affaire Sampanis et Autres c. Grèce*, id., Application No. 32526/05, Judgment of 5 June 2008 (final on 5 September 2008), para. 69 (in French).

towards a group within a given society,[129] while ethno-cultural bonds appeal to an internal sense of belonging in the face of pressure from the majority to conform to the dominant social pattern. From the perspective of contemporary international human rights law, Tanaka's comments may also suggest a broader conceptualisation of non-discrimination as an overarching jurisprudential theme affecting the position of minority groups.

In *Diergaardt*, the complainants, members of the Rehoboth Baster Community of Namibia, argued both on their own behalf and on behalf of their own group for a breach of Article 26 ICCPR, by contending that Namibia had denied them the use of their mother tongue in administration, justice, education and public life, as a result of declaring English the only official language of the state and failing to allow for the use of other languages. The HRC did not elaborate upon the contested language policies of Namibia per se, apparently justifying the notion that the use of an exclusive official language may be legitimate and does not automatically constitute discrimination against other languages. Nevertheless, based on evidence from the authors, it found an intentional targeting by public officials against the possibility to use Afrikaans when dealing with public authorities, in breach of Article 26 ICCPR. On a strict reading of the HRC's line, Judge Tanaka's 'exclusion' in *South West Africa* is detected in the form of a specific purpose to penalise Afrikaans speakers as such and non-discrimination is used as a construct that implicitly upholds language claims. It has been suggested that the HRC points in fact to a disproportionately negative impact on Afrikaans speakers resulting from the restriction on the use of Afrikaans.[130] The dissent led by Mr Bhagwati strongly dismissed the majority's finding, noting that all languages other than English were treated on the same footing and that the contested specific provision regarding the authors' language was necessary because such

[129] In *Malawi African Association and Others v. Mauritania* (Comm. Nos. 54/91, 61/91, 98/93/, 164/97 à 196/97 and 210/98 (2000), the AfrCommHPRs found that 'for a country to subject its own indigenes [i.e. Black Mauritanians from the South] to discriminatory treatment only because of the colour of their skin is an unacceptable discriminatory attitude and a violation of the very spirit of the African Charter and of the letter of its Article 2', *ibid*, para. 131. In *East African Asians v. United Kingdom*, the EurCommHR held that 'publicly to single out a group of persons for differential treatment on the basis of race might, in certain circumstances, constitute a special form of affront to human dignity', (1973) 3 EHRR, para. 207; the point was confirmed by the EurCrtHR in *Moldovan v. Romania*, (2007) 44 EHRR, 16. The concept of direct discrimination on racial grounds has also been considered by the ECJ in the context of the interpretation of the 2000 EC Race Directive: Case C-54/07, *Centrum voor gelijkheid van kansen en voor racismebestrijding v. Firma Feryn NV*, 10.07.08.

[130] S. Joseph, J. Schultz & M. Castan, *The International Covenant on Civil and Political Rights*, *supra* note 52, p. 712.

language used to be the official language of Namibia.[131] This case exemplifies the complexities of non-discrimination and the role of judicial discourse in generating an understanding of its implications that may reach out to critical spheres of minority identity.

The importance of the interpretive approach to minority issues in this context can be highlighted by a comparison of *Lyng v. Northwest Indian Cemetery Protective Association* before the US Supreme Court and *Minority Schools in Albania* before the PCIJ. In *Lyng*, Indian applicants argued that the First Amendment's Free Exercise Clause prohibited the government from authorising timber harvesting and road construction on a federal area that had been traditionally used for religious purposes by members of American Indian tribes of north-western California. Writing for the majority, Justice O'Connor, while acknowledging the area as a traditional site for Indian religious practices and even assuming the 'extremely grave' effects[132] on some religious practices that could derive from those activities, held that 'government simply could not operate if it were required to satisfy every citizen's religious needs and desires... [t]he First Amendment must apply to all citizens alike, and it can give to none of them a veto over public programs that do not prohibit the free exercise of religion'.[133] In short, the notion of 'identical treatment' of indigenous and non-indigenous religious practices under the Constitution concealed the distinctive pre- and post-colonial indigenous experience and the reality of an imbalance between their protections under property rights regimes. The 'indigenous' and 'non-indigenous' were made to coalesce into a factually and legally indistinguishable set of (religious) 'needs and desires'[134] towards which, as Justice Brennan's dissenting opinion put it, government was exhorted, at best, 'to be sensitive'.[135]

In *Minority Schools*, Albania offered a conceptually similar argument by claiming that, since the closing of all private schools embraced by the Constitution applied to both the majority and minorities in that country, such measure guaranteed full equality of all Albanian nationals and therefore was in line with Article 5 of the Declaration signed by the Albanian representative before the Council of the League of Nations in October 1921. By rejecting this perspective, the PCIJ distinguished factual from merely ostensible equality – a notion already embraced over a decade earlier in *Questions relating*

---

[131] Comm. No. 760/1997, Views of 25 July 2000, CCPR/C/69/D/760/1996, Dissenting Opinion of Messrs Bhagwati, Lord Colville, and Yalden, paras. 7–9.

[132] 485 U.S. 439 (1988), p. 451.

[133] *Ibid.*, p. 452.

[134] *Ibid.*

[135] *Ibid.*, p. 473.

to Settlers of German Origin in Poland[136] – and held that the closing of the minority schools was incompatible with equality of treatment, notwithstanding the majority private schools would *not* be allowed to stay. The dissent led by Sir Hurst echoed the more than half of a century older *Lyng* decision in that Article 5 of the Declaration was construed as mandating complete uniformity of minority and non-minority nationals, any other modification of the non-discrimination requirement to take the specific situation of minority groups into account amounting, in their view, to an 'unconditional right'[137] to maintain and create minority institutions. In essence, the PCIJ recognised the non-discriminatory enjoyment of the right of members of minorities to set up their own educational and religious institutions, which had been curtailed by unequal measures:

> The abolition of these institutions, which alone can satisfy the special requirements of the minority groups, and their replacement by government institutions, would destroy this equality of treatment, for its *effect* would be to deprive the minority of the institutions appropriate to its needs, whereas the majority would continue to have them supplied in the institutions created by the State... [t]he idea embodied in the expression "equal right" is that the right thus conferred on the members of the minority cannot in any case be inferior to the corresponding right of other Albanian nationals. In other words, the members of the minority must always enjoy the right stipulated in the Declaration, and, in addition, any more extensive rights which the State may accord to other nationals.[138]

Seen retrospectively, and in contrast with *Lyng*, *Minority Schools* expanded on the view of non-discrimination against minority groups based on a comparison between the majority and the minority (and by implication, between minority groups themselves), both in relation to established rights (e.g. freedom of religion in *Lyng*) and other 'more extensive' rights that impact on the needs of the group. In *Belgian Linguistics*, the EurCrtHR made two points that are important to this discussion. The first is that equality under Article 14 ECHR *is* compatible with difference in treatment in the exercise of the ECHR rights, as long as certain conditions are met, notably that a reasonable and objective justification is provided and a relationship of proportionality between the means employed and the aim sought to be realised is established. The second is that distinctions falling within the ambit of the ECHR and failing to pass such test may indirectly produce discrimination contrary to Article 14, even though no violation of the related substantive right can be found. On this approach, one perspective that might be brought to bear directly,

---

136 Advisory Opinion of 2 March 1923, Ser. B., No. 6, 1925, p. 24.
137 *Ibid.*, p. 25.
138 *Ibid.*, p. 20 [author's emphasis].

though implicitly, on the protection of minority identity is that of unreasonable distinctions resulting from state measures.

The EurCrtHR's proposition that no right to mother tongue education could be established on the basis of Article 2 of Protocol No. 1, alone or in conjunction with Article 14 ECHR, did not amount to precluding any assessment of Belgian language policies against the anti-discrimination parameter set out in the ECHR. And indeed, the EurCrtHR did assess those policies in relation to Article 14, finding that overall they pursued a legitimate aim and did not reveal any arbitrary measures that run counter to the ECHR. Even so, it found that access to education based solely on residency resulted in unreasonable distinctions on linguistic grounds against French-speaking children living in the Dutch unilingual region. From the perspective of minority identity, this line of reasoning may be broadly interpreted as two-pronged: the ECHR is *not* indifferent to the possible discriminatory effects on minority groups that may have been generated by official (language or otherwise) policies, but, on the contrary, prohibit them; proactive domestic policies that appear *prima facie* in line with the ECHR must be corrected so as to remove the source of discrimination against minority groups in breach of Article 14.

Clearly, the conceptual theme of this jurisprudence taps into wider tendencies, both within and outside the convention regime, enabling a finding of discrimination through a contextual assessment of the distinctive position of individuals or groups vis-à-vis the contested measures. In the case of *Thlimmenos v. Greece*,[139] the EurCrtHR not only confirmed its earlier view of non-discrimination, it expanded on it by making the additional point that the right not to be discriminated against in the enjoyment of the ECHR rights 'is also violated when States without an objective and reasonable justification fail to treat differently persons whose situations are significantly different'. Central to this proposition is the notion that state measures can generate discrimination even though they are neutral on their face. In *Kelly v. United Kingdom*,[140] involving an alleged discriminatory use of lethal force against the Catholic or nationalist community in Northern Ireland by British security forces, the EurCrtHR openly admitted in principle that 'where a general policy or measure had disproportionately prejudicial effects on a particular group, it is not excluded that this may be considered as discriminatory notwithstanding that it is not specifically aimed or directed at that group'.

---

[139] Application No. 34369/97, Judgment of 6 April 2000, para. 44.

[140] Application No. 30054/96, Judgment of 4 May 2001, para. 148; see also *Hugh Jordan v. UK*, Application No. 24746/94, Judgment of 4 May 2001, para. 154.

This concept was reaffirmed in *DH and others v. The Czech Republic*,[141] in connection with a claim that the system of special schools in the Czech Republic produced disproportionately harmful effects on Roma children and, in point of fact, amounted to racial segregation. Like *Kelly, DH and others* failed on the merits before a Chamber, which set a problematically high probatory standard to establish discrimination on account of race (or indeed ethnic or national origin). The Grand Chamber remarkably reversed the Chamber's decision to uphold the notion of indirect discrimination without the need to prove discriminatory intent.[142] The Grand Chamber's focus was, not on the wording of the statutory provisions governing placements in special schools, but on whether the manner in which that legislation had been applied in practice had resulted in a disproportionately high number of Roma pupils being placed in special schools without justification.[143]

The point was brought home that, in contemporary societies 'exclusion' or 'segregation' in Judge Tanaka's sense in *South West Africa* may be the function of more subtle policies than apartheid or the doctrine of 'separate, but equal' under the pre-*Brown v. Board of Education* US Constitution – a doctrine itself superseded at a later stage by an opposite construction of the (textually unchanged) equal protection clause. This issue had come to the fore in a number of cases, such as *Nachova and others v. Bulgaria*[144] and *Bekos*

---

[141] Application No. 57325/00, Judgment of 7 February 2006 [C] and Judgment of 13 November 2007 [GC]; see also *Hoogendijk v. The Netherlands*, Application No. 5864/00, Judgment of 6 January 2005 [sex discrimination].

[142] Until recently, it was correctly noted that 'the Court does not generally recognize indirect discrimination', G. Gilbert, 'The Burgeoning Minority Rights Jurisprudence of the European Court of Human Rights', *supra* note 104, p. 747.
On evidential matters, see *infra*, Chapter 5.

[143] Application No. 57325/00, Judgment of 13 November 2007, paras. 184–185. Note that the notion of indirect discrimination was based on a wealth of international, supranational and domestic jurisprudence, especially in Parts IV, V, and VI of the judgment (relevant law and practice). Along broadly similar lines, the EurCrtHR found indirect discrimination against Roma children who had been sent to separate classes in what was otherwise a mainstream primary school in a Greek municipality: *Affaire Sampanis et Autres c. Grèce*, Application No. 32526/05, Judgment of 5 June 2008 (final on 5 September 2008), para. 96 (in French). In the *Case of Oršuš and Others v. Croatia*, Application No. 15766/03, Judgment of 17 July 2008, involving the placement of Roma pupils in Roma-only classes within certain local primary schools on the basis that the pupils' knowledge of the Croation language was inadequate, the EurCrtHR's First Section did not find a breach of Article 14, but applicants successfully requested that the case be referred to the Grand Chamber, claiming indirect discrimination (on the basis of *DH et others* and *Sampanis*) and even the possibility of direct discrimination on account of race or ethnicity.

[144] Applications Nos. 43577/98 and 43579/98, Judgment of 6 July 2005, paras. 160–168.

and Koutropoulos v. Greece[145] under the ECHR involving acts of violence by state officials against persons of Roma origin. The EurCrtHR has importantly redefined the functioning of non-discrimination on procedural grounds, by reading an implicit and separate duty to investigate into possible racist motives behind those acts into Article 14, in conjunction with the relevant substantive provision. The (unprecedented) 'proceduralisation' of Article 14, coupled with the landmark account of non-discrimination in *DH and others*, illustrate the capacity of the concept of non-discrimination to intervene in cases of suspected indirect institutional racism.

In *L.R. et al. v. Slovak Republic*,[146] the CERD found that an act of indirect racial discrimination attributable to the state party had occurred as a result of a municipal council revoking, on the basis of a discriminatory petition submitted to it, a previously approved resolution that instructed the local mayor to draw up a project aimed at securing governmental finance set up to alleviate housing problems of the Roma community. In *Legal Resources Foundation v. Zambia*,[147] the AfrCommHPRs concluded that there was no evidence that the Constitution of Zambia Amendment Act 1996 – which provided that anyone who wished to contest the office of the President had to prove that both parents had Zambian nationality by birth or descent – was intended 'to affect adversely an identifiable group of Zambian citizens by reason of their common ancestry, ethnic origin, language or cultural habits'.[148] In *Singh Bhinder v. Canada*,[149] the HRC accepted the applicant's principled consideration that the legislative requirement of wearing safety headgear in the workplace, while neutral on its face, did discriminate against persons of the Sikh religion who wear a turban in their daily life.[150] At the European Union level, the ECJ openly embraced the notion of indirect discrimination in *O'Flynn v. Adjudication Officer*,[151] involving a comparison of national and migrant workers under national law based on actual or anticipated harm, which was subsequently taken up in the so-called Race Directive of 2000.[152]

145 Application No. 15250/02, Judgment of 13 December 2005.

146 Comm. No. 31/2003, Opinion of 7 March 2005.

147 Comm. No. 211/98 (2001).

148 *Ibid.*, para. 73.

149 Comm. No. 208/86, Views of 9 November 1989, (1990) Annual Report 50.

150 The HRC more clearly upheld the notion of indirect discrimination in *Althammer v. Austria*, Comm. No. 998/2001, Views of 8 August 2003; the earlier *Diergaardt* has also been interpreted as a case of indirect discrimination: S. Joseph, J. Schultz & M. Castan, *The International Covenant on Civil and Political Rights, supra* note 52, p. 712.

151 Case C-237/94 [1996] ECR I-2617, paras. 20–21.

152 European Community Council Directive implementing the principle of equal treatment between persons irrespective of racial or ethnic origin, Article 2(2), 2000/43, 29 June 2000, O.J. 2000 L180 22; the *Thlimmenos* argument was broadly confirmed by the ECJ in *Garcia*

As these examples show, judicial discourse has increasingly broadened the measure of non-discrimination, not by stretching the inherently limited notion of open or overt discrimination, but by constantly and circumstantially re-assessing the area of what may generate discriminatory effects as a result of *Lyng*-type 'neutral' state policies.

But while the subject- and effects-based ramifications of this interpretive process are virtually open-ended, *Belgian Linguistics* signals an actual or potential significance of the right to non-discrimination to the accommodation of specific interests or needs of minority groups. Unlike *Belgian Linguistics*, *Thlimmenos*, involving a Jehovah's Witness who had been denied registration as a chartered accountant because of his conviction by Greek courts for refusing on religious grounds to wear a military uniform, did not call for an assessment of specific group policies, but nevertheless did find a breach of Article 14 (in conjunction with Article 9) as a result of Greece's failure to accommodate the religious position of Jehovah's Witnesses under the relevant Greek law. Neither case questioned state laws per se. Rather, they both looked for areas where corrections or improvements were needed. In a sense, this line partly underpinned *DH and others* as well, to the extent that the issue was not whether a system of special schools – or indeed any particular schooling system – was in itself incompatible with the ECHR, but rather whether the actual schooling arrangements for Roma children in the Czech Republic took their special needs into account and could be justified as compared to the treatment received by children belonging to the majority population who were in a similar situation.[153]

A somewhat converging approach is reflected in *Diergaardt* and *Waldman v. Canada*[154] before the HRC. In *Diergaardt*, the HRC did not dismiss Namibia's language policy, yet it found aspects of it to be prejudicial to the Rehoboth Baster Community's language interests. In *Waldman*, the HRC observed that the exclusive funding of Roman Catholic minority schools in Ontario went beyond what Canada was specifically obliged to under the ICCPR. Nevertheless, it stressed that 'if a State party chooses to provide public funding to religious schools, it should make this funding available without discrimination'.[155] Having determined that there was no reasonable and objective basis for the distinctions between those minority schools and minority schools of different religious denomination, the HRC concluded that

Avello v. Belgium, [2003] ECR I-11613, para. 31; for earlier case law, see e.g. Case 170/84, *Bilka-Kaufhaus GmbH v. Karin Weber von Hartz* [1986] ECR 1607.

153 Application No. 57325/00, Judgment of 13 November 2007, e.g. paras. 183, 205, 207.

154 Comm. No. 694/1996, Views of 3 November 1999, UN Doc. CCPR/C/67/D/694/1996 (1996).

155 *Ibid.*, para. 10.6.

a breach of Article 26 had occurred. A similar case against discrimination has been made in Latvia with regard to provisions of the 1998 Education Law debarring minority private schools, but not Latvian-speaking private schools, from seeking state financial support.[156] As noted, both *Podkolzina* and *Antonina Ignatane* turned on inappropriate language tests, but the applicants had also made the point that the requirement of a high proficiency or third-level knowledge of Latvian to stand as a candidate for general and local elections was disproportionate to the aims pursued, implying indirect discrimination against non-Latvian people.

The EurCrtHR's and HRC's reasoning exemplified by *Belgian Linguistics* and *Waldman* respectively, may well prove important to adjusting domestic policies – originally addressing only the language or otherwise needs of the majority or certain minority groups – in a way that the needs of the group(s) that had been previously discriminated against are equally accommodated. Being concerned with the *ex post facto* implications of state measures, this approach is roughly comparable to the principle of reasonable accommodation which has been upheld by the Supreme Court of Canada in matters of religious discrimination, and eventually endorsed in Canadian legislation in 1998. At the core of that principle is that freely adopted regulations or practices by the state or private companies that indirectly affect individuals' freedoms (such as freedom of religion) are not per se unlawful, but must be adjusted to account for those individuals' particular needs, unless the demanded accommodation can be refused on other grounds (such as proportionality, respect for rights of others, or excessive financial burden).[157]

The judicially-driven accommodation process is not merely incidental to the right to non-discrimination but it may, and does result in deeply transformative understandings of the very essence of the protected entitlement. In *Yatama*, the IACrtHR in effect upheld a reading of the right to political participation in Article 23 ACHR that accommodated both indigenous and non-indigenous perspectives in the electoral processes on the basis of substantive equality. The re-conceptualisation of property rights under the same system, with its attendant reform of domestic property rights regimes, while entailing a separate human rights discourse, clearly flows from this identity related construction of non-discrimination. The equality assumptions behind the recognition of indigenous property alongside traditional (majority) systems

---

156 See *supra*, note 105.

157 J. Woehrling, 'L'obligation d'accommodement raisonnable et l'adaptation de la société à la diversité religieuse', (1998) 43 *Revue du droit de McGill*, pp. 325–401; the concept of (denial of) reasonable accommodation (as discrimination) is introduced in Article 2 of the UN Convention on the Rights of Persons with Disabilities, UNGA, 13 Dec. 2006.

of private property, in the jurisprudence of the IACrtHR, were most clearly expounded by IACommHR in *Maya*, which found a breach by Belize of the right to non-discrimination in Article II ADRDM to the detriment of the Maya people of the Toledo District, 'by failing to provide them with the protections necessary to exercise their right to property fully and equally with other members of the Belizean population'.[158]

It is precisely the right to non-discrimination that has triggered off conceptions of indigenous land and indeed property rights, both internationally and domestically. In line with the *Maya* decision, the Supreme Court of Belize has understood indigenous property both on its own terms and as the subject of discriminatory policies against the Maya claimants.[159] In the landmark *Mabo* case,[160] the High Court of Australia revised Australian property law and recognised aboriginal title as a result of a reformulation of the concept of property under common law informed by the international law standard of non-discrimination.

On this understanding of the connection between non-discrimination and substantive equality, what starts as an assumption of mainly indirect discrimination tends to turn into a finding of positive duties which can be derived from that connection. *Minority Schools'* concept of equality in fact as a bar to the seemingly neutral educational policy of Albania is a classical case in point. International judicial discourse has started to unearth the relationship between indirect discrimination and positive equality, though it is usually (and correctly) suggested that the two notions, while deeply interconnected, do retain a separate import.[161]

Interestingly, *Waldman* applied to a case of inter-minority discrimination what the PCIJ had already implied in *Minority Schools* by referring to 'more extensive' rights that the state may have granted to 'other nationals',[162] though at that juncture the PCIJ was essentially referring to persons belonging to the majority. Three years earlier, in *Treatment of Polish Nationals and Other Persons of Polish Origin or Speech in the Danzig Territory*,[163] the PCIJ had used the same notion in relation to the treatment of ethnic Poles who did not belong to the Polish minority in the Free City of Danzig. As noted earlier, proactive measures adopted as a matter of general policy – be they the financial support for the Roman Catholic minority within the public

158 Report No. 96/03, Case 12.053, October 24, 2003, para. 170.

159 *Aurelio Cal et al. v. The Attorney General of Belize and the Minister of Natural Resources and Environment*, Claims Nos. 171 and 172 of 2007, Judgment of 18 October 2007, para. 114.

160 No. 2, 175 CLR 1 (1992).

161 See *infra*, Chapter 4.

162 Advisory Opinion of 23 January, 1935, Ser. A./B., No.64, 1935, p. 20.

163 Ser. A./B., No. 44, 1933, pp. 40–41.

educational system in Canada (*Waldman*), the residency-based access to secondary education in Belgium (*Belgian Linguistics*), or the additional rights for the non-minority Albanian nationals (*Minority Schools*) – are therefore made subject to the test of non-discrimination even though they are not per se required by international law.

The conceptual link between non-discrimination and minority identity depends on the extent to which the discrimination analysis is comprehensive and nuanced. In footnote four of *United States v. Carolene Products Co.*,[164] the US Supreme Court held that the possibility of a failure of the political process to protect 'religious, national or racial minorities' raises the question of whether 'prejudice against discrete and insular minorities... may call for a correspondingly more searching judicial inquiry'.[165] Although the *Carolene Products* footnote echoed the national and international experience of the time, it has undoubtedly inspired the strictest scrutiny test that the US Supreme Court has applied over time to visible forms of discrimination against minority groups, as part of a wider three-level system of review.[166] It has been suggested, though, that the rigidity of this three-level approach, coupled with a broader re-appraisal of discrimination that emphasises the effects deriving from legislative or otherwise measures that appear neutral on their face, can explain the more limited influence of the *Carolene Products* jurisprudence on minority issues in recent times.[167] To be sure, cases such as *Wisconsin* and *Santa Clara Pueblo v. Martinez*,[168] showed attention to, or non-interference with, group identity matters, but have not had any major repercussions on the conception of equality.[169]

The *Lyng* decision and the later *Employment Division v. Smith*[170] seem to confirm it. In the latter case, the Supreme Court determined that the state of Oregon was permitted to fire Native Americans for violating a state prohibition

---

164 304 U.S. 144 (1938).

165 *Ibid.*, p. 152, fn. 4. See also R. Cover, 'The Origins of Judicial Activism in the Protection of Minorities' (1982) 91 *Yale Law Journal*, p. 1287 et seq.

166 J. H. Gerards, 'Intensity of Judicial Review in Equal Treatment Cases', (2004) *Netherlands International Law Review*, pp. 144–149; see further id., *Judicial Review in Equal Treatment Cases* (Leiden/Boston, 2005).

167 Id., 'Intensity of Judicial Review in Equal Treatment Cases', *supra* note 166, p. 150.

168 98 U.S. 167 (1978). For an account of this case, see *infra*, Chapter 4.

169 The admittedly important concept of indirect discrimination in US jurisprudence has always appeared a somewhat free-standing category: J. Ringelheim, *Diversité Culturelle et Droits de l'Homme: L'Émergence de la Problématique des Minorités dans le Droit de la Convention Européenne des Droits de l'Homme* (Bruxelles, 2006), pp. 336–337; D. Schiek, L. Waddington & M. Bell (eds.), *Cases, Materials and Text on National, Supranational and International Non-Discrimination Law*, (Oxford: Hart Publishing, 2007), pp. 348–349.

170 494 U.S. 872 (1990).

on use of the peyote drug, and to deny them unemployment benefits because of such use, even though the ingestion of peyote was part of the sacramental requirements of the Native American Church. Just as *Lyng*, *Employment Division* minimised the impact of general laws on indigenous identity in the name of equal compliance with those laws, and left possible accommodation to the political process[171] – arguably the same process that, in terms of the *Carolene Products* footnote, had failed to secure accommodation of precisely indigenous religious practices.

This narrative can be usefully contrasted with the approach to non-discrimination underlying *Andrews v. Law Society of British Columbia*[172] before the Supreme Court of Canada. Whereas *Lyng* and *Employment Division* embraced a narrow understanding of equality, the *Andrews* decision, striking down a bar against non-citizens lawyers in British Columbia, somewhat re-framed the American judicial debate on non-discrimination (including the *Carolene Products* footnote) by looking at the position of the affected group (*in casu*, non-citizens) in a purposive and comprehensive manner. In contrast with the mechanical (three-level) approach reflected in the American equality jurisprudence, Judge Wilson referred to the need to interpret section 15 of the Canadian Charter of Rights and Freedoms 'with sufficient flexibility to ensure the "unremitting protection" of equality rights in the years to come'. In short, the decision called for a nuanced analysis of discrimination that accounts for the position of several non-dominant groups in contemporary societies.

Unsurprisingly, context and substantive equality have acquired a prominent place in Canadian case law concerning minorities' identity. For example, in *Multani v. Commission scolaire Marguerite-Bourgeoys*,[173] the Supreme Court did hold that freedom of religion was not absolute, yet it implicitly valued such freedom and protection of minority groups by arguing, *inter alia*, that the issue of whether the applicant, an orthodox Sikh student, could be allowed to wear his kirpan at school was to be decided through a contextual analysis under section 1 of the Canadian Charter, not on the basis of a priori, principled determination of internal limits on freedom of religion.[174] In *Arse-*

---

[171] *Ibid.*, p. 890; see also *Lyng v. Northwest Indian Cemetery Protective Association*, 485 U.S. 439 (1988), pp. 451–452.

[172] [1989] S.C.R. 143.

[173] [2006] SCC 6.

[174] *Ibid.*, pp. 24–27. Compare with *Leyla Sahin v. Turkey* before the EurCrtHR, Application No. 44774/98, Judgment of 10 November 2005 [ban on wearing the Islamic headscarf in universities is not in breach of freedom of religion in Article 9 ECHR]; disagreeing with the majority's view that the ban was justified in the name of gender equality and secularism, Judge Tulkens noted that '[it] is not the Court's role to make an appraisal of…a religion or religious practice, just as it is not its role to determine in a general and abstract way the signi-

nault-Cameron v. Prince Edward Island & Ors,[175] the same court dismissed a formal vision of equality that treats majority and minority groups alike by emphasising the special requirements of minority language rights protection under section 23 of the Canadian Charter. Most importantly, it echoed the PCIJ line in *Minority Schools* based on effective interpretation and protection, in that it made clear that such requirements were in fact not met by means of 'objective standards, which assess the needs of minority language children primarily by reference to the pedagogical needs of majority language children'.[176] It is precisely such appreciation of context that also lies behind the above-mentioned notion of reasonable accommodation developed by the Supreme Court in relation to religious discrimination, whereby the rigid neutrality of the law becomes contained by discrete adjustments that are deemed justifiable (and indeed required) under the circumstances.

A more flexible and contextual model of reviewing this type of cases often calls for a complex balancing exercise. In *Chapman*, the EurCrtHR in practice conceded a wide margin of appreciation in matters of national planning, while in principle the scope of this margin was apparently limited by recognition of Roma identity and needs. Competing factors generated competing visions as to the intensity of judicial review of minority issues under the ECHR, and therefore the most appropriate margin of appreciation to be accorded to states parties. Central to expanding the conceptual reach of non-discrimination is its comparative dimension. In *R. v. Drybones*,[177] Justice Hall rejected the notion that protection against discrimination could be ensured if it merely implied a comparison of Indians with Indians under the contested provision of the Indian Act, and therefore allowed no consideration of the position of non-Indians under comparable federal law. Nearly twenty years later, Justice McIntyre in *Andrews* boldly took issue with the proposition that persons who are 'similarly situated be similarly treated' and those who are 'differently situated be differently treated':

---

fication of wearing the headscarf or to impose its viewpoint on the applicant..., a young adult university student', *ibid.*, Dissenting Opinion of Judge Tulkens, para. 12. Commenting on this case, Mullaly argues that the 'denial of autonomy by the state and ultimately the European Court represents an appeal to perfectionism...that...goes beyond the limits of permissible regulation', S. Mullaly, 'The UN, Minority Rights and Gender Equality: Setting Limits to Collective Claims', in G. Pentassuglia (ed.), 'Reforming the UN Human Rights Machinery: What Does the Future Hold for the Protection of Minorities and Indigenous Peoples?' (2007) 14 *International Journal on Minority and Group Rights*, Special Issue, p. 282.

175 [2000] S.C.R. 3.

176 *Ibid.*, para. 31.

177 [1970] S.C.R. 282.

> The test…is seriously deficient in that it excludes any consideration of the nature of the law. If it were to be applied literally, it could be used to justify the Nuremberg laws of Adolf Hitler. Similar treatment was contemplated for all Jews. The similarly situated test would have justified the formalistic separate but equal doctrine of *Plessy v. Ferguson*.[178]

He arguably captured, quite emphatically, the core of the matter: any analysis of possible discriminatory effects against individuals or groups requires a critical and comprehensive understanding of the group of persons with whom the complainants are to be compared within the relevant social and legal context.[179] What is 'similarly situated' and 'differently situated' (as upheld, for example, by European anti-discrimination jurisprudence) needs to be unpacked and problematised on a case-by-case basis. As also implied by Justice McIntyre's comments, courts do possess discretion in this regard that should be carefully exercised, since the extent of their discretion impacts directly upon the conceptualisation and applicability of substantive equality. This is of course not unique to minority issues. For example, in *Gruber v. Silhouette International Schmied GmbH & Co KG*,[180] the ECJ was faced with the question of whether Ms Gruber, who had resigned from employment because of maternity, should be compared, as she claimed, with those who resigned from employment for 'important reasons', under the terms of the Austrian legislation in question, or simply with those who resigned without 'important reasons', as the employer contended. The ECJ accepted the latter argument and found no sex-based discrimination, but this would not have been the case had the court embraced the complainant's perspective. Advocate General Lèger disagreed with the ECJ's understanding of the comparator group. In *Ballantyne*, which turned on the question of whether a Quebec law prohibiting commercial advertising outdoor in a language other than French discriminated against the authors – English-speaking individuals engaged in trade – the HRC was satisfied that the law applied to both French and English speakers and thus raised no issue of discrimination. On this approach, both French and English traders were 'similarly situated' before the law – in a sense, they created an indistinguishable 'whole'. Their comparatively different situation given the actual impact of that law on English speakers as opposed to French speakers was not taken into account. The case of minority identity, though, exposes non-discrimination as a comparative concept even further. In *Treatment of Polish*

[178] [1989] 1 S.C.R. 143, p. 28.

[179] On the role of comparison in the case law of the EurCrtHR, see e.g. M. Janis, R. S. Kay & A. W. Bradley, *European Human Rights Law: Texts and Materials* (Oxford, 3rd edition, 2008), pp. 474–485.

[180] Case C-249/97 [1999] ECR I-5295.

Nationals,[181] the PCIJ distinguished under the relevant instruments minorities 'in the narrow sense' (Danzig nationals belonging to the Polish minority in the Free City) from minorities 'in the wide sense' (Polish nationals, whether or not belonging to minorities in Poland, and other non-Danzig persons of Polish origin or speech) to articulate a distinction – contested by the Polish government – between specific minority guarantees for the former and protection against discrimination for the latter. In so doing, it identified the groups that were relevant to a comparative non-discrimination assessment.

In the far more recent *Gorzelik*[182] before the EurCrtHR, the Polish government argued that the registration of the applicants' association of Silesians would make the group – which it considered simply one of several ethnic groups of Polish citizens – gain the status of a national minority, thereby producing 'adverse consequences' for the rights of 'other ethnic groups' in Poland – such as the Highlanders, Kashubinas and Mazurians – in violation of the principle of equality. The applicants objected that it could not be prejudged as to whether these groups would really be discriminated against, as it first should be established that they had similar aspirations and that those aspirations had been denied.

For their part, both the Chamber and Grand Chamber accepted the notion that Poland had acted to protect, *inter alia*, the rights of others, without considering, though, the groups between which a comparison was appropriate, and the very reason for such comparison. The Grand Chamber stressed that Polish authorities had consistently recognised the existence of a Silesian 'ethnic minority' and the right of Silesians to associate with one another. Yet, it offered no analysis as to whether there was any basis for distinguishing this group from recognised national minorities. In fact, a more comprehensive and contextual approach might well have pointed to inequality of treatment, not between the Silesians and those groups mentioned by Poland, but between the former and the groups that had already been recognised as national minorities, both in terms of group status per se and in terms of the benefits provided for under Polish electoral law for registered associations of national minorities. If the Silesians could be (potentially) regarded as a national minority an instance of discrimination against them would have to be found contrary to Article 14 ECHR (at least with regard to electoral matters), in line with the EurCrtHR's jurisprudence on domestic policies going beyond what the ECHR specifically requires.

181 Ser. A./B., No. 44, 1933, pp. 38–41.
182 Application No. 44158/98, Judgment of 20 December 2001 [C] and 17 February 2004 [GC].

Chapter 4

Mediation

Minority claims typically – though by no means exclusively – reflect wider competing interests of the affected minority group(s) and the majority. As discussed in the previous chapter, judicial discourse is capable of elaborating and expounding general human rights categories in order to accommodate minority interests and needs. Equally importantly, judicial discourse has engaged in mediating competing claims without necessarily advancing any specific substantive solutions. It might be argued that, the more minority claims expose the central legal themes of minority protection the more that discourse is likely to acknowledge the resulting complexities by turning to an essentially procedural approach whose central concern is to ensure the openness, effectiveness or otherwise legality of the political decision-making process. As discussed in the following two sections, this can be noted in relation to both distinctive minority provisions and general provisions that are claimed in connection with individual minority concerns.

Moreover, conflicts internal to the community over claims affecting individuals and/or the community as a whole have exposed a mediating dimension of judicial discourse which is as important as the one which is reflected within the context of state-group disputes. The remaining sections of the chapter address the issue of 'minorities within minorities' in connection with questions of gender equality and representation in the face of internal dissent.[1] Judicial discourse has shown further potential for mediation within the framework of human rights law. Interestingly, such discourse has not limited itself to setting out procedural benchmarks, it has also embraced substantive strategies impinging on the relationship between identity and equality, as well as the ramifications of rights protection across the community.

---

[1] A. Eisenberg & J. Spinner-Halev (eds.), *Minorities within Minorities: Equality, Rights and Diversity* (Cambridge, 2005).

Reconciling majority and minority interests

Involvement in the decision-making process

A first indication of this line is provided by the jurisprudence under Article 8 ECHR. Aside from conceptual advances on earlier case law, the EurCrtHR has mostly upheld the margin of appreciation doctrine in assessing the impact of the respondent state's measures on the way of life of Roma/Gypsy individuals.

In fact, while showing deference to state concerns and policies, the EurCrtHR has also attempted to identify constrains on state action. In *Chapman*, it conceded that the implementation of certain general laws might have an incidence on the Roma/Gypsy traditional lifestyle, and defined a positive obligation to facilitate the Roma/Gypsy way of life in terms of giving 'some special consideration' to their needs and different lifestyle 'both in the relevant regulatory planning framework and in arriving at the decisions in particular cases.'[2] It may be questioned whether this requirement had been actually met by the government as the EurCrtHR noted that there was no provision of an adequate number of caravan sites that could be accepted by these people and on which they could lawfully camp at a price affordable to them.[3] The joint dissent confirmed that 'during the planning procedures it was acknowledged that there were no alternative sites available for the applicant to go to either in the district or in the county as a whole', and other sites, such as private residential ones, were in practice unavailable. However, the majority did argue that the 'applicant's personal circumstances had been taken into account in the decision-making process'.[4]

The EurCrtHR had in effect indicated in *Buckley* that both the regulatory framework and the process leading up to the contested decision should give proper regard to the individual's interests as protected by Article 8, in order to justify an interference under Article 8 (2). But the point here was solely procedural in character and thus divorced from the material situation of Roma/Gypsies as such, while *Chapman* arguably offers an adjustment of this thinking by implying *in principle* a link between procedural elements and substantive considerations of identity.[5] *DH and others*, while not based on

---

2 *Chapman v. United Kingdom*, Application No. 27238/95, Judgment of 18 January 2001, para. 96. See also *Connors v. the United Kingdom*, Application No. 66746/01, Judgment of 27 May 2004, para. 84.

3 *Chapman v. United Kingdom*, Application No. 27238/95, Judgment of 18 January 2001, para. 97.

4 *Ibid.*, para. 110.

5 These two perspectives re-emerged in *Connors v. UK*, Application No. 66746/01, Judgment of 27 May 2004, paras. 83, 84.

Article 8, built upon this line to establish the need to provide appropriate procedural safeguards when making schooling arrangements for Roma children in the Czech Republic, which essentially revolved around culturally-sensitive pedagogical tests and effective involvement of the children's parents.[6] In short, the EurCrtHR has appeared to value the distinctive situation of minority members, not so much in terms of a particular substantive outcome to their benefit, as in relation to participatory elements that could secure a (more) minority-conscious decision-making process.

In the case of *Noack v. Germany*,[7] involving a contested relocation of a Sorbian village in order to permit mining for lignite, the EurCrtHR held that a decisive factor in declaring the application inadmissible was that the decision-making process leading up to the relocation had lasted for several years and had involved all interested parties. More specifically, it was noted that the residents of the village in question would be transferred 'après avoir été consultés quant au choix de leur lieu de destination', and that after the transfer (within the traditional Sorbian area of settlement) they would continue to enjoy minority rights as guaranteed by the Constitution of the Land of Brandenburg. Whereas *Chapman* is unclear as to what exactly the 'special consideration' criterion should entail in practice, *Noack* – by appealing to 'un plus grand devoir de vigilance de la part de la Cour' given the involvement of members of the Sorbian community – seems more openly to offer prior consultation and continuing protection of the minority group's way of life as a possible yardstick to measure the proportionality of state conduct under Article 8.

In *Hingitaq*, the EurCrtHR did not pronounce on the interferences with the proprietary interests and way of life of the Thule tribe of Greenland per se, but found that the national courts had struck a 'fair balance' in their judgment on the competing claims of the group and the Danish authorities. Although the EurCrtHR did not resort to ILO Convention 169 and its participatory thrust, it noted that the forced relocation of the Inughuit had been declared by the national authorities to constitute 'a serious interference and unlawful conduct towards them',[8] and that financial compensation and substitute housing and facilities for the villagers had been provided. Whether or not the Thule tribe constituted a distinct community within Greenland for purposes of ILO Convention 169 (which had been conceded by the High Court but dismissed by

---

[6] *DH and others v. The Czech Republic*, Application No. 57325/00, Judgment of 13 November 2007 [GC], paras. 181, 200, 203.

[7] *Noack v. Germany*, Application No. 46346/99, Admissibility Decision of 25 May 2000 (available in French), para. 1 (*En Droit*).

[8] *Hingitaq 53 and others v. Denmark*, Admissibility Decision of 12 January 2006, Application No. 18584/04, section A.

the Supreme Court), the EurCrtHR's procedural line in fact echoed, at least implicitly, the minority themes of participation and sustainability of identity related practices as a result of governmental decision-making processes.

Interestingly, this approach comes close to that of the HRC in the *Länsman* cases, brought by Sami reindeer herders of Finland. The HRC applied the test of consultation and proportionality based on economic sustainability, to development activities conducted by private parties and authorised by the state.[9] The aim was to determine whether there had been a failure to protect the complainants' specific indigenous economy against 'denial' in Article 27 CCPR, by eroding its actual capacity to sustain their right to enjoy their own culture. In the first *Länsman* case, the HRC concluded that:

> [T]he interests of the Muotkatunturi Herdsmen's Committee and of the authors were considered during the proceedings leading to the delivery of the quarrying permit, that the authors were consulted during the proceedings, and that reindeer herding in the area does not appear to have been adversely affected by such quarrying as has occurred.

In all other cases regarding the impact of logging activities on Sami reindeer herding in Finland, the HRC has used the consultation and sustainability parameters, thereby establishing its monitoring role in relation to both the decision-making process leading up to the impugned measures and the effects of such measures on the way of life of the people concerned once they have been implemented. The procedural element of participation was broadly touched upon in *Apirana Mahuika et al. v. New Zealand*, involving the assessment of a comprehensive settlement between the government of New Zealand and the Maori people as a whole, which had been entered into in light of the Treaty of Waitangi signed in 1840 between the Maori and the British Crown:

> [T]he Committee has emphasised that the acceptability of measures that affect or interfere with the culturally significant economic activities of a minority depends on whether the members of the minority in question have had the opportunity to participate in the decision-making process in relation to these measures and whether they will continue to benefit from their traditional economy
>
> ...
>
> In the consultation process, special attention was paid to the cultural and religious significance of fishing for the Maori, *inter alia*, to securing the possibility of Maori individuals and communities to engage themselves in non-commercial

[9] *I. Länsman v. Finland*, Comm. No. 511/1992, Views of 26 October 1994, (1995) II Annual Report 66, paras. 9.6, 9.8; *J. I. Länsman v. Finland*, Comm. No. 671/1995, Views of 30 October 1996, (1997) II Annual Report 191, paras. 10.4–10.7; HRC General Comment No. 23 (50), 1994, para. 7.

> activities...the Committee concludes that the State party has, by engaging itself in the process of broad consultation before proceeding to legislate, and by paying specific attention to the sustainability of Maori fishing rights, taken the necessary steps to ensure that the...Settlement and its enactment through legislation...are compatible with article 27.[10]

Aside from questions of fact regarding either the level of effectiveness of the consultation process or the actual repercussions of the contested measures on the minority group's way of life, clearly the discursive focus shifts from an abstract and a priori content of the right to identity to the procedural ramifications of the process on the basis of which the contours of that right are supposed to be given substance. Unsurprisingly, cases of blatant denial of participation in governmental decisions to permit oil and gas exploration deeply affecting the group's way of life, have led to a finding of a breach of the identity related right.[11] But as the dispute between the majority and minority incrementally brings the complexities of their claims to the fore, judicial discourse tends to mediate the competing claims by exposing the fluid confines of the right and positioning itself – somewhat re-orienting the rationale of the *Carolene Products* jurisprudence of the late 1930s – as the guarantor of a political process that does account for minority identity. In *Marshall et al. v. Canada*,[12] the authors complained that the indigenous group of which they were representatives had not been invited to attend constitutional conferences that were designed to identify and clarify the indigenous rights recognised in the Canadian Constitutional Act of 1982. The HRC took a classical 'either/or' approach to the matter and concluded that there was no unconditional right for a group of citizens to choose the modalities of participation in the conduct of public affairs in Article 25 ICCPR. In the more complex Article 27 cases, the HRC implicitly upholds the relative indeterminacy of the right to enjoy one's identity in ways that make the reach of such right mostly a function of meaningful forms of effective involvement in the relevant decision-making exercise.

The recognition of indigenous property rights by the IACrtHR and IACommHR provides further illustration of the mediating role of judicial discourse based on effective participation. The re-conceptualisation of property, discussed above, has been in fact related, not to a pre-defined or automatic association of the right to property with any particular tracts of land, but to

[10] Comm. No. 547/1993, Views of 27 October 2000, CCPR/C/70/D/541/1993, paras. 9.5, 9.8.

[11] *Bernard Ominayak, Chief of the Lubicon Lake Band v. Canada*, Comm. No. 167/1984, Views of 26 March 1990, (1990) II Annual Report 1; *The Social and Economic Rights Action Center for Economic and Social Rights v. Nigeria*, Comm. No. 155/96, 2001.

[12] *Marshall et al. v. Canada*, Comm. No. 205/1986, Views of 4 November 1991, (1992) Annual Report 201.

a duty on the state to delimit, demarcate and title the territory belonging to the group as a result of full consultations with the latter. To put it differently: the Inter-American organs, faced with complexities arising from indigenous and non-indigenous property claims, have established a procedural framework within which indigenous property rights must be realised and the state and indigenous groups must settle their differences. This approach, already reflected in the *Mayagna* decision (against the background of claims from indigenous communities other than Awas Tingni),[13] was explicitly embraced by the IACommHR in *Maya*:

> [T]he Commission must clarify that it does not purport through this report to define and demarcate the precise territory to which Maya property rights extend. Rather, as discussed below, this is an obligation that must be fulfilled by the State in full collaboration with the Maya people and in accordance with their customary land use practices
>
> ...
>
> Accompanying the existence of the Maya people's communal right to property under Article XXIII of the Declaration is a correspondent obligation on the State to recognise and guarantee the enjoyment of this right. In this regard, the Commission shares the view of the Inter-American Court of Human Rights that this obligation necessarily requires the State to effectively delimit and demarcate the territory to which the Maya people's property right extends including official recognition of that right. In the Commission's view, this necessarily includes engaging in effective and informed consultations with the Maya people concerning the boundaries of their territory, and that the traditional land use practices and customary land tenure system be taken into account in this process.

In the earlier *Mary and Carrie Dann*, the IACommHR had taken a similar line in relation to the lack of participation of the claimants in the Indian Claims Commission process set up by the United States in order to consider historic grievances by indigenous communities. The government had conceded, and the US judiciary confirmed, that the Western Shoshone community used to have title to their ancestral lands, but that such title had extinguished as a result of the findings of the Indian Claims Commission. This time what was at stake was not the determination of indigenous property claims per se, but rather the continuing validity of indigenous title. Like in other land rights cases, though, IACommHR responded by setting out procedural benchmarks against which the legality of the (extinguishment) process should be assessed. In other words, the IACommHR did not take issue with the possibility of extinguishment, but with the 'broad manner in which the State has purported to extinguish indigenous claims, including those of the Danns, in the entirety

---

[13] *Mayagna (Sumo) Awas Tingni Community v. Nicaragua*, Judgment of 31 August 2001, Series C No. 79, sec. VII(f).

of the Western Shoshone territory'.[14] While emphasising that it was not for it to determine 'whether and to what extent the Danns may properly claim a subsisting right to property in the Western Shoshone ancestral lands',[15] the IACommHR found nevertheless a duty on the state to guarantee:

> a process of fully informed and mutual consent on the part of the indigenous community as a whole. This requires, as a minimum, that all of the members of the community are fully and accurately informed of the nature and consequences of the process and provided with an effective opportunity to participate individually or as collectives.[16]

In interpreting the judgment in *Moiwana*,[17] the IACrtHR emphasised the participatory element which had been arguably left unexplained in *Mayagna*, in the context of Article 21 ACHR:

> [T]he Court deems pertinent to point out that, by recognizing the right of the Moiwana community members to the use and enjoyment of their traditional lands, the Court has not made any determination as to the appropriate boundaries of the territory in question. Rather, in order to render effective "the property rights of the members of the Moiwana community in relation to the traditional territories from which they were expelled", and having acknowledged the lack of "formal legal title", the Court has directed the State, as a measure of reparation, to "adopt such legislative, administrative and other measures as are necessary to ensure" those rights, after due consultation with the neighbouring communities. If said rights are to be properly ensured, the measures to be taken must naturally include "the delimitation, demarcation and titling of said traditional territories", with the participation and informed consent of the victims as expressed through their representatives, the members of the other Cottica N'djuka villages and the neighbouring indigenous communities. In this case, the Court has simply left the designation of the territorial boundaries in question to "an effective mechanism" of the State's design.[18]

In short, the main theme of such discourse is not so much a consideration of legal arguments *in abstracto*, but the procedural management (and thus mediation) of specific proprietary interests in accordance with international human rights law.[19] *Yakye Axa* and *Saramaka* expanded on this line to include competing claims, land restitution and compensation for the lack of

---

[14] *Mary and Carrie Dann v. United States*, Report No. 75/02, Case 11.1140, December 27, 2002, para. 145.

[15] *Ibid.*, para. 171.

[16] *Ibid.*, para. 140.

[17] Interpretation of the Judgment of Merits, Reparations and Costs, Judgment of 8 February 2006, Series C No. 145.

[18] *Ibid.*, para. 19.

[19] For a discussion of standards relating to participation, see S. Wheatley, *Democracy, Minorities and International Law*, (Cambridge, 2005), Chapter 3.

available lands, as well as additional requirements for legitimate restrictions on indigenous property rights, as further ramifications of what is essentially a participation-based process. The choice and delivery of alternative lands (when restitution of the ancestral lands is not possible), the payment of just compensation or both 'should be realized with the agreement of the interested people, in accordance with their own consulting procedures, values, uses and customary law'.[20] Here participation becomes the distinguishing feature of a procedural framework where reparation, in the form of *restitutio in integrum* or compensation, is closely linked to the reading of indigenous property claims themselves. Indeed, effective participation of the group takes centre stage in relation to any restrictions on the enjoyment of indigenous property rights, particularly those resulting from activities of exploration and extraction of certain natural resources that are found on indigenous land.[21] The very 'preliminary' act of delimiting, demarcating and titling the lands can itself prove contentious as it intersects with private property that is already recognised. The IACrtHR has established guidelines to deal with the possibility of expropriating privately owned land and the extent to which private property may not prevail over indigenous property under the ACHR.[22] In a second decision following a request for interpretation of the 2005 judgment in *Yakye Axa*,[23] the IACrtHR responded to concerns voiced by the representatives of the victims that Paraguay was ignoring the group's demands by reaffirming the duty on the state to physically identify the lands subject to effective consultation with the groups and accommodation of those concerns.

A broadly comparable procedural line is offered by the Canadian Supreme Court's interpretation of the duty of consultation with indigenous communities.[24] In essence, this court has embraced a sliding scale approach to

---

20 *Yakye Axa Indigenous Community v. Paraguay*, Judgment of 17 June 2005, Series C No. 125, paras. 149–151.

21 *The Saramaka People v. Suriname*, Judgment of 28 November 2007, Series C No. 172, paras. 129, 133–137. The all-encompassing nature of the requirement of effective participation was confirmed in the later *Saramaka* decision regarding *Interpretation of the Judgment on Preliminary Objections, Merits, Reparations, and Costs*, Judgment of 12 August 2008, Series C No. 185, paras. 16–17. Further elaborating on the specific aspect of prior environmental and social impact assessments (ESIAs), the IACrtHR noted that 'the State's obligation to supervise the ESIAs coincides with its duty to guarantee the effective participation of the Saramaka people in the process of granting concessions', *ibid.*, para. 41.

22 *Yakye Axa Indigenous Community v. Paraguay*, Judgment of 17 June 2005, Series C No. 125, para. 217.

23 Interpretation of the Judgment of Merits, Reparations and Costs, Judgment of February 6, 2006, Series C No. 142, para. 26.

24 See e.g. *Delgamuukw v. British Columbia*, [1997] S.C.R. 1010; *Haida Nation v. British Colum-*

participatory rights. Property rights are to be protected through robust forms of consultations, including full consent to decisions which significantly affect those rights; absent specific property titles, consultation must be proportionate to the strength of the indigenous claim. Like in the Inter-American case law, the right still provides the benchmark, but the precise level of protection of that right against interference (whether it's a property right *stricto sensu* or other land-based identity claim) does in practice arise out of the participatory process which is inextricably linked to it. Judicial discourse mediates by guaranteeing the fairness of the process, including a heavy or less heavy burden of justification for interference falling on the state.

More generally, these examples show that the line of argumentation is not about consultation (and sustainability) per se, but rather about attempting a balancing act between the interests of the general community and the rights of the group's members. So long as the contested measures do not amount to a denial of rights, it does not pre-judge any particular outcome of the decision-making process – in essence, it puts the understanding of competing perspectives in context.

In *Lyng*, the US Supreme Court left the scope of the political process intact but appeared more than reluctant to mediate the competing claims through strong benchmarks against which that process was to be assessed. The court noted that the affected individuals would not be coerced by the government's action into violating their religious beliefs. It clearly refused to engage with the competing claims involving different conceptions of land and to uphold consultation with Native American religious leaders as required by the American Indian Religious Freedom Act 1996. As pointed out by Justice Brennan, the Supreme Court had valued, though, the overall repercussions of a state compulsory school attendance law on the Amish way of life in *Wisconsin v. Yoder*.[25] In *Lubicon Lake Band*, the HRC similarly assessed the impact of development activities on the band's way of life against a failure of the political process to involve the band in the decisions that affected them. In short, it was a contextual analysis of the effects on minority identity, rather than an affirmative coercive element, that led to a decision in favour of the group and its members. Of course, a balancing act sets limits on governmental action, which was precisely what the US Supreme Court was *not* inclined to do in *Lyng*. In *Buckley*, the EurCommHR referred to the margin of appreciation accorded to the domestic authorities but concluded that the 'interests of

bia (Minister of Forests), [2004] SCC 73; *Taku River Tlingit First Nation v. British Columbia (Project Assessment Director)*, [2004] SCC 74; *Mikisew Cree First Nation v. Canada*, [2005] S.C.R. 388.

25 485 U.S. 439 (1988), pp. 466–468 [citing *Wisconsin* 406 U.S. 205 (1972)].

the applicant in this case outweigh the general interest'; more specifically, it stated that special considerations arise in the planning sphere regarding the needs of Roma/Gypsies (as also confirmed by the EurCrtHR in *Chapman*), and that 'the correct balance...between the rights of an individual gypsy or gypsy family and the interests of the general community will depend always on the particular facts of the case'.[26] In her concurring opinion, Ms Liddy reiterated the fundamental point that in this sort of cases Article 8 must be read in terms of striking a fair balance between the competing interests of the individual and that of the national community as a whole. The joint dissent in *Chapman* made a similar argument by calling for an adequate protection of the applicants 'with different needs and values from the general community'. In *Kayano*, the Sapporo District Court engaged in a lengthy and comprehensive comparative balancing of the interests held by the Ainu group and the public benefits believed to derive from the Nibutani dam in the Hokkaido region. This court recognised the discretional authority of the public entity that authorised construction of the dam, but it also noted that:

> [T]here may be cases where, in making this judgment, the administrative entity unjustly and carelessly makes light of various factors and values which deserve the utmost regard from the start, with the result that where the greatest consideration is obviously due, it lacks instead. And there may be cases where less significant matters, which from the start were being considered, were overvalued.[27]

Clearly, the balancing of competing claims does not imply that the minority claim must always prevail. For one thing, arguments based on domestic law cannot justify limitations on rights protected under international law. *Kayano* incorrectly suggested that ICCPR Article 27 rights could be limited by the Japanese Constitution in the name of the public welfare as long as any limits were kept to the narrowest degree necessary.[28] On the other hand, the impact of domestic measures varies depending on the circumstances. In the first *Länsman* case, the HRC stated that the freedom of a state to pursue its own interests, such as development or economic activities by enterprises, should not be assessed by reference to an ECHR-style margin of appreciation, as contended by Finland, but by reference to whether the exercise of that freedom amounted to a denial of ICCPR Article 27 rights. Nevertheless, the theme of the *Länsman* decisions was that a limited impact on a minority group's way of life is not necessarily in breach of Article 27, while the

---

[26] *Buckley v. United Kingdom*, Report of 11 January 1995, (1995) 19 E.H.R.R. CD 20, para. 84.

[27] Judgment of the Sapporo District Court, Civil Division No. 3, 27 March 1997, (1999) 38 ILM, p. 416.

[28] *Ibid.*, para. 418. Vienna Convention on the Law of Treaties, 1969, Article 27: see generally I. Brownlie, *Principles of Public International Law* (Oxford, 6th edition, 2003), pp. 34–35.

cumulative effect of different activities, amounting *de iure* or *de facto* to large scale actions, may well erode Article 27 rights.[29] In *G. and E. v. Norway*, the EurCommHR's similarly held that the consequences for the complaining Norwegian Sami arising from the construction of the hydroelectric plant in question did interfere with their minority private way of life under Article 8 ECHR, but were very limited ones, given 'the vast areas in northern Norway which are used for reindeer breeding and fishing' and the only 'comparatively small area which will be lost for the applicants, for such purposes.'[30] A certain leeway conceded to states by judicial discourse in any particular case, before a right violation can be determined, is probably in itself a reflection of the mediating role being played by such discourse while balancing out competing interests. This may well prove inevitable, for judicial discourse is built around interpretation of facts and evidence.

At the same time, the criterion of effective involvement of the affected group in the decision-making process, as implicitly found in most of the above-mentioned provisions, suggests a predominantly procedural bearing of jurisprudential analyses. In *Kayano*, the Sapporo District Court did not openly address the issue of Ainu involvement,[31] but it acknowledged this aspect in a later case, in which Ainu applicants challenged a governmental procedure to return assets to the Ainu people under the Ainu Culture Promotion Law.[32] Just as in *Kayano*, the case raised issues under Article 13 of the Constitution (right to life and liberty) and 27 ICCPR. Applicants importantly interpreted *Kayano* in the sense of guaranteeing participation of the group in the decisions affecting it and claimed, *inter alia*, that the governmental procedure had not guaranteed this participation. The court rejected the claim, on the grounds that Ainu participation had been actually secured in the process.

The relevant degree of participation tends to compensate for uncertainties surrounding the precise operational scope of the right at issue. In this sense, the HRC line on consultation appears to be more rudimentary than the Canadian Supreme Court's to the extent that the level of effective participation is not

[29] See also *Anni Äärelä and Jouni Näkkäläjärvi v. Finland*, Comm. No. 779/97 Views of 24 October 2001, CCPR/C/73/D/779/1997.

[30] *G and E v. Norway*, Applications Nos. 9278/81 and 9415/81, DR, vol. 35, p. 36.

[31] The court held that the measures authorising construction of the Nibutani dam, though illegal, could not be reversed because of a number of practical and financial factors. However, it also noted that efforts to preserve Ainu culture were underway. Judgment of 27 March 1997, Civil Division No. 3, 27 March 1997, (1999) 38 ILM, pp. 428–429.

[32] For details of this case, see M. Levin & T. Tsunemoto, 'Symposium: The Indian Trust Doctrine after the 2002–2003 Supreme Court Term: A Comment on the Ainu Trust Assets Litigation in Japan' (2003) 39 *Tulsa Law Review*, p. 399 et seq.; G. Stevens, '*Ogawa v. Hokkaido (Governor)*, the Ainu Communal Property (Trusts Assets) Litigation' (2005) 4 *Indigenous Law Journal*, p. 1 et seq.

articulated in connection with the specific magnitude of the proposed activity or the scope or strength of the right or claim in question, but still arguably endorses a sliding scale approach to consultation by distinguishing minor (sporadic or isolated) from serious (consistent or cumulative) impact of state action on the group's way of life. More elaborated constraints on state action are set in *Saramaka* before the IACrtHR, which reproduces, and expands on the theme of effective participation in at least three ways. First, it reinforces the consultation duty by defining minimal, acceptable parameters of the consultation procedure.[33] Second, it singles out large scale development or investment projects as activities whose major impact on indigenous property requires, not just consultation, but free, prior and informed consent from the group in accordance with its customs and traditions.[34] This argument is regarded as an implication of the wider notion underlying the sliding scale approach that the level of effective participation is essentially a function of the nature and content of the rights and activities in question.[35] Third, it assesses the effects of any development activities on the group's territory and way of life also on the basis of the extent to which the group is allowed to reasonably share the benefits of those activities.[36] Where taken together, these elements inform a procedural and contextual management of competing claims in ways that effectively strike a balance between the group's perspective and wider concerns.

The mediating role of judicial discourse is also exemplified by pronouncements on self-determination in relation to minority groups. Despite long-standing controversies over the personal and material scope of the

[33] Judgment of 28 November 2007, Series C No. 172, para. 133: 'This duty requires the State to both accept and disseminate information, and entails constant communication between the parties. These consultations must be in good faith, through culturally appropriate procedures and with the objective of reaching an agreement. Furthermore, the Saramakas must be consulted, in accordance with their own traditions, at the early stages of a development or investment plan, not only when the need arises to obtain approval from the community, if such is the case. Early notice provides time for internal discussion within communities and for proper feedback to the State. The State must also ensure that members of the Saramaka people are aware of possible risks, including environmental and health risks, in order that the proposed development or investment plan is accepted knowingly and voluntarily. Finally, consultation should take account of the Saramaka people's traditional methods of decision-making'. See also *supra*, note 21.

[34] *Ibid.*, para. 134. Somewhat echoing earlier international jurisprudence, emphasis was put on the need to assess the individual and cumulative impact of existing or proposed development activities: *Interpretation of the Judgment on Preliminary Objections, Merits, Reparations, and Costs*, Judgment of August 12, 2008, Series C No. 185, para. 41.

[35] *Ibid.*, para. 137.

[36] *Ibid.*, paras. 129, 138–140.

international norm on self-determination, there can be little doubt that the ICJ captured its general thrust in the need, as it put it in *Western Sahara*,[37] 'to pay regard to the freely expressed will of peoples'. In other words, far from detailing the substantive contours of self-determination and the institutional or constitutional design resulting from it, the ICJ pointed to a recurrent procedural core underlying that norm, which was based on participation of the inhabitants of the relevant territorial unit. Unsurprisingly, the specific outcome of the self-determination process was entirely left to the political realm.[38] The participation parameter took on a special, mediating twist in the opinion delivered by the Supreme Court of Canada in *Reference Re Secession of Quebec*.[39] The proceedings arose from a reference by the federal government in relation to the secession of Quebec. A key question put to the Supreme Court was whether there was a right to self-determination under domestic and international law that would give Quebec the right to unilateral secession from Canada. The Supreme Court held in no uncertain terms that there was no such right from both a domestic and international legal perspective. Nevertheless, it did engage with the complex issues arising from the position of Quebec within Canada in ways that essentially established a constitutional process involving 'all participants in Confederation.'[40] Despite the lack of provision on secession in the Constitutional Act of 1982, the Supreme Court found an implicit, 'unwritten' constitutional duty to negotiate a possible secession of Quebec as being incumbent upon the latter, the other provinces and the federal government as well, following a clear majority vote in that province favouring secession. Interestingly, this line based on participation through good faith negotiations at the central and local levels, appeared to acknowledge the ethno-cultural distinctiveness of Quebec within the wider federal structure:

> The principle of federalism facilitates the pursuit of collective goals by cultural and linguistic minorities which form the majority within a particular province. This is the case in Quebec, where the majority of the population is French-speaking, and which possesses a distinct culture. This is not merely the result of

[37] Advisory Opinion, 1975 ICJ 12, para. 70.

[38] So much so that consultation itself, while acknowledged as being of paramount importance to any process of self-determination, came to be mediated by the ICJ as part of wider considerations of the General Assembly regarding the precise forms and procedures by which the right was to be realised. This line generated an implicit attempt to relate the participatory element of decolonisation of Western Sahara to its pre-colonial cultural and legal ties with Morocco and Mauritania; for comments, see for example, K. Knop, *Diversity and Self-determination in International Law* (Cambridge, 2002), pp. 163–164.

[39] [1998] S.C.R. 2.

[40] *Ibid.*, paras. 88, 149.

> chance…The federal structure adopted at Confederation enabled French-speaking Canadians to form a numerical majority in the province of Quebec, and so exercise the considerable provincial powers conferred by the Constitution Act, 1867 in such a way as to promote their language and culture.[41]

Although the constitutional dimension focussed on the possibility of secession of Quebec, not on the right of Quebec to (re-)negotiate its place within the federal structure without having to secede, it might be argued that the Supreme Court also pointed to a comprehensive process of internal self-determination (that is, short of secession) in accordance with international law. As phrased by the court:

> [I]nternational law expects that the right to self-determination will be exercised by peoples within the framework of existing sovereign states and consistently with the maintenance of the territorial integrity of those states.[42]

Apart from discussing 'exceptional circumstances' under which an international right to secession might arise, but which does not apply to Quebec (even assuming their positive recognition in international law), the Supreme Court's approach to internal self-determination echoed the participatory themes of its constitutional law discourse. While it declined to determine whether Quebec was a 'people' in the sense of international law, the Supreme Court noted that 'there [was] no necessary incompatibility between the maintenance of the territorial integrity of existing states, including Canada, and the right of a "people" to achieve a full measure of self-determination'.[43] Its discourse came to mediate the competing claims (of Quebec and the other parties to the federation) by providing a participation-based constitutional framework that effectively intersected the *procedural* ramifications of (internal) self-determination derived from *Western Sahara* and contemporary international law practice.[44] A broadly comparable (*mutatis mutandis*) structure of thinking is reflected in *Opinion No. 2* of the Badinter Commission, established by the European Community to address legal differences or issues relating to the crisis

---

[41] *Ibid.*, para. 59.

[42] *Ibid.*, para. 122. Further elaboration is likely to come from the ICJ in the context of an advisory opinion which has been requested by the UN General Assembly on *Accordance with International Law of the Unilateral Declaration of Independence by the Provisional Institution of Self-Government of Kosovo*, Order of 17 October 2008.

[43] *Ibid.*, para. 130.

[44] Interestingly, in *Katangese Peoples' Congress v. Zaire* (Comm. No. 75/92 (1995)), concerning a claim that Katanga was entitled to independence under Article 20 ACHPR, the AfrComm-HPR declined to determine whether the Katangese 'consist[ed] of one or more ethnic groups'. At the same time, it arguably exposed, albeit implicitly, a connection between the still existing political rights of the Katangese and the possibility for them to achieve internal self-determination in its multiple variants (paras. 4–6).

in Yugoslavia.[45] Faced with the question of whether the Serbian populations in Bosnia-Herzegovina and Croatia had the right to self-determination, the Commission first acknowledged that 'international law as it currently stands does not spell out all the implications of the right to self-determination', while noting that 'changes to existing frontiers at the time of independence (*uti possidetis iuris*)' were not permitted 'except where the States concerned agree otherwise'.[46] Similarly to *Reference Re Secession of Quebec*, a distinction was made between unilateral independence for minority groups (which remained unrecognised in international law) and mutually agreed border changes (which presupposed a procedural context for negotiated solutions to be sought by the groups, or at least on their behalf). The core part of the opinion focussed on the protection of minority groups within a wider process of self-determination that stops short of independence. First, the Commission controversially found that several instruments on minority protection were binding on Bosnia-Herzegovina and Croatia as part of peremptory norms of general international law (*ius cogens*). Second, it understood the role of minority protection on the basis of a fundamental connection between self-determination and human rights:

> [W]here there are one or more groups within a State constituting one or more ethnic, religious or language communities, they have the right to recognition of their identity under international law
>
> ...
>
> The right to self-determination serves to safeguard human rights. By virtue of that right, every individual may choose to belong to whatever ethnic, religious or language community he or she wishes.[47]

Here again, the substantive contours and operational design of the construction remain unexplored, as judicial discourse approaches the borderline with the political process. In essence, all the Commission did was to mediate the claims by finding benchmarks for governmental action, the most crucial of which was the right of minority groups to participate in that process in order to have their ethno-cultural identity effectively protected as a major component of a broader human rights framework. In a way, this line can be regarded as a more sophisticated elaboration of the two widely known UN reports on the *Aaland Islands* question in the early 1920s.[48] While they appeared to diverge

---

45 European Community Arbitration Commission, Opinion No. 2, 11 January 1992, (1992) 31 ILM 1497.

46 *Ibid.*

47 *Ibid.*, p. 1498.

48 Report of International Commission of Jurists on Legal Aspects of the Aaland Question, League of Nations Official Journal, Spec. Supp., No. 3, 3 (1920); Report of Commission of Rapporteurs on the Aaland Islands Question, League of Nations Doc. B7 21/68/106 (1921).

on the issue of 'remedial secession', with the second report favouring separation in the event of serious abuses against the Aaland population, they both recognised the lack of a positive right to independence for minority population groups, and distilled from law and policy a fundamental procedural principle which was designed to bring self-determination into line with minority protection, regardless of issues of detail. That principle was the entrenchment (conventional, constitutional or otherwise) of the Aalanders' civil liberties and identity rights within Finland.

The emphasis on process in most of the cases discussed so far, namely on the procedural steps that have to be taken to make that process legally acceptable, does not (and should not) do away with a substantive core as the outer limit of the mediation exercise generated by judicial discourse. In this sense, the basic point of major pronouncements on (internal) self-determination, including autonomy regimes, is not only that an adequate procedural framework must exist, but also that such framework must meet the most basic requirements of international human rights law in terms of individual rights and group protection.[49] Along comparable lines, the entire Inter-American jurisprudence on indigenous property rights (loosely understood as a key element of indigenous self-determination) rests on the notion that, while a specific participation-based process within the state is needed to make practical sense of an otherwise merely abstract recognition of indigenous lands, it is still for the Inter-American organs to determine whether such process achieves the objective of respecting those rights.[50] In *Apirana Mahuika*, the HRC concluded that the settlement reached between the government of New Zealand and the Maori people was compatible with Article 27 ICCPR, principally on the grounds that it was the end result of a broad consultation process that had taken account of Maori interests and needs. But it also held that this process could not substitute for the parallel rights of other members of the minority group – the 'dissenters' Maori[51] – that remained to be protected.

Conversely, judicial discourse can use core entitlements to define the content of the procedural test of involvement, thereby further refining the scope of its mediating intervention. For example, as hinted at earlier, the Supreme Court of Canada's sliding scale approach to consultation with indigenous groups is based on a distinction between cases where property rights must be upheld

[49] See also the position of the Council of Europe's Venice Commission on the right to autonomy set forth in Article 11 of Recommendation 1201, which was adopted by the Parliamentary Assembly in 1993: CDL-MIN (1996) 4, pp. 4–5.

[50] *Yakye Axa Indigenous Community v. Paraguay*, Judgment of 17 June 2005, Series C No. 125, para. 215; *Yakye Axa Indigenous Community v. Paraguay*, Interpretation of the Judgment of Merits, Reparations and Costs, Judgment of 6 February 2006, Series C No. 142, para. 22.

[51] On the issue of 'minorities within minorities' see below in the chapter.

and cases where they cannot be established. Within the first set of cases, the degree of consultation is said to vary depending on the seriousness of the issue and the expected level of interference with property rights. A less heavy yet effective test of consultation, must still be passed by the state if property rights are not at stake, and the case focuses only on the actual use of the land.

(Positive) equality as a justificatory test

The question of reconciling minority and majority interests through a mediating line of judicial discourse also arises in the context of *positive* equality as opposed to non-discrimination (or negative equality) discussed in the previous chapter. Indeed, the dimension of differential treatment benefiting minority groups raises particularly problematic issues. By way of illustration, the following analysis primarily draws on the jurisprudence under the ECHR and ICCPR.

An attempt at reconciling those interests underlies the jurisprudential theme of whether Article 14 ECHR, besides outlawing unreasonable distinctions, generates a positive duty to achieve equality. In *Belgian Linguistics*, the EurCrtHR incidentally acknowledged that sometimes different legal solutions are 'called for' in order to correct factual inequalities.[52] *Thlimmenos*, involving a Jehovah's Witness who had been denied registration as a chartered accountant because of his conviction by Greek courts for refusing on religious grounds to wear a military uniform, led the EurCrtHR to find a breach of Article 14 (in conjunction with Article 9) for failure by the respondent state 'to introduce appropriate exceptions to the rule barring persons convicted of a serious crime from the profession of chartered accountants'.[53] It did so on the assumption, previously recalled, that significantly different situations should be treated differently in order to comply with Article 14. For one thing, the implied language of positive distinctions that are reasonable and objective appears to be in line with the EurCrtHR's increasingly embraced understanding of the ECHR as not ruling out positive obligations for the parties.[54] And yet, this case can hardly reflect recognition of an automatic general duty to ensure positive equality, which may directly benefit minority groups along with other groups under the ECHR. First, the EurCrtHR does not point to a direct entitlement to differential treatment, but rather to the effects on equality deriving from the lack of such treatment, which arguably does not necessarily exceed the

[52] Judgment of 23 July 1968, Series A, No. 6., para. 34.

[53] Application 34369/97, Judgment of 6 April 2000, para. 48.

[54] In the context of freedom of religion, see e.g. *Jewish Liturgical Ass'n Cha'are Shalom ve Tsedek v. France*, Application No. 27417/95, Judgment of 27 June 2000.

view of indirect discrimination already encompassed by the *Belgian Linguistics* and other decisions. Second, the 'reasonable and objective' test leaves the parties a margin of appreciation in assessing the situations in question, and in practice the EurCrtHR has not been always keen to intrude upon the parties' assessment on issues involving Article 14. Third, the individual-oriented characterisation of the situations leading up to a differential treatment (the focus is indeed on 'persons' in analogous or significantly different situation) seems to suggest that the impact of the EurCrtHR's proposition on group considerations may be more limited. And some post-*Thlimmenos* case law provides indication of that.

For example, in *Podkolzina* the EurCrtHR did not address the claim made by the applicant, that the 'third-level knowledge' of the Latvian language as a legislative requirement for standing as a candidate in parliamentary elections was manifestly disproportionate to the legitimate aim of securing an appropriate functioning of Parliament, suggesting indirect discriminatory practices against non-Latvian speaking people such as members of the Russian-speaking group, particularly on account of association with a national minority. No reference was made by the EurCrtHR to a positive duty to secure special arrangements to tackle the 'significantly different' situation of the affected people. In *Chapman* and similar cases, the EurCrtHR held the view that according protection under Article 8 to Roma/Gypsy individuals in unlawful residence in a caravan on their land would raise 'substantial problems' under Article 14 in relation to non-Roma/Gypsy individuals who were still prevented from establishing their houses on their land in the same area, whereas the joint dissent pointed to the applicant's specific lifestyle as precisely the additional factor justifying the application of Article 14 as interpreted in *Thlimmenos*. This latter theme was amplified by the dissent in relation to the more general question regarding the relationship between the ECHR and Council of Europe standards on minority protection, but was certainly made explicit by the Chamber's dissent in *DH and others*, with regard to increased resources and sustained action to improve access to education by Roma children in the Czech Republic. In this case, Judge Cabral Barreto clearly regarded post-*Thlimmenos* Article 14 as generating both negative and positive duties of protection against discrimination.[55] By contrast, Judge Costa noted in his concurring opinion that, in his view, 'up till now this Court ha[d] refused to consider [positive discrimination] a State obligation'.[56] In the case of *Refah*

[55] Application No. 57325/00, Judgment of 7 February 2006, Dissenting Opinion of Judge Cabral Barreto, paras. 4–6.

[56] *Ibid.*, Concurring Opinion of Judge Costa, para. 7.

Partisi (The Welfare Party) and others v. Turkey, concerning the dissolution of a major Muslim political party that advocated, *inter alia*, the establishment of a plurality of personal law regimes along religious lines, the EurCrtHR stated firmly that the envisaged difference in treatment was incompatible with Article 14 ECHR,[57] *a fortiori* setting aside *Thlimmenos* as a source of mandatory group-oriented and active measures in this context.

Seen retrospectively, the *Thlimmenos* argument seems to have exposed the outer limits of an understanding of discrimination that is still defined primarily by a 'negative' vision of equality. In other words, the fundamental rationale for the case is that, differential treatment may be necessary to prevent or remove (essentially indirect) discrimination, but is not, or not necessarily, envisaged under the ECHR as an a priori and structural element of public policy. Echoing the almost forty years older obiter in *Belgian Linguistics*, the EurCrtHR (Grand Chamber) in *DH and others* explained that 'Article 14 *does not prohibit* a member State from treating groups differently in order to correct "factual inequalities" between them'.[58] Following up on *Thlimmenos* and more group-oriented case law on indirect discrimination,[59] it also implied that a failure to adopt differential treatment can still be defended on reasonable and objective grounds unrelated to the discriminatory ground at issue. In this sense, judicial discourse may step in to assess the damage, if any, caused by state action or inaction, not to enforce a pre-defined European theory of how states parties must actively address inequalities within their own societies. Unsurprisingly, a distinction between indirect discrimination and a specific obligation to achieve effective equality is reflected in the EC Race Directive on the basis of the ECJ's jurisprudence.[60]

Though based on a particular instrument (i.e. the ECHR), this discourse illustrates real and potential (at least operational) difficulties associated with a

---

[57] Applications Nos. 41340/98, 41342/98, 41343/98 and 41344/98, Judgment of 31 July 2001 [C], para. 70, and Judgment of 13 February 2003 [GC], para. 119.

[58] Application No. 57325/00, Judgment of 13 November 2007, para. 175 [author's emphasis]. See also *Affaire Sampanis et Autres c. Grèce*, Application No. 32526/05, Judgment of 5 June 2008 (final on 5 September 2008), para. 68 (in French).

[59] See *supra*, Chapter 3.

[60] European Community Council Directive of 29 June 2000 implementing the principle of equal treatment between persons irrespective of racial or ethnic origin, EC Directive 2000/43 of 29 June 1996, O.J. 2000 L 180, 22, Article 5. On indirect discrimination and positive action under EC law, see generally D. Schiek, L. Waddington & M. Bell (eds.), *Cases, Materials and Text on National, Supranational and International Non-Discrimination Law*, (Oxford: Hart Publishing, 2007), p. 352 et seq., and p. 801 et seq. On the approach of the ECJ in relation to the equality directives, see D. Caruso, 'Limits of the Classic Method: Positive Action in the European Union After the New Equality Directives' (2003) 44 *Harvard International Law Journal*, p. 331 et seq.

pro-minority group approach to equality that is based on the recognition of a distinctive positive duty on states. It may be useful to note that, for example, in *Morton v. Mancari*,[61] the US Supreme Court upheld special measures to the benefit of federally-recognised members of Indian groups on the basis of arguments which were not derived from human rights and positive equality but from the unique position of Indians in the United States. From a broader perspective, a fundamental distinction should also be made between the sort of 'special measures' envisaged by general anti-discrimination clauses and the positive action conceptualised by the minority protection discourse. In *Minority Schools*, the PCIJ arguably used the notion of equality to call for measures that could remedy the structural imbalance within the majority and the minority in areas critical to the preservation of cultural integrity. The focus was on 'result' (as opposed to opportunity) and 'equilibrium between different situations' rather than incidental or transient elements of state policies. CERD and the Committee on the Elimination of Discrimination against Women have increasingly linked indirect discrimination and positive equality but generally concentrate on specific areas or aspects and fall short of indicating comprehensive structural policies.[62]

Admittedly, the notion of 'special measures' reflected in jurisprudential assessments may occasionally rely on anti-discrimination measures to advance, in effect, identity related rights. A case in point is *Gerhardy v. Brown*,[63] in which the High Court of Australia referred to Article 1(4) ICERD to conclude that a South Australian piece of legislation that had restored land rights to an indigenous community did not discriminate against non-members of that community. In *Saramaka*, the IACrtHR broadly construed the right to juridical personality for the benefit of the Saramaka people as a special measure owed to them as a way of protecting their lands and thus their identity.[64] Generally speaking, though, special measures essentially constitute tools for temporary affirmative action treatment, whereas the minority related positive action serves *au fond* the specific and sole objective of governing the complexities posited

[61] 417 U.S. 535 (1974).

[62] D. Schiek, L. Waddington & M. Bell (eds.), *Cases, Materials and Text on National, Supranational and International Non-Discrimination Law*, *supra* note 59, pp. 340–341; K. Henrard, 'The Protection of Minorities Through the Equality Provisions in the UN Human Rights Treaties: The UN Treaty Bodies', in G. Pentassuglia (ed.), 'Reforming the UN Human Rights Machinery: What Does the Future Hold for the Protection of Minorities and Indigenous Peoples?' (2007) 14 *International Journal on Minority and Group Rights*, Special Issue, pp. 156–176.

[63] 159 CLR 70 (1985).

[64] Judgment of 28 November 2007, Series C No. 172, paras. 172, 103.

by the existence of a minority community as an ethno-cultural group. Thus, such positive action may well be of a permanent nature, as long as it is in tune with the principle of equality. It may be argued that a reading of Article 14 ECHR that implies a direct and general duty to reasonably differentiate, though not precluding minority identity considerations, would be likely to constrain them because of the most basic character of positive discrimination under international human rights law.

A second approach reflects a line of mediation of competing claims that reserves to judicial discourse a justificatory rather than prescriptive role. The HRC has appeared quite assertive on positive action under Article 27 ICCPR (aside from protection in the private sphere), but the core discourse has been mostly framed in terms of justifying, rather than systematically subsuming, positive measures under that provision. In the *Länsman* cases, the criterion of involvement of the affected group seems to be construed more as a flexible material parameter to determine 'non-denial' and less as a prior strict legal requirement to protect minority identity. In *Apirana Mahuika*, the HRC held that the settlement reached between the government of New Zealand and the Maori people regarding Maori fishing rights as a fundamental component of their economic and cultural activities was 'compatible' with Article 27 as it passed the test of consultation and economic sustainability applied in the *Länsman* cases (though New Zealand had directly presented it as action taken in fulfilment of positive obligations under Article 27). In short, this line does not propose hard and fast rules on positive measures to be enforced at the state level, but rather mediates the claims through a contextual assessment of the decision-making process *ex post facto*. To be sure, the HRC's view of Article 27 is incremental in nature, and an ever higher number of affected states parties is subscribing to the notion that Article 27 does entail positive identity obligations as such. Clearly, the base line from which to assess existing positive measures in connection with Article 27 is the complex of anti-discrimination clauses, by analogy with *Diergaardt* and *Waldman* as commented in the previous chapter.

On the justificatory approach, states are normally left free to decide if and when positive action is necessary or required, though a solid equality benchmark is offered as to *how* such action, where it takes place, must be shaped. This is where judicial discourse turns, or may turn, the justificatory perspective into a mediating tool. In *Belgian Linguistics*, the EurCommHR observed that a territorially-based linguistic system was not necessarily incompatible with the ECHR:

> [U]n régime linguistique de l'enseignement organisé sur une base territorialiste ne serait pas nécessairement contraire à la Convention. Un tel systéme pourrait se justifier par des considérations d'ordre administratif, financier ou autre.

> La Commission ne croit pourtant pas devoir entrer dans la discussion de la légitimité des differentes conceptions sur lesquelles un régime linguistique peut être édifié.[65]

By combining *Belgian Linguistics* and *Thlimmenos*, it might be contended that special language rights for members of a minority group, including a territorially-based linguistic system encompassing mother tongue education and/or mother tongue communication with public authorities, designed to remedy in a reasonable and objective manner the structural imbalance between persons belonging to the minority and those belonging to the majority in areas critical to the preservation of cultural integrity, would not be in breach of Article 14 ECHR. In *The Liberal Party, Mrs R. and Mr P. v. United Kingdom*,[66] the EurCommHR indirectly indicated that special voting laws aimed at enhancing the election prospects of a religious or ethnic minority could be allowed under the ECHR, in those cases where a minority could never be represented in the legislature 'because there was a clear voting pattern along these lines in the majority'. Similarly, the dissenting judges in *Mathieu-Mohin and Clerfayt v. Belgium*,[67] implicitly justified special electoral arrangements that could remove what they believed to be language-based discriminatory effects against the French speakers elected in *Halle-Vilvoorde*, in Belgium.

In line with further European anti-discrimination law instruments, this approach does not insist on the existence of an obligation to adopt positive measures to achieve full and effective equality, yet it does acknowledge that de facto inequalities suffered by certain groups or categories of persons may constitute justifications for adopting them.[68] Here judicial discourse interposes itself between the sphere of public policy-making and the human rights-based arguments of the group by providing an *ex post facto* and case-by-case analysis of existing or prospective minority regimes. In a string of cases involving pro-Kurdish political movements in Turkey, the EurCrtHR did uphold the notion that territorial autonomy (or even secession) for a minority group was one of the several possible consequences of allowing for a process of democratic deliberation to flourish as required by the ECHR.[69] Admittedly, as already implied by *Belgian Linguistics*, the lack of positive treatment does

---

65 Report of 25 June 1965, para. 405.

66 Application No. 8765/79, 21 DR 211.

67 Judgment of 2 March 1987, Series A, No. 113.

68 Pre-existing forms of autonomy or power-sharing may also provide a basis for such a justification: for comments on the European context, see W. Kymlicka, *Multicultural Odysseys: Navigating the New International Politics of Diversity* (Oxford, 2007), p. 242.

69 See e.g. G. Pentassuglia, 'Minority Issues as a Challenge in the European Court of Human Rights: A Comparison with the Case Law of the United Nations Human Rights Committee' (2003) 46 *German Yearbook of International Law*, p. 404.

not in itself breach the equality principle, as such treatment may not be *claimed* on the basis of that principle. That also means, by contrast, that the existence of such treatment may or may not be justified on equality grounds. For example, whereas the Romanian Constitutional Court, in a remarkable decision from 1999,[70] held that the right to mother tongue education in so-called 'multicultural universities' under the statutory regulation in question did not discriminate against other Romanian citizens but in fact realised equality between members of national minorities and ethnic Romanians, one year before the Slovakian Constitutional Court had applied a merely negative concept of equality by striking down provisions of the local self-government electoral law of 1998 which set up a system of ethnic proportional representation in local elections.[71]

The mediating space created by judicial discourse becomes all the more significant as the permissibility of minority regimes is increasingly upheld. If it is accepted that difference in treatment is permissible and does not necessarily amount to discrimination, on language, religious or other grounds, then a circumstantial inquiry into whether and to what extent pro-minority group differential treatment is consistent with equality captures a key feature of the jurisprudential exercise.

Indeed, the measure of such permissibility came to the fore, albeit indirectly, in the *Refah Partisi* case. In 1998, the Turkish Constitutional Court dissolved the Refah Party – by that time the majority party in Parliament and leading partner of a coalition government. In the Grand Chamber's analysis (quoting verbatim from the earlier decision of the Chamber), one basic reason for this was that Refah had been proposing a plurality of legal systems along religious lines:

> [T]he Court considers that Refah's proposal that there should be a plurality of legal systems would introduce into all legal relationships a distinction between individuals grounded on religion, would categorise everyone according to his religious beliefs and would allow him rights and freedoms not as an individual but according to his allegiance to a religious movement.
>
> The Court takes the view that such a societal model cannot be considered compatible with the Convention system, for two reasons.

[70] Dec. No. 114 of 20 July 1999, at www.eurac.edu/miris.

[71] Dec. 19/98 of 15 October 1998, in *Bull. Constitution. Case Law* 3 (1998) 460–462, SVK-1998–3–010. More generally, on the reluctance to embrace positive equality, see the Decision of the Slovak Constitutional Court of 18 October 2005 transposing the EU Race Directive, PL ÚS 8/04; for a commentary, see A. Bröstl, 'Positive Action and the Principle of Equality: Discussing a Decision of the Constitutional Court of the Slovak Republic' (2005/6) 5 *European Yearbook of Minority Issues*, p. 377 et seq.

> Firstly, it would do away with the State's role as the guarantor of individual rights and freedoms and the impartial organiser of the practice of the various beliefs and religions in a democratic society, since it would oblige individuals to obey, not rules laid down by the State in the exercise of its above-mentioned functions, but static rules of law imposed by the religion concerned. But the State has a positive obligation to ensure that everyone within its jurisdiction enjoys in full, and without being able to waive them, the rights and freedoms guaranteed by the Convention
>
> ...
>
> Secondly, such a system would undeniably infringe the principle of non-discrimination between individuals as regards their enjoyment of public freedoms, which is one of the fundamental principles of democracy. A difference in treatment between individuals in all fields of public and private law according to their religion or beliefs manifestly cannot be justified under the Convention, and more particularly Article 14 thereof, which prohibits discrimination. Such a difference in treatment cannot maintain a fair balance between, on the one hand, the claims of certain religious groups who wish to be governed by their own rules and on the other the interest of society as a whole, which must be based on peace and on tolerance between the various religions and beliefs...[72]

These comments have been criticised on points of evidence and substance.[73] The joint dissent in the Chamber's judgment maintained that it was not necessary to examine the precise nature or effect of the multi-juridical society in question since there was no evidence that the contested statements advocating this kind of society posed a genuine threat to the secular order in Turkey and, in any event, that any concrete steps had been taken to introduce it by Refah once in government. In fact, the EurCrtHR's basic assumptions, namely that Refah's model curtailed individual freedom, covered all fields of public and private law, and denied the state the role of guarantor of rights and freedoms, could hardly be established. Ironically, Refah argued that it had promoted a private law system based on freedom of contract that conformed with individuals' religious norms and practices, not public laws meant to revise the relationship between individuals and the state.

But even assuming the existence of those features in Refah's conception of legal pluralism, the question arises as to whether those comments were intended to cover Refah's model (as perceived by the EurCrtHR) and indeed *any* type of plurality of legal systems designed to accommodate ethno-cultural communities. In his concurring opinion, Judge Klover noted that it is well-established in ancient and modern legal theory and practice that in certain cases 'members of minorities of all kinds may have more than one type of

[72] Applications Nos. 41340/98, 41342/98, 41343/98 and 41344/98, Judgment of 13 February 2003, para. 119.

[73] For a critique, see K. Boyle, 'Human Rights, Religion and Democracy: The Refah Party Case' (2004) 1 *Essex Human Rights Law Review*, p. 1 et seq.

personal status', thereby calling for an analysis more complex than the one offered by the EurCrtHR on the competing interests of the communities concerned and civil society as a whole. From a justificatory perspective, a way of reconciling the EurCrtHR's approach with the criticisms generated by its apparently sweeping propositions on legal pluralism is to distil from such propositions at least three elements that, *a contrario*, the EurCrtHR would use to uphold forms of autonomy (whether on religious grounds or otherwise) benefiting minority groups in multinational states. That is, freedom of choice for group members to be bound by the community rules; narrow accommodation of the group's autonomy granted by the state to protect the group members' legitimate interests and needs; and safeguard of the role of the state as the ultimate guarantor of rights and freedoms. Interestingly, in *Jewish Liturgical Ass'n Cha'are Shalom ve Tsedek v. France*,[74] the EurCrtHR did recognise a French law which allowed the Jewish community to have its own religion-based laws regarding the slaughtering of animals, even though they conflicted with French law. Cast in the language of a positive undertaking to secure religious freedom under Article 9 ECHR, that implied recognition of a measure of autonomy over religious matters as being compatible with the ECHR. This line is all the more significant, given the EurCrtHR's consistent emphasis on *organisational* rather than *personal* autonomy in a stream of cases involving the collective dimension of freedom of religion.[75] As will be discussed below, domestic jurisprudence from countries such as India, Tanzania or South Africa have equally (at least implicitly) upheld personal law regimes while at the same time securing protection of women's rights. Whether or not the resulting division of jurisdictional spheres proves workable in any particular case,[76] *Refah Partisi* (paradoxically) deepens the discourse about equality in ways that provide important guidance to acceptable principles and limits of minority regimes.

In fact, a judicial space for mediating majority and minority interests is generated not only by a direct justification for the pro-minority measures but also

[74] Application No. 27417/95, Judgment of 27 June 2000.

[75] J. Ringelheim, *Diversité Culturelle et Droits de l'Homme: L'Émergence de la Problématique des Minorités dans le Droit de la Convention Européenne des Droits de l'Homme* (Bruxelles, 2006), pp. 110–111; M. Iovane, 'The Universality of Human Rights and the International Protection of Cultural Diversity: Some Theoretical and Practical Considerations', in G. Pentassuglia (ed.), 'Reforming the UN Human Rights Machinery: What Does the Future Hold for the Protection of Minorities and Indigenous Peoples?' (2007) 14 *International Journal on Minority and Group Rights*, Special Issue, pp. 256–258. For a general discussion of personal autonomy, see M. Suksi, 'Personal Autonomy as Institutional Form – Focus on Europe Against the Background of Article 27 of the ICCPR', *ibid.*, (2008) 15, p. 157 et seq.

[76] A. Shachar, *Multicultural Jurisdictions: Cultural Differences and Women's Rights* (Cambridge, 2001).

by a finding of a breach of the principle of proportionality. The theme of *Refah Partisi* may be viewed as peculiar to the structure of personal law regimes, but it did most certainly expose, along with earlier ECHR jurisprudence, the role of judicial *control* over the boundaries or ramifications of the minority regime in question vis-à-vis the rights of others. In *Ford*,[77] the Supreme Court of Canada held that provisions of the Charter of the French Language prohibiting the use of any language other than French in commercial signs and firm names infringed the guarantees of freedom of expression recognised in the Canadian Charter of Rights and Freedoms and the Quebec Charter of Human Rights and Freedoms, as well as the guarantee of non-discrimination provided in the latter instrument. On the one hand, the Supreme Court acknowledged the crucial importance of language and language rights to the sense of collective and individual identity of both the francophone community and non-francophones of Quebec (and by implication, of the whole of Canada). On the other hand, it concluded that the exclusivity of the French language in that context was clearly disproportionate to the legitimate aim of promoting and maintaining a French *visage linguistique* in Quebec. Interestingly, the equality argument, broadly considered to underpin the distinctive position of the French-speaking community of Quebec, came to be used this time against itself. Indeed, the Supreme Court noted that although s. 58 of the Charter of the French Language applied to everyone, the requirement of the exclusive use of French, regardless of their language of use, could not be justified:

> It has the effect...of impinging deferentially on different classes of persons according to their language of use. Francophones are permitted to express themselves in their language of use while anglophones and other non-francophones are prohibited from doing so....because of its differential effect or impact on persons according to their language of use, s. 58 creates a distinction based on language within the meaning of s. 10....[t]he human right or freedom in issue here is the freedom to express oneself in the language of one's choice....[t]he distinction based on language of use created by s. 58 has the effect of nullifying the right to full and equal recognition and exercise of this freedom. Section 58 is therefore of no force or effect as infringing s. 10 of the Quebec *Charter*. The same conclusion applies to s. 69 of the *Charter of the French Language*.[78]

This line echoes the theme of the similar *Ballantyne* case before the HRC, in which the government of Quebec argued, *inter alia*, that the Charter of the French Language applied the notion of *de facto* equality to protect the cultural

[77] [1988] 2 SCR 712.
[78] *Ibid.*, para. 82.

identity of French speakers. The HRC did not uphold the ramifications of the language restrictions in the private sphere, though the decision was on freedom of expression, not indirect discrimination:

> The Committee believes that it is not necessary, in order to protect the vulnerable position in Canada of the francophone group, to prohibit commercial advertising in English. This protection may be achieved in other ways that do not preclude the freedom of expression, in a language of their choice, of those engaged in such fields as trade. For example, the law could have required that advertising be in both French and English. A State may choose one or more official languages, but it may not exclude, outside the spheres of public life, the freedom to express oneself in a language of one's choice. The Committee accordingly concludes that there has been a violation of article 19, paragraph 2.[79]

These examples point to two distinct yet interrelated aspects of the justificatory (and mediating) role of judicial discourse regarding equality. For one thing, anti-discrimination provisions provide fundamental base lines for weighing up minority and majority interests; if it is accepted that a positive understanding of equality can justify minority regimes within states, it must be also accepted that limits on such regimes are inherently built into that same notion. Judicial discourse thus mediates the claims by oscillating between acceptance and rejection, thereby keeping the relevant system or set of provisions constantly open to review. This also applies to complex power-sharing arrangements involving several ethnic communities. In case 5/98,[80] the Bosnian Constitutional Court considered whether the state and sub-state institutional structures based on ethnic proportional representation and established under the Dayton Agreement were in breach of Article 3 of Protocol 1 ECHR, which provides for periodic elections ensuring the free expression of the people in the choice of the legislature. The Bosnian Court concluded that the system of ethnic representation was not per se in violation of that provision. Nevertheless, it held that the ECHR clause was seriously impaired by the combination of such system and the veto power of ethnically defined 'majorities' which were in fact minorities in Parliament and in the country as a whole. In essence, the court attempted a mediation between the upholding of the power-sharing arrangement and the equal rights of all citizens, regardless of ethnic group membership.

The level of intrusiveness of judicial discourse inevitably varies as the legal assessment moves from less to more integrated legal orders. Within the EC context, such cases as *Criminal Proceedings against Otto Bickel and Ulrich*

[79] Communications Nos. 359/1989, 385/1989, Views of 31 March 1993, para. 11.4.

[80] Partial Decision of 1 July 2000, at www.ustavnisud.ba.

Franz,[81] *Roman Angonese v. Cassa di Risparmio di Bolzano SpA*,[82] and *Criminal Proceedings against Robert Heinrich Maria Mutsch*,[83] illustrate the variations on the equality theme generated by the supranational logic of internal market and free trade. In all these cases, the minority regime came under scrutiny in relation to the position of persons who came from outside the region in which the group has traditionally lived. All of them were said to enjoy freedom of movement under EC law in conjunction with the principle of non-discrimination on grounds of nationality. The ECJ upheld the equality argument in a way that either extended the minority regime to non-minority members (*Bickel and Franz, Mutsch*) or found that an element of that regime did not apply to those individuals as it was incompatible with EC anti-discrimination law (*Angonese*). It would appear that, unlike the Quebec decisions, where the autonomous equality-based rationale for minority regimes is left largely unaffected by the recognition of limits to their permissibility, the ECJ judgments in effect superimpose the economic integration-oriented conception of equality over distinctive and human rights-based concerns for minority identity. An attempt to combine EC equality and cultural (national) identity concerns was reflected in *Groener v. Minister for Education*,[84] in which the ECJ regarded the Irish language requirement for teachers, including foreign nationals, in vocational education as not amounting to discrimination. Even so, it has been argued that the decision in practice led to a hybrid redefinition of language requirements that ultimately limited their identity related impact.[85]

At the same time, the proportionality argument that is embraced in different ways by the above decisions to reject certain pro-minority elements indirectly mediates the majority-minority (or by analogy, non-minority members-minority members) competing claims by *confirming* the overall legitimacy of the minority regime. In this sense, *Refah Partisi*, the Quebec cases as well as the ECJ jurisprudence, suggest varying degrees of judicial justification for forms of protection of minority groups that are in line with the principle of equality.

---

[81] Case 274/96 [1998] ECR I-7637.

[82] Case 281/98 [2000] All ER (EC) 577.

[83] Case 137/84 [1985] ECR 2681.

[84] Case 379/87 [1989] ECR 3967.

[85] D. Caruso, 'Limits of the Classic Method: Positive Action in the European Union After the New Equality Directives', *supra* note 60, p. 358. In the *Avello* case (*Carlos Garcia Avello v. Belgium*, Case 148/02, Judgment of 2 October 2003), involving a refusal by Belgian authorities to change children's surname to include the name of their father – a Spanish national residing in Belgium who wanted their children's surname to conform to Spanish practices – the Advocate General appealed to non-discrimination in relation to freedom of movement and respect for cultural diversity to challenge the Belgian position (para. 72). The ECJ deemed such refusal to be in breach of EC law by emphasising the children's perspective and the implications of EU citizenship rights.

While *Refah Partisi* seems to allow for such a justification inferentially, the Quebec cases and the ECJ jurisprudence openly start from the premise that the minority regime in question is *not* in itself incompatible with human rights law or EC law, though certain aspects of it are. In *Ballantyne*, the HRC made it clear that the francophone community of Canada had the right to protect its own identity under Article 27 ICCPR, and implicitly accepted the wider justifications for the Quebec law on outdoors commercial advertising. Still, it noted that such protection '[could] be achieved in other ways that [did] not preclude the freedom of expression'.[86] In *Bickel and Franz*, in response to the point made by the Italian government that the rules at issues were meant 'to protect the ethno-cultural minority residing in the province' and therefore should not be extended to outsiders who happened to be present in the region occasionally and temporarily, the ECJ sought to balance out the competing claims:

> Of course, the protection of such a minority may constitute a legitimate aim. It does not appear, however, from the documents before the Court that that aim would be undermined if the rules in issue were extended to cover German-speaking nationals of other Member States exercising their right to freedom of movement.[87]

In *Groener*, the ECJ held that the EC Treaty did not prohibit 'the adoption of a policy and promotion of a language of a member state which is both the national language and the first official language'.[88] In terms of the protection and promotion of *minority* languages, *Bickel and Franz* (and related jurisprudence) does not prohibit the differential treatment generated by a language (or otherwise) regime benefiting minority groups, which is therefore implicitly recognised despite the ultimately homogenising imperatives of the Community legal order. Rather, it offers a test of proportionality on the basis of which individual ramifications of that regime are assessed against wider EC objectives.[89]

In short, the scope of the justificatory perspective on minority related equality matters is a function of the legal system within which it is designed to work, though its fundamental mediating thrust can arguably be regarded as a diffused theme of judicial discourse.

---

[86] Communications Nos. 359/1989, 385/1989, Views of 31 March 1993, para. 11.4.

[87] Case 274/96 [1998] ECR I-7637, para. 29.

[88] Case 379/87 [1989] ECR 3967, para. 19.

[89] For a discussion, see D. Caruso, 'Limits of the Classic Method: Positive Action in the European Union After the New Equality Directives', *supra* note 60, p. 344; R. Hofmann, 'National Minorities and European Community Law' (2002) 2 *Baltic Yearbook of International Law*, p. 159 et seq.

Reconciling interests within the group

Women and the group

The case of gender equality within minority groups has brought up complex issues regarding the scope and boundaries of identity based protections. Although the interplay of equality and identity claims ultimately underpins the whole architecture of rights that are variably associated with ethno-cultural minority groups, inter-communal disputes turning on the role and status ascribed to women within the community expose the tension between those two claims from a human rights perspective. The mediating role of judicial discourse can be assessed against different adjudicatory approaches, which prioritise the group or the individual respectively.

In *Canada AG v. Lavell*,[90] the Supreme Court of Canada dismissed Jeanette Lavell's claim that the Indian Act entailed discrimination on grounds of sex since it denied membership status to those women who married non-Indian men, and the children born to these marriages, while preserving group status for the male members who married non-Indian women. The rationale for this is broadly captured by the later *Martinez* case[91] before the US Supreme Court. Julia Martinez was a member of the Santa Clara Pueblo who was married to a non-Santa Claran. Two years before this marriage, the Pueblo passed a tribal ordinance denying membership to children of female members who married outside the Santa Clara Pueblo, while extending membership to children of male members who married outside the community. As a result of this ordinance, the Martinez children had been denied admission to the tribe, and were consequently excluded from active and passive voting rights, as well as residence and inheritance rights in the event of her mother's death. The Supreme Court upheld the tribe ordinance by embracing what might be characterised as the privatising view of non-interference. The District Court for the District of New Mexico had judged in favour of the group, noting that membership rules were 'basic to the tribe's survival as a cultural and economic entity'[92] and that '[t]o abrogate tribal decisions [was] to destroy cultural identity under the guise of saving it'.[93] The Court of Appeals disagreed on the merits as a result of a strict scrutiny equality test based on the presumptively invidious nature of sex discrimination, but the Supreme Court eventually reversed this decision. Like in *Canada AG*, the fundamental narrative was the distinctive identity of indigenous communities and the related

[90] [1974] S.C.R. 1349.
[91] 98 U.S. 1670 (1978).
[92] *Ibid.*, p. 1675.
[93] *Ibid.*

imperative of non-interference with their customs and values. Indian tribes were recognised as '"distinct, independent political communities, retaining their original natural rights" in matters of local self-government'.[94] Applying a sort of ECHR-style margin of appreciation doctrine at sub-national level, the Supreme Court stated that tribal forums were in a better position than federal courts to evaluate questions of indigenous identity. Judicial intervention, the court pointed out, would 'substantially interfere with a tribe's ability to maintain itself as a culturally and politically distinct entity',[95] running counter to the legislative intent of Congress. The group's ordinance went in effect unchecked. The minority within minority dispute was regarded as a purely internal matter. The group identity discourse hinged on arguments peculiar to the US system rather than specific notions of human rights, though *Canada AG* concluded that a similar provision in the Indian Act was not per se in breach of the principle of equality in the Canadian Bill of Rights.

The universalistic framework of human rights is precisely what has inspired an opposite line of discourse, that is, one based on the individual right of non-discrimination. This was certainly a major dimension of *Ephrahim v. Pastory*,[96] in which the High Court of Tanzania held that Haya customary law, which barred women, unlike men, from selling clan land violated the prohibition of discrimination on account of sex as enshrined in the Constitution and several international instruments to which Tanzania was a signatory, including the Universal Declaration of Human Rights, the Convention on the Elimination of All Forms of Discrimination Against Women, and the ICCPR. Interestingly, by appealing to non-interference with the groups' practices, earlier cases had showed reluctance on the part of the Tanzanian judiciary to intervene in this sort of inter-communal disputes.[97] Somewhat echoing the same non-interventionist line, a few years later the Supreme Court of Zimbabwe upheld a customary rule that gave preference to males in inheritance.[98] A similar outcome had been claimed by the applicant in *Lau Wong Fat v. Attorney General* before Hong Kong courts.[99] As an indigenous inhabitant of the New Territories, he sought to prevent the government of Hong Kong adopting legislation that would allow women, in the absence of a will, to have the same rights to inherit rural land in the New Territories as men, thereby conforming to the general regimes applicable in the rest of Hong Kong. Diametrically opposed to the discourse in *Ephrahim*, the Zimbabwean

[94] *Ibid.* (quoting from earlier US jurisprudence).
[95] *Ibid.*, p. 1684.
[96] (1992) 87 ILR 106.
[97] *Ibid.*, pp. 110–116.
[98] *Magaya v. Magaya*, [1999] 3 LRC 35.
[99] [1997] HKCA 199.

court dismissed the legal effect of international human rights instruments to which Zimbabwe was a party, thereby shielding tribal customary laws from gender equality arguments (already precluded by the Constitution). In contrast, the Court of Appeal of Hong Kong did use the Hong Kong Bill of Rights Ordinance giving effect to the ICCPR to consider the applicant's claim that the new legislation on land inheritance was incompatible with the protection of minority groups. The court held that the argument was 'wholly untenable' because that legislation was meant to remove one instance of discrimination against women, fully in line with international standards.

The universalising logic of human rights broadly reflected in *Ephrahim* substantially differs from the privatising view of non-interference underlying the above-mentioned jurisprudence at least in two fundamental respects. First, it importantly locates the inter-minority conflict within the frame of domestic and international human rights law as opposed to one of simply political or constitutional expediency. Second, it focuses on individuals within the group as bearers of general human rights entitlements, regardless of their minority status. On the other hand, these two lines, where strictly applied, come to crystallise a binary choice between some kind of unbounded group autonomy and classical or minimalist conceptions of equality. In terms of narratives, they suggest either exclusionary ethnos or classical demos.

Moving beyond the interventionist/non-interventionist dilemma, judicial discourse can in fact mediate the claims in ways that account for the complexities arising from the conflict between minority women and the group as a whole. The case of *Sandra Lovelace v. Canada*,[100] seems to illustrate this. As is widely known, the complainant was a Maliseet Indian. Under the Indian Act, she had lost her status as an Indian as a result of her marrying a non-Indian. After divorcing her husband, she wanted to go back to the Tobique reserve, the place where she was born and brought up. She had been denied the right to reside on a reserve and to benefit from federal services that were being made available only to persons with Indian status. In sum, the case was very similar to *Canada AG*, but this time the Indian Act was being challenged before the HRC, on the basis of a number of ICCPR provisions, most notably the anti-discrimination clauses in Articles 2 (1), 3 and 26, as well as minority rights in Article 27. The HRC could have arguably chosen either of the approaches illustrated above. Indeed, it could have construed the case very much in line with *Canada AG* and *Martinez* and justified *mutatis mutandis* a non-interventionist line, on account of group autonomy (ex Article 27) or non-discrimination (namely, on the grounds that minority related sex-based

[100] Comm. No. 24/1977, Views of 30 July 1981, (1981) Annual Report 166; (1983) Annual Report 248.

distinctions did not amount to discrimination). Conversely, the HRC could have upheld Lovelace's claim on strict equality grounds, reading the case solely from the general angle of non-discrimination against individuals.

The decision in fact embraced neither of these lines. For one thing, the HRC appeared to accept the notion, as further explained in later case law, that restrictions on individual rights could be justified by the legitimate aim of minority group survival and well-being pursued through proportional means. The level of protection for the group's interests and values as articulated in the Indian Act was made a function of compliance with the ICCPR by Canada:

> Restrictions on the right to residence, by way of national legislation, cannot be ruled out under article 27 of the Covenant. This also follows from the restrictions to article 12(1) of the Covenant set out in article 12(3). The Committee recognises the need to define the category of persons entitled to live on a reserve, for such purposes as those explained by the Government regarding protection of its resources and preservation of the identity of its people. However, the obligations which the Government has since undertaken under the Covenant must also be taken into account.[101]

On the other hand, the HRC considered that the essence of the complaint was the denial of Lovelace's Article 27 rights in the face of her cultural ties with the group and her wish to return to the reserve:

> Persons who are born and brought up on a reserve, who have kept ties with their community and wish to maintain these ties must normally be considered as belonging to that minority within the meaning of the Covenant. Since Sandra Lovelace is ethnically a Maliseet Indian and has only been absent from her home reserve for a few years during the existence of her marriage, she is, in the opinion of the Committee, entitled to be regarded as 'belonging' to this minority and to claim the benefits of article 27 of the Covenant
>
> ...
>
> The case of Sandra Lovelace should be considered in the light of the fact that her marriage to a non-Indian has broken up. It is natural that in such a situation she wishes to return to the environment in which she was born, particularly as after the dissolution of her marriage her main cultural attachment again was to the Maliseet band.[102]

More than that, Lovelace's claim was meant to challenge the assumption of the Canadian government (and the majority of indigenous organisations which supported it), that Maliseet society was patrilineal. Lovelace argued that the nature of the group was in fact matrilineal, and that the Indian Act had endorsed a distorted, colonial reading of Indian traditions. In other words, Lovelace's argument was part of a wider effort to restore pre-colonial legacies

101 *Ibid.*, para. 15

102 *Ibid.*, paras. 14, 17.

by emphasising the role of women within that particular context. By finding a clash of identity claims between the Indian Act and the ICCPR (via Article 27), the HRC implicitly upheld this debate internal to the community. They concluded that the denial to Sandra Lovelace to live on the Tobique reserve was neither reasonable nor necessary in order to preserve the identity of the tribe and constituted an unjustifiable impairment of her Article 27 rights, read in the light of other provisions, including the equality guarantees between men and women in Articles 2 (1), 3 and 26.

The theme of gender equality has been confirmed in subsequent HRC practice, and can therefore be regarded as an established feature of its own approach to the protection of minority groups under the ICCPR. At the same time, the equality component of the *Lovelace* rationale was clearly intended to back up a specific discourse about minority identity and how to address an inter-minority dispute revolving around cultural claims. Unlike the non-interventionist and sex-discrimination strategies, the HRC's view mediated the claims by upholding a nuanced 'insider' perspective on group identity, according to which individual minority rights must be recognised on a non-discriminatory basis. This identity-equality construct ultimately interposed itself between the privatising view of non-interference and the identity *un*related understanding of sex-discrimination in relation to minority women. Article 27 was not used to dilute the impact of the general provisions against discrimination; it set out a benchmark against which minority laws could be measured, for the benefit of community members and the community as a whole. The recognition that such laws may have within themselves the possibility of more egalitarian outcomes while respecting all members' right to identity, was a major part of that perspective.

An example of a similar mediating line is offered by the decision of the Supreme Court of India in the case of *Mohammed Ahmed Khan v. Shah Bano Begum.*[103] Shah Bano, Mohammed Khan's former wife, claimed maintenance payment against him on the basis of the general law (Section 125 of the Code of Criminal Procedure), which applied to everybody regardless of religion. Her former husband argued that the general law was irrelevant, since the responsibility of the husband to maintain a divorced wife was determined by the Muslim Personal Law and was limited to a three-month period subsequent to divorce (*iddat).* As explained by the All Indian Muslim Personal Law Board on behalf of the petitioner, the personal law arrangements included the payment of dower and support from the extended family. In essence, the dispute turned on the scope and boundaries of a minority personal law vis-à-vis a general law. Like the HRC in *Lovelace*, and perhaps even more clearly than

[103] A.I.R. 1985 945, Judgment of 23 April 1985.

in that case, the Supreme Court could have joined the earlier *Martinez* non-interventionist line by acknowledging complete autonomy of the personal law in the matter. Alternatively, it could have upheld Shah Bano's claim to maintenance based on the general law, and indeed the need to secure legal uniformity in this area in line with the Constitution. This second line would have framed the equality point made by Shah Bano in the context of a wider discourse about the applicable legal regulation, entirely divorced from the experience of the parties as members of a minority group.

Here again, like the HRC in *Lovelace*, the Supreme Court did not embrace either of these lines. Instead, its discourse took a mediating twist in that it sought to establish that, while the general obligation to prevent vagrancy and destitution prevailed over personal laws in the event of conflict, Shari'ah law should be read in a way as to make it compatible with Section 125 of the Code of Criminal Procedure. Indeed, based on several sources and more evolutionary understandings of Shari'ah law, the Supreme Court concluded that the duty on the husband to provide maintenance to his divorced wife was not limited to the period of *iddat*, nor could such a short time period be compensated by the payment of dower and support from the extended family network. The duty to make provision for a divorced wife who could not maintain herself, far from conflicting with the Muslim Personal Law, derived directly from the Holy Quran.

Although the 1986 Muslim Women Protection of Rights Divorce Act, following pressure from conservative voices within the Muslim community, attempted to reverse the Supreme Court judgment, it was again this court which returned to the issue of maintenance in 2001 in relation to a challenge of constitutionality brought against the 1986 Act in *Danial Latifi and Anr v. Union of India*.[104] Conflicting interpretations of this Act had emerged in several high courts as to whether or not the husband's duty to maintain his divorced wife was limited to the period of *iddat*. The All Indian Muslim Personal Law Board intervened in the case and argued again for a restrictive interpretation of the Act as a way of protecting the personal law regime and the identity of the Muslim community. The Supreme Court concluded that the duty to pay maintenance was limited to the period of *iddat*, but that the Act could not be presumed to be contrary to the anti-discrimination clauses contained in the Constitution, since Section 125 of the Code of Criminal Procedure (i.e. the general law brought up in Shah Bano) applied equally to all non-Muslim women belonging to different religious communities. In short, the Supreme

[104] A.I.R. 2001 S.C. 3958, Judgment of 28 September 2001.

Court upheld the constitutionality of the 1986 Act and read it in conjunction with the pre-existing statutory law and the Constitution.[105]

In both *Mohammed Ahmed Khan* and *Danial Latifi*, judicial discourse mediated the inter-minority conflict raised by the tension between ethno-cultural identity and gender equality. They did so by valuing the equality dimension as part of a reformed reading of Islam and the Muslim personal laws. Unlike the privatising logic of non-interference, such discourse did not leave the minority regime unchecked; it measured it against human rights principles. Unlike a strictly construed anti-discrimination approach, it viewed women's rights both on their own terms and as being internal to a distinctive, dynamic process of re-assessment and re-definition of the community's identity.[106] In this respect, it might be argued that *Ephrahim* itself does reflect a mediating element, despite its appeal to classical (apparently culture-blind) standards prohibiting sex discrimination. It ultimately *adjusted* the rules of inheritance based on tribal customary law to recognise to both males and females equal rights to inherit and sell clan land. Under Haya law, any other clan members could redeem the sale made without the consent of the clan by payment of the purchase price to the external purchaser. 'That' – the High Court held – 'now applies to both males and females'.[107] Equally implying the need for local adjustments, the Court of Appeal of Hong Kong in *Lau Wong Fat* noted that the challenged legislation did not preclude an indigenous inhabitant of the New Territories from making a will in favour of male descendants in line with the indigenous custom in that part of Hong Kong, but rather dealt with expanding the scope of the land inheritance regime to the whole of Hong Kong.

The above examples also suggest that the judicial recognition of the complexities posed by inter-communal disputes is inevitably linked to the context within which such recognition occurs. *Lovelace* was decided against the peculiar backdrop of indigenous autonomy, while the Indian, Tanzanian and Zimbabwean jurisprudence reflected the specific experience of legal pluralism defined by personal laws and the resulting inter-communal dynamics. For example, both the *Mohammed Ahmed Khan* and *Danial Latifi* decisions were

---

[105] A similar line seems to have been taken in relation to aspects of community customary law applicable to the Scheduled Tribes of India. In *Madhu Kishwar and ors v. State of Bihar and ors* (1991 (2) SCALE 148 [794]), the Supreme Court considered state legislation that, in the name of long-established customary law, prevented women from named tribes from acquiring or transferring property. The Court did not challenge that body of law as such, but did hold that Scheduled Tribes were entitled to benefit from the guarantees of the Constitution.

[106] For a similar approach by Pakistani higher courts, see S. Mullaly, *Gender, Culture and Human Rights: Reclaiming Universalism* (Oxford/Portland Oregon, 2006), pp. 181–188.

[107] *Supra* note 96, p. 119.

affected by potential restrictions on the claims of the Muslim minority group that could be promoted by the dominant Hindu community in the name of universal human rights. The move away from an 'either/or' approach to the inter-minority controversy reflected concerns for a specific communal set up. Still, they highlight a model of discourse that could be used in other settings as well, both international and domestic. It may be interesting to note that the Constitutional Court of South Africa has recently appealed to the notion of 'living indigenous law' to argue for a different understanding of communal customary law, particularly in respect of differential treatment between men and women in the area of succession.[108] On the one hand, the Court values indigenous law as part of the Constitution's deeper commitment to cultural diversity; at the same time, it promotes internally generated changes to this body of law as community members change their patters of life by replacing traditional extended families with nuclear families. Reminiscent of the Supreme Court of India's attempt to provide internal yet new meanings of Shari'ah law in *Mohammed Ahmed Khan*, the South African Constitutional Court proposes dynamic readings of indigenous law that can be reconciled, not only with the Constitution and the international law that is part of the South African legal order, but also with the changing needs and circumstances of the community itself:

> The exclusion of women from heirship and consequently from being able to inherit property was in keeping with a system dominated by a deeply embedded patriarchy which reserved for women a position of subservience and subordination and in which they were regarded as perpetual minors under the tutelage of the fathers, husbands, or the head of the extended family.[109]

As the inferences from *Refah Partisi* under the ECHR show, the boundaries between minority regimes and the sphere of general (or secular) law – that is, the scope of multicultural arrangements within a state – may have to be constantly negotiated and re-considered. The mediating line of judicial discourse has applied human rights law in ways that have proved conducive to unearthing diversity within minority communities while still preserving the distinctiveness of minority identity.

---

[108] *Nonkululeko Letta Bhe, the Women's Legal Centre Trust et al. vs Magistrate Khayelitsha, the President of the Republic of South Africa, the Minister for Justice and Constitutional Development et al.*, CCT 49/03; *Charlotte Shibi vs Mantabeni Freddy Sithole, the Minister for Justice and Constitutional Development et al.*, CCT 69/03; *South African Human Rights Commission and Women's Legal Centre Trust vs the President of the Republic of South Africa, the Minister for Justice and Constitutional Development et al.*, CCT 50/03, Constitutional Court of South Africa, Judgment of 15 October 2004.

[109] *Ibid.*, para. 78.

Dissenters and group representation

Another cause of inter-group friction has been exposed by applications in which claimants rejected being represented by certain community leaders in dealing with public authorities or have claimed protection as a distinctive element of the community in question because of diverging practices of the respective organisational bodies.

For example, in *Marshall et al. v. Canada*[110] the authors emphasised that the indigenous group of which they were representatives had not conferred any right to represent their members on the Assembly of First Nations (AFN), one of the four major indigenous associations invited by the Canadian government to attend constitutional conferences which were designed to identify and clarify the rights afforded to indigenous communities under the Constitutional Act of 1982. In *Apirana Mahuika*, the applicants challenged a comprehensive settlement between the government of New Zealand and the Maori people as a whole as overriding their claims and those of the majority of their particular Maori tribes. In *Cha'are Shalom ve Tsedek*, filed with the EurCrtHR, the dispute revolved around allowing for religious pluralism within the Jewish community in France in the face of diverging practices of religious rites by a sector of such a community compared to those of mainstream Jewish associations. These cases do not reflect a radical rift between the group and the complaining members such that the basic identity aspirations of the group themselves are called into question, so much as illustrate how the issue of representation can indirectly manifest itself as a matter of fine-tuning or adjustment between mainstream group leadership and certain sectors of the group over individual matters, namely over the extent of rights believed to be needed to meet the demands of the group and/or some of its members. They also suggest that this type of conflict is only one among many others which are conceivable along the broad spectrum of inter-communal disputes, in which even serious questions of elite accountability – involving suspected self-appointed ethnic entrepreneurs – must be framed in terms of adequate internal decision-making and the recognition of the group's representatives.

In *Marshall* and *Cha'are Shalom ve Tsedek* the HRC and EurCrtHR, respectively, essentially assumed the external representative role of the mainstream associations concerned.[111] While the EurCrtHR's majority in *Cha'are Shalom ve Tsedek* characterised the contested interference as of 'limited effect' and

[110] Comm. No. 205/1986, Views of 4 November 1991, [1992] Annual Report, 201.

[111] As noted in Chapter 1, the EurCrtHR has been more cautious in cases where associations have argued for the very existence of a minority group, which they claimed to embody: see also *infra*, Chapter 6. For examples of internal debates, see J. Ringelheim, *Diversité Culturelle et Droits de l'Homme*, *supra* note 75, pp. 376–377.

the difference of treatment as 'limited in scope',[112] the joint dissent valued the inter-communal dispute by arguing that it is not for the EurCrtHR 'to substitute its assessment of the scope or seriousness of an interference for that of the persons or groups concerned', and concluded that the approval of certain ritual slaughters that mainstream Jewish associations had received and the applicant association had not, lacked a reasonable and objective justification, thereby failing to secure true religious pluralism. In fact, their line on internal pluralism offered a mediating strategy between the state's and group's concerns. For one thing, they recognised the role of mainstream organisations in their dealings with the state:

> We certainly do not disregard the interest the authorities may have in dealing with the most representative organisations of a specific community. The fact that the State wishes to avoid dealing with an excessive number of negotiating partners so as not to dissipate its efforts and in order to reach concrete results more easily, whether in its relations with trade unions, political parties or religious denominations, is not illegitimate in itself, or disproportionate....[113]

However, they argued that France had deprived the minority within the Jewish community of the possibility to act as a religious body, and called for internal pluralism as a way of securing representation of that minority in terms of religious practices. The issue is ultimately tied up with the wider question of guaranteeing effective participation of minority groups, both externally *and* internally. Indeed, effective participation may be said to entail both the right of minority members to have a real say vis-à-vis public authorities in the processes affecting their distinctive identity, and the right to be involved in the mechanisms of decision-making and representation *within* the group itself.[114] In this sense, *Marshall* appeared to expose both such dimensions, though the HRC found no violation of Article 25 (a) ICCPR in Canada's failure to invite the authors to attend the constitutional conferences in question. The *Länsman*

---

[112] Application No. 27417/95, Judgment of 27 June 2000, paras. 84, 87.

[113] *Ibid.*, Dissenting Opinion of Judges Bratza, Fischbach, Thomassen, Tsatsa-Nikolovsak, Pantion, Leints and Traja, Section 2.

[114] In a report delivered by the Dutch Advisory Committee on Human Rights and Foreign Affairs regarding indigenous groups, the minimum requirement for testing representation is suggested to the effect that 'the position of a representative should not be controversial, or should not be contested by the people in question. In cases of reasonable doubt, it should also be possible to require a representative to make plausible his claim to represent an indigenous people': Advies Commissie Mensenrechten, *Indigenous Peoples*, Report No. 6, 1993, pp. 22–23. This criterion has been mainly submitted in relation to the external recognition of indigenous community leaders before international forums, but it could also provide a more general base line from which to assess the level of participation and inclusiveness in decision-making within the community, and thus the claims which ensue.

test under Article 27 would arguably question the *Marshall* approach in that it emphasises the importance of meaningful involvement of, and within the group, while still acknowledging (like in *Cha'are Shalom ve Tsedek*) the views of the minority group's main organisations. It is in this context that the criterion of effective participation mediates the inter-minority divergences on a procedural level.

In *George Howard v. Canada*,[115] the author, a member of the Hiawatha First Nation, argued that the so-called Williams Treaties, which had been concluded in 1923 between the Crown and the Mississauga First Nations (to which the author's community belonged), were the only treaties that had extinguished aboriginal hunting and fishing rights, and that in any event those treaties had not been properly negotiated with the Mississauga.[116] This seemed to suggest either disagreement with the group's ancestors who signed the William Treaties or lack of effective involvement of the negotiators in the process leading up to the signing of such treaties. The HRC did not engage with complex issues of fact and evidence, and addressed the case only in relation to later Ontario fishing legislation as applied to the author. On the other hand, it did not comment on the determination of Canadian courts to the effect that the William Treaties had extinguished the right of the Nation to which the author belonged to fish outside their reserves or their adjacent waters.

Whereas *George Howard* incidentally raised questions of representation and participation going back to the early decades of the 20th century, more contemporary processes bring to the fore the mediating impact of the participation test within the wider community. As noted, *Apirana Mahuika* turned on the effects on the 'dissenting' Maoris of a far-reaching agreement between New Zealand and the Maoris as a whole that re-arranged the fishing quota management system adopted in the 1980s. As in the *Länsman* cases, the test of consultation and sustainability was applied when considering the contested measures. But this time, the HRC valued the test in terms of both the relationship between the government and the group and the decision-making process or mechanisms of representation internal to the group itself. Indeed, it regarded the agreement compatible with Article 27, not simply because it was meant to protect an essential element of a minority group's identity, but because the process of consultation had involved virtually all Maori communities and national organisations. For one thing, it characterised the divisions amongst Maori as a 'matter of concern'; at the same time, it noted that New Zealand had nevertheless engaged in a process of 'broad consultation' with

---

[115] Comm. No. 879/1999, Views of 26 July 2005, CCPR/C/84/D/879/1999.

[116] *Ibid.*, paras. 3.2, 9.7, 11.3.

the Maori people before proceeding to legislate on the settlement in order to secure 'broad Maori support'.[117] In short, the HRC stressed the importance of consultations involving all the main actors, or at least of securing sufficiently adequate representation of the views of the group's associations. By so doing, it appeared to understand the participation parameter as an element that can mediate internal differences by providing a framework for wide and open discussions within the group, not only between the group and the state.

This is evident in the case of *Mary and Carrie Dann*. As noted earlier, the IACommHR, based on international human rights standards, found that any determination of indigenous title to land must be based on a process of 'fully informed and mutual consent on the part of the indigenous community as a whole'. Interestingly, this state duty was not limited to providing opportunities for indigenous representatives to engage in consultations with the public authorities, it primarily implied an obligation to ensure that the decision-making and/or mechanisms of representation internal to the group were such as to guarantee an effective level of participation and inclusiveness amongst the various sectors of the community:

> In the case of the Danns, however, the record indicates that the land claim issue was pursued by one band of the Western Shoshone people which no apparent mandate from the other Western Shoshone bands or members. There is also no evidence on the record that appropriate consultations were held within the Western Shoshone at the time that certain significant determinations were made. This includes in particular the [Indian Claims Commission's] finding that the entirety of the Western Shoshone interest in their ancestral lands, which interests affect the Danns, was extinguished at some point in the past
>
> ...
>
> In the Commission's opinion and in the context of the present case, this was not sufficient in order for the State to fulfil its *particular obligation* to ensure that the status of the Western Shoshone traditional lands was determined through a process of informed and mutual consent *on the part of the Western Shoshone people as a whole.*[118]

The lack of representation before a quasi-judicial body such as the Indian Claims Commission also raises, indirectly, the question of group representation in relation to complaints proceedings – an issue addressed by the HRC

117 Comm. No. 547/1993, U.N. Doc. CCPR/C/70/D/547/1993 (2000), paras. 9.6, 9.8.

118 Report No. 75/02, Case 11.1140, December 27, 2002, paras. 140, 141 [author's emphasis]. This obligation can arguably be seen as involving both a measure of direct engagement by the state with all the group's components, and a somewhat 'horizontal' duty to facilitate or promote an open dialogue within the group, while still refraining from substituting for the latter's traditions and decision-making processes (on this point, see also *The Saramaka People v. Suriname, Interpretation of the Judgment on Preliminary Objections, Merits, Reparations, and Costs*, Judgment of 12 August 2008, Series C No. 185, para. 26).

in its case law. In *George Howard*, the HRC declared inadmissible the claim made by the author on behalf of his Fist Nation as he had not provided any authorisation from the other members of the group nor had he offered any arguments to justify such claim even without an explicit mandate from the group.[119] This line echoes earlier HRC jurisprudence on self-determination claims, although it has long been clarified that no such claims may be brought under the First Optional Protocol, regardless of the existence of a genuine collective representation of the complaint. On the other hand, in *Saramaka* the IACrtHR presented a more fundamental way of addressing controversies over representation, aside from prior authorisations which are not required under the ACHR.[120] Suriname had objected to considering the Association of Saramaka Authorities as well as the twelve Saramaka captains who had petitioned the IACommHR as the true representatives of the community. While the controversy was framed in terms of competing views of the state and those Saramakas who were involved in the proceedings rather than an inter-communal dispute, the IACrtHR construed recognition of juridical personality for the benefit of the community as a whole as an important way of transcending external or internal frictions that affected the actual capacity of the Saramakas to enjoy certain rights in a communal manner and to defend them in court. Here the parameter of (internal and external) participation and respect for the group's traditions and decision-making processes supports a reading of Saramaka juridical personality and judicial protection in Articles 3 and 25 ACHR, respectively, as a special and mediating measure that is intended to overcome divisions while securing effective rights protection.[121]

In the event of inter-communal disputes, judicial discourse can also mediate on a more substantive level. In other words, whereas the above examples turn on the 'preliminary' procedural question of whether effective participation has occurred, both with the state and within the group, or even whether conditions have been created for judicial representation of the group as a result of such participation, in other cases mediation, and thus accommodation, is sought in terms of diversifying the substance of rights protection. In *Apirana Mahuika*, the HRC importantly concluded that the settlement reached between the government of New Zealand and the Maori people regarding Maori fishing rights as a fundamental component of their economic and cultural activities was compatible with Article 27, but it also held that the parallel rights of other members of the minority group should be protected as well, pointing

[119] Comm. No. 879/1999, Views of 26 July 2005, CCPR/C/84/D/879/1999, para. 8.3.
[120] See *infra*, Chapter 5.
[121] Judgment of 28 November 2007, Series C No. 172, paras. 169–172.

to the need for a sustainable, though diversified, way of securing protection of Maori identity:

> The Committee has noted the authors' claims that they and the majority of members of their tribes did not agree with the Settlement and that they claim that their rights as members of the Maori minority have been overridden. In such circumstances, where the right of individuals to enjoy their own culture is in conflict with exercise of parallel rights by other members of the minority group, or of the minority as a whole, the Committee may consider whether the limitation in issue is in the interests of all members of the minority and whether there is reasonable and objective justification for its application to the individuals who claim to be adversely affected.
>
> ...
>
> The Committee emphasises that the State party continues to be bound by article 27 which requires that the cultural and religious significance of fishing for Maori must deserve due attention in the implementation of the... Act.... the Committee emphasises that in order to comply with Article 27, measures affecting the economic activities of Maori must be carried out in a way that the authors continue to enjoy their culture, and profess and practice their religion in community with other members of their group. The State party is under a duty to bear this in mind in the further implementation of the... Act.[122]

In essence, the impact of Article 27 on the inter-minority dispute was *not* construed in terms of a choice between the group's pro-settlement tribes and the authors' dissenting voices. Rather, it entailed protection for both of them, though the ramifications of such protection *varied* depending on the beneficiary within the group. A similar line was implied by the dissent's argument in *Cha'are Shalom ve Tsedek*, that internal religious pluralism should be guaranteed within the Jewish community in France. They argued that the exclusive right to authorise ritual slaughters conferred by France on mainstream Jewish associations did not secure equality of treatment between them and the applicant association. Based on non-discrimination grounds, this approach in effect offered a reading that was not limited to ensuring a measure of representation for the dissenting minority in the public sphere; it reached out to the substance, and thus modalities, of religious freedoms enjoyed by the community as a whole.

[122] Comm. No. 547/1993, U.N. Doc. CCPR/C/70/D/547/1993 (2000), paras. 9.6, 9.9.

Chapter 5

Access to justice

The procedural component of judicial discourse discussed in Chapter 4 is defined by the notion that minority related provisions do not necessarily entail clear cut substantive outcomes, but may well (and in fact do) generate duties on states to secure an effective process in which minority voices are represented and minority claims are fully taken into account, and/or to monitor the compatibility of any resulting regime with the human rights of others. In short, the sort of 'proceduralism' involved in that discourse is most directly linked with the way in which relevant provisions are interpreted and applied to core substantive issues.

The following examines a different type of procedural approach – this time in a more conventional, judicial sense. This approach can take at least four distinct forms: internationally guaranteed access to internal dispute settlement mechanisms; expansion of international jurisdiction *ratione personae* and *ratione temporis*, and greater impact of minority issues on questions of evidence and burden of proof. Central to this assessment is the instrumental impact of rights on those issues as well as the way that wider community interests become implicated.[1]

---

[1] Like the previous chapters, the present one does not claim to be exhaustive in the analysis of the various aspects involved. In particular, it does not discuss the role of interim measures in relation to minority groups; international case law is evolving and probably still unsuited to a comparative discussion. Suffice it to say that interim measures are being increasingly requested or ordered to prevent irreversible damage to indigenous groups. For HRC practice, see e.g. *Bernard Ominayak, Chief of the Lubicon Lake Band v. Canada*, Comm. No. 167/1984, Views of 26 March 1990, (1990) II Annual Report 1; as for the Inter-American system, see e.g. *Kelyenmagategma Indigenous Community of the Enxet People v. Paraguay*, IACommHR Annual Report 2004; *Kankuamo Indigenous Peoples v. Colombia (Provisional measures)*, Order of 5 July 2004, IACrtHR Series E (2004); *Sarayaku Indigenous communities v. Ecuador (Provisional measures)*, Order of July 6, 2004, *ibid*. In the latter context, the notion of 'irreparable harm' is being re-interpreted to include not only the danger of death or physical abuse of individuals but also the deprivation of land and natural resources as they

Right to judicial protection

Article 6 (1) ECHR deals with the right to a fair and public hearing before an independent and impartial tribunal 'in the determination of... civil rights and obligations'. As clarified by the EurCrtHR, the Article 6 (1) right is not just a defendant's right, it is a plaintiff's right as well, including the right to effective enforcement of judgments. Also, the procedure about which the applicant is complaining must be decisive for the determination of the 'civil right' in question.

In *Canea Catholic Church v. Greece*,[2] the applicant church had been prevented from protecting its properties as a result of the refusal by a Greek civil court to recognise that the church had legal personality. The EurCrtHR held that such refusal was not justified and violated the very substance of the right to access to court under Article 6, taken alone or with Article 14 (based on comparisons with the treatment afforded to the Greek Orthodox Church and the Jewish community). The case indirectly signals the relevance of Article 6 to minority groups, in the sense of providing at least a procedural context within which minority issues in general, or even minority rights in particular, can be determined.

The EurCrtHR has also applied this provision to complaints of individuals who claim an interest in matters involving a relationship between the state and others. Interestingly, in the case of *Muonio Saami Village v. Sweden*,[3] the applicant Sami village complained about a decision regarding the granting of reindeer herding permits in the village for the year 1992, which accorded three of the total nine permits to people who were *not* members of the village and obliged the permit holders to jointly herd 1,600 reindeer belonging to others. The applicant alleged that it had been a victim of a violation of Article 6 ECHR in that there was no determination of the village's rights in respect of reindeer herding by an independent tribunal. The government maintained that reindeer herding constituted a right recognised under the 1971 Reindeer Herding Act which, subject to certain conditions, is afforded to members of a Sami village, and that this right were to be considered a 'civil right' within the meaning of Article 6 (1) ECHR. Since the government's decision on 19

---

affect whole communities. The procedural impact of interim measures on the representation of minority interests is likely to benefit from the current tendency to confer legally binding force on such measures: see e.g. *Dante Piandiang and Ors v. The Philippines*, Comm. No. 869/1999, HRC Views of 19 October 2000; *Mamatkulov and Askarov v. Turkey*, EurCrtHR, Applications Nos. 46827/99 and 46951/99, Judgment of 4 February 2005; *La Grand* (Germany v. United States), ICJ Reports 2001, p. 466.

[2] Judgment of 16 December 1997, Reports 1997–VIII.

[3] Application No. 28222/95, Judgment of 9 January 2001.

May 1993 upholding the prior administrative ruling on the 1992 permits was not open to a review on the merits by a court of law or any other 'tribunal' for the purposes of Article 6 (1), the government importantly admitted that there had been a violation of this provision. The application, already declared admissible by the EurCrtHR, was later on struck out because of a friendly settlement reached between the Swedish government and the applicant.

In effect, Article 6 (1)-type clauses may be read as a catalyst for the domestic enforcement of certain minority provisions even in the context of inter-communal matters. Along similar lines, the authors in *Apirana Mahuika* before the HRC, while arguing that the settlement between the government of New Zealand and the Maori people as a whole had infringed their own Article 27 rights, further claimed that such settlement – which they, as representatives of individual Maori tribes, opposed – prejudiced their own pending and future fishing minority claims in court, in violation of Article 14 (1) ICCPR.[4] However, the HRC dismissed this claim on the merits. In *Mary and Carrie Dann*, substantive and procedural claims are, again, strictly interrelated. The minority claim to property made by the Danns did not detract from a separate claim to a fair trial that can decide on their specific property interests. In the IACommHR's words:

> Based upon the record before it, the Commission finds that the determination as to whether and to what extent Western Shoshone title may have been extinguished was not based upon a judicial evaluation of pertinent evidence, but rather was based upon apparently arbitrary stipulations as between the US government and the Temoak Band regarding the extent and timing of the loss of indigenous title to the entirety of the Western Shoshone ancestral lands
>
> ...
>
> This effectively left the issue of title to Western Shoshone lands without definitive substantive adjudication by the US courts
>
> ...
>
> [T]he courts ultimately did not take measures to address the substance of these objections [i.e. that the ICC had not taken the interests of the Western Shoshone people as a whole into account, nor had it sought judicial review to support extinguishment of title] but rather dismissed them based upon the expediency of the ICC processes.[5]

The IACommHR ultimately relied on the right to a fair trial in Article XVIII ADRDM as a way of protecting (internationally) access to judicial review of minority claims (domestically):

---

4 Comm. No. 547/1993, Views of 27 October 2000, UN Doc. CCPR/C/70/D/541/1993, paras. 6.4, 6.5.

5 Report No. 75/02, Case 11.1140, December 27, 2002, paras. 137, 141.

> This requires in particular that the Danns be afforded resort to the courts for the protection of their property rights, in conditions of equality and in a manner that considers both the collective and individual nature of the property rights that the Danns may claim in the Western Shoshone ancestral lands.[6]

Similarly, in *Mayagna*, the property claims of the community were clearly linked to the deficiencies reflected in domestic judicial proceedings relating to land titling and the provision of effective remedies. Article 25 ACHR requires states to provide effective and rapid judicial procedures for determination of claims and provision of remedies in the event of violations. The IACrtHR found a breach of the right to judicial protection under the ACHR in that Nicaragua had not adopted adequate domestic legal measures to allow delimitation, demarcation, and titling of indigenous community lands, nor had it considered the amparo remedy filed by members of the Awas Tingni Community within a reasonable time.[7] Like in *Mayagna, Moiwana* showed a connection between the identity claim (defined by property rights) and the issue of internal judicial protection, though in this case the authorities' failure to investigate concerned the displacement of the community caused by an attack on their physical integrity.[8] Generally speaking, the IACrtHR has insisted on the notion that effective due process guarantees are essential to an appropriate articulation of indigenous claims and effective protection of their rights.[9]

In sum, access to court (and remedies) under either the ECHR or other (universal or non-European) human rights instruments provide a space for judicial discourse to look at minority issues procedurally, that is to say, by way of securing consideration of minority claims within a judicial setting. As noted, in *Muonio* Sweden plainly recognised the right in question as a 'civil right' in the sense of Article 6 (1) ECHR. Likewise, in *Mayagna*, there was little doubt that Nicaragua had recognised indigenous property rights in the Constitution and national legislation. In some cases, though, a prior question is precisely whether the complaint involves the determination of an actual 'right'.[10] In *Apirana Mahuika*, the authors argued that Maori fishing rights

---

6 *Ibid.*, para. 171.

7 Judgment of 31 August 2001, Series C No. 79, para. 137.

8 Judgment of 15 June 2005, Series C No. 124, para. 163; 'The facts demonstrate' – the IACrtHR noted – 'that they have been deprived of th[e] right [to property] to the present day as a result of the events of November 1986 and the State's subsequent failure to investigate those occurrences adequately', *ibid.*, para. 134.

9 *The Saramaka People v. Suriname*, Judgment of 28 November 2007, Series C No. 172, paras. 178, 185.

10 In *Masson & Van Zon v. The Netherlands* ((1995) 22 EHRR 491, para. 44), the EurCrtHR referred to 'a "right" which can be said, at least on arguable grounds, to be recognised under domestic law', implying a close assessment of the relevant national law sources. In a con-

were clearly 'rights...in a suit at law' within the meaning of Article 14 (1) ICCPR, while the HRC held that 'whether or not claims in respect of fishery interests could be considered to fall within the definition of a suit at law', the 1992 Treaty of Waitangi (Fisheries Claims) Settlement Act had extinguished the authors' pre-existing claims to fisheries in legal proceedings.[11] In fact, a major question here was whether access to court had been denied in respect of those claims. New Zealand stressed that Article 14 does not provide for a general right of access to court in the absence of rights and jurisdiction recognised by law. Its main argument was indeed that the discontinuance of the domestic judicial proceedings regarding the authors' claims to fisheries was justified by the fact that the 1992 Act was intended to settle all Maori claims to fisheries. In a similar vein, the US government argued in *Mary and Carrie Dann* that the extinguishment of Western Shoshone land title that had been determined by the Indian Claims Commission in consultation with the Temoak Band had superseded judicial proceedings regarding the Danns' property claims. In *Apirana Mahuika*, the HRC accepted New Zealand's argument about both pending and future claims to fisheries from the authors by noting that '[o]ther aspects of the right to fisheries, though, still give the right to access to court, for instance in respect of the allocation of quota and of the regulations governing customary fishing rights'.[12] In *Mary and Carrie Dann*, the IACommHR held that the features of, and background to the Indian Claims Commission process were such that this process did not legally exhaust judicial claims to property from an underrepresented sector of the Western Shoshone like the Danns. These cases show that an access to court question in general, and in relation to minority issues in particular, may have to be assessed not only against the existence of a right *tout court* but also against the actual justiciability of the specific aspects of an existing right that are to be determined in court.

The substance of the *Muonio* case can be usefully contrasted with the much earlier case of *Kitok v. Sweden* before the HRC:[13] whereas the former turned on the protection of a particular minority right under the Reindeer Herding Act, the latter raised the question whether this very Act, by depriving the author of his status as a Sami, violated the international rights recognised in Article 27 ICCPR. Although the focus in *Muonio* was on domestic minority

curring opinion, Judge de Meyer stated that any right which a citizen 'may feel entitled to assert', whether under national, supranational or international law, falls within the meaning of 'civil right' in Article 6 (1), thus favouring a more liberal and open interpretation (*Rolf Gustafsson v. Sweden*, Reports 1997-IV 1149, Concurring Opinion of Judge de Meyer).

[11] *Supra* note 4, paras. 6.4, 9.11.

[12] *Ibid.*, para. 9.11.

[13] Comm. No. 197/1985, Views of 27 July 1988, (1988) Annual Report 221.

provisions, the access to court issue may well arise from a claim to minority protection under international law, or a claim that is somewhat linked to such protection, as is illustrated by the two-tier structure of the complaint in *Apirana Mahuika* and *Anni Äärelä and Jouni Näkkäläjärvi* v. *Finland* (both establishing a connection between Article 27 claims and due process guarantees in domestic proceedings in Article 14(1) ICCPR),[14] as well as the above-mentioned cases under the Inter-American system. Indeed, *Mayagna*, *Moiwana* and *Mary and Carrie Dann*, they all relate the issue of domestic judicial protection to the substantive claim to indigenous property upheld in principle under Article 21 ACHR and XVIII ADRDM, respectively.

Here again, like in *Canea*- or *Muonio*-like situations, judicial discourse can bridge the gap between principled recognition of rights and their actualisation within domestic legal systems by guaranteeing impartial internal review of the particular claims at hand. In fact, as long as minority issues fall within the scope of the international right to judicial protection, the entitlement to a fair and independent judicial review of course does not entail any evaluation of the merits of the claim under the relevant human rights instrument (be it the ECHR or otherwise). Rather, the procedural fairness protected by access to court clauses guarantees a mechanism within the national legal system to settle minority claims by the people concerned in view of applicable domestic and international standards. On this reading, the above jurisprudence suggests that judicial discourse can use those clauses very much in the same (procedural) way that, for example, Article 14 (3) ILO Convention No. 169 points to domestic procedures. This provision requires the parties to secure adequate procedures to resolve those land claims as might exist, although this treaty is not intended to establish new land claims. In particular, those problematic land issues that are left unresolved by the treaty are referred to fair domestic mechanisms for legal determination. By analogy, international jurisprudence can rely on international provisions on access to justice to 'judicialise' certain minority claims (under domestic or international law) before national courts.

---

[14] In the second case (Comm. no. 779/1997, Views of 24 October 2001, UN Doc. CCPR/C/73/D/779/1997 (1997), the HRC importantly found a breach of Art. 14 (1) ICCPR in that a substantial award of costs had been imposed against the authors in domestic proceedings bringing a claim under Art. 27 ICCPR, without considering the specific circumstances of the group and the effect of this imposition on access to court of other similarly situated claimants. The HRC also found that the principle of equality of arms reflected in Art. 14 (1) had been violated, *ibid*., paras, 7.3–7.4.

Locus standi *and injured party*

A typical requirement for judicial-like models and discourse to be set in motion is that the case be brought up by those (be they individuals, groups of individuals or NGOs) who believe to have been victims of a rights violation under the applicable international human rights instrument. While this is not always a *sine qua non* for petitioning (or spurring judicial discourse itself), it is still an essential element that reflects the scope of human rights jurisdiction *ratione personae*, and the extent to which it relates to issues involving minority groups.

In general, the victim requirement by definition stands in the way of human rights actions being brought up on behalf of the public interest (*actio popularis*), or raised by third parties such as NGOs, without the victim's knowledge and authorisation, or otherwise actions concerning measures which, in the language of Article 230 (4) European Community Treaty, are of no 'direct and individual concern' to applicants. In *Korkmaz v. Commission*,[15] in which human rights organisations complained about Turkey's performance in the Kurdish-populated areas, the ECJ held that assessment by the Commission of whether or not this situation amounted to a lack of an 'essential element' for the European Community to continue granting pre-accession assistance to that country under an European Community regulation, could not produce legally binding effects capable of affecting the applicants' interests by bringing about a significant change in their legal position. In *Kurdistan Workers' Party (PKK) and Kurdistan National Congress (KNK) v. Council*,[16] the ECJ dismissed the claims for annulment of European Community decisions adopted pursuant to certain United Nations Security Council resolutions, because of a failure to establish proper judicial representation of the PKK, and the fact that neither KNK – an umbrella organisation defending Kurdish rights and interests – nor any of its members could be deemed to be individually concerned.

However, judicial discourse can certainly expand the ambit of international supervision with a view to allowing a greater measure of minority group representation. Within the same EC framework, for example, the ECJ has recently construed the notion of direct discrimination under the Race Directive in a way that does not necessarily require an identifiable complainant who claims to be a victim, as long as other actors (*in casu*, an NGO) have brought up the claim domestically.[17] This broad reading of the directive suggests an assertive

[15] Case T-2/40, Order of 30 March 2006.

[16] Case T-229/02, Order of 15 February 2005.

[17] *Centrum voor gelijkheid van kansen en voor racismebestrijding v. Firma Feryn NV*, Case C-54/07, 10.07.08.

role of the ECJ (and consequently national courts as well) in detecting cases of racial and ethnic discrimination that may well affect particular groups rather than individual victims.

At a deeper level, individual claims, such as those lying at the core of *Lovelace*, ultimately connect to wider notions of group identity and well-being that may manifest themselves in the form of genuinely collective complaints. In *Mikmaq Tribal Society v. Canada*,[18] the question was raised as to whether an individual was entitled to submit a complaint of a breach of the right to self-determination in Article 1 ICCPR on behalf of his group. The HRC concluded that the author had not proved that he had been authorised to represent the group to that effect. The lack of a representative mandate from the group was also found in *George Howard*, though the claim was that Article 27, not Article 1, had been violated. The procedural point here is that, while later self-determination claims have been declared inadmissible under the First Optional Protocol to the ICCPR on grounds which are quite different to the issue of representation, the HRC has recognised Article 27 complaints from groups of minority members who claim to be similarly affected.

The concept of collective communications was first elaborated in *Lubicon Lake Band* and then applied to a stream of cases, including *Diergaardt*, *Jouni Länsman, Eino Länsman and the Muotkatunturi Herdsmen's Committee v. Finland*,[19] and *George Howard*. As explained by the HRC, 'individuals' in the sense of Article 1 First Optional Protocol does not include legal persons, nor may individuals bring a claim on behalf of the group unless they are properly authorised by the latter to do so. In *Jouni Länsman*, the HRC found no indication that 'individual members of the Muotkatunturi Herdsmen's Committee had authorised it to bring a claim on their behalf, or that Jouni and/or Eino Länsman were authorised to act on behalf of the Herdsmen's Committee and its members'.[20] In *George Howard*, it also noted that the author had failed to provide 'any arguments to the effect that he would be in a position to represent before the Committee other persons without their authorisation'.[21] The possibility of collective communications, as defined in *Lubicon Lake Band*, may have been further refined, or made explicit by those cases. Arguably, *Jouni Länsman* seems to suggest that, if duly authorised, a minority association, such as the Muotkatunturi Herdsmen's Committee, might bring a claim on behalf of their members (as alleged victims), despite references in the First Optional Protocol to communications being lodged by 'individuals' (involving

[18] Comm. No. 78/1980, Views of 29 July 1984, UN Doc. A/39/40.
[19] Comm. No. 1023/2001, Views of 17 March 2005, CCPR/C/83/D/1023/2001.
[20] *Ibid.*, para. 6.1.
[21] Comm. No. 879/1999, Views of 26 July 2005, CCPR/C/84/D/879/1999, para. 8.3.

representatives as well). Also, *George Howard* appears to be (more openly) confirming *Lubicon Lake Band* and *Diergaardt* in that individual complainants might be in a position to represent the group of minority members even without a specific authorisation from them, somewhat implying that a mandate to this effect may be inferred from the author's status within the community or other factors. In short, HRC discourse, while retaining the victim requirement, has expanded the personal scope of jurisdiction primarily (though not exclusively) in the context of minority cases.

The CERD is also re-assessing that requirement under Article 14 (1) ICERD, which unlike Article 1 of the First Optional Protocol to the ICCPR, also refers to 'groups of individuals'. In the case of *The Documentation Advisory Centre on Racial Discrimination v. Denmark*,[22] lodged by a domestic NGO which claimed that a job advertisement published by a Danish firm in a Danish newspaper amounted to discrimination against persons of non-Danish origin, the CERD conceded that a group of persons may represent the interests of a minority group as long as the victim parameter has been satisfied:

> The Committee does not exclude the possibility that a group of persons representing, for example, the interests of a racial or ethnic group, may submit an individual communication, provided that it is able to prove that it has been an alleged victim of a violation of the Convention or that one of its members has been a victim, and if it is able at the same time to provide due authorisation to this effect.[23]

In *The Jewish Community of Oslo et al. v. Norway*,[24] it held that a breach of Article 4 (incitement to racial discrimination and racial hatred) and Article 6 had occurred as a result of a commemorative speech openly targeting the local Jewish community, including the authors, which had been delivered by a representative of a neo-Nazi organisation. The complaint had been brought before the CERD by individuals both on their behalf, and as representatives of their own organisations claming a breach of the ICERD in their own right. Interestingly, on the issue of admissibility, the CERD argued that, it was not necessary that each individual within the group be an individual victim for the group to be able to bring a claim. It concluded, contrary to the argument made by the state party, that 'bearing in mind the nature of the organisations' activities and the classes of person they represent, they too satisfied the 'victim' requirement in article 14'.[25] When combining *The Documentation Advisory*

---

[22] Comm. No. 28/2003, Opinion of 3 December 2002, CERD/C/63/D/28/2003.

[23] *Ibid.*, para. 6.4. For an expansive approach to *locus standi* in respect of ethnic/racial discrimination in a similar case under EC law, see *Feryn*, *supra* note 17.

[24] Comm. No. 30/2003, Opinion of 15 August 2005, CERD/C/67/D/30/2003.

[25] *Ibid.*, para. 7.4.

Centre and *The Jewish Community of Oslo*, it would appear that the CERD is deepening its understanding of 'groups of individuals' in order to ensure greater representation of minority interests; arguably, the ramifications may be manifold, and not all necessarily uncontroversial: 1) groups and associations (including NGOs) alleging to be a victim of a violation; 2) groups and associations (including NGOs) acting on behalf of each of its members (as alleged victims); 3) groups and associations (including NGOs) authorised to represent some of its members (as alleged victims); 4) organisations representing some individual victims and, at least indirectly, an entire class of persons. Clearly, the group dimension is being expanded, regardless of the specific contours of this jurisprudence.[26] This is further reinforced by the notion, upheld in *A. Koptova v. Slovakia*,[27] and *The Jewish Community of Oslo*, that complaints may involve not only actual but also *potential* victims as long as they are directly affected by wider measures exposing the group to discrimination.[28]

Of course, effective representation of minority issues does not always require collective complaints *stricto sensu*. For example, *Chapman* and a set of similar cases before the ECHR invited the EurCrtHR to address the specific situation of applicants, though against the backdrop of Roma identity and lifestyle. In this respect, *Chapman* echoes *Lovelace* in the sense that they both illustrate the individualistic profile of *locus standi* in respect of minority claims. Individual claims are not necessarily limited to individual circumstances. In *DH and others*, all applicants were Czech nationals of Roma origin who argued that they had been discriminated against in the enjoyment of their right to education on account of their ethnicity. While making a claim in their own right, the applicants raised the wider issue of whether the system of special schools established by the Czech Republic, overwhelmingly populated by Roma pupils, did indirectly amount to segregation affecting Czech Roma children as a whole. There can be little doubt that recognising judicial standing to greater numbers of minority members and their associations tends to make the claims transcend the situation of specific individuals.

In *Hingitaq 53*, over 400 hundred individuals from the Thule tribe of Greenland submitted their complaint regarding property rights together with a group representing the interests of relocated members of that tribe and their descendents. While this somewhat echoes the structure of HRC 'collective

---

[26] The ramifications of the CERD's position will need further clarification as they point to strict group claims, representation of the alleged victims, or class actions. The first ramification seems to be more difficult to sustain, given the lack of specific group rights under the ICERD.

[27] Comm. No. 13/1998, Opinion of 1 November 2000, CERD/C/57/D/13/1998.

[28] In *The Jewish Community of Oslo* the CERD embraced a line similar to the one upheld in general by the HRC and EurCrtHR; *supra* note 24, para. 7.3.

communications', it also suggests the additional representative dimension that minority institutions (as opposed to individual victims or their duly authorised representatives) can bring in under the ECHR. The EurCrtHR declared the application inadmissible on issues of substance, not for lack of jurisdiction *ratione personae.* Indeed, in cases such as *Metropolitan Church of Bessarabia*, *Canea* and *Muonio*, the EurCrtHR recognised the legal entities involved as applicants under Article 34 ECHR. This was due to the particular position of those entities. In *Muonio*, the EurCrtHR noted that it was the Sami village, not the Samis who comprised it, which enjoyed the right in question under the 1971 Reindeer Herding Act. In *Metropolitan Church of Bessarabia* and *Canea*, minority religious communities gained standing before the EurCrtHR through their religious institutions. The general point is that, the understanding and application of Article 34 ECHR in relation to NGOs and groups of individuals do affect the extent to which minority issues are, or can be discussed in judicial proceedings. In this context, though, the group dimension is not merely an indirect effect arising from judicial standing, but rather the consequence of the victim requirement. In *Johtti Sapmelaccat Ry and Others v. Finland*,[29] the first applicant was a Sami association promoting Sami culture; it brought a claim together with other Sami individuals. Although the case turned on the fishing rights of the Sami people under Finnish law as a distinctive component of Sami identity, the EurCrtHR held that, unlike the village's status in *Muonio*:

> [T]he first applicant association is not responsible for fishing within its respective area and does not represent its members in such matters. Moreover, the rights designated in the Fishing Act can be exercised by a Sámi only as a private individual. Therefore the Court considers that the first applicant, Johtti Sapmelaccat r.y., may not, for the purposes of Article 34 of the Convention, claim to be a "victim" of the violations alleged in the present application.

Similarly, in *Noack*, the EurCrtHR declared inadmissible a claim by Domowina, an organisation defending Sorb interests, because such claim concerned its members, not Domowina as such.

Under the Inter-American system of human rights protection, by contrast, there is no specific requirement to the effect that petitions with the IACommHR be lodged by persons, groups of persons, or NGOs claiming to be victims of a violation of the ACHR or ADRDM. Although the system as a whole retains a connection with the victim criterion by requiring that the alleged victims be at least identifiable, the relaxation of such requirement has provided an opportunity for the IACommHR to develop an expansive interpretation of the admissibility criteria *ratione personae.* In the context of the

[29] Application No. 42969/98, Admissibility Decision of 18 January 2005.

present study, the most typical petitioning pattern is that of claims made by NGOs and indigenous organisations on behalf of indigenous groups and their members, regardless of the latter's knowledge and consent. For example, in the cases of *Guahibo*[30] and *Yanomami*, groups of indigenous rights activists, alleged that serious human rights violations had been committed against the Guahibo Indians of Colombia and Yanomami Indians of Brazil, respectively. In *Moiwana*, Moiwana '86 – a human rights organisation which had been named after the attack by armed forces of Suriname on the N'djuka Maroon village of Moiwana in 1986 – submitted a petition on behalf of those Moiwana villagers who had died or become displaced as a result of that attack. In other cases, complaints have been submitted by both NGOs and the main indigenous associations representing the alleged victims. In *Maya*, the Indian Law Resource Center and the Toledo Maya Cultural Council submitted a petition to the IACommHR on behalf of the Mopan and Ke'kchi Maya People of the Toledo District of Southern Belize. In *Kichwa Peoples, Yatama*, and *Yakye Axa*, organisations of the affected communities lodged a petition together with a number of human rights NGOs. The *Sawhoyamaxa* case was initially taken to the IACommHR by an NGO representing the indigenous peoples living in the Chaco of Paraguay. In effect, the IACommHR has come to consolidate a flexible line on standing by accepting a progressive, though never complete, procedural disjunction of complainants and victims. This line has been buttressed by the IACrtHR, which goes as far as to recognise, not only petitions to the IACommHR which are submitted by specific group members on behalf of all members of the group regardless of any authorisation from the paramount leader of the community,[31] but also a basic, albeit qualified, entitlement of the alleged victims to participate in all stages of the IACrtHR's proceedings (*locus standi in iudicio*). This entitlement has been construed as a consequence of their right to access to justice under the Inter-American system and international human rights law in general.[32] There is no question that the IACommHR's and IACrtHR's view of standing has resulted in widening representation of indigenous claims, irrespective of considerations relating to the merits of each case.

Comparatively speaking, these petitions are broadly similar to the several communications accepted by the AfrCommHPRs on behalf of groups and individuals who had allegedly suffered gross human rights violations under the

[30] Case No. 1690 (Colombia).

[31] *The Saramaka People v. Suriname*, Judgment of 28 November 2007, Series C No. 172, para. 23.

[32] *Ibid.*, paras. 25–29. In essence, the alleged victims are allowed to inform the IACrtHR of any supervening facts, and argue for different rights or make different legal arguments based on the same facts as those presented by the IACommHR.

ACHPR. Facilitated by an already flexible approach to admissibility requirements under this instrument,[33] the AfrCommHPRs has accepted complaints from third-party NGOs and allowed the complainant(s) not to name all the victims of the alleged violations in the event of grave and massive abuses.[34] In *The Social and Economic Rights Center Action*, this body went as far as to characterise NGO petitioning which is unrelated to specific victims' names as the expression of an *actio popularis.*[35] But probably the gist of this jurisprudence lies as much in expanding the scope of third-party petitioning as it does in re-conceptualising the very (at least implied) notion of 'victim' under the communication procedure. Indeed, while most of the leading cases – such as the Mauritanian and Ogoni cases – have been submitted by NGOs, a deeper pattern seems to be at work that addresses a unique feature of the ACHPR, namely the recognition of peoples' rights. In *Katangese Peoples' Congress v. Zaire,*[36] a claim to self-determination was brought on behalf of the Katangese people by Mr Gerard Moke in his capacity as President of the Katangese Peoples' Congress. Although the AfrCommHPRs did not determine whether the Katangese consisted of one or more ethnic groups, it was prepared to consider internal self-determination (aside from secession) to the benefit of a distinctive sector of the population.[37] In *Malawi African Association* and *The Social and Economic Rights Action Center* as well as, more recently, *Anuak Justice Council v. Ethiopia,*[38] violations of (other) peoples' rights were claimed on behalf of collectivities – be they the Ogoni people of Nigeria, the black ethnic groups of Mauritania, or the Anuak community living in the Gabella region of Ethiopia – who are in fact part of wider multicultural entities. At least under certain circumstances, 'people(s)' has thus been understood to include sectors of the population within state polities as opposed to traditional notions of peoples' rights associated with whole national entities, or even the state.[39] This substantive point has fed into the communication procedure: by entertaining communications involving any such sections, as filed by third-party NGOs or

---

[33] Art. 56 (1) ACHPR.

[34] *Malawi African Association and Others v. Mauritania*, Comm. Nos. 54/91, 61/91, 98/93/, 164/97 à 196/97 and 210/98 (2000), para. 79.

[35] Comm. No. 155/96, 2001, para. 49.

[36] Communication 75/92 (1995).

[37] In its Advisory Opinion on *the United Nations Declaration on the Rights of Indigenous Peoples*, adopted in May 2007, the AfrCommHPR insists that self-determination must be exercised in a way which is compatible with the territorial integrity of the state: paras. 23–24, 27.

[38] Communication 299/2005, 20th activity report.

[39] As noted, the reassessment of 'people' under Article 20 ACHPR does not allow, though, a sector of the population to claim independence. For a traditional understanding of peoples' rights, see generally J. Crawford (ed.), *The Rights of Peoples*, Oxford, 1988.

the group's associations or representatives themselves, the AfrCommHPRs' discourse has pushed the boundaries of the ACHPR further.

An interesting and largely symmetrical ramification of the explicit or implicit expansion of the victim requirement or re-appraisal of the notion of victim of a right violation is provided by the increasingly collective role of reparations granted as a result of the adjudication of minority claims. Just as legal standing is being redefined to allow for greater access to international complaints mechanisms by minority groups, so too is the notion of injured party, particularly in relation to damages awarded to the benefit of those groups. This is certainly the case of indigenous communities in Latin America. In line with a typically assertive view of remedies under the ACHR,[40] the IACrtHR has recognised the collective dimension of reparations under Article 63 (1). In several cases including *Aloeboetoe*, *Yakye Axa*, and *Sawhoyamaxa*, the IACommHR has made the point that reparations should be considered not only from the perspective of the affected members of the group, but also in terms of the damage suffered by the community as a whole. Initially applied to a case of moral compensation for the murder of a group's member,[41] the IACommHR has consistently upheld this line in relation to more specific indigenous land disputes. While the IACrtHR has not ordered any reparations for the group as such, and insisted that the members of the group be regarded injured parties instead,[42] the collective nature of remedies has been openly emphasised. In *Aloeboetoe*, it ordered Suriname to reopen and staff the local school and make the medical dispensary available, 'as an act of reparation' to the benefit of all members of the group.[43] In *Yakye Axa*, it confirmed the 'special collective significance' of the reparations[44] and ordered Paraguay to provide compensation for material damage, to create a community development fund designed to back up the return of the land to the community, and to offer public apologies to it. Similar measures were ordered in *Sawhoyamaxa* and *Saramaka*, given the 'collective nature of the

---

[40] *Velásquez Rodríguez v. Honduras*, Judgment of 29 July 1988, Series C No. 4, para. 174.

[41] *Aloeboetoe and others v. Suriname*, Judgment of 10 September 1993 (Reparations), Series C No. 15.

[42] *Sawhoyamaxa Indigenous Community v. Paraguay*, Judgment of 29 March 2006, Series C No. 146, paras. 204–209; *The Saramaka People v. Suriname*, Judgment of 28 November 2007, Series C No. 172, paras. 188–189.

[43] In a very similar vein, moral damages for the benefit of the community were awarded in *Moiwana Village v. Suriname*, Judgment of 15 June 2005, Series C No. 124, para. 194.

[44] See also *Case of Massacre de Plan de Sánchez v. Guatemala*, Judgment of 19 November 2004 (Reparations), Series C No. 116, para. 86.

damage caused'[45] and the 'collective nature of reparations'.[46] Thus, on the IACrtHR's approach, reparation should not only take the form of *restitutio in integrum* (including through the medium of demarcation and titling of indigenous land), compensation for previous dispossessions, or guarantees of non-repetition in the event of interference with indigenous property rights, but should also include a further range of community-oriented measures, in an attempt to restore crucial elements of the group's identity while providing the people concerned with minimum socio-economic support (for example, access to housing or health services).[47]

This approach goes beyond the traditionally cautious deference of other bodies to the autonomy of states in choosing the general or individual measures that should be adopted at the domestic level to put an end to a human rights violation.[48] It does indicate, though, the potentially transformative role of judicial discourse in accommodating minority group perspectives in all stages of legal proceedings, namely as both carriers of claims and expression of distinctive (material and moral) damages.

Continuing effects of rights violation

Another interesting procedural area where judicial discourse appears to have generated greater concern for the situation of minority groups relates to the jurisdictional competence to determine the continuing effects of a right violation. This typically tends to raise the issue of whether the court has jurisdiction *ratione temporis* over facts which occurred prior to that court acquiring jurisdiction over the state, and/or more broadly an issue of inter-temporal law, namely of how to deal with past situations affecting the group.

[45] Judgment of 29 March 2006, Series C No. 146, paras. 224, 228.

[46] Judgment of 28 November 2007, Series C No. 172, paras. 188, 194–202; importantly, the point was also made that there is no need to individually name the beneficiaries of reparations as long as the members of the group are identifiable in line with the group's practices, para. 188.

[47] On the latter types of remedies, see also the AfrCommHPR's decision in *The Social and Economic Rights Action Center for Economic and Social Rights v. Nigeria*, Comm. No. 155/96, 2001.

[48] See e.g. the EurCrtHR in *DH and others v. The Czech Republic*, Application No. 57325/00, Judgment of 13 November 2007 [GC], Section IV A; however, a recent expansion of remedial powers, including a form of class action through so-called pilot judgments, may render the EurCrtHR more assertive: L. R. Helfer, 'Redesigning the European Court of Human Rights: Embeddedness as a Deep Structural Principle of the European Human Rights Regime' (2008) 19 *European Journal of International Law*, pp. 146–148.

As is widely-known, Arbitrator Huber in the *Island of Palmas Case*[49] expounded the doctrine of inter-temporal law by referring to the notion that a legally relevant fact be considered in the light of the law in force at the time the fact happened, while subjecting the 'continued manifestation' of a right to the 'evolution of the law'.[50] The interaction between the 'law of the time' and the evolving parameters of international law can be interpreted in terms of either limiting or replacing the 'old' right by means of the 'new' right for present purposes or restoring the *status quo ante* as a way of correcting past wrongs. For example, in *Western Sahara* Algeria's argument was that, although Spain had legitimate title to Western Sahara at the time of its colonisation, such title had become subject to the right to self-determination which accrued to the people of that territory.[51] On the other hand, Morocco claimed that the evolution of the law had invalidated Spain's title and restored its own titles to Western Sahara.[52]

From the perspective of minority groups, judicial discourse has proved capable of dealing with the past through the procedural opening provided by the doctrine of 'continuing violations' of rights. By analogy with Algeria's and Morocco's theses, the continuing violations approach may result in limiting existing titles and/or reinstating pre-existing entitlements. *Lubicon Lake Band* and *Mabo* are examples of this. In the first case, the HRC found a breach of Article 27 ICCPR on the basis of historical inequities deriving from Canada' s failure to protect the Band's land rights and the connection between such inequities and more recent industrial exploitation of resources in their traditional territories. Here the continuing violation of Article 27 rights was essentially equated with the lingering effects of historical dispossessions without implying any recognition of ownership rights per se. Rather, the point was that, the title to territory held by Canada had become subject to contemporary international human rights law in the form of respect for minority rights under the ICCPR. For its part, *Mabo* went beyond limiting state titles to territory by restoring the rights that were sacrificed to uphold colonial dispossession of indigenous land. In the words of Justice Brennan:

> [T]he fiction by which the rights and interests of indigenous inhabitants in land were treated as nonexistent was justified by a policy which has no place in the contemporary law of this country... Whatever the justification advanced in earlier days for refusing to recognise the rights and interests in land of the indigenous

[49] (Netherlands, USA) 1928, 2 *Reports of International Arbitral Awards*, p. 829.

[50] *Ibid.*, p. 845.

[51] Oral Statement of Mohammed Bedjaoui, 14 July 1975, *Western Sahara*, ICJ Pleadings, vol. IV, p. 448.

[52] Statement of Georges Vedel, 24 July 1975, *Western Sahara*, ICJ Pleadings, vol. IV, p. 151.

> inhabitants of settled colonies, an unjust and discriminatory doctrine of that kind can no longer be accepted.[53]

The notion that native title had survived the Crown's acquisition of sovereignty and 'radical title' to the land in effect came to combine the reinstatement of pre-existing rights with the continuing yet limited validity of the state's title. Both *Lubicon Lake Band* and *Mabo* explicitly or implicitly acknowledge ongoing repercussions of past wrongs.

Expanding jurisdiction *ratione temporis* is one way of addressing and remedying past violations. *Moiwana* exemplifies this approach. As mentioned earlier, the case originated in an attack on the N'djuka Maroon village, which had caused the forced displacement of the tribe from their traditional lands. The facts occurred at a time (1986) when Suriname, the respondent state, had neither ratified the ACHR nor accepted the jurisdiction of the IACrtHR. Unsurprisingly, Suriname argued that the IACrtHR was not competent to exercise jurisdiction *ratione temporis*. The IACrtHR rejected the argument on the grounds that the situation generated at the time continued to produce effects in the present:

> Moiwana community members continue to be either internally displaced within Suriname or to live as refugees in French Guiana. Thus, the Tribunal may properly exercise jurisdiction over the ongoing nature of the community's displacement, which – although initially produced by the 1986 attack on the Moiwana village – constitutes a situation that persisted after the State recognized the Tribunal's jurisdiction in 1987 and continues to the present day.[54]

In essence, the IACrtHR found a breach of property rights and other rights enjoyed by the tribe and their members by virtue of the continuing effects arising from the 1986 massacre. Looking back to past wrongs affecting a minority group, the IACrtHR allowed for historical perspectives on issues whose adjudication would have otherwise been precluded on strict procedural grounds. But exactly at what level of historical retrospection can or should judicial discourse pitch its assessment? While *Moiwana* dealt with events dating back to nearly twenty years before, the crux of indigenous claims is often based on much older forced dispossessions of ancestral lands which occurred at the time of colonisation, or otherwise at a much earlier stage compared to Moiwana-style situations of displacement. In these cases, establishing continuing effects of a right violation can be problematic and open to different interpretations. For example, in *Hingitaq 53* the EurCrtHR noted that the facts of the case occurred prior to the entry into force of the ECHR

[53] The High Court of Australia, No 2, 1992, 175 CLR 1., para. 42.

[54] Judgment of 15 June 2005, Series C No. 124, para. 108.

and Protocol 1 for Denmark, and that the substantial restriction of access of the Thule tribe to hunting and fishing as a result of the establishment of the Thule Air Base in 1951 as well as the relocation of the tribe from their settlement in Uummannaq in May 1953 were to be regarded instantaneous acts, namely acts with no continuing effects to be found in the present. By contrast, the ILO Committee of Experts, asked to pronounce on a similar claim under the 1989 ILO Convention 169, found that the effects of the 1953 relocation did persist because the relocated persons were not in a position to return to the Uummannaq settlement and thus the respective legal claims remained outstanding 'despite the fact that the relocation was carried out prior to the entry into force of the Convention'.[55] The notion of continuing effects is far from unknown to the EurCrtHR: in *Loizidou v. Turkey*,[56] it held that the right to property can be violated on a continuing basis if the land has not been returned to its legal owner. The restrictive approach in *Hingitaq 53* may have been due to the uncertainties surrounding the status of the Tribe, but clearly illustrates the competing understandings ('complete' or 'instantaneous' versus 'continuing' or 'ongoing' situation) that can arise from an issue of inter-temporal law involving minority groups.

The approach to historical dispossession of indigenous ancestral lands has been so far construed by judicial discourse, not on the basis of an automatic or direct connection with some kind of 'critical date' set by colonial or post-colonial history (i.e. in the form of a fully-fledged corrective justice-based approach to wrongful taking of lands), but through the medium of contemporary events or measures underlying the dispute at issue. *Lubicon Lake Band, Yakye Axa* and *Sawhoyamaxa*, for instance, – all of them involving forms of historical dispossession – defined the role of the past, not in isolation, but in terms of a marked connection with the present. *Sawhoyamaxa* importantly qualified the link with past dispossessions by pointing to the need to establish an existing material and/or spiritual relationship with ancestral lands.[57] In effect, the connection with past inequities, even when not explicitly relied upon (like in *Lubicon Lake Band*), has been implicitly used, regardless of the jurisdictional rule of *ratione temporis*. Indeed, both *Yakye Axa* and *Sawhoyamaxa* focused on facts which occurred at a time when Paraguay had already ratified the ACHR, notwithstanding the obvious relation of those facts to colonial dispossessions.[58] In *Mary and Carrie Dann*, the procedural issue

[55] Docs. GB.277/18/3, GB.280/18/5, 1999.

[56] Application No. 15318/89, Judgment of 18 December 1996.

[57] In this sense, it clarified the basis for some form of corrective justice which is left uncovered or unexplained in ILO Convention 169 and the UNDIP, respectively; see also the next section on standard of proof, and *supra* Chapter 2.

[58] See e.g. *Sawhoyamaxa Indigenous Community v. Paraguay*, Judgment of 29 March 2006, Series C No. 146, para. 125.

was not whether the IACommHR was competent *ratione temporis* to consider the property claims being brought against the United States (the case was decided under the terms of the ADRDM, adopted in 1948 within the OAS, and the competence of the IACommHR under the Inter-American system was not optional), but rather whether the petitioners were still being affected by the situation about which they were complaining. In many ways, this case captures the bottom line from which jurisprudential issues of inter-temporal law regarding minority groups can be tackled, suggesting a group-oriented reading of Arbitrator Huber's doctrine in the *Island of Palmas Case*:

> As for the alleged impermissible inter-temporal application of law, the State's submissions in this regard rely upon the mistaken premise that the Commission is addressing a "previously existing situation" in evaluating the Danns' complaint. While it may be the case that the ICC process itself took place more than 30 years ago, the Petitioners' complaints concerning indigenous title to the property, including alleged improprieties in the ICC process, remained the subject of controversy and continued to affect the Petitioners' interests at the time their petition was lodged and continue to do so. Moreover, the American Declaration, as an embodiment of existing and evolving human rights obligations of member states under the OAS Charter, is not to be interpreted and applied as the law that existed at the time of the Declaration's adoption but rather in light of ongoing developments in the rights protected under those instruments. Consequently, it is appropriate to evaluate the Petitioners' complaints in light of developments in the corpus of international human rights law more broadly since the American Declaration was first composed. To the extent that the Danns remain the victims of an on-going violations of their rights under Articles II and XXIII of the Declaration, then, the State is obliged to resolve the situation in light of its contemporary obligations under international human rights law and not those applicable at the time when the ICC process took place, to the extent that the law may have evolved.[59]

Evidence

The way in which judicial discourse deals with issues of evidence, including specific aspects relating to the burden of proof, may well reflect additional possibilities for advancing, albeit indirectly, minority claims. A first illustration of this is in terms of requiring stronger evidence to justify existing restrictions on minority related rights.

As previously discussed, the EurCrtHR has decided several cases involving either the dissolution of a political party that publicly advocated or embraced solutions for the benefit of a minority group, reaching out to fundamental

[59] Report No. 75/02, Case 11.1140, December 27, 2002, para. 167.

constitutional and territorial changes, or the manifestation or assertion of minority identity through the proclaimed objectives of an association, particular public meetings or the general activities of the group concerned. For one thing, in *Gorzelik* and more recently *The United Macedonian Organisation Ilinden and others v. Bulgaria*,[60] the EurCrtHR clarified that, in relation to Article 11 ECHR associations other than political parties, such as those seeking recognition of ethno-cultural minority identities, do play an important role in securing the proper functioning of democracy. On the other hand, all those cases have firmly established the notion that, while in principle the state may still set out limitations on such groups and their associative freedoms, particularly strong evidence is needed for these limitations to be regarded as compatible with Article 11:

> [T]he exceptions set out in Article 11 are to be construed strictly; only convincing and compelling reasons can justify restrictions on freedom of association. In determining whether a necessity within the meaning of Article 11 § 2 exists, the States have only a limited margin of appreciation, which goes hand in hand with rigorous European supervision embracing both the law and the decisions applying it, including those given by independent courts.[61]

The extent to which the EurCrtHR has been in practice consistently 'rigorous' in upholding this demanding evidentiary test – mainly built around rejection of the use or propagation of violence and endorsement of democratic principles – appears to be rather problematic in the context of particular cases, such as *Gorzelik, Refah* and *Leyla Sahin*,[62] as well as general considerations regarding the margin of appreciation and the relationship between the Strasbourg court and national judges. But aside from casuistic or systemic elements, the EurCrtHR's jurisprudence on Article 11 clearly illustrates an attempt to deal with the issue of evidence on minority related matters in ways that makes it less rather than more likely that the state's claim will succeed, at least in relation to situations affecting fundamental pre-conditions for the community to assert and articulate its own identity.

---

60 Application No. 59491/00, Judgment of 19 January 2006, para. 58.

61 *Ibid.*, para. 61 [quoting from *Sidiropoulos and others v. Greece*, Judgment of 10 July 1998, Reports 1998-IV].

62 Application No. 44774/98, Judgment of 10 November 2005 [ban on wearing the Islamic headscarf in universities is not in breach of the ECHR]; Dissenting Opinion of Judge Tulkens; see *supra*, Chapter 3, note 172; see also S. Spiliopoulou Åkermark, 'The Limits of Pluralism – Recent Jurisprudence of the European Court of Human Rights with Regard to Minorities: Does the Prohibition of Discrimination Add Anything?' (2002) 3 *Journal on Ethnopolitics on Minority Issues in Europe*, p. 1 et seq.

This line takes on even greater salience in respect of the state's inability or unwillingness to provide the evidence that is required. In *Velikova v. Bulgaria*[63] and *Anguelova v. Bulgaria*,[64] involving complaints of racial discrimination in the killings of persons of Roma origin while in police custody, the EurCrtHR adopted its typical standard of proof 'beyond reasonable doubt' in assessing evidence. However, it also noted that, in accordance with earlier case law, where the events are wholly or partially within the exclusive knowledge of the authorities, as in the case of injuries or death of persons under their control in custody, 'the burden of proof may be regarded as resting on the authorities to provide a satisfactory and convincing explanation' of those events.[65] In *Nachova*, a Chamber of the EurCrtHR recognised that 'specific approaches to the issue of proof may be needed in cases of alleged discriminatory acts of violence', especially those resulting from measures that are neutral on their face and yet have a disproportionately negative impact on a particular group:

> [T]he Court considers that in cases where the authorities have not pursued lines of inquiry that were clearly warranted in their investigation into acts of violence by State agents and have disregarded evidence of possible discrimination, it may, when examining complaints under Article 14 of the Convention, draw negative inferences or shift the burden of proof to the respondent Government, as it has previously done in situations involving evidential difficulties
>
> ...
>
> In these circumstances, the Court considers that the burden of proof shifts to the respondent Government, which must satisfy the Court, on the basis of additional evidence or a convincing explanation of the facts, that the events complained of were not shaped by any prohibited discriminatory attitude on the part of State agents.[66]

The Grand Chamber appeared to accept in principle the Chamber's point on burden of proof in cases of racial discrimination,[67] while falling short of upholding such a shift in the particular circumstances of the case:

> The Grand Chamber cannot exclude the possibility that in certain cases of alleged discrimination it may require the respondent Government to disprove an arguable allegation of discrimination and – if they fail to do so – find a violation of Article 14 of the Convention on that basis. However, where it is alleged – as here – that a violent act was motivated by racial prejudice, such an approach would amount to requiring the respondent Government to prove the

[63] Application No. 41488/98, Judgment of 18 May 2000.

[64] Application No. 38361/97, Judgment of 13 June 2002.

[65] *Ibid.*, para. 111.

[66] Applications Nos. 43577/98 and 43579/98, Judgment of 26 February 2004, paras. 169, 171.

[67] See also *Bekos and Koutropoulos v. Greece*, Application No. 15250/02, Judgment of 13 December 2005.

> absence of a particular subjective attitude on the part of the person concerned. While in the legal systems of many countries proof of the discriminatory effect of a policy or decision will dispense with the need to prove intent in respect of alleged discrimination in employment or the provision of services, that approach is difficult to transpose to a case where it is alleged that an act of violence was racially motivated. The Grand Chamber, departing from the Chamber's approach, does not consider that the alleged failure of the authorities to carry out an effective investigation into the alleged racist motive for the killing should shift the burden of proof to the respondent Government with regard to the alleged violation of Article 14 in conjunction with the substantive aspect of Article 2 of the Convention.[68]

In short, the Chamber did find evidence of racial discrimination (in conjunction with Article 2) based on the state's failure to conduct an investigation into the killings in question, whereas the Grand Chamber did not. The bottom line in this context is that, aside from general (non-minority related) issues of death or injury in police custody, arguable claims of (minority related) discrimination, that is, *prima facie* cases of such discrimination, may lead to a shift of the burden of proof on to the state, although the Grand Chamber's approach has in practice limited the possibility of the shift to facts that do not involve violent acts. By way of comparison, in the *Genocide* case the ICJ would seem to have been justified in not reversing the onus of proof as invoked by Bosnia for acts of genocide allegedly committed by Serbia, namely for acts aimed at bringing about denial of life, not of specific minority individuals, but of ethno-cultural groups as such, in whole or in part.[69] It should be pointed out that, both the Grand Chamber's decision in *Nachova* and the Chamber's line in the later *DH and others* reflected the Court's prudent consideration of issues of institutional racism. Both of them were essentially based on the notion that the burden of proof still lies with applicants and must be substantiated by specific evidence of racial prejudice or motive.[70] The Grand Chamber's judgment in *DH and others*, though, broke new ground in that it did overcome the Chamber's hesitancies by openly reaffirming, and elaborating on the point of the burden of proof made in *Nachova*. It did uphold such a shift in the event of a rebuttable presumption of indirect discrimination, without requiring proof of a discriminatory intent.[71]

---

68 Applications Nos. 43577/98 and 43579/98, Judgment of 6 July 2005 [GC], para. 157.

69 Judgment of 26 February 2007, paras. 204–206.

70 Application No. 57325/00, Judgment of 7 February 2006, paras. 49, 52 [racial prejudice]; Applications Nos. 43577/98 and 43579/98, Judgment of 6 July 2005 [GC], para. 157 [racial motive].

71 Paras. 184, 189, 194. This was confirmed in *Affaire Sampanis et Autres c. Grèce*, Application No. 32526/05, Judgment of 5 June 2008 (final on 5 September 2008), paras. 78, 79, 83 (in French). A similar argument was made in the *Case of Oršuš and Others v. Croatia*, Applica-

Regardless of the greater or lesser extent to which the burden of proof may, or will be shifted in the educational or other minority related spheres, the several complaints of abuse against the Roma community in Bulgaria that have been raised under the ECHR have generated a discourse geared towards a procedural (and substantive) rethinking of the EurCrtHR's approach to matters of discrimination against minority groups. In a sense, this discourse echoes the developing jurisprudence of the ECJ relating to the burden of proof in cases involving (mostly sex) discrimination, and which are now consolidated in Article 8 of the Race Directive.[72] Unsurprisingly, in *Hoogendijk v. The Netherlands*[73] – involving a claim of sex discrimination in respect of disability allowances introduced by national legislation – the EurCrtHR held that the burden of proof must shift on to the government if applicants are able to establish a *prima facie* case of sex discrimination on the basis of undisputed official statistics. This case was importantly recalled in the Grand Chamber's decision in *DH and others.*

As hinted at in *Nachova*, another procedural possibility generated by judicial discourse aside from the shift of the burden of proof is to draw negative inferences from the passive or uncooperative and/or unreliable attitude by state authorities. For example, in *Timishev v. Russia*,[74] concerning a denial of access to Kabardino-Balkaria by a Russian national of Chechen ethnic origin, the EurCrtHR supported the applicant's version of events turning on discrimination against Chechens who travelled by private car, following an analysis of the inconsistencies reflected in the factual findings put forward by the government. Whereas the burden of proof approach relates to the justifications for facts that are basically undisputed, such as the mistreatment or death of members of a minority group, this line is more focussed on establishing precisely the facts on which the minority claim is based. The HRC has frequently decided in favour of the complainants in the absence of any response from the state party on the issues raised by the claim. *Diergaardt* illustrates this in relation to minority issues:

> The authors have also claimed that the lack of language legislation in Namibia has had as a consequence that they have been denied the use of their mother tongue in administration, justice, education and public life. The Committee notes that the authors have shown that the State party has instructed civil servants

tion No. 15766/03, Request for Referral to the Grand Chamber on Behalf of the Applicants, 13 October 2008, para. 31.

[72] European Community Council Directive implementing the principle of equal treatment between persons irrespective of racial or ethnic origin, 2000/43 of 29 June 2000, O.J. 2000 L 180, 22.

[73] Appl. 5864/00, Judgment of 6 January 2005.

[74] Applications Nos. 55762/00 and 55974/00, Judgment of 13 December 2005.

> not to reply to the authors' written or oral communications with the authorities in the Afrikaans language, even when they are perfectly capable of doing so. These instructions barring the use of Afrikaans do not relate merely to the issuing of public documents but even to telephone conversations. In the absence of any response from the State party the Committee must give due weight to the allegation of the authors that the circular in question [issued by the Regional Commissioner, Central Region, Rehoboth, which explicitly excluded the use of Afrikaans during phone conversations with regional public authorities] is intentionally targeted against the possibility to use Afrikaans when dealing with public authorities. Consequently, the Committee finds that the authors, as Afrikaans speakers, are victims of a violation of article 26 of the Covenant.[75]

In essence, the HRC upheld the authors' position and evidence (a circular preventing the regional authority from using the authors' language) as a consequence of the state's failure to produce information rebutting the authors' allegation. This example also suggests that the impact of minority issues on points of fact largely depends on the kind and weight of evidence endorsed by judicial discourse to establish whether a right violation has occurred. In this sense, one important dimension of such discourse is the possibility for it to enlarge the range of evidentiary material that can be relied upon to uphold the claims, to include minority or minority-friendly sources.

For example, in *Delgamuukw v. British Columbia*,[76] involving the establishment of aboriginal title based on occupancy and land related Aboriginal practices recognised in Aboriginal law, the Supreme Court of Canada did expand the judicially relevant sources of evidence to account for the perspective of aboriginal communities:

> In practical terms, this requires the courts to come to terms with the oral histories of aboriginal societies, which, for many aboriginal nations, are the only record of their past. Given that the aboriginal rights recognised and affirmed by s. 35(1) are defined by reference to pre-contact practices or,...in the case of title, pre-sovereignty occupation, those histories play a crucial role in the litigation of aboriginal rights
>
> ...
>
> Many features of oral histories would count against both their admissibility and their weight as evidence of prior events in a court that took a traditional approach to the rules of evidence
>
> ...
>
> Notwithstanding the challenges created by the use of oral histories as proof of historical facts, the laws of evidence must be adapted in order that this type of evidence can be accommodated and placed on an equal footing with the

[75] Comm. No. 760/1997, Views of 25 July 2000, CCPR/C/69/D/760/1996, para. 10.10.

[76] [1997] 3 S.C.R. 1010.

types of historical evidence that courts are familiar with, which largely consist of historical documents.[77]

In essence, the Supreme Court reversed a lower court's decision to dismiss oral testimony as acceptable evidence on the grounds that it was hearsay, by pointing to the predominantly oral nature of indigenous traditions, and therefore the need to take that testimony (*in casu*, traditional songs referring to the territory's limits) into account when establishing the boundaries of the communities' lands. In *Mabo*, the High Court of Australia similarly used indigenous oral testimony to uphold aboriginal title and its specific scope. A comparable pattern is offered by the Court of the Navajo Nation in the United States, which exercises criminal and civil jurisdiction within the reservation or in respect of issues having an impact on the Navajos. In addition to the primary and secondary rules of the American legal system, this Court also applies Navajo common law, which includes reliance on oral traditions, such as ceremonies, songs or prayers, and related societal customs, mostly in connection with the articulation of Navajo claims to land.[78] Yet another example is given by the Waitangi Tribunal under the Treaty of Waitangi signed in 1840 between the Maori and the British Crown, which uniquely blends, in its findings of fact, distinctive Maori sources and more traditional court approaches to evidence.[79] Although the judicial discourse of both the Navaho and Waitangi bodies, unlike the Supreme Court of Canada's or the High Court of Australia's, is specifically meant to address the situation of the respective communities, their practice does illustrate the broader point about the treatment of minority evidence made above.[80]

Equally significant is the use of minority-friendly sources, ranging from statistics to expert testimony (in the form of amicus briefs). In *DH and others*, the EurCrtHR's Chamber did not uphold the applicants' argument that it was for the Czech Republic to disprove *prima facie* evidence of discrimination

[77] *Ibid.*, para. 84.

[78] J. Anaya, 'The Protection of Indigenous Peoples' Rights over Lands and Natural Resources under the Inter-American Human Rights System,' (2001) 14 *Harvard Human Rights Journal*, pp. 44–45. For the relevance of indigenous customary laws to the articulation of land claims by indigenous groups, see e.g. CERD's concluding observations on Guyana, UN Doc. CERD/C/GUY/CO/14, 4 April 2006, para. 16.

[79] For an overview, see M Te Whiti Love, 'The Settlement of Treaty of Waitangi Claims of Maori Groups in Aotearoa/New Zealand', in M. Boltjes (ed.), *Implementing Negotiated Agreements: The Real Challenge to Intrastate Peace* (The Hague, 2007), p. 229 et seq., at pp. 242–243.

[80] Oral evidence from community sources and/or expert evidence based on community practices have been widely admitted before the IACrtHR: see e.g. *Mayagna (Sumo) Awas Tingni Community v. Nicaragua*, Judgment of 31 August 2001, Series C No. 79; *Moiwana Village v. Suriname*, Judgment of 15 June 2005, Series C No. 124.

against Roma children being placed in special schools for pupils with learning disabilities. It was satisfied that, among other things, the system of special schools was not intended to cater for Roma pupils only, and that the applicants' parents did not behave in such a way as to suggest any concern that that system was being discriminatory against their children. As a matter of fact, the Chamber's point was not about the burden of proof, but about establishing the very existence of a *prima facie* case of indirect discrimination. The applicants argued that a presumption of discrimination could be based on statistical data, including reports from international organisations. The Chamber, while confirming in principle the concept of indirect discrimination, noted that 'statistics are not by themselves sufficient to disclose a practice which could be classified as discriminatory'.[81] This illustrates an important link between the establishment, and substantive import, of minority related facts and the type of evidence upheld by judicial discourse. Interestingly, Recital 15 of the EC Race Directive enables national law and practice to establish indirect discrimination by any means including on the basis of statistical evidence. For its part, the ECJ has used statistics in sex discrimination cases. In *Enderby v. Frenchay Health Authority*,[82] involving difference in treatment between men and women in matters of pay, it held that a *prima facie* case of discrimination had been established because 'significant statistics disclose an appreciable difference in pay between two jobs of equal value, one of which is carried out almost exclusively by women and the other predominantly by men'.[83] In later case law, the ECJ relied on statistical figures to determine that a far greater number of women than men had been affected by the measure in question, and clarified that valid statistical evidence should cover enough individuals, should not reflect occasional or short-term phenomena, and should be generally significant.[84] As alluded to earlier, the EurCrtHR had embraced a somewhat similar line on statistics in the *Hoogendijk* case, raising an issue of indirect discrimination against Dutch married women in relation to disability benefits. As stressed by Chamber Judge Barreto in *D.H. and others*, it had been confirmed that Roma pupils accounted between 80 and 90 per cent of the total cohort of Czech special schools – a figure that, by ECJ standards, would have justified a presumption of discrimination. In *Anguelova*, Judge Bonello argued for a lower standard of proof (aside from shifting the burden

[81] Application No. 57325/00, Judgment of 7 February 2006, para. 46 [citing *Hugh Jordan v. the United Kingdom*, Application No. 24746/94, Judgment of 4 May 2001, para. 154].

[82] Case C-127/92 [1993] ECR I-5535.

[83] *Ibid.*, p. 5573.

[84] *R v. Secretary of State for Employment, ex parte Seymour-Smith*, Case C-167/97 [1999] ECR I-623, at 683; *Nolte v. Landesversicherungsanstalt Hannover*, Case C-317/93 [1995] ECR I-4625.

of proof itself) in cases of ethnic discrimination, such as 'preponderance of evidence or...a balance of probabilities'.[85] Statistics would presumably be a major part of this test. In the wake of the ECJ's jurisprudence and the practice of several UN quasi-judicial bodies, the EurCrtHR's trajectory culminated in the Grand Chamber's approach in *D.H. and others*, which did accept 'less strict evidential rules...in cases of alleged indirect discrimination'.[86]

That judicial discourse can provide a procedural vehicle for deeper exposure of minority issues is further confirmed by the growing number of cases in which expert testimony from individuals and NGOs is accepted as being of special importance to establishing the facts and/or supporting claims of a right violation. For example, in *Mabo* the High Court of Australia used academic opinions, besides aboriginal oral sources, to establish indigenous land tenure systems. In *Mayagna*, the IACrtHR relied on several testimonies from the Awas Tingni and other indigenous communities, academics and NGOs, to establish the characteristics of the group, as well as the specific context of the dispute.[87] Most of the recent discrimination cases before the EurCrtHR have featured third-party interveners discussing notions of indirect discrimination, shift of the burden of proof, and the lowering of the standard of proof. In cases such as *Nachova* and *D.H. and others*, the third-party argument did raise a variety of aspects that were taken up, discussed or even upheld in the judgments.[88] It might be argued that those interventions are part of a wider developing judicial discourse about discrimination under the ECHR and other instruments and legal orders.[89]

Apart from expanding the types of minority and minority-friendly sources that can be used as admissible evidence, judicial discourse can have a major

[85] *Anguelova v. Bulgaria*, Application No. 38361/97, Judgment of 13 June 2002, Partly Dissenting Opinion of Judge Bonello, para. 18 [with particular reference to deprivation of life or inhuman treatment]. In the *Genocide* case before the ICJ, Bosnia argued for the same standard of proof in relation to acts of genocide, but the ICJ rejected the claim, Judgment of 26 February 2007, para. 208.

[86] *DH and others v. The Czech Republic*, Application No. 57325/00, Judgment of 13 November 2007 [GC], para. 186; the Grand Chamber broadly referred to 'various types of evidence' while still requiring proof which is based on strong, clear and concordant inferences, *ibid.*, paras. 178, 187.

[87] Judgment of 31 August 2001, Series C No. 79, sections V (B), and VII.

[88] Applications Nos. 43577/98 and 43579/98, Judgment of 6 July 2005, para. 143; and Application No. 57325/00, Judgment of 13 November 2007 [GC], paras. 161–174.

[89] Unsurprisingly, national jurisprudence figures highly alongside international case law, especially on questions of proof; see also the Dissenting Opinion of Judge Bonello in *Anguelova*, *supra* note 85. On seminal judicial ideas being taken up at a later stage in judicial discourse, see e.g. K. Knop, *Diversity and Self-Determination in International Law* (Cambridge, 2002), pp. 116, 128–129.

impact on the very substance that needs to be proven by minority groups. The focus here is not so much on *how* a particular claim can be established, namely on the evidentiary sources that can be relied upon for that purpose, but on *what* has to be established, that is to say, on the substantive requirements that must be met for the court to be able to uphold the claim. The issue of proving indigenous title by indigenous groups illustrates the point. While it has been argued that the *onus probandi* should fall on the non-indigenous element that claims a right to all or part of the land,[90] the gist of judicial assessment most typically revolves, *not* around a shift of the burden of proof on to the state (as advocated in some of the cases discussed above), but rather around the content of the proof to be provided by the indigenous claimant. From this perspective, judicial discourse has often been instrumental in easing the burden of proof placed on indigenous communities when claiming indigenous title under domestic jurisdictions. For example, the central common law requirement of a continuing occupation of the land has been frequently understood as not amounting to 'an unbroken chain of continuity' or uninterrupted material possession but as the proof of a 'substantial maintenance of the connection' between the people and the land.[91] In *Aurelio Cal et al.*,[92] the Supreme Court of Belize upheld a similar standard of proof to establish indigenous property under the Constitution in the face of claims by the state that occupation had not been exclusive and continuous. This is in line with international jurisprudence emphasising the diverse ties of indigenous communities to their traditional lands rather than a strictly construed physical relationship that inevitably disregards the impact of past disruptions of occupation for reasons outside the group's will.[93] As explained in *Mabo*, changes to the group's traditional way of life as it was at the time of colonisation do not affect the connection between the people and the land as long as such a connection has been maintained. The substance to be proven by the group has thus been re-conceptualised in relation to both the physical and identity dimensions of the attachment to the land. This dynamic understanding of the connection between the people and the land might even

---

90 J. Martinez Cobo, *Study of the Problem of Discrimination against Indigenous Populations*, UN Doc. E/CN.4/Sub.2/1983/21/Add.8, para. 519.

91 *Delgamuukw v. British Columbia*, [1997] S.C.R. 1010, para. 153 [quoting from Mabo]; *The Richtersveld Community and Others v. Alexkor Limited and the Government of the Republic of South Africa*, Case No. 488/2001, Judgment of 24 March 2003, para. 23; *R v. Marshall; R v. Bernard* [2005] 2 S.C.R. 220.

92 *Aurelio Cal et al. v. The Attorney General of Belize and the Minister of Natural Resources and Environment*, Claims Nos 171 and 172 of 2007, Judgment of 18 October 2007, paras. 24, 61.

93 For aspects relating to recognition, see *supra* Chapter 2.

be said to echo the rationale for the notion upheld by the HRC in one of the *Länsman* cases, that members of minority groups may invoke Article 27 ICCPR even though their way of conducting traditional activities has been adapted to modern technology.

On the other hand, Australian courts operating under the Native Title Amendment Act of 1998 have been more restrictive in defining the standard of proof required of indigenous communities, particularly on the issue of occupation. By requiring proof of a continuous occupation, the 1998 legislation sets out a high standard of proof which is hardly compatible with, not only the prevailing trend at common law, but also international jurisprudence. Indeed, the Australian case raises the issue of restrictive national approaches (whether or not judicially-generated or backed-up), and the extent to which they can be contained or modified by international law.[94]

A problematic issue is the extent to which international findings of fact uphold or depart from domestic ones in the relevant case. In *Gorzelik*, for example, the EurCrtHR's Grand Chamber stated that the ECHR left the national authorities a margin of appreciation in assessing whether a 'pressing social need' could justify a restriction on an ECHR right, while at the same time clarifying that this assessment was subject to its own scrutiny and included domestic court decisions.[95] In practice, it did assume the understanding of Polish law as provided by Polish courts, in relation to both the registration of associations (and the effects of the registration of the applicants' association), and recognition and classification of 'national' minorities and 'ethnic' minorities or groups in Poland. As discussed in Chapter 2, the EurCrtHR did not take issue with the apparently restrictive domestic courts' factual characterisation of 'national' and 'ethnic' minorities from the perspective of international law. Similarly, the HRC in *Jarle Jonassen*[96] declined to re-assess an 1897 decision of the Norwegian Supreme Court which the applicants – Sami reindeer herders of Norway – regarded as discriminatory against the Sami people:

> In respect of articles 26 and 2, the Committee notes the authors' arguments that the Supreme Court in the 'Aursunden Case 1997' attached importance to the Supreme Court decision in 1897, and that the latter decision was based upon discriminatory views of the Samis. However, the authors have not provided information which would call into doubt the finding of the Supreme Court in the 'Aursunden Case 1997' that the Supreme Court in 1897 was not biased against

[94] *Ibid.*

[95] Application No. 44158/9820, Judgment of 17 February 2004, para. 96.

[96] Comm. No. 942/2000, Views of 25 October 2002, UN Doc. CCPR/C/76/D/942/2000 (2000).

> the Samis. It is not for the Committee to re-evaluate the facts that have been considered by the Supreme Court in the 'Aursunden Case 1997'.[97]

These cases illustrate a certain degree of reluctance by international bodies to intrude upon the decisions of domestic courts on issues of fact and evidence, especially when combined with questions of internal law. The classical formal argument for justifying this approach is that international monitoring bodies are not 'fourth' courts of appeal for applicants. Those minority complaints thus got caught in procedural hurdles set out by an apparently lenient (pro-state) international judicial discourse. This need not always be the case, though. In *Sidiropoulos*, Greece argued that the Florina Court of First Instance and the Salonika Court of Appeal had made an accurate assessment of the factual circumstances of the case and established – based on what they deemed to be relevant evidence – that the association's real aim was to dispute the Greek identity of Macedonia and to sustain irredentist aspirations for the Greek province. Both the EurCommHR and the EurCrtHR did re-evaluate the facts by denying the association's separatist intentions, while the EurCrtHR even read the association's proposed activities through the lens of international standards on minority protection.[98] In other words, they provided an independent factual evaluation, which inevitably reflected on their substantive conclusions. A clear expansion of this approach is reflected in *Maya* and *Mary and Carrie Dann*. For one thing, *Maya* reaffirmed the autonomous role of international law (as interpreted by the IACommHR) in determining the existence of indigenous property rights:

> [T]he communal property right of the Maya people is not dependent upon particular interpretations of domestic judicial decisions concerning the possible existence of aboriginal rights under common law.[99]

On the other hand, *Mary and Carrie Dann* stressed the *procedural* autonomy of the IACommHR in addressing minority related issues of fact and evidence:

> The Commission also observes that many of the State's objections relate to the extent to which and manner in which the Commission evaluated issues, facts and evidence that, according to the State, had already been the subject of consideration and determination by the domestic courts. What the State must recognize in this connection, however, is that the Commission has an independent obligation to evaluate the facts and circumstances of a complaint as elucidated by the parties in light of the principles and standards under the American Declaration. This includes such matters as the adequacy of the procedures through which

97 *Ibid.*, para. 8.3.

98 Judgment of 10 July 1998, Reports 1998–IV, para. 44.

99 Report No. 96/03, Case 12.053, October 24, 2003, para. 130.

> the petitioners' property interests in the Western Shoshone ancestral land were purported to be determined. While proceedings or determinations at the domestic level on similar issues can be considered by the Commission as part of the circumstances of a complaint, they are not determinative of the Commission's own evaluation of the facts and issues in a petition before it.[100]

In essence, international judicial discourse, while traditionally sensitive to domestic findings, can still take a more independent approach to those issues, depending on the case and the system within which that discourse is generated. Obviously, an expansive approach to evidence does create opportunities for a more equalising perspective on the competing claims, as well as enlarging the range of minority related sources of evidence and the possibilities of interpretation, as indicated above.

Between acceptance and rejection of domestic factual findings is the possibility of valuing both parties' assessment of facts, without upholding either of them. For example, in *George Howard* and *Anni Äärelä and Jouni Näkkäläjärvi v. Finland*,[101] the question of whether or not the authors' Article 27 rights under the ICCPR had been violated depended on competing understandings and evaluations of factual circumstances. In the first case, the question was whether the author's right to fish on and adjacent to his First Nation's reserves, or to fish outside the reserves with a fishing licence, was sufficient for the author to enjoy this element of his culture in community with the other members of his group. The second case was similar to the *Länsman* cases, raising the issue of whether certain logging operations amounted to a breach of Article 27. In these cases, the HRC recalled the differing views of the parties on the real impact of the domestic measures in question on the authors' Article 27 rights, and stated that it was not in a position to draw independent conclusions on the factual circumstances regarding the author's complaints. At the same time, it did hold that, based on the information before it, no breach of Article 27 could be found.[102] A similar issue of evidence was raised before the AfrCommHPRs in *Malawi African Association* in respect of an allegation of a violation of the linguistic rights of black groups in Mauritania. The AfrCommHPRs – arguably more correctly than the HRC in the above cases – noted that there were no sufficient factual elements to determine *if* a violation had occurred.[103] It might be contended that the HRC cases reveal a fundamental tension between two different approaches to evidence. For one thing, the HRC appeared sensitive to the domestic findings, in line with the

[100] Report No. 75/02, Case 11.1140, December 27, 2002, para. 164.

[101] Comm. No. 779/97, Views of 24 October 2001, CCPR/C/73/D/779/1997.

[102] Comm. No. 879/1999, Views of 26 July 2005, CCPR/C/84/D/879/1999, paras. 12.11; Comm. No. 779/97 Views of 24 October 2001, CCPR/C/73/D/779/1997, para. 7.6.

[103] Comm. Nos. 54/91, 61/91, 98/93/, 164/97 à 196/97 and 210/98 (2000), paras. 136–139.

traditional approach – in *Anni Äärelä*, it even emphasised the Finnish higher court's (pro-state) line.[104] On the other hand, the HRC showed consideration for the author's different narrative and readings of facts by refraining from choosing either of the parties' perspective.[105]

---

104 Comm. No. 779/97, Views of 24 October 2001, CCPR/C/73/D/779/1997, para. 7.3.

105 In this sense, it is the petitioner's account that arguably makes it difficult for the HRC to accept the state's position: see H. J. Steiner, 'Individual Claims in a World of Massive Violations: What Role for the Human Rights Committee?', in P. Alston & J. Crawford (eds.), *The Future of UN Human Rights Treaty Monitoring* (Cambridge, 2000), pp. 33–34.

Part II

Chapter 6

Ethno-cultural diversity and international judicial discourse

The analysis has attempted to capture major dimensions of international jurisprudence concerning minority groups – what we have termed recognition, elaboration, mediation and access to justice. Each of these dimensions is primarily defined by a distinctive aspect of the process of adjudication relating to minority communities, be it their legal existence, their rights and interests, or their position and factual circumstances within the adjudicatory mechanism itself.

In essence, the role of judicial discourse has been brought to the fore from two crucial angles. First, the articulation of minority issues through decisions on competing claims has been explored. In this sense, the inquiry has consisted in a case-based analysis of a range of questions, such as way of life, property, language and participation, as well as the implications of the principle of equality, including issues of gender and religion. Second, judicial discourse has been discussed in terms of facilitating representation of minority concerns, rather than directly protecting or addressing specific minority rights. Examples of this approach have included the legal identification of a minority community, the upholding of general preconditions for enjoying minority identity, the expansion of judicial standing and/or consideration of minority related views, evidence and remedies, or the monitoring of aspects of the decision-making process affecting minority groups.

Dimensions of judicial discourse: preliminary observations

Judicial discourse does reveal multiple approaches to evaluating the position of minority groups. A very preliminary way of looking at it is by exposing elements seemingly underpinning most part of such discourse. They appear to be of a dialogical, contextual, or otherwise interpretive nature in a broad sense.

A dialogical line normally seeks to account for competing perspectives and claims as opposed to prioritising a definitive and one-sided understanding of the law. This goes some way to explaining why such an approach opens up important discursive spaces even though they may have to be conceptualised in terms of reasons and process rather than results. In *Western Sahara*, for example, the ICJ established the international legal significance of indigenous tribes in a non-European setting, while falling short of recognising them as international legal subjects. Both the majority and individual judges captured the identity of such tribes – and even wider historical identities affected by colonialism – through their interpretation of *terra nullius*, legal ties and legal entity, while rejecting Morocco's and Mauritania's claims to territory that included those tribes. In *Chapman*, the eventual reluctance of the EurCrtHR to uphold the applicant's claim to a distinctive identity did not prevent the majority from embracing the notion that minority issues do attract the guarantees of Article 8 and that the special needs and lifestyle of the Roma must be given special consideration in the decision-making process against the backdrop of a more general positive duty to facilitate the group's way of life. The strong dissent did add to what was effectively a dialogical acceptance and rejection of Roma views vis-à-vis state autonomy. Equally, the hesitancies of *Gorzelik* did not deter the Grand Chamber from openly recognising protection for ethno-cultural diversity as falling within the scope of the ECHR while still upholding state discretion. In *Reference Re Secession of Quebec*, the Supreme Court of Canada offered what could arguably be characterised as a classical exposition of a dialogical approach. It located Quebec's claim within a multiparty framework of negotiation involving the federal government, Quebec, the other provinces, and the indigenous groups living within Quebec. The significance of the decision does not lie in a merely technical legal response to the questions put to the Court but rather in the way that the perspectives of those actors are related to the Constitution and the international law of self-determination.

Leading cases decided by the HRC illustrate the importance of contextual assessments. It has been a constant argument of the HRC that Article 27 rights, apart from basic starting points, cannot be determined *in abstracto* – that is, on the basis of a pre-defined and fixed content of the right to enjoy ones' identity – but have to be placed in context. The equality-based recognition of an implicit right of a minority woman to reside on a reserve (*Lovelace)*, the distinction between disaggregated and cumulative impacts of development activities on the way of life of minority groups (*Länsman* cases), and the acknowledgment of a constructive relationship between comprehensive arrangements benefiting the group and individual claims from group members (*Apirana Mauhika*), are only some examples of the extent to which context-specific considerations have come to inform the understanding of Article 27 rights in ways that a strictly textual reading of those rights cannot.

Dialogical and contextual elements of course tap into the wider role of interpretation in connection with issues of both substance and procedure. The re-assessment of property rights under the ACHR to include indigenous systems of land tenure or the gradual expansion of the notion of non-discrimination to include both direct and indirect effects under the ECHR are obvious cases in point. Standing rules have been interpreted more generously, and so have the scope of relief measures and the methods and standard of proof in a number of jurisdictions.

But more than that, this way of looking at judicial discourse does not assume a clear-cut and tight distinction between the various elements that underpin it. Most of the above cases are effectively multidimensional. For example, the line in *Chapman* appears to be both interpretive (*stricto sensu*) and dialogical. Some principled concessions of a minority group's way of life under Article 8 ECHR are combined with the acceptance of the balance struck by the UK in favour of the general community interest. Most of the HRC cases elaborate upon Article 27 in a way that is context-specific. For example, echoing *Diergaardt, Apirana Mahuika* started from the rather innovative premise that the right to self-determination in Article 1 supports and partly deepens the understanding of Article 27, thereby establishing an overarching conceptual theme that ultimately informed more contextual considerations based on the parameter of participation.[1] *Reference Re Secession of Quebec* can be seen as both dialogical (in that it is based on the principle of mutual recognition and good faith negotiations in accordance with the Canadian Charter) and contextual (in the sense of setting out a framework for context-specific solutions that account for the interests of all actors involved). Other cases do combine all of the above elements, indigenous land rights being a most evident expression of this. The case law of the Inter-American system has expanded the notion of property rights, found context-specific positive duties of delimitation and titling, and established a participatory process designed to address all the ramifications of land claims, including restitution and compensation.

These and other aspects of international (and partly domestic) jurisprudence inevitably generate controversy over the latter's reach and function.

[1] Comm. No. 547/1993, Views of 27 October 2000, UN Doc. CCPR/C/70/D/541/1993, para. 9.2; *J. G. A. Diergaardt et al. v. Namibia*, Comm. No. 760/1997, Views of 25 July 2000, CCPR/C/69/D/760/1996, para. 10.3; on a similar theme, see also *Marie-Hèlene Gillot et al. v. France*, Comm. 932/2000, Views of 15 July 2002, UN Doc. CCPR/C/75/D/932/2000 (2000), para. 13.4.

In Europe, for example, the jurisprudence of the EurCrtHR has come under intense scrutiny as a result of an expanding framework of minority protection. Cases such as *Gorzelik, Refah Partisi* and the 2006 Chamber's decision in *DH and others* have been used as examples of judicial self-restraint in relation to issues as different as the existence of a 'national minority', the establishment of ethnic parties, or indirect discrimination supported by statistical data.[2] To the extent that they appear more lenient towards state interests, they are also said to compare unfavourably with non-judicial mechanisms such as the Framework Convention's Advisory Committee. In reality, broad generalisations based on specific decisions claim to prove more than other aspects of the same decisions, or simply other jurisprudence, seem to allow.[3]

The key point is that, regardless of the way in which we read or classify individual cases, a conceptual analysis that is driven solely by empirical (case-based) findings, while offering an understanding of how courts and court-like bodies construe minority issues for purposes of human rights law, cannot in itself provide an account of the potentialities and limitations of that discourse in general. In other words, the conceptual dimensions of recognition, elaboration, mediation and access to justice discussed in the previous chapters do expose different moments of judicial intervention in matters relating to minority groups, but their exposition does not explain the extent to which each of those dimensions relates to more principled or normative arguments about judicial discourse. Moreover, confining the assessment to a number of legal settings that are most directly relevant to minority groups overlooks the impact of adjudication of (other) human rights within different yet comparable contexts. With this in mind, the remainder of the chapter will first outline the main themes of the theoretical debate over judicial review and its impact on issues of group diversity or identity in plural societies. Then, it will discuss

[2] S. Spiliopoulou Akermark, 'The Framework Convention for the Protection of National Minorities and the Future of Minority Protection in Europe', paper presented at Liverpool Law School on 1 December, 2006 (on file with author).

[3] As discussed in Chapter 2, judicial discourse can prove conducive to group recognition in multiple ways. Acceptance of the Polish argument in *Gorzelik* is countered by the broad recognition of the principle of ethno-cultural diversity in the Grand Chamber's judgment and the several pro-Kurdish cases where the possibility of advanced domestic schemes of minority protection, including special language rights and territorial autonomy, was recognised. Assuming *Refah Partisi* reflects an hostility *tout court* towards religious or ethnic parties, it does not follow that courts cannot take a different line on the subject. The widely known case concerning *The Status of the Movement of Rights and Freedom (MRF)* decided in 1992 by the Bulgarian Constitutional Court does point in a different direction (*supra*, Chapter 3). *A fortiori*, this applies to the complete reversal of the Chamber's approach in *DH and others* by the Grand Chamber in 2007 against the backdrop of other judicial approaches in favour of indirect discrimination and statistics-based evidence.

the role of adjudication of socio-economic rights in certain national jurisdictions against the backdrop of some of the theories of judicial review. Finally, it will re-assess the conceptual dimensions of international jurisprudence on minority issues in the light of these theoretical and comparative insights.

Courts in plural societies

The theoretical debate

This is obviously not the place for a detailed discussion about the theories of judicial review that have been presented over the years by several scholars from the perspective of constitutional law and political philosophy.[4] Most of these theories are thoroughly analysed elsewhere and there is no need for us to rehearse all components of this long-standing debate. They invariably reflect wider conceptions of law. All of them, by definition, account for the internal dynamics of democracy and the rule of law, not the peculiar configuration of the international legal order. On the other hand, respect for international human rights lies primarily with state authorities, including courts. Moreover, the impact of international human rights bodies has expanded to such an extent that it is appropriate – indeed necessary – to look at some elements of the debate over the role of domestic courts (mostly constitutional courts) as a way of deepening our understanding of international judicial discourse per se.

There are by and large two aspects, or a combination of them, that should be considered for the purposes of our discussion, namely the indeterminacy of constitutionally protected human rights (or fundamental rights, in constitutional language) and the question of judicial review in the face of societal pluralism. Scholars like Ronald Dworkin and Michael Perry recognise the open-textured nature of constitutional provisions and argue for judicial activism as a response to the inadequacy of merely textual readings. In connection with his widely known theory of 'rights as trumps', i.e. as core limits on government's power, Dworkin sees judicial review as a way of protecting private autonomy from state coercion. In addition to text and precedent, Dworkin's judge is crucially guided by moral principles in discovering the content of a right as part of coherent whole defining the political, legal and constitutional order.[5] In his early and recent work, Perry, like Dworkin,

---

[4] In line with traditional terminology, 'judicial review' will be used precisely within that context. As indicated in Chapter 1, 'judicial discourse' is a broader concept for the purposes of the analysis, reflecting the more general role of international jurisprudence.

[5] R. Dworkin, *Taking Rights Seriously* (Harvard, 1978); id., *Law's Empire* (Harvard, 1986).

rejects the notion that legislatures can attend to fundamental moral principles underlying constitutionally protected human rights, and emphatically asserts the role of constitutional courts in specifying the meaning of those rights by weighing up the ethical and political values that inform them and the community's life as a whole. In his own words:

> The challenge of specifying an indeterminate human right, then, is the challenge of deciding how best to achieve, how best to "instantiate", in the particular context at hand, the political-moral value (or values) at the heart of the right…; it is the challenge of discerning, in the context at hand, what way of achieving that value, what way of embodying it, best reconciles all the various and sometimes competing interests at stake in the context at hand.[6]

Whereas Dworkin's judge embarks on the Herculean task of achieving moral coherence and integrity through legal interpretation, Perry's judge specifically anchors her interpretive role to the unearthing of an objective set of values on behalf of a pre-defined community.[7] Both judges are the guardians of the 'morality' of the constitution and both of them are capable of providing right answers to judicial questions in their own distinctive ways. Dworkin's basis of judicial review is primarily respect for the rights of minorities, at least in the classical liberal sense.[8] Perry's judge is driven by particular political and religious traditions. Despite their differences, both judges ultimately engage in morally-informed interpretations of the law that struggle to come to terms with the reality of ethical pluralism and ethno-cultural diversity.

It is precisely because of deep disagreement over moral, political and cultural issues in contemporary pluralistic societies that Jeremy Waldron strongly argues against the danger of judicial paternalism implied by the above theories.[9] He maintains that giving judges the power to determine the content of human rights is deeply undemocratic as it bypasses representative legislative assemblies. For Waldron, disagreement can and should be channelled into deliberative processes of majoritarian decision-making culminating in electoral processes in which all citizens are allowed to take part. The right of participation, notably the right to vote as opposed to judicial interventionism, is the mantra of Waldron's approach. Generalising from the US constitutional experience, Waldron assumes that judicial review requires judges to have the ultimate say in the matter, including issues of high principle such as human

---

[6] M. J. Perry, *Toward a Theory of Human Rights: Religion, Law, Courts* (Cambridge, 2007), p. 93.

[7] Id., *Morality, Politics, and Law* (Oxford, 1988), p. 135 et seq.

[8] See, by contrast, W. Kymlicka, *Multicultural Citizenship: A Liberal Theory of Minority Rights* (Oxford, 1995).

[9] J. Waldron, *Law and Disagreement* (Oxford, 1999); id., 'The Case Against Judicial Review' (2006) *Yale Law Journal*, p. 1348 et seq.

rights. Other constitutional models effectively suggest that constitutional judicial decisions over fundamental rights are not necessarily non-revisable, but are rather part of a conversation between judges and elected officials.[10] But the fundamental problem with Waldron's model is that it downplays the role of power within simple majoritarian democracy and its structural implications for all sorts of political minorities.

The need to safeguard the role of accountable legislative assemblies against the intrusiveness of an unaccountable judiciary ultimately makes Waldron hostile towards any approach to judicial review, be it substantive or procedural. John Hart Ely goes beyond the search for ethical coherence at the basis of Dworkin's and Perry's theories and Waldron's democracy-based objections to judicial review *tout court* by favouring a procedural approach to the role of courts. While he accepts the indeterminacy of constitutional provisions (especially on questions of values), he argues that judicial review is not undemocratic as long as it is concerned with securing the procedural conditions for a proper and effective democratic process. Ely adopts a 'participation-oriented, representation-reinforcing approach to judicial review',[11] in the sense of assigning to courts the role of guardians, not of substantive values, but of procedural fairness in the process of representation. Drawing on the *Carolene Products* case, Ely's argument is centred on the need for judicial review to scrutinise laws which are directed at 'religious, national or racial minorities', and may indeed reflect prejudice against them or the apparently wider category of 'discrete and insular minorities'. In the final analysis, Ely's model is based on a fundamental disjunction between procedure and substance – the process' 'malfunctioning' (to be censored judicially) and its material outcome (to be left to democratic participation). While courts should not interfere with the substantive outcomes of participatory processes, they must guarantee that such processes do not systematically exclude minority communities from the interest group bargaining which, in Ely's view, captures the essence of a pluralist democracy.

Jürgen Habermas builds upon Ely's approach within the context of a deliberative theory of rights and democracy. For one thing, he argues that, while human rights are normally anchored to universally upheld democratic values

[10] For example, the British Human Rights Act 1998 does not allow the judiciary to strike down legislation that is deemed to be incompatible with the human rights at issue. Courts may only interpret the legislation as to make it compatible with those rights (s.3) or issue a declaration of incompatibility (s.4). In both cases, Parliament remains free to further amend the law or refrain from amending it as signalled by the judiciary. In Canada, section 33 of the Constitutional Act of 1982 enables Parliament to override a Supreme Court's judgment that a particular law violates the Act (so called 'notwithstanding clause').

[11] J. H. Ely, *Democracy and Distrust: A Theory of Judicial Review* (Harvard, 1980), p. 136.

embodied in international human rights instruments, their precise scope, their exact contours, must result from open, consensus-seeking processes of democratic deliberation.[12] Guided by the principle of substantive legal equality, Habermas' law rests on the notion that 'all who are possibly affected could assent as participants in rational discourses'.[13] In this sense, laws affecting ethno-cultural minority groups, on both Habermas' and Ely's accounts, must not ignore the perspectives of such groups in the political (deliberative) decision-making process, if those laws are to gain democratic legitimacy. For Habermas, it is the function of constitutional review precisely to guarantee the openness of that process, to rejuvenate deliberative democracy. Unlike Ely, though, he argues for a more complex role of such review beyond the straitjacket of refereeing the interest group bargaining and policing elections. In *State v. Makwanyane*,[14] the Constitutional Court of post-apartheid South Africa stated:

> The very reason for establishing the new legal order, and for vesting the power of judicial review of all legislation in the courts, was to protect the rights of minorities and others who cannot protect their rights adequately through the democratic process. Those who are entitled to claim this protection include the social outcasts and marginalised people of our society. It is only if there is a willingness to protect the worst and the weakest amongst us, that all of us can be secure that our own rights will be protected.[15]

The case led to a pronouncement of unconstitutionality of the death penalty under the transitional 1993 Constitution, but the language of the decision did not simply account for basic technical elements of civil rights protection, it reached out to, and was effectively informed by, concerns for social (in)equality and poverty in South Africa. This suggests that protecting minority groups through the judicial process can and should have multiple dimensions, well beyond securing the right to vote.[16]

Habermas' model of judicial review reflects the complexities of contemporary democracies. For him, constitutional review needs to secure both civil and political rights and social (or socio-economic) rights; it needs to scrutinise the constitutional justifications for governmental interferences; it needs to make sure that the 'weak' public spheres of civil society are made able to

---

[12] J. Habermas, *The Inclusion of the Other: Studies in Political Theory* (Harvard, 1998), p. 190.

[13] Id., *Between Facts and Norms: Contributions to a Discourse Theory of Law and Democracy* (Cambridge/Malden, 1996), p. 458.

[14] Case No. CCT/3/94, [1995] 1 LRC 269.

[15] *Ibid.*, para. 64.

[16] Unsurprisingly, this court has taken the lead in developing a discourse about socio-economic rights, as discussed later in the chapter.

generate meaningful influence over the 'strong' public spheres built around administrative, economic, or social powers. All of this does not make a case for a substantive conception of judicial review which is designed to substitute for the democratic process:

> Rather, the source of legitimacy includes, on the one hand, the communicative presuppositions that allow the better argument to come into play in various forms of deliberation and, on the other, procedures that secure fair bargaining conditions.[17]

In reality, Habermas' vision of judicial review, in spite of its broader procedural scope compared to Ely's, is more confident than the latter in the relative determinacy of norms:

> [R]ulings on constitutional complaints and the concrete constitutional review initiated by individual cases are both *limited* to the *application* of (constitutional) norms presupposed as valid
>
> ...
>
> The court reopens the package of reasons that legitimated legislative decisions so that it might mobilize them for a coherent ruling on the individual case in agreement with existing principles of law; it may not, however, use these reasons in an implicitly legislative manner that directly elaborates and develops the system of rights.[18]

These procedural models of judicial review, particularly Habermas' wider deliberative theory, have had a profound influence over current discourses about law, courts and democracy. Yet, aspects of these theories have been exposed to criticism or re-adjustment. There are two points that should be briefly highlighted here. One is the strict distinction between procedure and substance on which both theories rest. The other relates to Habermas' emphasis on consensus-seeking procedures of deliberation, which essentially assumes that, as long as time and good will are available, deliberative processes will produce societal agreement in the form of rationally accepted outcomes and set out the role of constitutional courts accordingly.

The validity of a clear-cut distinction between process and outcome has been questioned. Commenting on Ely's theory, Sandra Fredman argues that such distinction is 'impossible to sustain'.[19] For Fredman, Ely downplays the role of power and access to resources as a precondition for genuine representation, as well as the function of human rights as a 'value pre-commitment' by which society is bound and which judicial review should properly mirror. As she

---

[17] J. Habermas, *Between Facts and Norms, supra* note 13, pp. 278–279.

[18] *Ibid.*, pp. 261–262.

[19] S. Fredman, *Human Rights Transformed: Positive Rights and Positive Duties* (Oxford, 2008), p. 110.

puts it, 'for judicial review to be legitimate in a democratic sense, it is neither possible nor necessary to sterilize its role of all evaluative content'.[20] For its part, Habermas' judicial proceduralism is said to be premised on an overly optimistic view of the applicability of constitutional provisions (including human rights norms) following processes of democratic will-formation. As noted by Zurn, the key starting point of all main theories of judicial review (expect Habermas'), whether substantive or procedural, acknowledges that 'crucial constitutional provisions are deliberately open-textured and the specific meaning of their content... is often the subject of reasonable and deep disagreement'.[21]

Contrary to Habermas, Jeremy Webber takes the openness of norms and the consequent openness of judicial decision-making as his point of departure for suggesting a model of judicial review that speaks to the competing perspectives of individuals and groups within plural societies. He rejects the procedure/substance distinction by arguing that judges 'cannot help but adjudicate among contending conceptions of justice' due to 'the law's open texture', the consequent need to draw on considerations that 'lie beyond the text' and the fact that 'in a pluralistic age, we disagree, sometimes fiercely over what those considerations should be'.[22] He argues for a judicial method that, as a response to gender, class or cultural bias or preconceptions, makes a genuine effort to understand the contending visions and seeks to transcend them through a synthesis that all parties can substantively recognise. For Webber, though, this method serves as a regulative ideal; 'the test of the process cannot be full substantive agreement', but rather 'the opportunity for and the quality of one's participation in the decision'.[23] In the final analysis, Webber's judge is still constrained by the constitution, the legislature, and the parties' conceptions of justice, yet strives to dialogically, thus creatively, embrace the latter's perspectives as much as possible by allowing them to participate fully and on equal terms in the process and eventually assuming their points of view as the basis for the final decision.

Other theorists have equally dismissed a fundamental distinction between procedure and substance as a viable approach to legal adjudication, but unlike Webber, who appeals (in a vaguely Dworkinian sense) to extra-legal considerations for solutions that are responsive to the litigants' positions, they firmly locate the interplay of substantive and procedural elements of judicial review

---

20 *Ibid.*

21 C.F. Zurn, *Deliberative Democracy and the Institutions of Judicial Review* (Cambridge, 2007), p. 248.

22 J. Webber, 'A Judicial Ethic for a Pluralistic Age', in O. A. Payrow Shabani (ed.), *Multiculturalism and Law: A Critical Debate* (Cardiff, 2007), p. 100.

23 *Ibid.*, p. 99.

within a revised conception of Habermas' deliberative theory of democracy. Indeed, while conceding the frequent indeterminacy of law and an inevitable degree of 'creative' judicial interpretation, they see courts as both deliberative actors and part of a wider network of deliberative actors involving the legal community (i.e. other courts, relevant institutions, and so on) and the public at large. For them, the key point is not that the litigants recognise the decision as the reflection of a dialogical conception of justice, but rather that the decision is based on solid legal reasoning which is legitimate in the eyes of the legal community and can be exposed to public criticism and possible revision over the longer-term.[24] In cases affecting ethno-cultural minority groups, Webber's judge would uphold the group's claim in whole or in part and would be driven by the need to deliver justice in dialogue with the parties. On the deliberative view of judicial review, reasoned argument rather than the parties' perspectives takes centre stage, in dialogue with other legal actors and the public. The final decision may or may not be in favour of the group, but is still subject to the ramifications of public discourse. Simone Chambers offers the example of *Delgamuukw* before the Supreme Court of Canada,[25] where the obvious bias against Aboriginal views in the original trial ruling were later on overturned as a result of severe public criticism.[26] Conversely, she uses the growing use of the 'cultural defence' argument in the American criminal court system as an illustration of the need to subject judges to public scrutiny also when they seem to have reversed the bias, subordinating the victims of crimes (women and children, for example) to broader collective claims.

If this line of thinking connects judicial review to Habermas' deliberative model, James Tully expands on such model in ways that, instead of idealising consensus, starts from the reality of disagreement in multicultural and multinational societies, while still retaining a crucial role for courts and policy-makers. Tully's approach is many ways a constructive criticism of Habermas' from the perspective of political theory. For one thing, tensions in Habermas' approach to consensus have surfaced in scholarly debates. To oversimplify, his insistence on consensus or unanimity as the outcome to be achieved under the best of circumstances in the deliberative process of democratic will-formation has been said to either downplay the often insurmountable difficulties posed by substantive disagreement or to run the risk of excluding irreconcilable views from the realm of 'reasonable disagreement' that Habermas nevertheless

---

24 O. A. Payrow Shabani (ed.), *Multiculturalism and Law, supra* note 22, pp. 101–125.

25 [1997] 3 S.C.R. 1010.

26 S. Chambers, 'It is Not in Heaven! Adjudicating Hard Cases', in O. A. Payrow Shabani (ed.), *Multiculturalism and Law, supra* note 22, pp. 121–122.

concedes as a matter of practical reasoning.[27] Minority claims often do involve positions that are difficulty to reconcile with those of the majority. A classic example of this is the clash between the indigenous views of land tenure and spirituality and the commercial understanding of property by the state and private companies that are engaged in mining and other development activities,[28] or otherwise the resistance of minority groups to any deliberative process that would grant the majority the power to control a minority group's way of life.[29] Central to Habermas' model is that, whatever the areas of reasonable disagreement, there can still be consensus on the procedures of dialogue, namely on what counts as process, and as claims and counter-claims within that process.

In Tully's conception of 'struggles over recognition' in multicultural and multinational societies, particularly in relation to ethno-cultural groups,[30] lack of consensus is assumed to be inevitable. Tully's approach deals with contestation or (reasonable) disagreement as a structural element – it does not seek or assume consensus as the expression of definitive solutions in the discursive process. In this sense, his view of reasonable disagreement seems to better encompass those minority views which are irreconcilable with the dominant ones. For Tully, disagreement involves not only substantive values (somewhat conceded by Habermas, as a matter of practical reasoning), but extends to procedural mechanisms as well, that is, to the procedural rules with which negotiations over the terms of recognition began. As he puts it, 'reasonable disagreement [over procedures] will persist, and there will be an indeterminate plurality of reasonable procedures'.[31] This dialogical model assumes disagreement over substance and procedure, yet starts from basic parameters of constitutional identity that includes what Tully terms 'principles, values and goods'. Drawing on the decision of the Supreme Court of Canada in *Reference Re Secession of Quebec*, he explains:

---

[27] J. Raz, 'Disagreement in politics', (1998) 43 *American Journal of Jurisprudence*, p. 33.

[28] For a review of domestic debates and jurisprudence, see e.g. R. Ahdar, '*Indigenous Spiritual Concerns and the Secular State: Some New Zealand Developments*', (2003) 23 *Oxford Journal of Legal Studies*, pp. 611–637; W. L. Cheah, '*Sagong Tasi* and Orang Asli Land Rights in Malaysia: Victory, Milestone or False Start?', (2004) 2 *Law, Social Justice & Global Development Journal*, at http://www/go.warwick.ac.uk/elj/lgd/2004_2/cheah.

[29] *Minority Schools in Albania*, Advisory Opinion of 23 January, 1935, PCIJ, Ser. A./B., No. 64, 1935.

[30] J. Tully, 'The Practice of Law-Making and the Problem of Difference: An Introduction to the Field', in O. A. Payrow Shabani (ed.), *Multiculturalism and Law*, *supra* note 22, p. 22.

[31] *Ibid.*, p. 33. See also D. Owen & J. Tully, 'Redistribution and recognition: two approaches', in A. S. Laden & D. Owen (eds.), *Multiculturalism and Political Theory*, (Cambridge, 2007), p. 286.

> These principles, values and goods do not form a determinate and ordered set of principles of justice to which all the members agree. Rather, they are many, none is trump, different ones are brought to bear in different cases, and there is reasonable disagreement and contestation about which ones are relevant and how they should be applied in any case.[32]

On this broad model (whose full articulation cannot be accounted for here), struggles for recognition are conducted through inclusive dialogues or 'multilogues' where democratic participation – rather than identities per se (always exposed to change and reconstruction as a result of such dialogues) – is key:

> The primary aim will be to ensure that those subject to and affected by any system of governance are always free to call its prevailing norms of recognition and action coordination into question; to present reasons for and against modifying it; to enter into a dialogue with those who govern and who have a duty to listen and respond; to be able to challenge the prevailing procedures of negotiation in the course of the discussions; to reach or fail to reach an imperfect agreement to amend (or overthrow) the norm in question; to implement the amendment; and then to ensure that the implementation is open to review and possible renegotiation in the future. This is the fundamental democratic freedom of citizens – of having an effective say in a dialogue over the norms through which they are governed.[33]

So, what is for Tully the role of courts in multicultural and multinational societies? Within this framework, courts come into play from two essential angles. First, they are viewed as still crucial to the process of participation envisaged above. To the extent that they are not seen in opposition to the role of citizens engaged in democratic deliberations, and that all relevant actors work towards agreements on recognition which will always be 'less than perfect' because of irreducible disagreement, they can, and often do provide a valuable input that is capable of broadening the boundaries of public discourse. As Tully notes, 'while [courts] do not have the final word, neither do the citizens engaged in the dialogue nor any particular institutional set of procedures'.[34] The point of this is not to celebrate contestation, let alone foment instability through contempt for the will of the majority, but rather to set out a broad system of cheques and balances driven by democratic participation, including the right to initiate change. Seen from this perspective, courts, like policy-makers or theorists, help shape the debate in dialogue with those involved in the struggles over recognition, by explaining claims and/or addressing procedural

---

32 J. Tully, 'Introduction', in A. Gagnon & J. Tully (eds.), *Multinational Democracies* (Cambridge, 2001), p. 11.

33 Id., 'The Practice of Law-Making', *supra* note 30, p. 35.

34 *Ibid.*, p. 38.

questions that arise from those struggles. Echoing the deliberative view of judicial review discussed earlier, courts are an important part of the 'multilogues' generated by the participatory process. Their decisions, their points of closure, are always subject to revision over time and are always exposed to public scrutiny, just as they are (or should be) a counterbalancing force in the wider debate over the circumstances of recognition (or lack of it). For Tully, *Reference Re Secession of Quebec* epitomises the kind of systemic guidance a constitutional court can offer, but equally importantly (constitutional) courts, together with several other (non-judicial) institutions on a both national and international level, can provide important checks and balances against the distortions or manipulations of popular deliberation.

Indeed, this is linked to the second angle from which judicial review is conceptualised in Tully's model. Not only are courts part of this dynamic framework, they also provide alternative avenues for bringing about change to the norms of recognition. An essential distinction is made between a broad framework of dialogue and actual decision-taking. For a number of reasons, (poor resources or argumentative skills, lack of power, lack of time, and so on), this dialogue may prove limited in terms of altering the dominant groups' perceptions or prejudices against minority groups; '[i]n these circumstances a majority decision-making rule...just leaves an oppressed minority hostage to the majority at the end of the discussions'.[35] It is at this point that courts, together with other national, trans-national or international institutions, come to represent alternative decision-taking forums as long as they, too, are open to challenge in turn.

An example of the role courts can play within this polycentric and dynamic framework is given by the *Delgamuukw* case. For one thing, the much criticised words chosen by Judge McEachern in the initial 1991 ruling to describe indigenous way of life and its comparative worth were later on overturned by the Supreme Court's groundbreaking recognition of aboriginal title to land on the basis of indigenous history as oral evidence. The initial decision had sparked off a robust public debate over the recognition of indigenous peoples and their land under the Canadian Charter, generating reflection and change. As noted by Simone Chambers, the judge's depiction of aboriginal life 'forced debate to confront and articulate background biases and to engage in criticism'.[36] At the same time, the 1997 Supreme Court's decision served as an alternative form of recognition of indigenous identity following a ten-year long attempt by indigenous organisations to secure a constitutional amendment

[35] *Ibid.*, p. 39.

[36] S. Chambers, 'It is Not in Heaven! Adjudicating Hard Cases', *supra* note 22, p. 122.

to that effect.[37] In this sense, *Delgamuukw* provided an avenue for political change which was no longer available within the wider discursive process.

A broadly comparable dynamic can be noticed in relation to the landmark judgment of the Malaysian state of Selangor's High Court in *Sagong Tasi and Ors v. Negeri Kerajaan Selangor and Ors*,[38] against the background of the Malaysian Constitution. Malaysia is one of the few Asian countries which explicitly recognise indigenous peoples (Orang Asli) in the Constitution, yet it does not contain any formal provision for indigenous land rights. *Sagong Tasi* originated from forced evictions of the Orang Asli Temuan tribe from their ancestral land for the construction of a highway to the Kuala Lumpur International Airport. Part of that land fell within the limited purview of the Aboriginal Peoples' Act. Effectively responding to the traditional political marginalisation of the Orang Asli in modern Malaysia and international and comparative developments regarding indigenous communities, the High Court recognised aboriginal title to ancestral lands under common law and found a duty upon the government to pay compensation.[39] It did so on the basis of a creative interpretation of the interaction amongst the common law, the Aboriginal Peoples' Act and the Constitution. Just as *Delgamuukw* before the Supreme Court of Canada, *Sagong Tasi* before the Malaysian High Court broke a pattern of isolation of indigenous views and changed the 'norms of recognition' in Tully's sense. But just as the initial ruling in *Delgamuukw*, *Sagong Tasi* does reflect important flaws. Indeed, the recognition of aboriginal title to land is not matched with any recognition of the specificities of indigenous land rights under international and comparative law. The key point of the decision is that Orang Asli native title does exist at common law, but is no different from 'ordinary' private land rights for the purpose of the Land Acquisition Act. Consequently, monetary compensation for acquired land applies to indigenous property on the same basis as non-indigenous property. Despite the Court's drawing on international developments in the field, the judgment fails to account for the non-market-value of land for indigenous groups, and the need (indeed, the international legal obligation, based on ILO 169 and reinforced by the UNDIP) to engage in consultation with the community in order to obtain its consent to relocation and to offer alternative

[37] It should be noted that *Delgamuukw* culminated a judicial process initiated by earlier decisions in the 1990s, including *R. v. Van der Peet* [1996] S.C.R. 507 and *R. v. Sparrow* [1990] S.C.R. 1075.

[38] [2002] 2 CLJ 543.

[39] By recognising an aboriginal right to the land as such, the Court went beyond the scope of an earlier decision in *Adong Kuwait v. Kerajaan Negeri Johor* [1997] 1 MLJ 418, *ibid.*, para. 45.

lands of equal quality before any consideration of financial compensation may be entertained.[40]

The Court's commercial understanding of indigenous land taps into an 'irreducible disagreement' which is at the heart of most state-indigenous group disputes. The judgment advances matters, but stops half way. On Tully's model, *Sagong Tasi* does not, cannot have the last word on the matter. Rather, it represents an avenue for recognition which, like all other procedural or institutional avenues, is bound to prove 'less than perfect', generating disagreement, further debate, and revision or adjustment over the longer term.

The case of socio-economic rights

As hinted at earlier, the internal debate over judicial review in pluralistic societies has also been driven by human rights other than those which are most directly relevant to the identity of minority groups. More specifically, the adjudication of socio-economic rights in a number of national jurisdictions has opened up a wider discursive space about the justiciability of such rights and the quality of judicial intervention. Despite the obvious distinctiveness of the rights involved, a brief analysis of such jurisprudence can deepen our understanding of the role of courts against the backdrop of the theories of judicial review sketched out in the previous section, and provide further insights (*mutatis mutandis*) into the role of international judicial discourse within the context of minority protection.

Indeed, analyses of minority issues and socio-economic rights have been typically built around a number of broadly similar generalisations. The relevant rights (for example, under the UN Covenants on Human Rights as well as national constitutions and laws) require positive measures rather than solely abstention from interference. On a practical level, the question of socio-economic rights, being mostly directed at vulnerable groups, resonates with the structural non-dominance of the ethno-cultural communities which enjoy protection under international human rights law.[41] The latter are quite often the beneficiaries of social programmes aside from measures which are designed to protect and promote their identity. At the same time, questions

---

40 As we have seen, under the Inter-American system, *Yakie Axa* and *Saramaka* set out further specific requirements involving the relationship between consultation and consent with regard to third-party activities affecting indigenous land, expropriation of privately owned land or withdrawal of private concessions.

41 See e.g. M. A. Baderin, 'The African Commission on Human and Peoples' Rights and the Implementation of Economic, Social, and Cultural Rights in Africa', in M. A. Baderin & R. McCorquodale (eds.), *Economic, Social and Cultural Rights in Action* (Oxford, 2007), p. 139 et seq.; V. Gómez, 'Economic, Social, and Cultural Rights in the Inter-American system', *ibid.*, p. 166 et seq.

and concerns have been raised regarding the content of both categories, the level of financial and/or political commitment required to realise the rights, and consequently the capacity of courts to intervene in the face of demands on the democratic decision-making process.

In *Olga Tellis v. Bombay Municipal Corporation*,[42] the Supreme Court of India decided a case brought up by pavement and slum dwellers of Bombay who argued that the city corporation's announced plan to evict them and deport them to their places of origin was in breach of the right to life in Article 21 of the Constitution. In particular, the petitioners sought a judgment that they could not be evicted without being offered alternative accommodation, and made a crucial connection between the right to life and the means of livelihood, that is, the means by which a life can be lived. It should be pointed out that the Indian Constitution does not make direct provision for socio-economic rights, although it does recognise socio-economic issues under its Directive Principles of Social Policy as an integral part of the founding text. The Supreme Court has been very keen to interpret civil and political rights in the context of the directive principles, or otherwise to regard the latter, as they put it in *Olga Tellis*, 'as equally fundamental in the understanding and interpretation of the meaning and content of fundamental rights'.[43] Indeed, the Court accepted that Article 21 – read in conjunction with the directive principles on the right to an adequate means of livelihood (Article 39(a)) and the right to work (Article 41) – does include the right to livelihood, going beyond the traditionally narrower conception of the right to life as entailing solely an obligation on the state not to arbitrarily deprive individuals of their life:

> If the right to livelihood is not treated as a part of the constitutional right to life, the easiest way of depriving a person of his right to life would be to deprive him of his means of livelihood to the point of abrogation.[44]

The petitioners argued that their life depended on their living close to their places of work and through begging in their dwellings or on pavements. The broad reading of the right to life effectively turned a classical, 'negative' civil right into a pro-active entitlement with a strong social component. As the Court confirmed ten years later, the Article 21 right 'derives its life-breath from the directive principles of State policy'.[45] In *Olga Tellis*, the Court also

---

[42] [1985] 3 S.C.C. 545.

[43] *Ibid.*, para. 32. In *Mohini Jain v. Karnataka*, the Court went as far as to make a connection between freedom of expression and the right to education (A.I.R. 1993 S.C. 2178).

[44] *Supra* note 42, para. 32.

[45] *Consumer Education & Research Centre v. Union of India* A.I.R. 1995 S.C. 922, at 25; the judicial interpretation of Article 21 has reached out to environmental rights and aspects of

found that the procedure for eviction, while not in itself unreasonable or unjust, was defective because of a failure to provide notice:

> Notice would give an opportunity for response and argument, for dialogue preceding the eviction action which might thereby be judged to be arbitrary. It heightened the chance of law observance and accuracy of judgment of the state authority.[46]

The Court ultimately granted judicial relief in that it recognised a duty on the state authorities to engage in consultations with the individuals concerned, and ordered that the pavement and slum dwellers be afforded an opportunity for alternative pitches or accommodation.

The experience of South Africa is also of particular interest to our discussion, given the express recognition of socio-economic rights in the Constitution along the lines of the International Covenant on Economic, Social and Cultural Rights (ICESCR).[47] The Constitutional Court has undoubtedly taken the lead in adjudicating such rights. Its somewhat innovative jurisprudence has been the subject of extensive analysis in legal and policy circles. Three major cases – *Soobramoney v. Minister of Health,*[48] *Government of South Africa v. Grootboom*[49] and *Minister of Health v. Treatment Action Campaign*[50] – largely reflect the Court's dynamic understanding of its role. *Soobramoney* involved an individual who suffered from chronic kidney failure and his life could only be prolonged by regular dialysis treatment. As a result of resource constraints generated by the provincial health department's financial policy, the public hospital to which the appellant had turned for such treatment had refused it based on guidelines that limited dialysis to those patients with acute renal failure who could be treated and remedied. He argued that the hospital's refusal amounted to a breach of the right to life and the right to emergency health care in Sections 11 and 27(3), respectively. The Court dismissed this line and dealt with the case in terms of the right to have access to health care in Section 27(1), which was understood, on the basis of the second paragraph, as a duty 'to take reasonable legislative and other measures, within its available resources, to achieve the progressive realisation of this right'. The Court was

---

education: C. Foster & V. Jivan, 'Public Interest Litigation and Human Rights Implementation: The Indian and Australian Experience' (2008) 3 *Asian Journal of Comparative Law*, pp. 4–5.

[46] *Supra* note 42, para. 37.

[47] It is also important to note that South African courts must consider international law when interpreting constitutional rights (Article 39 (1) of the Constitution) and apply that body of law as it becomes applicable within the South African legal order (Articles 231–233).

[48] 1998 (1) SA 176 (CC).

[49] (11) BCLR 1169 – hereafter referred to as '*Grootboom*'.

[50] (2) 2002 (5) SA 721 (CC) – hereafter referred to as '*TAC* case'.

satisfied that the need to ration the availability of dialyses machines due to resource constrains was clear and consistently applied. It did not judge the allocation of resources per se, deferring to the 'rational decisions taken in good faith by the political organs and medical authorities whose responsibility it is to deal with such matters'.[51]

In *Grootboom* and *TAC*, the Court moved away from a mere rationality standard of review to embrace a more substantive notion of reasonableness. *Grootboom* was litigated on the basis of the right to adequate housing in Section 26. The case concerned a group of people who had been living in extremely poor conditions in a squatter settlement near Cape Town. Such conditions had become so intolerable as to force them to set up dwellings on private land. Eviction proceedings led to the destruction of the dwellings, and triggered legal action against the government to provide the petitioners with basic shelter. The High Court found in favour of the latter and the government appealed the decision. The Constitutional Court recognised that a governmental housing development policy was in place whose medium and long terms objectives were irreproachable. However, it did find that such policy lacked any provision for those who were in desperate need. The Court made two key points. First, it held that it was not necessary to determine in the first instance the minimum core of the right to adequate housing, and that it was more important to establish whether the measures at issue were reasonable, in line with Section 26(2) (whose wording is identical to that of Section 27(2) mentioned earlier). On this approach, the right must be progressively realised on the basis of a reasonable and comprehensive housing programme, though it is not for the court to substitute for the political process:

> [T]he precise contours and content of the measures to be adopted are primarily a matter for the legislature and the executive... A court considering reasonableness will not enquire whether other more desirable or favourable measures could have been adopted, or whether public money could have been better spent... It is necessary to recognise that a wide range of possible measures could be adopted by the state to meet its obligations. Many of these would meet the requirement of reasonableness.[52]

Second, the Court upheld reasonableness on the basis of the substantive values of 'human dignity, freedom and equality'.[53] In other words, the proceduralism implied by the test was nevertheless linked to a substantive assessment of governmental measures – an element clearly lacking in *Soobramoney*. The specific point was made that a housing programme which excludes a

[51] 1998 (1) SA 176 (CC), para. 29.
[52] (11) BCLR 1169, para. 23.
[53] *Ibid.*, para. 44.

'significant segment of society cannot be said to be reasonable'.[54] Everyone, said the Court, must be treated with care and concern, and this is even more so in relation to those 'whose needs are the most urgent and whose ability to enjoy all rights is most in peril'.[55] In short, the existing programme failed to meet the requirement of reasonableness, though the exact scope of the plan to be adopted in order to tackle the situation of those in desperate need and the precise budget allocation for that were left to the government.

The test of reasonableness was confirmed in the *TAC* case. It arose out of restrictions imposed by the South African government on the provision of an antiretroviral drug which was meant to diminish the risks of mother-to-child transmission of HIV/AIDS. This policy, which limited the availability of the drug to a number of specially designated research and training sites, was challenged as amounting to a violation of the right to have access to health care in Section 27. The Court rejected the notion put forward through amicus briefs that the first paragraph of that section should be read as a free-standing right (in conjunction with Section 7(2)), and was thus not subject to the qualification of its second paragraph. Instead, it confirmed the inextricable link between sections 27(1) and 27(2) and reaffirmed *Grootboom* in the sense of construing the right as a duty on the state to adopt measures that meet the test of reasonableness. It recognised that it is not equipped to make wide ranging factual and political enquiries, and that the inevitable budgetary implications of determinations of (un)reasonableness are merely coincidental and do not derive from the fact that judgments are directed at rearranging budgets. In any event, the drug had been offered free of charge for five years by the manufacturer, which made cost immaterial to the decision. Rather, the Court looked at the efficacy of the treatment (or lack of it). Based on medical evidence suggesting the enormous cost in human life resulting from the restrictions in question, the Court concluded that they were not reasonable and in fact required the government to revise its policy comprehensively, including an extension of the testing and counselling facilities beyond the areas where they already existed. Like in *Grootboom*, the Court used the extent of exclusion of significant parts of society from the state programme as a powerful indicator of its unreasonableness.

That the test tends in effect to intersect with equality considerations is confirmed by *Khosa v. Minister of Social Development*[56] involving measures limiting child and old age benefits to citizens of South Africa. The applicants were Mozambican citizens who had acquired the status of permanent resi-

[54] *Ibid.*, paras. 43–44.

[55] *Ibid.*

[56] 2006 (4) SA 505 (CC).

dents in South Africa. They argued that their exclusion from access to those benefits was in breach of the right of 'everyone' to social security in Section 27. The Court struck down the scheme on the grounds that it was unreasonable to differentiate between citizens and permanent residents in relation to social assistance. It held that, in most respects, permanent residents had similar obligations to citizens, and South African society catered to the basic needs of non-citizens. The increase in the cost of social grants was negligible, while the impact of exclusion of permanent residents was considerable. As the Court put it, 'the denial of the right is total and the consequences of the denial are grave. They are relegated to the margins of society and are deprived of what may be essential to enable them to enjoy other rights vested in them under the Constitution'.[57] In essence, the Court did not challenge the need to differentiate between groups in order to allocate social benefits. Rather, it regarded the differential treatment in question to be unjustified.

What does this brief account of national jurisprudence on socio-economic rights tell us about the role of courts in complex pluralistic societies? Somewhat echoing the debate over judicial review discussed in the previous section, the Indian and South African case law seems to suggest multiple combinations of procedural and substantive elements. The Indian experience is based on a re-conceptualisation of civil and political rights rather than an elaboration on socio-economic rights *stricto sensu*. The *Olga Tellis* reading of the right to life epitomises the expounding role of the Supreme Court in connection with the (non-justiciable) directive principles. It confirms human rights provisions as living instruments defined by a degree of judicial elaboration. At the same time, this judicial intervention does not substitute for the political process but sets out the framework of legality for governmental action. The newly found right to livelihood of pavement dwellers was essentially understood as entailing a duty to consult with these people before any lawful removal could take place, including an opportunity for alternative accommodation.

The South African constitutional adjudication of socio-economic rights is even more interesting because of the explicitly recognised justiciability of such rights. The presence of specific clauses on socio-economic matters does not dispense with judicial conceptualisation. For one thing, the test of reasonableness upheld by the Constitutional Court of South Africa is presented as an alternative to the minimum core thesis of the UN Committee on Economic, Social and Cultural Rights[58] to advance a procedural understanding of the

[57] *Ibid.*, para. 77.

[58] See in particular General Comment No. 3 (1990); for a critique of the South African court's stance on the minimum core approach, see D. Bilchitz, *Poverty and Fundamental Rights: The Justification and Enforcement of Socio-Economic Rights* (Oxford, 2007), Chapter 5. On

socio-economic rights at issue. For the Court, the real issue is not to engage in the difficult task of pre-determining the content of the right *in abstracto* but to judge the reasonableness of the programme that is intended to realise it. While the test may or may not result in a deferent standard of review in any particular case, overall the line suggests an attempt to mediate human rights claims and governmental autonomy. The complexities deriving from the implementation of socio-economic rights has thus prompted the Court to establish basic guidelines which can facilitate the realisation of the right while still seeing the specific contours and content of the measures as a matter for the government. On the other hand, reasonableness is far from devoid of any substantive import. The test effectively impinges on the values of human dignity, freedom and, above all, equality, as the fundamental yardsticks against which governmental action must be measured.

Equality is not only a substantive value which defines the procedural parameter of reasonableness. It is *au fond* the expression of a free-standing procedural approach to substantive treatment, which concentrates on the beneficiaries of treatment rather than on treatment itself. As Baroness Hale remarked in *Ghaidan v. Godin-Mendoza* with regard to Article 8 ECHR:

> Everyone has the right to respect for their home. This does not mean that the state – or anyone else – has to supply everyone with a home. Nor does it mean that the state has to grant everyone a secure right to live in their home. But if it does grant that right to some, it must not withhold it from others in the same or an analogous situation. It must grant that right equally, unless the difference in treatment can be objectively justified.[59]

As *Khosa* shows, the judicial approach to equality gains in strength when it is combined with a particular substantive right. Here the predominantly procedural dimension of equality provides an indispensable standard by which respect for a free-standing right (*in casu*, the right to social security) can be judged.

In short, it is a complex interplay of substance and procedure, of substantive and procedural readings that appears to underpin the above jurisprudence. See

---

the other hand, in General Comment No. 9 (1998) the ICESCR Committee notes that 'there is no Covenant right which could not, in the great majority of systems, be considered to possess at least some significant justiciable dimension' (para. 10). For recent UN work on the drafting of an optional protocol to the International Covenant on Economic, Social and Cultural Rights establishing a complaints procedure, see e.g. *Report of the Open-ended Working Group on an optional protocol to the International Covenant on Economic, Social and Cultural Rights on its fifth session*, UN Doc. A/HRC/8/7. The optional protocol to the ICESCR was adopted by the General Assembly in December 2008, which recommended that it be open for signature in 2009: General Assembly GA/10795 (Doc. A/63/435).

[59] [2004] UKHL 30; [2004] 2 A.C. 557, at 135.

from this perspective, Ely and Habermas provide a narrower account of judicial review in pluralist democracies, to the extent that substantive perspectives on rights and their realisation are either rejected or deemed fundamentally unnecessary. In the context of socio-economic rights in national jurisdictions, that interplay reveals a more complex role of courts as the guardian of the political process, and deliberative democracy in particular. For one thing, the South African experience goes beyond Ely's minimalist procedural fairness designed to protect minority groups against discrimination in the interest bargaining of democracy. As Sandra Fredman notes, accountability, equality and deliberative elements are crucially reflected in the socio-economic rights jurisprudence of the Constitutional Court of South Africa.[60] While 'accountability' – in the sense of scrutinising the reasons for the state's failure to act or the state's choice to act in a particular way – arguably resembles Ely's test of review inspired by *Carolene Products*, it is the substantive equality perspective that enriches what is paradoxically still a procedural reading. Both *Grootboom*, *TAC* and *Khosa* relate the notion of reasonableness to the impact of exclusion on particular and most vulnerable sectors of society. There is a move beyond Ely's neutrality 'to openly endorse the substantive value of equality in protecting minorities'.[61]

At the same time, the interaction of procedural and substantive dimensions points to an expansive vision of the role of courts within the framework of deliberative democracy. Unlike Habermas' approach to judicial review which is limited to the application of fundamental rights norms in order to secure external processes of democratic will-formation, the socio-economic rights jurisprudence provides a richer account of judicial intervention as part and parcel of the deliberative effort. Access to court has been facilitated by public interest litigation in South Africa and India. Buttressed by such constitutional provisions as the directive principles, the Indian model has gone as far as to produce a variety of major procedural changes, including the relaxation of standing and initiating proceedings requirements, greater recourse to an inquisitorial approach as an alternative means of fact-finding, and the use of a wide range of remedies that may even dispense with the principle of *res judicata*.[62] Central to this scheme of 'social action litigation'[63] is the possibility for anyone acting bona fide, particularly NGOs, to establish proceedings

[60] S. Fredman, *Human Rights Transformed*, *supra* note 19, 113–123.

[61] *Ibid.*, p. 112.

[62] C. Foster & V. Jivan, 'Public Interest Litigation and Human Rights Implementation: The Indian and Australian Experience', *supra* note 45.

[63] U. Baxi, 'Taking Human Suffering Seriously: Social Action Litigation Before the Supreme Court of India', in N. Tiruchelvan & R. Coomaraswamy (eds.), *The Role of the Judiciary in Plural Societies* (New York, 1987).

on behalf of those persons who are unable to approach the Court for relief 'by reason of poverty, helplessness or disability or socially or economically disadvantageous position'.[64] While the South African judiciary remains fundamentally anchored to the traditional adversarial process, on James Tully's model, both Indian and South African public interest litigation can be regarded as a necessary procedural adjustment within struggles over recognition – this time in relation to resource distribution rather than identity. Wider standing and/or initiating proceedings rules result in wider discursive spaces for those individuals and groups whose perspectives will be represented in court. But most crucially, both the South African and Indian highest courts have endorsed the deliberative approach in ways that favour dialogue between the government and civil society both within and outside the courtroom.

The *TAC* case, for example, enabled an NGO to represent those who had had no voice in the political decision-making process by engaging the government in a discussion over HIV/AIDS policies in the country. The test of reasonableness mediated the claims by requiring the government to provide convincing explanations for those policies in the face of demands from civil society being backed up by medical evidence. In short, the Court facilitated genuine deliberation by involving those women who were most affected by the restrictions on the use of the antiretroviral drug. Major elements of deliberative democracy are also evident in cases involving eviction. In the recent *Occupiers of 51 Olivia Road v. City of Johannesburg*,[65] concerning occupiers of buildings in central Johannesburg facing eviction by the City's authorities, the Cape Town High Court issued an interim order calling upon the parties 'to engage with each other meaningfully' to resolve the dispute in the light of the Constitution and statutory provisions. As noted, in the much earlier *Olga Tellis* the Supreme Court of India found a duty to consult with the pavement dwellers to be a requirement of legality for any eviction proceedings. Equally importantly, judicial remedies have been provided in the form of orders to take action and report back to the court within a pre-defined timetable on the extent of compliance, thereby ensuring that the decision-making process continues and involves the applicant and other parties concerned.[66]

There are of course limits to such participation, some of which have proved controversial. For example, in *Olga Tellis* the Court did not go as far as to specifically mandate the provision of alternative pitches as condition prior to eviction and the necessary outcome of consultations. In another major public litigation case concerning the construction of a dam on the Narmada River in

[64] Justice Bhagwati in *S.P. Gupta v. Union of India* A.I.R. 1982 S.C. 149.
[65] Case No. CCT 24/07 Interim Order, 30 August 2007.
[66] S. Fredman, Human Rights Transformed, *supra* note 19, pp. 121, 126–128.

India,[67] an environmental group claimed *inter alia* that the right to life of the indigenous communities living in the area at issue would be breached because of the significant impact of the planned resettlement on those communities' way of life. While questioning the petitioners' credentials in representing the groups, the Court dismissed the claim on the grounds that the relocation would give these people better amenities and would facilitate their assimilation into the mainstream of society. This is not surprising, given India's still paternalistic attitude towards its indigenous groups (Adivasi) in the context of ILO Convention 107, the only one of the two ILO conventions (together with ILO Convention 169) which India has ratified.[68] More importantly, the Court took that view without giving the groups an opportunity to articulate their position first; they were heard only after the construction project and its concomitant resettlement had been allowed.[69] On a systemic level, these aspects tap into a wider set of problematic issues surrounding public interest litigation in India, ranging from the loose scope and representation of the public interest to the reluctance to challenge governmental policies which are backed up by strong political and economic forces, to the at times exceedingly pervasive nature of the judicial intervention in defiance of the separation of powers.[70]

But it is precisely because of these aspects that, on the deliberative model discussed in the previous section, the Indian and South African courts can represent deliberative actors as long as they, too, become exposed to public scrutiny and criticism. Discussing the Indian model, Christine Forster and Vedna Jivan have identified a range of beneficial extra-judicial effects of public interest litigation in relation to human rights compliance:

> These include PIL's ability to, first, mobilise human rights activists, civil society groups, lawyers and academics into a visible and persuasive movement; second, the creation of a forum and nexus where a number of powerful social actors, institutions and systems are forced to interact and consider human rights issues; and third, a capacity to engender awareness raising… [e]ven when public interest litigation has been unsuccessful…[71]

---

67 *Narmada Bachao Andolan v. Union of India* [2000] 10 S.C.C. 664.

68 For the conceptual underpinnings and implementation of ILO Convention 107, see L. Rodríguez-Piñero, *Indigenous Peoples, Postcolonialism, and International Law* (Oxford, 2005).

69 For an account of the *Narmada* case and related cases, see S. Fredman, *Human Rights Transformed, supra* note 19, pp. 138–141, 145–147.

70 *Ibid.*, pp. 124–149; C. Forster & V. Jivan, 'Public Interest Litigation and Human Rights Implementation', *supra* note 62.

71 C. Forster & V. Jivan, 'Public Interest Litigation and Human Rights Implementation', *supra* note 62, p. 31.

Most of these elements are reflected in the South African experience as well, though the procedural development of Indian public interest litigation remains unparalleled, due to inevitable differences in socio-political conditions. As mentioned earlier, James Tully, on his broad reading of participatory democracy in a pluralistic setting, sees courts as being not only part of such dynamic framework, but also as alternative catalysts for change. The *TAC* case illustrates the point in the context of socio-economic rights. On the one hand, the Court afforded an opportunity to the most affected by the antiretroviral drug restrictions, and ultimately civil society, to reverse governmental policies in the development of which they had had no role. In this sense, the courtroom served as an alternative avenue for change, just as in *Delgamuukw* before the Supreme Court of Canada or *Sagong Tasi* before the Malaysian state of Selangor's High Court indigenous groups used judicial intervention to their benefit in the face of gaps in the political process. At the same time, the South African Court issued a mandatory order, including the lifting of the restrictions and widespread testing and counselling in the public sector, which was based on the need for further deliberation and participation by all relevant bodies and actors concerned. The Court did not claim to have the last word on the matter; it was conscious that its avenue for recognition was, in Tully's words, 'less than perfect' and possibly in need of revision in accordance with human rights principles:

> A factor that needs to be kept in mind is that policy is and should be flexible. It may be changed at any time and the executive is always free to change policies where it considers it appropriate to do so. The only constraint is that policies must be consistent with the Constitution and the law. Court orders concerning policy choices made by the executive should therefore not be formulated in ways that preclude the executive from making such legitimate choices.[72]

Although the lack of supervisory content has been criticised, and other South African courts have introduced such content in later cases,[73] the order nevertheless provides an important indication of the role of judicial decisions on socio-economic rights (and other human rights) as part of a wider discursive exercise to which they can contribute procedurally and/or substantively.

International jurisprudence re-assessed

The fast-developing jurisprudence on socio-economic rights in the midst of controversies over the need for a court-like mechanism to realise those rights

---

[72] (2) 2002 (5) SA 721 (CC), para. 114.

[73] S. Fredman, *Human Rights Transformed, supra* note 19, p. 121.

nationally and internationally, effectively challenges traditional assumptions about the (in)ability of judicial discourse to engage with the complexities of human rights protection. The jurisprudence on minority issues examined in this book seems to reinforce the point, at least in empirical terms. But how exactly should we look at the conceptual dimensions of recognition, elaboration, mediation and access to justice illustrated in the previous chapters, in the light of the theoretical and practical insights into the role of courts that we have just discussed?

When we move from the domestic to the international realm, what Alexander Bickel famously described as 'counter-majoritarian difficulty' to capture the power of constitutional courts to override legislative measures adopted by elected representatives,[74] raises the question, *mutatis mutandis*, of the degree to which minority related judicial discourse is compatible with state sovereignty and the internal political processes that generated consent to the (human rights) treaty under which that discourse forms. On a procedural, Ely-style view, the need to counter the danger of judicial-like paternalism and law-making against the will of the parties arguably justifies judicial discourse solely to the extent that it serves minimum objectives which are embodied in the treaty, such as securing non-discrimination in the enjoyment of rights and facilitating the political process as the fundamental vehicle for the realisation of those rights. Indeed, if we assume some broadly understood notion of democracy to be one of the underlying objectives and upshots of human rights provisions, especially under general human rights treaties involving countries in transition towards more open systems,[75] then it can be argued that international jurisprudence is legitimate to the extent that it upholds rather than undermines the internal democratic process.

Seen from this perspective, the international jurisprudence on minority groups represents a fundamentally procedural exercise in that it sets limits on state intervention with a view to securing a fair and inclusive political process. Its aim is not to substitute for that process, but rather to rejuvenate it through human rights protection. The dimensions of judicial discourse discussed in Chapters 2–5 variably reflect this model. Whether it is pro-Kurdish movements in Turkey, minority organisations in Bulgaria, Greece or Poland, or minority churches in Moldova and elsewhere, the several cases decided under the ECHR regarding freedoms of association and expression, and/or freedom of religion, expose the role of the EurCrtHR as the guardian of the democratic process, regardless of the degree to which specific minority

[74] A. Bickel, *The Least Dangerous Branch: the Supreme Court at the Bar of Politics* (Indianapolis, 1962), p. 17.

[75] S. Marks & A. Clapham, *International Human Rights Lexicon* (Oxford, 2005), pp. 61–70.

claims are upheld in the relevant domestic legal orders. In *Gorzelik*, the Grand Chamber captured this aspect by referring to the essential role being played by minority associations 'to the proper functioning of democracy' and embracing the notion that 'pluralism is also built on the genuine recognition of, and respect for, diversity and the dynamics of cultural traditions'. The point of this case law is not to be found in the rather advanced levels of minority protection (or even secessionist options) that the applicants advocated in their own context, but in the constraints being placed on the government by the EurCrHR in defence of a democratic process within which substantive claims to minority protection can be made. This procedural approach anchored to the notion of democratic participation is not merely an upshot of the lack of minority provisions in the ECHR, but as we have seen, reflects a deeper element of international jurisprudence concerning minority groups.

For example, Article 27 ICCPR and indigenous land claims under the Inter-American system have generated a discourse revolving around fundamental procedural benchmarks against which state interference is to be judged. The test of consultation set out by the HRC in the *Länsmann* or *Apirana Mahuika* cases under the minority rights provision of the Covenant exemplifies the participation-oriented approach to minority issues which is effectively geared towards facilitating an open deliberative exercise between the parties at the domestic level. In this sense, the HRC is concerned with the fairness and effectiveness of the participatory process while leaving the specific contours and content of the arrangements to direct state-group negotiations.

The theme of democratic participation is reinforced by the broader narrative of self-determination, both within and outside the ICCPR. In *Katangese Peoples' Congress*, involving a claim to independence by the province of Katanga under Article 20 ACHPR, the reference by the AfrCommHPR to the right of the Katangese to participate in government was in fact permeated by the recognition of the internal dimension of self-determination in its multiple variants.[76] In the *Ogoni* case, one of the key elements leading up to a finding of a breach of Article 21 was that 'the government did not involve the Ogoni Communities in the decisions that affected the development of Ogoniland'.[77] The case of indigenous property rights in several instances

[76] Comm. No. 75/92 (1995): '[S]elf-determination may be exercised in any of the following ways independence, self-government, local government, federalism, confederalism, unitarism or any other form of relations that accords with the wishes of the people'. In the AfrCommHPR's Advisory Opinion on *the United Nations Declaration on the Rights of Indigenous Peoples*, adopted in May 2007, the participatory content of indigenous self-determination short of secession is strongly reaffirmed (para. 27).

[77] *The Social and Economic Rights Action Center for Economic and Social Rights v. Nigeria*, Comm. No. 155/96, 2001, para. 55.

before the IACommHR and IACrtHR represents an even more sophisticated effort to spell out the procedural requirements of the decision-making process relating to land disputes. While indigenous consultation and informed consent stand out as the most veritable mantra of the Inter-American land rights jurisprudence, the actual content of indigenous property rights hinges on an 'effective mechanism'[78] through which the group's traditional land use practices feed into the process of identifying indigenous territories and their exact boundaries, and relate to any outstanding inter-community claims and claims from private parties. This somehow echoes the housing related dispute in *Grootboom* before the South African Constitutional Court, in that the complexities deriving from the implementation of the right to housing prompted the Court to provide basic guidelines which could facilitate the realisation of that right, while still seeing the details of the housing programme as a matter for the government.[79] On the other hand, the judicial intervention in *Grootboom* supported the democratic process by building a solid element of accountability into the design of public policies by the state.

Indeed, aside from participation, equality exposes another major procedural dimension embraced by judicial discourse to secure effective decision-making. At the domestic level, *Khosa* before the South African Constitutional Court and *Ghaidan* before the British House of Lords – both with significant socio-economic overtones – clearly illustrate the point by concentrating, not on the need or a duty to provide certain benefits, but on the ways in which those benefits have been granted. At the international level, *Broeks v. The Netherlands*,[80] reproduces this approach in the context of social security:

> The Committee observes in this connection that what is at issue is not whether or not social security should be progressively established in the Netherlands, but whether the legislation providing for social security violates the prohibition against discrimination contained in Article 26 of the International Covenant on Civil and Political Rights and the guarantee given therein to all persons regarding equal and effective protection against discrimination.[81]

More importantly, this line has direct resonance with retrospective interventions designed to generate adjustments to pro-active political processes that are fundamentally unfair towards certain ethno-cultural minority groups or persons belonging to them. The argument was squarely made in *Waldman*,

---

[78] *Moiwana Village v. Suriname*, IACrtHR, Judgment of 15 June 2005, Series C No. 124, para. 19.

[79] As noted, *Olga Tellis* before the Supreme Court of India also exposes the dimension of consultation/due process, though the lack of mandatory alternative accommodation falls behind the requirement of alternative land in indigenous jurisprudence.

[80] Comm. 172/1984, Views of 9 April 1987, (1987) Annual Report 139.

[81] *Ibid.*, para. 12.5.

involving a constitutionally protected preferential treatment accorded to the Roman Catholic minority schools compared to other minority schools:

> In this context, the Committee observes that the Covenant does not oblige States parties to fund schools which are established on a religious basis. However, if a State party chooses to provide public funding to religious schools, it should make this funding available without discrimination.[82]

A similar pattern is reflected in cases where more articulated minority regimes have been established by the state. For example, in *Ballantyne* (and related Canadian jurisprudence) the HRC did not challenge the legitimacy or overall legality of Quebec's autonomy, it only policed the boundaries of that regime in ways that secured equal protection for the rights of the English-speakers living in the province. Broadly comparable narratives underpin jurisprudential interventions in the complex relationship between minority protection and women's rights. On a positive reading of *Refah Partisi* before the EurCrtHR, equality – especially in terms of gender and individual freedoms – becomes the most crucial 'democratic' test for personal law regimes once the state has freely chosen to adopt them. *Lovelace* before the HRC, and by analogy *Shah Bano* before the Supreme Court of India, can be seen as interventions aimed at correcting, not contesting or replacing, minority legislation in order to enhance the quality of the protective measures.

In short, on an expanded view of Ely's 'representation-reinforcing' theory of judicial review, and more generally Habermas' model of deliberative democracy, significant aspects of international jurisprudence relating to minority issues resonate with the role of judicial discourse as the guardian of the political process within states parties. Central to this perspective is the acknowledgment of a political space that interposes itself between that discourse and the actual realisation of rights. *Chapman* on Roma issues and especially *Noack* regarding the Sorbian minority in Germany, do not go as far as to intervene in the domestic debate over the most appropriate level of protection to be afforded to the group, but effectively require an open and pluralistic decision-making process that duly accounts for the minority perspective. From this point of view, the EurCrtHR facilitates democratic deliberation in Habermas' sense, thereby refraining from upholding specific substantive outcomes. The various duties upon the state regarding land demarcation, titling, and redress found by both the IACommHR and the IACrtHR in an ever greater number of indigenous disputes, are illustrations of the degree to which judicial discourse does provide procedural guidance to the political process in ways

[82] Comm. No. 694/1996, Views of 3 November 1999, UN Doc. CCPR/C/67/D/694/1996 (1996), para. 10.6.

that facilitate (and indeed require) direct engagement by the state with the groups concerned. So much so that, as discussed in Chapters 3 and 4, the IACrtHR has even set forth benchmarks for the state to be able to examine equally valid indigenous and private claims to the land, and therefore to determine on a case-by-case basis the 'legality, necessity and proportionality' of expropriation of privately owned land as a way of attaining a legitimate objective in a democratic society.[83]

Tests of proportionality or reasonableness have equally come to define the procedural dimension of judicial discourse with a view to implicitly upholding spheres of autonomy for policy-makers. For example, in *Bickel and Franz* before the ECJ did not declare the minority regime in South Tyrol as being *tout court* incompatible with EC law, but did conclude that denial of extension of that regime to German-speaking nationals of other member states was in breach of the EC right to freedom of movement. By regarding minority protection as a 'legitimate aim' and setting out a proportionality requirement, the ECJ deferred to internal political processes and defined the boundaries of its own intervention from the perspective of the Community legal order. The test of reasonableness established by the South African Constitutional Court in relation to socio-economic rights reflects a largely comparable approach in its own context: the Court assumed in *Grootboom* that the government was free to develop a comprehensive housing programme out of a 'wide range of possible measures', and that considering reasonableness would not involve a decision of whether other more effective or useful measures could have been adopted. In their own distinctive ways, both *Bickel and Franz* and *Grootboom* exemplify *ex-post-facto* interventions over matters whose contours and content are bound to remain within the domain of the government. It could be said that 'proportionality' (broadly understood) has mainly served as a regulatory criterion for either securing participation of minority groups in the political process (under the ECHR, for example)[84] or exposing – in synergy with the principle of equality – the outer limits of the legal space left for a permissible minority regime under the relevant instruments.

To the extent that international jurisprudence on minority issues can be loosely justified on the basis of Ely's and Habermas' model of judicial review, that is, on the basis of that jurisprudence's (minimalist) contribution to upholding the internal democratic process, it crucially involves the

[83] *Yakye Axa Indigenous Community v. Paraguay*, Judgment of 17 June 2005, Series C No. 125, para. 217.

[84] As mentioned in earlier chapters, the HRC has used a proportionality test in the sense of assessing the impact of state measures on the continuing protection of the group following the process of consultation.

more general question of constraining state discretion, or – in the language of the EurCrtHR – the state's margin of appreciation. For, surely, judicial discourse can prove lenient towards state autonomy in a way that the balance of competing claims is more easily struck in favour of the public authorities than the group. As mentioned in Chapter 3, in *Otto-Preminger-Institut*, the confiscation by the Austrian authorities of a film that the Roman Catholic Church deemed offensive to the Catholic religion was principally justified by the EurCrtHR on the grounds that the vast majority of people living in Tyrol professed that religion and that, consequently, the national authorities were in a better position to assess the necessity of the interference with freedom of expression. This obvious – and rightly criticised – case of 'moral majoritarianism'[85] somewhat resonates with the kind of leeway enjoyed by the state vis-à-vis ethno-cultural groups in a number of practical instances. For example, in *G and E* the EurCommHR concluded that the construction of the hydroelectric plant in question did interfere with the minority group's way of life but could be justified because of the economic well-being of the country. Comparatively speaking, the narrative of economic development is a most powerful theme in the *Narmada* case considered in the previous section, where the Supreme Court of India held that the relocation of the indigenous communities concerned would even facilitate their assimilation into mainstream society, in line with the paternalistic rationale of ILO Convention 107.[86] In *Gorzelik*, the EurCrtHR eventually rejected the applicants' claim that denial of registration as a national minority violated Article 11 ECHR by stressing that they should be prepared to limit their freedoms for the stability of the country, defined by the protection of Poland's electoral system. Along broadly similar lines, in *The Gypsy Council and others v. the United Kingdom*,[87] the EurCrtHR held that the Horsmonden Horse Fair was indeed a traditional gathering of longstanding and considerable cultural importance to the Roma/Gypsy group, but the prohibition order complained of was proportionate in terms of Article 11 as it was intended to respond to the legitimate interests of the community as a whole. In *Chapman*, the EurCrtHR clung on to the state's margin of appreciation to dismiss a duty to make available to the group a number of suitably equipped caravan sites in parallel to the implementation of general planning policies.

---

85 G. Letsas, A *Theory of Interpretation of the European Convention on Human Rights* (Oxford, 2007), pp. 120–123; E. Benvenisti, 'Margin of Appreciation, Consensus and Universal Standards' (1998–1999) 31 *New York Journal of International Law and Politics*, p. 843 et seq.

86 S. Fredman, *Human Rights Transformed, supra* note 19, p. 142.

87 Application No. 66336/01, Admissibility Decision of 14 May 2002.

If on the procedural model, minority related judicial discourse serves as the guardian of a fair and inclusive, political – essentially deliberative – process, how can this same model respond to the possibility of pro-state (and effectively majority)-indulgences of that discourse? The question may seem redundant as long as every uncritically pro-state balancing act is taken to simply reflect the body's failure to perform the role assigned to it under the procedural model. In fact, it is especially relevant to those – rather numerous – minority group cases that reveal (or are believed to reveal) some degree of genuine empirical uncertainty.

Some examples come to mind. In *DH and others* the EurCrtHR was asked, not to determine the most appropriate educational system capable of accommodating minority interests, but to address the more difficult question of establishing the impact that a particular system of special schools was having on the Roma community in the country. In *Mary and Carrie Dann*, the key issue was whether or not indigenous property title had extinguished as a result of an internal process that had taken place several decades earlier. In *Gorzelik*, a variety of empirically controversial aspects was raised directly or indirectly, including the existence of a national minority, the group's 'real' intentions in relation to the benefits that accrued to registered national minorities under Polish electoral law, and the repercussions of the group obtaining such benefits on other groups deemed to be in a comparable situation. In the *Länsman* cases, the HRC was confronted with the factually problematic issue of determining the extent to which economic activities by enterprises had encroached on the Samis' way of life. So, how to contain state discretion in this sort of cases from a procedural perspective? How to tackle the practical uncertainty posed by establishing the effectiveness of a particular educational system in relation to a particular minority community, the actual existence of such community, an earlier extinguishment of an indigenous property title, or the real level of intrusiveness of external economic development activities on a minority group's way of life?

Based on international and European case law, Julian Rivers has usefully broken down the concept of margin of appreciation to include at least three forms of state discretion: policy-choice discretion, cultural discretion, and evidential discretion.[88] The first form turns on the range of necessary policy options which may variably affect the enjoyment of a right; the second form points to the hierarchies of values upheld by the state in relation to the limitation of the right; the third type is concerned with the factual basis for justifying

[88] J. Rivers, 'Proportionality and Discretion in International and European Law', in N. Tsagourias (ed.), *Transnational Constitutionalism: International and European Perspectives* (Cambridge, 2007), p. 107 et seq., at 113–122.

that limitation. The latter type of discretion becomes crucially important as costs and benefits implied by the first two types rely on assumptions which may be difficult to prove. While all of these types of discretion are measured against the test of proportionality, most notably the extent to which a rights interference pursues a legitimate aim, and reflects a proper relationship between the measures adopted and the aim sought to be realised, each type of discretion does affect the balancing act required by the proportionality review in ways that allow for a greater or lesser margin of appreciation for the state. It should be noted that several cases involving minority issues expose some, if not all of those forms of state discretion. For example, in the first *Länsman* case, the HRC recognised that Finland was entitled 'to encourage development or allow economic activity by enterprises', but it went on to say that the scope of such freedom was not to be assessed by reference to a margin of appreciation, but by reference to the obligations deriving from Article 27 ICCPR. In other words, there is no room for cultural discretion in the event of an encroachment on Article 27 rights. At the same time, the focus shifted to evidential matters as the HRC affirmed that the central issue in the case was whether the impact of the quarrying on Mount Riutusvaara was 'so substantial' as to effectively amount to a denial of the authors' minority rights.

Limits on cultural discretion should thus be seen to include any improper interference with group diversity at the sub-national level. The recent case law of the EurCrtHR regarding freedom of association and expression can be taken to imply a solid rejection of any form of cultural discretion that is paradoxically used to suppress the manifestation of cultural diversity within the state; equally importantly on a conceptual level, *Chapman* does recognise protection of a minority group's way of life in the context of Article 8 ECHR. On the other hand, the ECJ in *Bickel and Franz* upholds minority protection as a (positive) variant of cultural discretion at the level of the member states, while still stressing the need to achieve a stricter degree of uniformity at the level of the Community legal order.

From the procedural perspective under discussion, a key form of the margin of appreciation is evidential discretion. While constraints on cultural discretion may result in a stringent evidential test as the limitation affects basic human rights such as freedom of association, evidential matters acquire special significance whenever the case reflects empirical difficulties which are linked to wider issues of policy, and thus calls for a more complex balancing act. It is at this point that we should return to the question raised earlier: assuming a minimalist, procedural role for minority related international jurisprudence, how do we deal with problematic dimensions such as the impact of a particular educational system or a particular development project on a minority group, the actual existence of a minority group and its relationship with other groups, or an earlier extinguishment of an indigenous property title?

As explained by Julian Rivers on the basis of the jurisprudence of the HRC, the EurCrtHR and the ECJ, the proportionality review relating to evidential discretion mainly revolves around the reliability of factual judgments, or more broadly, the quality of the internal process leading up to the decision-taker's assessment:

> The deference that the court shows to primary decision-takers is thus not intrinsic or uniform, but it is a willingness to believe the decision-taker's assessment of the likelihood of gains, a willingness which should reduce with the seriousness of the limitation of the right in question and increase with the demonstration that the decision-taker adopted processes more likely to reach right answers to the relevant empirical questions.[89]

Aside from the precise – at times controversial – level of review under particular instruments,[90] a scrutiny which is anchored to the plausible, process-based character of factual prognoses seems to provide an important principled test for limiting state discretion in the context of minority disputes. Indeed, on the procedural model espoused above, not only is such scrutiny inherently necessary, it arguably requires careful assessment of the level of involvement of the affected group (or group member) in the deliberative process that informed the state's factual analysis and consequently the measures under review. Recent international jurisprudence on minority issues confirms the importance of this evidential test.

In *DH and others*, the Czech Republic argued that the difference in treatment between Roma children and non-Roma children was justified on the basis that the education system required special schools to be made available for those children – most of them of Roma origin – with special needs. They defended their general statements about the situation of Roma children by invoking psychological tests of these children's intellectual capacities and parental consent to them being placed in the special schools at issue. Having established a *prima facie* case of indirect discrimination against Roma children, the Grand Chamber did not discuss the suitability of special schools in the abstract, but recognised – somewhat in line with the Chamber's decision – a certain margin of appreciation in the government's desire to respond to the situation of children with particular educational needs. However, what the Grand Chamber did investigate was the very factual basis for such a difference

[89] *Ibid.*, p. 122; a practical example might be *Evans v. UK* (2006) 43 EHRR 41, p. 79, where the EurCrtHR was satisfied that legislation on assisted reproduction had been passed following 'an exceptionally detailed examination of the social, ethical and legal implications of developments' in the field.

[90] J. Rivers, 'Proportionality and Discretion in International and European Law', *supra* note 88, pp. 120–129.

in treatment, or more generally, the adequacy of the process that had led up to the adoption of the contested measures. Seen from this perspective, the Grand Chamber concluded that neither the psychological tests nor the parental consent invoked by the government reflected a reliable basis for justifying the system of special schools. As for the tests, it observed that there was a 'danger that [they] were biased and that the results were not analysed in the light of the particularities and special characteristics of the Roma children who sat them'.[91] More importantly, it was found that the parents of the Roma children had not been put in a position to fully and effectively participate in this process. In fact, the authorities had taken no 'additional measures to ensure that the Roma parents received all the information they needed to make an informed decision or were aware of the consequences that giving their consent would have for their children's futures'.[92]

A broadly similar procedural line is reflected in *Mary and Carrie Dann* before the IACommHR, in relation to the United States' contention that the property title of the Western Shoshone had extinguished several decades earlier following the findings of the Indian Claims Commission. While the United States had invoked the internal process, including domestic court findings, as providing the factual basis for its position vis-à-vis the applicants, the IACommHR limited state discretion by addressing the question in terms of the reliability of that process and the factual judgments that it had generated:

> This includes such matters as the adequacy of the procedures through which the petitioners' property interests in the Western Shoshone ancestral land were purported to be determined. While proceedings or determinations at the domestic level on similar issues can be considered by the Commission as part of the circumstances of a complaint, they are not determinative of the Commission's own evaluation of the facts and issues in a petition before it…The Commission hastens to add in this connection that, contrary to what the State appears to contend in its response, the domestic courts did not reach consistent or clear decisions on certain central aspects of the petitioners' complaints relating to the Western Shoshone ancestral land, including particularly the question of whether the alleged extinguishment of indigenous title in the land had ever been litigated before domestic authorities as well as whether the Danns' due process rights were properly respected in the domestic process.[93]

---

[91] Application No. 57325/00, Judgment of 13 November 2007 [GC], para. 201.

[92] *Ibid.*, para. 203. A similar approach to the nature and content of such tests as well as the quality of parental consent was taken in *Affaire Sampanis et Autres c. Grèce*, Application No. 32526/05, Judgment of 5 June 2008 (final on 5 September 2008), paras. 90, 92, 94 (in French). A similar claim is being currently made by applicants in the *Case of Oršuš and Others v. Croatia*, Application No. 15766/03, Request for Referral to the Grand Chamber on Behalf of the Applicants, 13 October 2008, paras. 15, 16, 20, 21, 33.

[93] Report No. 75/02, Case 11.1140, December 27, 2002, para. 164.

Reaffirming one of the general themes of the land rights jurisprudence, the quality of the process is once again measured against the level of involvement of the group in it. In this respect, the IACommHR found that that process had 'proved defective':

> That only proof of fraud or collusion could impugn the Temoak Band's presumed representation of the entire Western Shoshone people, and that Western Shoshone General Council meetings occurred on only three occasions during the 18 year period between 1947 and 1965, fails to discharge the State's obligation to demonstrate that the outcome of the ICC process resulted from the fully informed and mutual consent of the Western Shoshone people as a whole.[94]

In other cases, constraints on state discretion have been set by refraining from making a choice between the state's and the group members' perspectives in circumstances where the internal process is not sufficiently reliable. In *George Howard* and *Anni Äärelä*, both decided by the HRC, the different views of the parties were accounted for in relation to the actual impact of the measures in question on the authors' Article 27 rights. The HRC concluded that it was unable to reach independent conclusions on the matter, because national courts were either silent on the relevant questions of fact or did not appear to be sufficiently convincing. In *Anni Äärelä*, the HRC noted that the authors had been consulted in the development of the logging plans by the Forestry Service and that the lower and higher courts had taken different views of the expert evidence produced. The reliability of factual judgments assumed by the state was implicitly questioned without conceding a breach of Article 27. By contrast, in the *Länsman* cases before the HRC, and *Noack* before the EurCrtHR, the state's argument was accepted precisely because, in circumstances of disagreement over empirical questions, the internal process leading up to the relevant decisions was deemed sufficiently plausible. In other words, the problematic evidential matters raised by these cases were ultimately addressed, not in terms of the exact and incontrovertible nature of facts, but in terms of an adequate assessment of the issues involved, including an opportunity for the group as a whole to effectively have its own perspective fed into such process. In *Noack*, the EurCrtHR referred to its 'plus grand devoir de vigilance' in such matters, and noted the extensive debate that had been conducted over the past several years over whether to relocate the Sorbian minority, which had included consultation with the group and an assessment of the implications of the relocation for the continuing enjoyment of its distinctive way of life. The first *Länsman* case captures this procedural line by inferring the reliability of the process from the group's involvement

[94] *Ibid.*, para. 165.

and other plausible indicators of the limited impact of the mining activities on the Sami community.

If review of process and its malfunctioning can be regarded as the bottom line of a procedural approach inspired by Ely's participation-oriented theory of judicial review and Habermas' conception of deliberative democracy – particularly in circumstances of disagreement over the empirical basis for considering minority issues and the extent to which evidential state discretion can and should be limited – then *Gorzelik* appears to defy this approach in one important respect. While the EurCrtHR relied on domestic court findings to respond to the claim made by the applicants that the Silesians constituted a national minority, and limited in principle state discretion by appealing to 'rigorous' European supervision, in practice it failed to assess the adequacy of the internal process that was at the very basis of the controversial empirical assumptions made by Poland. The EurCrtHR had noted that there was no internal mechanism through which national minority status could be sought, though there did exist legislation allocating electoral benefits to registered associations of national minorities. No specific evidence had been produced by the government of the impact that national minority status for the Silesians could have on the groups it referred to in the proceedings. The electoral benefits possibly resulting from recognition of the Silesians as a national minority were based on purely speculative reasoning as to the intentions of the applicants. The EurCrtHR conceded that the lack of an internal mechanism for obtaining national minority status, while not the subject of an international obligation incumbent upon Poland, did represent a lacuna in Polish law. However, it failed to link this element to the reliability of the general statements made by the government and domestic courts on the matter. The Grand Chamber made no attempt to investigate into the plausibility of the distinction between 'national minorities' and 'ethnic minorities' in Article 35 of the Polish Constitution from the perspective of international law,[95] the adequacy of the understanding of national minority espoused by Polish courts, the equality implications of such understanding in relation to the legislation on electoral benefits for registered national minorities, and above all, the lack of opportunity for the Silesians (and possibly other groups as well) to participate in the process that informed the factual analysis.[96] Poland's wide margin of appreciation was upheld because it was perceived that protecting

[95] 'National minority' in Article 14 ECHR arguably qualifies as an autonomous concept and its core meaning cannot be reduced to merely national perspectives. On the doctrine of autonomous concepts, see G. Letsas, 'The Truth in Autonomous Concepts: How To Interpret the ECHR', (2004) 15 *European Journal of International Law*, pp. 279–305.

[96] G. Pentassuglia, 'Inside and Outside the European Convention: The Case of Minorities Compared' (2006) 6 *Baltic Yearbook of International Law*, p. 285, note 76.

a country's electoral stability outweighed the claim made by the Silesians – a group already recognised as an 'ethnic' minority – to call themselves (and be recognised as) a 'national' minority. Yet, evidential state discretion did appear rather uncontrolled in the face of empirical uncertainty.

Expanding on the procedural model

This procedural reading involves not only the elaboration of human rights provisions and the mediating role of that discourse in connection with complex human rights claims, but also the dimensions of recognition and access to justice.

As mentioned in Chapter 2, the EurCrtHR has hardly addressed the specific question of whether the community concerned is a minority group in the sense of international law. However, it has upheld freedom of association (and expression) as a fundamental element of an open society in which national and sub-national identities can be freely asserted and debated, and for which protection can be sought. As the EurCrtHR put it in *Stankov*:

> Freedom of assembly and the right to express one's views through it are among the paramount values of a democratic society. The essence of democracy is its capacity to resolve problems through open debate. Sweeping measures of a preventive nature to suppress freedom of assembly and expression other than in cases of incitement to violence or rejection of democratic principles – however shocking and unacceptable certain views or words used may appear to the authorities, and however illegitimate the demands made may be – do a disservice to democracy and often even endanger it. In a democratic society based on the rule of law, political ideas which challenge the existing order and whose realisation is advocated by peaceful means must be afforded a proper opportunity of expression through the exercise of the right of assembly as well as by other lawful means.[97]

In *Gorzelik*, the Grand Chamber established a crucial connection between associations 'seeking an ethnic identity or asserting a minority consciousness' and the quality of the democratic process:

---

[97] Applications Nos. 29221/95 and 292225/95, Judgment of 2 October 2001, para. 97; see also *United Communist Party of Turkey and others v. Turkey*, Judgment of 30 January 1998, Reports 1998-I: 'The Court considers one of the principal characteristics of democracy to be the possibility it offers of resolving a country's problems through dialogue, without recourse to violence, even when they are irksome. Democracy thrives on freedom of expression. From that point of view, there can be no justification for hindering a political group solely because it seeks to debate in public the situation of part of the State's population and to take part in the nation's political life in order to find, according to democratic rules, solutions capable of satisfying everyone concerned' (para. 57).

> It is only natural that, where a civil society is functioning in a healthy manner, the participation of citizens in the democratic process is to a large extent achieved through belonging to associations in which they may integrate with each other and pursue collectively common objectives.[98]

By emphasising the role of free and equal citizens engaged in public debate over identity issues and claims, the EurCrtHR arguably approximates Habermas' deliberative model based on consensus-seeking processes of democratic deliberation – this time in relation to group recognition. A distinctive feature of this approach is its insistence that, aside from the established set of decision-making procedures and institutions, democracy is ultimately a function of genuine participation of civil society (or the 'weak' public spheres of civil society, in Habermas' sense) in a broadly understood deliberative process. As Seyla Benhabib explains:

> Deliberative democracy focuses on social movements, and on the civil, religious, artistic, and political associations of the unofficial public sphere, as well. The public sphere is composed of the anonymous and interlocking conversations and contestation resulting from the activities of these various groups.[99]

When applying this model to cultural disputes, she defines groups' claims and status as being the result of complex societal (political and moral) dialogues where identities, far from being immutable and monolithic, are acknowledged or re-invented.[100] In other words, the key point for Benhabib is not the defence of group identities per se, but rather the creation of conditions under which those identities can be appropriated or re-appropriated through public discourse. Seen from this perspective, the above-mentioned ECHR jurisprudence can be said to promote deliberative democracy to the extent that it facilitates the conditions for an exchange of perspectives on the understanding of national identity and the existence of groups struggling for recognition within the state.

At the same time, *Gorzelik* arguably exposes the limits of a deliberative model that endorses a somewhat rigid separation between courts and civil society. The EurCrtHR refrained from providing guidance on the status of the Polish Silesians, on the assumption that this matter would be openly debated within Polish society and that the ECHR rights to freedom of expression and association would enable this debate to develop within the canons of democratic discourse and deliberation. While formally safeguarding the political process, the EurCrtHR overlooked the reality of an unbalance between the role

[98] Application No. 44158/9820, Judgment of 17 February 2004 [GC], para. 92.

[99] S. Benhabib, *The Claims of Culture: Equality and Diversity in the Global Era* (Princeton, 2002), p. 21.

[100] *Ibid.*, pp. 70–71.

of civil society (including minority associations) and governmental (majority)-decision making. The lack of an objective mechanism to seek and obtain recognition as a national minority status in spite of legislation conferring particular benefits on registered national minorities underscored the unilateral rather than dialogical character of the internal process. Seeing courts as being somewhat in opposition to, or divorced from the deliberative exercise that is due to take place in the political arena may well deprive individuals and groups of indispensable checks and balances involving the way public discourse and deliberation are actually conducted. It is entirely possible that, in circumstances like those underlying *Gorzelik*, majority-decision making will leave the minority group unrecognised just as it was at the start of any public discourse about recognition. As aptly noted by Steven Wheatley, '[t]he fact of procedural inclusion [of ethno-cultural minority groups] is unlikely to alter the outcomes of decision-making processes'.[101]

We need an enriched account of the procedural reading of judicial discourse that is based on an expansive view of the discursive or communicative approach. There are interesting parallels here with James Tully's insights into the dynamic of decision-making processes. As mentioned earlier, while a staunch advocate of participatory democracy centred on the driving force of civil society, he makes a crucial distinction between public discourse and actual decision-taking:

> The power of the exchange of reasons among the members of an association to unsettle the prejudices and alter the outlooks of the most powerful groups is limited... [t]herefore, minorities need to be able to appeal to other decision-taking institutions at the end of the dialogue, such as courts, parliaments, international human rights regimes, non-partisan adjudicators or mediators, global transnational networks and so on. These too are imperfect and need to be open to challenge in turn, but they provide indispensable checks and balances on the powers of the dominant groups to manipulate the dialogue and manufacture agreement.[102]

Thus, for Tully a civil society-based approach to public deliberation, involving struggles over recognition, still requires a variety of actors including domestic and international adjudicators, to act as countervailing forces to a public discourse controlled by the majority because of its structural (financial, political, argumentative) dominance. More importantly, judicial discourse should be regarded as part of wider 'multilogues' generated by that public process. On Tully's approach, courts can and should play a more active role than Habermas or Benhabib would be probably prepared to concede. They

[101] S. Wheatley, *Democracy, Minorities and International Law*, (Cambridge, 2005), p. 160.

[102] J. Tully, 'The Practice of Law-Making', *supra* note 30, p. 39.

help shape the debate in dialogue with the actors concerned, and do represent alternative (though 'less than perfect') avenues for recognition through participation. As he explains, there is no reason to believe that the participatory process should take place only by means of particular formal or informal sets of procedures. '[T]he discussions, negotiations and contestations take place in a variety of practices and procedures, and the legitimacy of these is itself part of the discussion'.[103] Reasonable disagreement can thus be detected at the level of both substance and procedure.

In parallel with this view of the discursive model, an enriched procedural account of the international jurisprudence on minority issues can be offered in terms of both recognition and access to justice. We have already mentioned the impact of domestic courts on recognition of groups and claims in a number of jurisdictions. *Delgamuukw* culminated a litigation strategy aimed at achieving an alternative form of recognition for indigenous communities and their land under the Canadian Charter; *Kayano* culminated a process of recognition of the Ainu in Japan as a minority group; *Sagong Tasi* recognised (limited) protection for indigenous land rights in Malaysia.[104] Broadly comparable examples are offered by the domestic jurisprudence on socio-economic rights.[105] International supervisory bodies, too, can represent alternative avenues for obtaining that group status or protection which is being questioned or denied by the political process. For example, as discussed in Chapter 2, in both *Moiwana* and *Saramaka* the IACrtHR recognised the groups at issue as distinct tribal communities similar to indigenous peoples, despite their not being indigenous to their traditional territories.[106] Interestingly, Suriname had argued in *Saramaka* that the Saramaka people did not make up a coherent community qualifying for protection because some of their members lived outside of the traditional Saramaka territory. The IACrtHR dismissed the argument by focusing on the Saramakas' special attachment to their land and therefore applying – like in *Moiwana* – the notion of indigenous property rights under Article 21 ACHR. As we have seen, judicial discourse can impact on group recognition in a variety of other ways, including the upholding of the group's structures and legal personality as a way of effectively enjoying human rights protection. More generally, international jurisprudence has made a contribution to exposing spaces of identity within the legal sphere.

---

[103] Id., 'Introduction', *supra* note 32, p. 20.

[104] See *supra* in this chapter, and Chapter 2.

[105] See e.g. the *TAC* case, (2) 2002 (5) SA 721 (CC).

[106] Within the African context this line is echoed by the AfrCommHPR's understanding of indigenousness as not being limited to 'first inhabitants': Advisory Opinion of the African Commission on Human and Peoples' Rights on *The United Nations Declaration on the Rights of Indigenous Peoples*, May 2007, paras. 9–13.

Western Sahara, for instance, unearthed the indigenous experience suppressed by the experience of European colonialism and found 'legal ties' between the nomadic tribes of the territory and other tribes of neighbouring regions.

The central point is that, from a procedural perspective, this jurisprudence can contribute within certain limits to changing Tully's 'norms of recognition' by enabling minority groups as such to enter the legal and political space in ways that provide an essential benchmark within a wider international and domestic human rights discourse. It is not just that consensus cannot be achieved and reasonable disagreement requires judicial intervention, let alone that such intervention is meant to substitute for the political process. Rather, international jurisprudence can be appreciated (also) in terms of ensuring that the group acquire legal significance to such an extent as to be recognised within the participatory process.

Indeed, if it is accepted that international supervisory bodies can and should be seen – like domestic courts – as both alternative deliberative actors and part of a wider network of deliberative actors involving the legal community and the public at large, then rules governing standing, intervention, evidence and remedies stand out as particularly crucial procedural tests of the ability of judicial discourse to respond to the participatory challenges posed by minority groups and third-parties concerned. As demonstrated in Chapter 4, several human rights supervisory organs have not only guaranteed wider access to internal dispute settlement procedures or expanded their own jurisdiction *ratione temporis*, but have also adjusted (or are now adjusting) their rules of procedure – to a greater or lesser extent – in an attempt to allow for better representation of the group's perspectives. In terms of *locus standi*, the practice of the HRC, CERD, Inter-American system and the African system have provided important illustrations of this trend. Despite the obvious specificities of each of these mechanisms as defined by the treaty under which they have been established, they all reflect an effort to enlarge the boundaries of effective participation of minority groups within the context of their own complaints procedures. They form a continuum in terms of the intensity of the victim requirement and the level of representation brought about by the petitioning from minority organisations and NGOs. Interestingly, the more relaxed the victim requirement and the higher the degree of group representation – for example, under the Inter-American and African systems – the more the adjudicatory mechanism echoes the South African, and most notably (judicially-generated) Indian experience of public interest litigation which we discussed earlier in this chapter. As noted, procedural changes have allowed a greater measure of collective representation, particularly through NGOs, in relation to socio-economic claims, and can be regarded necessary procedural adjustments within struggles over recognition defined by resource distribution. Both the Constitutional Court of South Africa and the Supreme Court of India have taken centre stage in a process of dialogue with the government, vulnerable communities and civil society at large. While none of the above-mentioned international mechanisms comes anywhere near the generosity of the Indian model, especially (though not exclusively) on initiating proceedings and fact-finding,[107] it can be argued that the Inter-American indigenous land rights jurisprudence, as well as the African jurisprudence (as illustrated by *The Social and Economic Rights Action Center*) can and should be viewed in the light of the experience of those domestic jurisdictions.

An expansive approach to *locus standi in judicio* (most crucially by way of third-party intervention) and evidence have equally widened (directly or indirectly) minority participation, whether it's through NGO intervention,[108] expert testimony from the group and other communities, academics and NGOs,[109] admission of group representatives to all stages of proceedings,[110] acceptance of a shift in the burden of proof and statistical evidence,[111] or even acceptance of oral evidence from community sources.[112]

Elements of the jurisprudence on socio-economic rights are an important demonstration of the way in which a court can use orders, mostly of a remedial nature, to facilitate dialogue between the parties concerned, both before and after delivering its judgment on the merits.[113] Central to the use of remedial orders in both South Africa and India has been the development of supervisory powers over the implementation of the obligations contained in the judgment and/or order, based on participation by all actors involved. A key aspect of this approach is the court's ability to keep the case open by requiring continuing reporting by the government on the extent of compliance. Interestingly, a similar advanced pattern can be noticed in relation to leading indigenous land rights cases decided within the Inter-American system. For example, the IACrtHR delivered in 2007 a decision requesting

---

[107] C. Forster & V. Jivan, 'Public Interest Litigation and Human Rights Implementation', *supra* note 62, pp. 16–18. For more traditional approaches to those aspects under international human rights complaints procedures, see H. Hannum (ed.), *Guide to International Human Rights Practice* (Philadelphia, 2nd edition, 1992), Parts II and III.

[108] E.g. *Nachova and others v. Bulgaria*, EurCrtHR, Applications Nos. 43577/98 and 43579/98, Judgment of 6 July 2005.

[109] E.g. *Mayagna (Sumo) Awas Tingni Community v. Nicaragua*, IACrtHR, Judgment of 31 August 2001, Series C No. 79.

[110] E.g. *The Saramaka People v. Suriname*, IACrtHR, Judgment of 28 November 2007, Series C No. 172.

[111] E.g. *DH and others v. The Czech Republic*, EurCrtHR, Application No. 57325/00, Judgment of 13 November 2007 [GC].

[112] See *supra*, Chapter 5.

[113] E.g. *Occupiers of 51 Olivia Road* (Case No. CCT 24/07 Interim Order, 30 August 2007) and *TAC* ((2) 2002 (5) SA 721 (CC)).

Paraguay to report on the measures adopted in order to comply with the 2006 judgment in *Sawhoyamaxa*, and reaffirmed its authority to provide continuing monitoring over the full execution of that judgment.[114] In *Saramaka*, it established a similar reporting obligation and reaffirmed that the case would be closed only as a result of full compliance by the state.[115] Generally speaking, the IACrtHR monitors the extent of compliance by ordering the state to submit periodic reports to that effect, which the members of the community concerned are then allowed to comment upon.[116] As in previous cases, in *Saramaka* a range of community-oriented measures was ordered as a form of collective reparation for the Saramaka people and a three-member implementation committee was tasked with managing the projects for which damages had been awarded. The IACrtHR explained that, not only had the committee to include a representative appointed by the victims, it also had to consult with the Saramaka people before making any decisions on those projects. Finally, the IACrtHR reserved to itself the power to convene a meeting to facilitate agreement between Suriname and the representatives of the Saramaka people on the composition of the implementation committee.

Here again, the expansion of the participatory process through some kind of conversation with the government and civil society is expected to give minority groups a more effective voice.[117] Far from insulating minority issues from the political process, judicial discourse becomes very much part of articulated multilogues that feed into that process.

Between substance and procedure

So far, the dimensions of judicial discourse discussed in Chapters 2–5 – i.e. recognition, elaboration, mediation and access to justice – have been (re-) examined through the lens of a procedural model that is primarily built

[114] Monitoring Compliance with Judgment, Order of 2 February 2007.

[115] Judgment of 28 November 2007, Series C No. 172, para. 214. See also the subsequent decision in *Interpretation of the Judgment on Preliminary Objections, Merits, Reparations, and Costs*, Judgment of 12 August 2008, Series C, No. 185, para. 57.

[116] *Mayagna (Sumo) Awas Tingni Community v. Nicaragua*, Monitoring Compliance with Judgment, Order of 7 May 2008; *Sawhoyamaxa Indigenous Community v. Paraguay*, Monitoring Compliance with Judgment, Order of 2 February 2008; *ibid.*, Order of 8 February 2008; *Yakye Axa Indigenous Community v. Paraguay*, Monitoring Compliance with Judgment, Order of 8 February 2008.

[117] Aside from the Inter-American system, it is worth noting that in the leading *Ogoni* case under the ACHPR, the AfrCommHPR indicated remedies that involved the community in the process of gathering and sharing information on health and environmental risks associated with any further oil drilling activities in Ogoniland.

around minimal objectives of securing non-discrimination in the enjoyment of rights and facilitating the political process as the fundamental vehicle for the realisation of those rights. We noted that, on this model, the legitimacy of judicial discourse under the relevant (human rights) treaty, and thus the basis of its harmonious relationship with state sovereignty, is largely a function of the extent to which that discourse upholds rather than undermines internal democratic participation.

More than that, such model defines the boundaries of judicial discourse. In terms of constitutional and political theory, the most typical account of the procedural approach to judicial review is that fundamental rights, as essential conditions for public processes of participation must either be automatically applied by courts or, if they are open to contestation, the determination of their scope or content, especially on questions of identity, must be left to the political process.[118] In terms of international human rights law, this view can only in part be related to the question of general law-making effects of judicial discourse beyond the will or original intentions of the parties to a treaty. In most cases, the decisions rendered by supervisory bodies are either not legally binding (for example, the HRC views) or entail binding effects only for the parties to the dispute (for example, the EurCrtHR judgments). True, individual decisions may have more general effects and therefore influence the way that the treaty as a whole is interpreted and applied,[119] but treaty amendment (or re-interpretation) remains possible as a result of widespread objection from the parties. In practice, the relationship between supervisory bodies and states parties is a dynamic, not static one. Far from reflecting a fundamental clash with state consent, experience shows that international jurisprudence is normally assumed to have been accepted by states as it develops and takes roots within domestic legal systems.[120] Although some human rights courts have increasingly provided remedies for particular treaty violations, international supervisory bodies cannot per se override national legislation, which is the distinguishing feature of most constitutional courts instead.

Of more critical importance is the notion implied by the classic procedural model based on Ely's and Habermas' theories of judicial review and

118 J. Habermas, *Between Facts and Norms, supra* note 13; J. H. Ely, *Democracy and Distrust, supra* note 11; for a recent elaboration on this approach, see S. Wheatley, 'Minorities under the ECHR and the Construction of a "Democratic Society"' (2007) *Public Law*, pp. 784–792.

119 This may derive from contentious or advisory proceedings, or even decisions delivered within specific supra-national settings, such as ECJ preliminary rulings under Article 234 EC Treaty.

120 See e.g. D. Armstrong, T. Farrell & H. Lambert, *International Law and International Relations* (Cambridge, 2007), pp. 169–170.

democracy, that human rights provisions, whether domestic or international, can only exist through participatory practices within society. As recently explained by Steven Wheatley in relation to the 'constitutional' dimension of the EurCrtHR's decisions:

> Constitutional norms and rights remain subject to contestation by reasonable persons... in domestic democratic settings, meaning and content only becomes clear through a process of democratic will-formation: there can be no democracy without rights and no rights without democracy.[121]

The general implication of this view is straightforward: it is not just a question of setting limits on judicial discourse in order to protect the consensual foundations of the treaty under which that discourse forms, it is the very nature of human rights norms (and indeed any norm of a somewhat 'constitutional' significance)[122] that requires supervisory bodies to step back and let society decide what such norms must entail. For Wheatley, the EurCrtHR can and should only 'destabilise' domestic arrangements affecting minority groups but cannot and should not respond to the complexities arising from human rights norms as they apply to those groups. Rather, the judgment provides 'the basis for critical self-reflection by the party concerned'.[123] In essence, Wheatley applies Ely's and Habermas' theories to international human rights litigation in ways that dispense with, or contain as much as possible, the interpretive, *substantive* ramifications of judicial discourse. On this view, internationally recognised human rights, or at least those that are most relevant to the distinctive ethno-cultural identity of minority groups, are ultimately what the political process wants them to be, leaving it to international jurisprudence the role of monitoring the implementation of the treaty understood as a set of merely general propositions that require further elaboration and discussion within the relevant polity for them to be given substance, and thus a life of their own. This approach goes beyond the question of whether or not a human rights provision is self-executing; it speaks to the very function of human rights litigation in plural societies.

As illustrated in the previous sections of this chapter, international jurisprudence can usefully be seen from a procedural perspective, whether in terms of recognising a minority group as a major actor in the legal and political discursive space, setting out benchmarks against which to measure

---

[121] S. Wheatley, 'Minorities under the ECHR and the Construction of a "Democratic Society"', *supra* note 118, p. 784.

[122] For a discussion in relation to human rights, see e.g. S. Gardbaum, 'Human Rights as International Constitutional Rights' (2008) 19 *European Journal of International Law*, p. 749 et seq.

[123] *Ibid.*, p. 791.

state conduct and mediate conflicting claims, or valuing minority grievances and perspectives through an expanded view of jurisdiction. But should that jurisprudence be viewed as serving *solely* procedural objectives? The procedural model may prove limited in practice: the *Carolene Products* case used by Ely to develop his own 'representation-reinforcing' theory of judicial review has unsurprisingly proved weak on substantive equality and/or indirect discrimination.[124] Habermas' model of deliberative democracy which is arguably reflected in *Gorzelik* before the EurCrtHR, leaves state discretion under the ECHR essentially unchecked. The more general questions are: To what extent are substantive readings of minority related human rights provisions reflected in international judicial practice? To what extent can they be justified as a matter of principle?

The procedural view generally recognises the all too frequently open-textured or indeterminate nature of human rights provisions. For Wheatley, for example, the problem is not with acknowledging this state of affairs, but rather with identifying a proper relationship between judicial and political discourse about human rights issues. As noted earlier, all main theories of judicial review (with the exception of Habermas'), assume constitutional provisions, or even norms in general, to be often the subject of deep disagreement as far as their applicability to a new set of circumstances is concerned. International law, too, does recognise the complexities of interpretation through Articles 31 and 32 of the Vienna Convention on the Law of Treaties. The basic rules of treaty interpretation include not only the 'ordinary meaning' to be given to the terms used in the relevant provision, they crucially involve the context of the treaty as a whole in ways that broadly encompass any agreement, practice, rule or understanding – internal or external, preceding or subsequent, to that treaty – which may directly or indirectly relate to it. The jurisprudence of the EurCrtHR provides the most obvious example of the centrality of interpretation. For the EurCrtHR, the ECHR 'is a living instrument which must be interpreted in the light of present-day conditions', and therefore cannot be read 'solely in accordance with the intentions of their authors'.[125] While suggesting that the ECHR provisions do reflect core meanings agreed upon at the time the ECHR was adopted, this statement more generally acknowledges the indeterminacy of the text when dealing with contemporary issues and

---

[124] S. Fredman, *Human Rights Transformed, supra* note 19, pp. 109–113; J. H. Gerards, 'Intensity of Judicial Review in Equal Treatment Cases' (2004) *Netherlands International Law Review*, p. 150. See *supra*, Chapter 3, especially the US Supreme Court's decisions in *Lyng* and *Employment Division.*

[125] *Loizidou v. Turkey (Preliminary Objections)* (1995) 20 EHRR 99, 71. See generally A. Mowbray, 'The Creativity of the European Court of Human Rights' (2005) 5 *Human Rights Law Review*, p. 57 et seq.

controversies. It is no coincidence that the EurCrtHR has engaged in intense elaboration on a variety of human rights themes, and progressively insulated the treaty from meanings, concepts or definitions upheld under the domestic law of the party concerned.[126]

Mayagna and *Maya* illustrate the significance of these approaches to a human rights discourse which is more directly related to ethno-cultural minority groups. In *Mayagna*, the IACrtHR interpreted the right to property in Article 21 ACHR by assuming the dynamic and relative openness of human rights provisions in the interpretive process:

> The terms of an international human rights treaty have an autonomous meaning, for which reason they cannot be made equivalent to the meaning given to them in domestic law. Furthermore, such human rights treaties are live instruments whose interpretation must adapt to the evolution of the times and, specifically, to current living conditions
>
> ...
>
> Through an evolutionary interpretation of international instruments for the protection of human rights, taking into account applicable norms of interpretation and pursuant to article 29(b) of the Convention.... [i]t is the opinion of this Court that article 21 of the Convention protects the right to property in a sense which includes, among others, the rights of members of the indigenous communities within the framework of communal property, which is also recognized by the Constitution of Nicaragua.[127]

In *Maya*, the IACommHR echoed this line in the context of the ADRDM and the Inter-America system as a whole:

> [T]he organs of the Inter-American human rights system have recognized that the property rights protected by the system are not limited to those property interests that are already recognized by states or that are defined by domestic law, bur rather that the right to property has an autonomous meaning in international human right law... [i]n this sense, the jurisprudence of the system has acknowledged that the property rights of indigenous peoples are not defined exclusively by entitlements within a state's formal legal regime, but also include that indigenous communal property that arises from and is grounded in indigenous custom and tradition.[128]

---

[126] See e.g. *Selmouni v. France*, Application No. 25803/94, Judgment of 28 July 1999, para. 101 [concept of torture]; *Dudgeon v. UK*, (1982) 4 EHRR 149 [homosexuality in relation to private life]; for the theory of autonomous concepts, see G. Letsas, 'The Truth in Autonomous Concepts: How To Interpret the ECHR', *supra* note 95. Although the EurCrtHR's interpretation of the ECHR has often taken national standards of protection into account, its teleological approach to the treaty has generally not involved a systematic consideration of domestic practices in the European legal space.

[127] Judgment of 31 August 2001, Series C No. 79, paras. 146, 148.

[128] Report No. 96/03, Case 12.053, October 24, 2003, para. 116.

It can be contended that the points on the autonomy and dynamism of international human rights law (*in casu*, property rights) reflect a much deeper aspect of interpretation, namely an inevitably – and indeed inherently – substantive dimension of international jurisprudence. As explained by Oscar Schachter:

> [T]he line between interpretation and new law is often blurred. Whenever a general rule is construed to apply to a new set of facts, an element of novelty is introduced; in effect new content is added to the existing rule. This is even clearer when an authoritative body re-defines and makes precise an existing rule or principle.[129]

It is precisely this process of re-conceptualisation and ultimately subsumption[130] which has informed a considerable part of the above-mentioned international judicial discourse, particularly in relation to general human rights standards. As noted in Chapter 3, traditional human rights entitlements have been somewhat re-read to accommodate minority needs and demands. Basic layers of protection affecting a minority group's way of life and well-being have been progressively construed through wider notions of private life, family life and/or right to life to embrace key claims to identity, economic self-sufficiency and even environmental protection. In many ways, 'life' as a human rights concept has come to form a continuum in terms of legal meanings and levels of engagement with the minority experience. Property, participation, education, language, they are all further general categories of human rights protection whose reach has been amplified to varying degrees and in different settings by the distinctive position of ethno-cultural groups or otherwise the reality of cultural diversity. *Ballantyne* before the HRC read a linguistic element into freedom of speech; *Cyprus* before the EurCrtHR added a mother tongue claim to the right to education under particular circumstances; *Yatama* and the several cases on land rights before the Inter-American organs expanded the meaning of political participation and property, respectively. Many more examples were discussed earlier in the book. Interestingly, elaboration on human rights provisions is also taking the form of a re-assessment of constitutional rights. *Kayano* before the Sapporo District Court elaborated on the right to life and liberty in Article 13 of the Japanese Constitution on the basis of Article 27 ICCPR. This same right was interpreted by the Supreme Court

[129] O. Schachter, *International Law in Theory and Practice* (The Hague, 1991), p. 87. For a thoughtful overview of the 'law-making' impact of interpretation by international jurisprudence across several areas, see A. Boyle & C. Chinkin, *The Making of International Law* (Oxford, 2007), pp. 244–247 and Chapter 6, particularly section 4.

[130] R. Alexy, 'On Balancing and Subsumption. A Structural Comparison' (2003) 16 *Ratio Iuris*, p. 433 et seq.

of Belize in *Aurelio Cal et al.* to include 'the very lifestyle and well-being' of the group, thereby echoing the decision of the IACommHR in *Maya.*[131] More generally, the case heavily relies on international standards, including the UNDIP, to inform the Court's interpretation of the Constitution.[132]

There can be little doubt that the international jurisprudence on minority issues does reflect major substantive elements. In this sense, the procedural reading espoused above arguably overlooks the necessity and inevitability of the interpretive exercise through judicial discourse. The fundamental role of human rights supervisory organs is to ensure the effective implementation of the treaty under which they operate. Unsurprisingly, their jurisdiction typically extends to all matters concerning the 'interpretation and application' of the relevant convention[133] and thus requires the supervisory body to examine the extent to which a state is bound by a particular provision.[134] As the experience of the ECHR clearly shows, it would be difficult, if not impossible, to imagine human rights treaties (and indeed any human rights instrument) having any meaningful impact without the interpretive substance ascribed to them as a result of the supervisory process. Minority related international jurisprudence is no exception in this regard. It ultimately expresses a connection between human rights norms and jurisprudential concretisation as being inherent to the logic and functioning of any adequate human rights (treaty) regime.

More importantly, the conceptual analysis of the jurisprudence discussed in the preceding chapters provides a view of judicial discourse that defies a rigid disjunction of substantive and procedural elements, substance and process, articulation of standards and support for the political process. This seems to cut across general values, criteria of adjudication and/or specific readings of rights. The EurCrtHR's jurisprudence on freedom of association (and related freedoms) is most certainly an example of a re-assessment of the ECHR in relation to minority issues in a way that blends substantive consideration of standards and a more general procedural concern for the proper functioning of a democratic system. Indeed, not only has the EurCrtHR emphasised the centrality of such freedoms to an open and genuinely pluralistic society, it has effectively re-interpreted those freedoms to include both substantive aspects previously unexplored (protection of pro-minority political parties, protection of minority structures and events, self-identification) and substantive values

---

131 Claims Nos. 171 and 172 of 2007, Judgment of 18 October 2007, para. 117; the Court also embraced the understanding of property rights upheld in *Maya, ibid.*, paras. 99–100, 102.

132 *Ibid.*, paras. 118–132; see also *Sagon Tasi, supra* note 38, and *infra* note 147.

133 See e.g. Article 32(1) ECHR and 62(3) ACHR. See also in general, *supra* note 129.

134 See e.g. HRC General Comment No. 24 (52), November 1994, para. 1.

informing the connection between associative freedoms and minority related claims (non-violence and respect for democratic principles).

The equality jurisprudence is another case in point. On the one hand, equality serves as a basic procedural criterion of adjudication in the context of retrospective interventions regarding positive regimes that the state has adopted for the benefit of one or more minority groups or the majority.[135] At the same time, equality itself does inform a substantive reading of rights to the extent that it provides a solid yardstick against which (non-)discrimination can be assessed. In *Thlimmenos*, the EurCrtHR indirectly re-interpreted freedom of religion in the light of an expanded (essentially indirect) view of discrimination to cover persons belonging to a particular religious group. In *Belgian Linguistics*, the right to education in Article 2 of Protocol 1 to the ECHR was given more substance within an identity related setting as a result of an interaction between that right and, again, Article 14 ECHR. Still, in both cases, equality was used as a fundamental procedural benchmark for policing the autonomy enjoyed by the state under the ECHR in matters of religion and education, respectively.[136] In *Lovelace* the HRC used (gender) equality to affirm yet problematise the material parameters of minority rights protection in Article 27 ICCPR. Just as the Indian jurisprudence in *Mohammed Ahmed Khan* and *Danial Latifi*, *Lovelace* established a connection between the procedural criterion of (gender) equality and wider dialogues over the substance of minority identity and the terms of more just multicultural arrangements.[137]

A similar interplay of substance and process can be noted at the level of more specific identity aspects of rights protection. In the *Lansmann* (and related) cases involving the impact of national measures on a minority group's way of life, the HRC's reasoning revealed two basic and intertwined ramifications. For one thing, it re-conceptualised 'culture' to include economic activities that are part and parcel of the group's identity.[138] On the other hand, it established procedural parameters to assess whether or not 'denial' of ICCPR Article 27 rights had occurred. The discussion of process was thus premised on a fundamental expansion of the right's substantive scope; no test of consultation and economic sustainability could have ever been upheld in this context unless a connection between identity and economic self-sufficiency was read

[135] For example, in relation to the Quebec and South Tyrol cases.

[136] See *supra* in the chapter, and Chapter 4.

[137] S. Mullaly, 'The UN, Minority Rights and Gender Equality: Setting Limits to Collective Claims', in G. Pentassuglia (ed.), 'Reforming the UN Human Rights Machinery: What Does the Future Hold for the Protection of Minorities and Indigenous Peoples?' (2007) 14 *International Journal on Minority and Group Rights*, Special Issue, pp. 263–283.

[138] This built on the earlier *Kitok*: Comm. No. 197/1985, Views of 27 July 1988, (1998) Annual Report 221; *Diergaardt* further elaborated on the matter, see *supra* Chapter 2.

into the indeterminate text of Article 27. This is all the more significant given the empirical uncertainty often surrounding such cases, as indicated earlier. The dismissal of the margin of appreciation argument made by Finland still allowed the HRC to uphold a process-based analysis of facts that linked the reliability of the state's perspective with a more substantive concern for the protection of traditional minority activities. In short, procedure follows on from a clarification of substance.

This line can be compared with the ECHR and Inter-American jurisprudence. In *Chapman* and *Noack*, the EurCrtHR accepted in principle to recognise the protection of a minority group's identity as being private and family life for purposes of Article 8 ECHR prior to any assessment of the extent to which that group's needs and demands had been given proper consideration during the decision-making process. The shift to a more direct relation between Article 8 and minority groups paves the way for a procedural (participation-oriented) approach to the state's margin of appreciation. At the same time, such shift does limit the reach of procedural considerations in the name of a specific substantive right. The Inter-American jurisprudence on indigenous land rights provides an even more vivid illustration of the role of judicial discourse in generating complex relationships between articulation of standards and support for the political process. The multifaceted and participatory process that is designed to deal with land disputes between the state and the group concerned, involving delimitation and titling of the land, redress for dispossessions, and/or guarantees against unlawful exploitation of natural resources found on indigenous land, can only be justified on the basis of a substantive reading of property as an identity concept under Article 21 ACHR. Not only is that process not meant to substitute for the newly expanded right at issue – its role being rather to reinforce it and support it – it is the entire jurisprudence on property rights that forms a continuum of substantive and procedural elements that makes it difficult to strictly separate conceptual aspects and operational requirements. For example, the procedural requirements established in *Sawhoyamaxa* regarding recovery of ancestral lands were based on a substantive effort to (re-)conceptualise 'traditional possession' and the type of relationship between the group and the land. The additional procedural requirements found in *Saramaka* regarding restrictions on property rights in relation to natural resources were also informed by substantive elements involving the scale of the activity at issue and more general entitlements to control over land use and respect for the environment.[139]

The said interplay of substantive and procedural elements in international judicial discourse importantly echoes two aspects which were discussed earlier.

[139] Judgment of 28 November 2007, Series C No. 172, paras. 129–140.

First, on an empirical level, the substance/procedure dynamic seems to be broadly comparable to that which is reflected in the domestic jurisprudence on socio-economic rights. Just as both socio-economic and minority issues have raised questions as to how their relate to the role of courts and court-like bodies mainly in connection with fears of judge-made social and group policies, so both of them have in practice proved receptive to judicial interventions in ways that expose, within their own context, several combinations of substantive and procedural perspectives. For example, *Olga Tellis*, with its re-conceptualisation of the right to life and finding of a duty to consult with the people concerned, hardly differs in approach from the various national and international decisions on minority issues that involve a re-reading of the right to life and/or establish pro-minority procedural duties as part of the decision-making process. The relationship between accountability and equality that is aptly emphasised when discussing the South African jurisprudence in *Grootboom* and related cases,[140] arguably confirms the reality and complexities of group-oriented adjudication through a blend of substance and procedure in explaining the scope of norms. Finally, greater openness of the interpretive process combines with, and is effectively induced by an expansive approach to *locus standi* and remedies as part of a wider participatory exercise – elements that we have already discussed in relation to minority issues.

The second aspect is a more theoretical one. As noted earlier, an important strand of legal and political theory discourse about the role of courts in plural societies, not only acknowledges the open-textured nature of crucial constitutional provisions and the concomitant societal conditions of reasonable disagreement or normative pluralism that most frequently surround them, it recognises – directly or indirectly – the inevitable role of judicial review in providing responses to the challenges that pluralistic societies face. While taking different approaches to legal interpretation and adjudication, these writers do converge on the notion that judicial review and the decision-making that it entails cannot be understood solely in the sense of upholding procedural fairness within the political arena or providing litigants with an opportunity to participate in the decision, but have to somehow engage with the substance of claims generated by conditions of normative pluralism. In this regard, Tully's discursive or 'agonistic' understanding of democracy within multinational and multicultural societies, exemplifies the complex role of judicial discourse in both supporting the political process and directly engaging in a dialogue with the parties involved over the substantive claims and procedural questions that are meant to inform that process. We have argued that this line has interesting parallels to the *practice* of minority related

[140] S. Fredman, *Human Rights Transformed, supra* note 19.

international jurisprudence, as it seems to reflect, *mutatis mutandis*, a similar type of interplay of substantive assessment of claims and wider demands for recognition and participation within the state.

Interpretation as cross-fertilisation

But one of the most significant aspects of the interpretive interplay of substance and process, (re-)conceptualisation of rights and procedural (participatory) dimension, is the extent to which international standards and/or principles are being used to reinforce and explain existing norms.[141] In other words, more than the fact of regarding human rights provisions as living instruments in ways that allow for new substantive and procedural meanings to be given to them through interpretation, it is *how* this is being done that both confirms the substance/procedure interaction and reflects the actual or potential role of minority related international jurisprudence. Examples can be offered that are the expression of two basic tendencies. One is to use additional provisions *within the treaty* as being instrumental in expanding the scope of the provision in question. The other is to achieve a similar objective by relying on provisions *external* to the treaty.

As noted earlier, the HRC has repeatedly stated that the right to self-determination in Article 1 ICCPR may affect the interpretation of 27. Clearly, the overarching theme that results from this construction, as defined by the requirement of participation, is bound to have an impact on more advanced notions of minority rights under the treaty, particularly in terms of autonomy or self-government for indigenous minority groups. Unsurprisingly, this notion was emphasised in *Apirana Mahuika* where a comprehensive settlement between the government and the Maori people established a new framework for Maori autonomy in areas critical to their cultural integrity. By considering that settlement compatible with Article 27, the HRC linked the narrative of minority identity with that of (internal) self-determination, while providing procedural criteria to govern such connection. On this approach, Article 1 paradoxically looses an autonomous role as it provides additional content for enlarging the boundaries of minority rights.[142] In *The Social and Economic Rights Action Center* – the Ogoni case – the AfrCommHPR took a

---

[141] It should be noted that a broadly similar phenomenon is affecting other areas where fundamental interests of individuals and groups are at stake: see e.g. M. Iovane, 'La participation de la société civile a l'elaboration et a l'application du droit international de l'environnement' (2008) 3 *Revue Générale de Droit International Public*, section II.2.

[142] The rationale for internal self-determination as reflected in *Katangese Peoples' Congress* before the AfrCommHPR is arguably very similar: see e.g. P. Macklem 'The Wrong Vocabulary

similar line by both recognising substantive rights which were not explicitly mentioned in the ACHPR – such as the right not to be subjected to forced evictions – and implicitly articulating the scope of Article 21 in a way that resonated with separate provisions, most notably in relation to property, health and the environment. Although there is no indication that this decision was informed by external international standards, the AfrCommHPR has more recently confirmed the existence of indigenous groups within the African continent and emphasised the importance of the UNDIP as an interpretive tool within the African system.[143] In its Advisory Opinion on this declaration, adopted in May 2007, the AfrCommHPR translates major entitlements to self-determination and land protection under that instrument as a 'series of rights' relative to self-government (as opposed to secession or independence), culture and control over natural resources which are said to reinforce those which are set forth in the ACHPR.[144] Future jurisprudence will inevitably draw on pertinent universal (or regional) practice as setting the stage for an analysis under the African regime.[145]

---

of Right: Minority Rights and the Boundaries of Political Community' (2005) *University of Toronto Legal Studies Series*, Research Paper No. XX–05, p. 18.

143 ACHPR/Res 65 (XXXIV) 03 Resolution on the Adoption of the Report of the African Commission's Working Group on Indigenous Populations/Communities,(2003) at http://www.achpr.org/english/resolutions/resolution70_en.html; ACHPR/Res.121 (XXXXII) 07 Resolution on the United Nations Declaration on the Rights of Indigenous Peoples, 28 November 2007, at <http://www.achpr.org/english/resolutions/resolution121_en.htm>; Advisory Opinion of the African Commission on Human and Peoples' Rights on *The United Nations Declaration on the Rights of Indigenous Peoples*, May 2007. In *Malawi African Association and Others v. Mauritania* (Comm. Nos. 54/91, 61/91, 98/93/, 164/97 à 196/97 and 210/98 (2000), the AfrCommHPRs also used the UNDM to articulate fundamental principles of non-discrimination and respect for group existence, *ibid.*, para. 131.

144 Advisory Opinion of the African Commission on Human and Peoples' Rights on *The United Nations Declaration on the Rights of Indigenous Peoples*, May 2007, especially paras. 23–24, 27, 35. The AfrCommHPR insists that self-determination must be exercised in a way which is compatible with the territorial integrity of the state.

145 In the pending case of *Cemiride (on Behalf of the Endorois Community) v. Kenya* (Comm. 276/2003), the claims relate to the establishment of a Game Reserve on traditional indigenous land. The Endorois, a pastoralist community, were evicted from their traditional land during the 1970s and 1980s; private concessions were also granted to a private company for ruby mining. Applicants claim *inter alia* a breach of property rights (Article 14), right to disposition of natural resources (Article 21) and cultural rights (Article 17). The application submitted to the AfrCommHPR heavily draws on Inter-American jurisprudence on property rights, HRC jurisprudence on Article 27 ICCPR, and general instruments such as ILO Convention 169 and the 1986 UN Declaration on the Right to Development (A/RES/41/128). More generally, Article 60 ACHPR allows the AfrCommHPR to draw inspiration from a variety of international law instruments in the field, particularly those which have been adopted within the African context.

It is precisely the use of external human rights instruments that provides an additional dimension to judicial discourse in this context. Domestically, such a process is emerging in the form of a conversation between courts and international human rights bodies. In *Kayano* and *Aurelio Cal et al.* mentioned earlier, international standards and jurisprudence applicable to minority groups prove essential to expounding constitutional norms on human rights.

Internationally, the use of such standards lies at the intersection of multiple regimes. Whereas *Saramaka* before the IACrtHR echoes the themes of participation, benefit-sharing and environmental impact which had arguably been highlighted to a greater or lesser degree in *The Social and Economic Rights Action Center*,[146] this time the analysis of the right to property is deeply permeated by the logic and spirit of a variety of international standards which are not contained in the ACHR. Central to this approach is Article 29(b) which establishes that no provision thereof may be interpreted as 'restricting the enjoyment or exercise of any right or freedom recognized by virtue of the laws of any State Party or by virtue of another convention to which one of the said states is a party'. The IACrtHR has consistently interpreted this clause as enabling it to read the ACHR in the light of standards upheld by the party outside the framework of the treaty. Here again, the UNDIP has been openly relied upon in connection with development projects affecting natural resources owned by indigenous communities. In general, as discussed in Chapter 3, indigenous land rights have been considered by the Inter-American organs in relation to not only ILO Convention 169, the UNDIP, and the Draft American Declaration on the Rights of Indigenous People, but also the right to self-determination set forth in the UN Covenants, Article 27 ICCPR, and elements of regional or national jurisprudence.[147] The interaction between the universal, regional and national could not be any clearer: the substantive and procedural aspects of Article 21 ACHR have come to embrace elements that elaborate and expand on the jurisprudence of other bodies. In *Saramaka*, notions of economic self-determination and identity, natural resources as part of (indigenous) property and the additional requirements of consultation or consent, benefit-sharing and environmental and social impact assessment for lawful restrictions on the (indigenous) right to property, are crucially borrowed from multiple jurisdictions, thereby making the treaty a proxy for cross-fertilisation processes.[148]

---

[146] Comm. No. 155/96, 2001, paras. 53, 55, 58; and *supra* Chapter 1.

[147] See also *Mary and Carrie Dann v. United States*, Report No. 75/02, Case 11.1140, December 27, 2002, paras. 124, 131; and *Maya*, Report No. 96/03, Case 12.053, October 24, 2003, paras. 85, 111–119; *Garifuna Community of Cayos Cochinos and its members v. Honduras*, Report No. 39/07, Petition 1118-03, Admissibility, 24 July 2007, para. 49.

[148] Judgment of 28 November 2007, Series C No. 172, paras. 92–96, 103, 118–123, 128–140. For a broadly similar line under the ICERD, see e.g. CERD's concluding observations on

The second example of this tendency is provided by the jurisprudence of the EurCrtHR. Although this court – despite its teleological approach to interpretation – has been reluctant to build minority related provisions of the ECHR around external standards, it, too, has implicitly acknowledged the inevitable intrusion of (some) such standards into its interpretive function. In *Sidiropoulos*, the EurCrtHR referred to (then) CSCE standards to uphold the right to freedom of association of minority members under the treaty.[149] By appealing to a 'strictly supervisory role' (essentially in the procedural sense described earlier in the chapter), the majority in *Chapman* refrained from using the Framework Convention for the Protection of National Minorities as a substantive interpretive tool. Still, it relied on an 'emerging international consensus recognising the special needs of minorities and an obligation to protect their security, identity and lifestyle'[150] to accept the argument that a minority group's way of life may attract the guarantees of Article 8 ECHR and arguably attempt to limit state discretion in the decision-making process. More positively than in *Chapman*, the EurCrtHR (Grand Chamber) in *Gorzelik* quoted from the Framework Convention to further articulate the substance of Article 11 ECHR, and by implication, the more general procedural significance of freedom of association within a democratic society.[151] In *DH and others*, the EurCrtHR openly drew on findings relating to the Framework Convention's monitoring process, and upheld the substantive notion of indirect discrimination and its procedural ramifications in the wake of leading domestic, international and European jurisprudence on the subject.[152]

---

the United States, UN Doc. CERD/C/USA/CO/6, 8 May 2008 [the UDIP should be used as a guide to interpret the ICERD's obligations relating to indigenous peoples]. With regard to indigenous participation and benefit-sharing as well as environmental concerns, note also Article 8(j) of the 1992 Convention on Biological Diversity in the context of so-called traditional knowledge; see generally M. Fitzmaurice, 'The Dilemma of Traditional Knowledge: Indigenous Peoples and Traditional Knowledge' (2008) 10 *International Community Law Review*, p. 255 et seq.

[149] Judgment of 10 July 1998, Reports 1998–IV, para. 44 [citing the Copenhagen Document on the Human Dimension and the Charter of Paris for a New Europe].

[150] Application No. 27238/95, Judgment of 18 January 2001, para. 93.

[151] Application No. 44158/9820, Judgment of 17 February 2004 [GC], para. 93.

[152] Application No. 57325/00, Judgment of 13 November 2007, *passim*, especially paras. 192, 200 [quoting from the Framework Convention's process]. In *Affaire Sampanis et Autres c. Grèce*, Application No. 32526/05, Judgment of 5 June 2008 (final on 5 September 2008), the EurCrtHR also relied on Parliamentary Assembly resolutions when discussing the status of Roma communities in Europe, para. 72 (in French).

On judicial persuasiveness

Tully's central idea that courts, together with other decision-taking institutions within a pluralistic system, cannot and should not have the last word, but should be viewed as part of a more general network of actors that are engaged in, or affected by struggles over (minority group) recognition, somewhat resonates with a distinctive aspect of judicial discourse, namely the quality of its legal reasoning. The necessity or desirability of revising earlier jurisprudential pronouncements as a result of wider public discourses is very often a function of the authority that those decisions can carry with them. The point is not whether judicial activism over substantive (minority) issues should give way to a strictly procedural, Ely-style approach to judicial discourse, or whether constitutional courts' judgments can or should be made revisable by Parliament,[153] but rather whether the decision (substantive or procedural, or a combination of both) is ultimately persuasive, though not necessarily acceptable to all the parties concerned. In response to the extra-legal inclinations of the synthesis method of adjudication proposed by Jeremy Webber, Kenneth Baynes emphasises the role of the legal community broadly understood in upholding the parameters of judicial discourse. For her, what holds this community together, is:

> [a]n overarching commitment to the idea of legal fidelity and legal argumentation, along with a complementary acknowledgment that the relevant norms governing the community (or more distinct discursive institutions) can themselves change, albeit in accordance with other legal processes and constraints. Within this broader conception of the law (or legal community), a judge... should be constrained by a set of legal norms relevant to her decision and... prepared to offer reasons that she reasonably believes the legal community would recognize. No doubt, she should also consider the situation of the litigants – including their interests and concerns... [b]ut her primary or overarching responsibility or judicial duty should be fidelity to the recognized standards of legal reasoning and her judgement should represent a 'good faith' effort to apply those legal standards.[154]

Whether and to what extent extra-legal considerations may weaken rather than strengthen judicial reasoning very much depends on the circumstances of the case. *Western Sahara*, for example, including the individual opinions of the ICJ's judges, arguably represents a subtle interpretive effort to combine considerations of group identity, accepted international legal categories and demands for more inclusive, post-colonial understandings of international

[153] *Supra* note 10.

[154] K. Baynes, 'Disagreement and the Legitimacy of Legal Interpretation', in O. A. Payrow Shabani (ed.), *Multiculturalism and Law, supra* note 22, p. 108.

law.[155] But aside from how the complexities of each case have been addressed, there is no question that the 'persuasive authority' of international jurisprudence, particularly on human rights matters, and therefore its ability to be active (yet inevitably 'less than perfect') part of wider discursive networks in Tully's sense, hinge on the quality of the legal argumentation that such jurisprudence is capable of generating.

Commenting on the jurisprudence of the EurCrtHR and ECJ, Anne-Marie Slaughter and Laurence Helfer note:

> We suggest that the precise nature of the reasoning involved, whether deductive, syllogistic, analogical, or some combination of these styles, is less important than that judicial decisions *be reasoned* in the first place: Reasons should explain why and how a particular conclusion was reached. To reason, in this context, means to give reasons for a particular result, regardless of the logic or mode of reasoning underlying those reasons... [M]any commentators seeking to analyze the success of the ECJ and the ECHR emphasize the fact of legal reasoning, in the sense that judicial opinions are reasoned at all, as much as the quality of that reasoning.
>
> Both courts provide reasons for their decisions and create a framework within which reasoned debate can be conducted by acknowledging the weight of precedent.[156]

Unsurprisingly, other bodies' 'persuasive authority' has been sometimes questioned on the grounds that the style and quality of the decisions were allegedly deficient. For example, Henry Steiner has lamented, *inter alia*, that HRC views have too frequently revealed an imbalance between background information and the 'terse statement' of the conclusions they contain, providing little room for elaborating on issues and arguments.[157] In terms of minority rights jurisprudence, *Lubicon Lake Band* might be said to be a case in point.[158] But similar criticisms have been made in relation to particular decisions or

[155] K. Knop, *Diversity and Self-Determination in International Law* (Cambridge, 2002), pp. 110–150.

[156] L. R. Helfer & A. M. Slaughter, 'Toward a Theory of Effective Supranational Adjudication' (1997) 107 *The Yale Law Journal*, pp. 320, 323; R. Bernhardt, 'The Convention and Domestic Law', in R. St. J. Macdonald, F. Matscher & H. Petzold (eds.), *The European System for the Protection of Human Rights* (Boston/Dordrecht, 1993), p. 45. In more general terms, Boyle and Chinkin write: 'Any court's role in the law-making process is likely to be accepted if it is perceived by the international community as a credible, impartial and legitimate institution which reaches reasoned decisions in accordance with accepted legal principles', *The Making of International Law, supra* note 129, p. 301.

[157] H. J. Steiner, 'Individual Claims in a World of Massive Violations: What Role for the Human Rights Committee?', in P. Alston & J. Crawford (eds.), *The Future of UN Human Rights Treaty Monitoring* (Cambridge, 2000), p. 42.

[158] Comm. No. 167/1984, Views of 26 March 1990, Annual Report, vol. II, 1990, 1, paras. 32.2–33.

aspects of them. Gerald Neuman has taken issue with the way in which the IACrtHR presented its conclusions on the scope and status of the principle of non-discrimination in its 2003 Advisory Opinion on the *Juridical Condition and Rights of Undocumented Migrants*.[159] On the notion upheld by the IACrtHR that non-discrimination is part of *ius cogens*, he writes:

> The breath of these conclusions might take one to pause to inquire whether they could be justified on either consensual or suprapositive grounds. That is, has the international community adopted a peremptory norm of the scope the Court identified, or should it do so?... Why is non-discrimination in all matters affecting human rights a *ius cogens* norm? The Court cited a wide range of international instruments prohibiting discrimination in a variety of contexts, or on the basis of a number of different criteria. But, even taking these instruments at face value, the fact that many forms of discrimination are internationally forbidden does not demonstrate that all forms of discrimination violate a fundamental value of the international community.[160]

This point seems to echo earlier debates over the persuasiveness of the proposition made in 1992 by the European Community Arbitration Commission on Yugoslavia that the rights of minorities were embodied in peremptory norms of international law – a proposition which was hardly explained or supported by positive evidence.[161] But whether or not we agree with the above assessments, it is clear that the practical impact that any (human rights) decision is likely to have on the legal community and the public at large largely depends on the degree of its conceptual, systemic or temporal consistency. This holds particularly true in respect of general notions or values that may be extracted from the corpus of human rights standards and the bearing they may have on conflicting claims.[162] This is not to suggest that a reasoned approach automatically yields persuasive reasons. For example, one might raise the question of whether the IACrtHR's interpretation of Article 29 (b) ACHR to justify a broader understanding of property (and other) rights in relation to indigenous communities is in fact allowed by the letter or rationale of that provision.[163] What a reasoned, articulated approach to interpretation

---

159 AO OC-18/03, Series A, No. 18.

160 G. L. Neuman, 'Import, Export, and Regional Consent in the Inter-American Court of Human Rights' (2008) 19 *European Journal of International Law*, p. 120.

161 G. Pentassuglia, *Minorities in International Law: An Introductory Study* (Strasbourg, 2002), p. 111.

162 On the 'quality control' of the interpretive process, see e.g. M. Iovane, *supra* note 141, section II.2.5.

163 It has been usually argued that this type of clause only deals with the 'negative' side of the equation, namely that of disallowing the use of the instrument as a pretext for cutting down higher levels of protection being provided outside that instrument. For a discussion in a different setting, see Liisberg, 'Does the EU Charter of Fundamental Rights threaten

does reveal, though, is the capacity of judicial discourse – as Anne-Marie Slaughter and Laurence Helfer put it – 'to create a framework within which reasoned debate can be conducted', especially by way of acknowledging and considering competing perspectives and values in ways that help expound the international instrument concerned. Arguing for an expounding role of the HRC, Henry Steiner writes:

> Expounding a constitution or basic law making treaty…requires judges to use appropriate cases to elucidate the instrument that they are applying, to interpret and explain it. Committee members must employ such cases to probe the basic purposes of the Covenant, to show its significance for the life and needs of the peoples it is meant to serve. Such an understanding of the role of opinions will often require acknowledgment of the difficulties in reaching a judgement, the consideration of alternative grounds, and some form of justification for the decision reached. In the novel and vexing cases, it will always require reasoned argument rather than the terse and opaque application of norm to facts. The Committee must act as a deliberative body that is sensitive to the legitimate and immense possibilities of its role in the human rights movement.[164]

Aside from wider proposals for reform, it has been increasingly accepted that, in spite of existing flaws, the HRC views – coupled with individual members' opinions and general comments – have made an important contribution to explaining the scope of the ICCPR.[165] From the standpoint of minority issues, a string of cases arguably reflects an increasingly sophisticated discursive style that has come to represent the very foundations of any understanding of those issues under the ICCPR.[166] As we have seen, notions of non-discrimination and identity have been progressively defined by more contextual analyses that value and discuss the competing claims.

An important indicator of their persuasiveness is provided by their gradual recognition within national legal orders as significant statements of the ICCPR

---

the supremacy of Community law? Article 53 of the charter: a fountain of law or just an inkblot?' (2001) 04/01 *Harvard Jean Monnet Working Papers*, p. 1 et seq.

164 H. J. Steiner, 'Individual Claims in a World of Massive Violations: What a Role for the Human Rights Committee?', *supra* note 157, p. 39.

165 L. R. Helfer & A. M. Slaughter, 'Toward a Theory of Effective Supranational Adjudication', *supra* note 156, pp. 356–358; H. Steiner, 'Individual Claims in a World of Massive Violations: What a Role for the Human Rights Committee?', *supra* note 157, p. 44.

166 See e.g. *Sandra Lovelace v. Canada*, Comm. No. 24/1977, Views of 30 July 1981, (1981) Annual Report 166; (1983) Annual Report 248; *I. Länsman v. Finland*, Comm. No. 511/1992, Views of 26 October 1994, (1995) II Annual Report 66; *J. I. Länsman v. Finland*, Comm. No. 671/1995, Views of 30 October 1996, (1997) II Annual Report 191; *Apirana Mahuika et al. v. New Zealand*, Comm. No. 547/1993, U.N. Doc. CCPR/C/70/D/547/1993 (2000); *J. G. A. Diergaardt et al. v. Namibia*, Comm. No. 760/1997, Views of 25 July 2000, CCPR/C/69/D/760/1996; *Waldman v. Canada*, Comm. No. 694/1996, Views of 3 November 1999, UN Doc. CCPR/C/67/D/694/1996 (1996).

law on the subject. Aside from the more or less successful implementation of individual decisions or persisting disputes over the edges of minority protection, it is fair to say that the core HRC views concerning Article 27 have developed indispensable minimum benchmarks at the domestic level.

The European and Inter-American experiences are equally important in this regard. As for the EurCrtHR, the amply documented high level of compliance with its judgments is only one aspect (albeit a crucial one) of its success story. More often than not, states prove ready to respond to criticisms generated by the case, regardless of its outcome. For example, Poland adopted in 2005 The Act on National and Ethnic Minorities as well as Regional Language, as a response (at least in part) to concerns expressed by the EurCrtHR in *Gorzelik* regarding the lack of legislation on national minorities in the country. The Czech Republic had abolished the system of special schools (with an overwhelming cohort of Roma pupils) even before the Grand Chamber's judgment held in 2007 that such system was in breach of the right to non-discrimination taken in conjunction with Article 2 Protocol 1 (right to education).[167] National authorities are also starting to accept (however grudgingly) the obligations deriving from the decisions on indigenous communities under the Inter-American system, at least in terms of adopting new legislation and providing compensation for victims. Although implementation issues figure highly on the Inter-American bodies' agenda, the IACrtHR has enhanced its authority by affirming its competence to closely monitor the extent of compliance through periodic reports that the respondent state is required to submit to that effect, and by making the closure of the case dependent on full execution of the judgment.[168] More than this, the impact of international jurisprudence can be inferred from by the ever greater 'traffic in persuasive decisions' between international bodies and between the latter and national courts, as indicated in the previous section.

Aside from empirical aspects of national implementation, judicial persuasiveness, on a more conceptual level, inevitably depends on the way in which ambitious legal interpretations are combined with the acknowledgment of state sensitivities. For their part, the Inter-American organs have not only interpreted the ACHR and ADRDM within a wider framework of conventional

[167] *DH and others v. The Czech Republic*, Application No. 57325/00, Judgment of 13 November 2007.

[168] See e.g. *Mayagna (Sumo) Awas Tingni Community v. Nicaragua*, Monitoring Compliance with Judgment, Order of 7 May 2008; *Sawhoyamaxa Indigenous Community v. Paraguay*, Monitoring Compliance with Judgment, *ibid.*, Order of 2 February 2008; *ibid.*, Order of 8 February 2008; *Yakye Axa Indigenous Community v. Paraguay*, Monitoring Compliance with Judgment, Order of 8 February 2008; *The Saramaka People v. Suriname*, Judgment of 28 November 2007, Series C No. 172, para. 214.

or general international human rights norms and jurisprudence relevant to ethno-cultural minority groups, in line with interpretive trends in human rights discourse.[169] They have also emphasised the respondent state's consent to (or support for) the relevant standards as they become applicable to the case at issue.[170] Recent developments under the African system may well point in the same direction. The AfrCommHPR is starting to engage with external standards, particularly the UNDIP, in an attempt to both explain their relation to the ACHPR and reconcile such expanded readings with the position of African states.[171] A telling illustration of the AfrCommHPR's approach is provided by the above-mentioned understanding of the right to self-determination under the UNDIP in the sense of self-government, land and ultimately cultural rights, as opposed to (external) self-determination in the sense of independence. As is widely known, no positive right of this kind has ever been recognised to 'minorities' as such, the UNDIP itself clearly disallows any secessionist claims in Article 46, and the entire body of jurisprudential references to indigenous self-determination effectively collapses into limited analyses of identity rights, whether they turn on land, participation or otherwise. In its 2007 Advisory Opinion, the AfrCommHPR clarified the scope of both the UNDIP and its own jurisprudence (notably *Katangese Peoples' Congress*) by insisting that self-determination for indigenous peoples must be exercised in a way which is compatible with the territorial integrity of the state, thereby putting concerns about a potential expansion of the corresponding provisions of the ACHPR that could threaten the 'national unity' of African countries to rest. Interestingly, an earlier version of Article 46 UNDIP was further amended as a result of this clarification.

These examples show that international supervisory bodies have the ability to enhance the quality and ramifications of their legal reasoning in ways that both expound the instrument in question through reasoned interpretation and enable the parties' perspectives to be valued and assessed within a regional and global discursive network.

---

169 G. Pentassuglia, *Minorities in International law, supra* note 161, pp. 109–110.

170 Compare *Mayagna (Sumo) Awas Tingni Community v. Nicaragua*, Judgment of 31 August 2001, Series C No. 79, paras. 152–153 and *The Saramaka People v. Suriname*, Judgment of 28 November 2007, Series C No. 172, paras. 92–92, 131; *Mary and Carrie Dann v. United States*, Report No. 75/02, Case 11.1140, December 27, 2002, paras. 124, 131; *Maya Indigenous Communities of the Toledo District v. Belize*, Report No. 96/03, Case 12.053, October 24, 2003, paras. 85, 111–119.

171 For example, in its 2007 Advisory Opinion on *The United Nations Declaration on the Rights of Indigenous Peoples* the AfrCommHPR emphasises the overwhelming support for the UNDIP from the African states (ACHPR/Res.121 (XXXXII) 07 Resolution on the United Nations Declaration on the Rights of Indigenous Peoples, 28 November 2007) and articulates meanings of the instrument that respond to the concerns expressed by some of the three abstaining states from Africa (Burundi, Kenya, and Nigeria).

The interplay of substance and procedure in international jurisprudence concerning minority groups can hardly be dismissed, as it forms, *at least in practice*, the core of any meaningful interpretive exercise by international supervisory bodies.[172] From a conceptual point of view, it is submitted that such complex role of jurisprudential assessments should not be viewed in opposition to public discourses about the contours of human rights. On the contrary, drawing on Tully's approach to democratic participation within national and international settings and more general theories of legal adjudication in plural societies, those assessments – whatever their reach at the level of the distinctive regime within which they operate – should be regarded more broadly as helping to shape the debate in dialogue with the legal community and the public at large, while at the same time enabling individuals and groups to bring up claims which have remained unheard within a majority-dominated state system. It is not a question of transposing theoretical (or institutional) constructs to the international plane 'lock, stock and barrel'. It is more a way of acknowledging the reality of non-dominance that by definition informs the minority experience at the domestic and global level, and the extent to which courts and court-like bodies can become implicated in it.

In spite of disagreement over values or conceptions of justice, judicial decisions – like any other type of public deliberation – must be taken and followed through.[173] As part of wider public discourses, such decisions will be directly or indirectly exposed to scrutiny by a variety of state and non-state actors (practitioners, academics, public agencies, NGOs and IGOs, other courts or quasi-judicial bodies, etc.); more than exploring possibilities for treaty amendment, the quality of their legal reasoning will be discussed on the basis of traditional and contemporary methods of international law interpretation. Far from substituting judicial discourse for the political process, each decision will inevitably prove 'less than perfect' (i.e. it will generate a measure of agreement and disagreement), creating a framework for further debate and possible revision or adjustment over the longer term.[174]

---

172 A similar claim could be made in the context of constitutional jurisprudence affecting minority groups.

173 See e.g. Fredman, *Human Rights Transformed, supra* note 19, p. 119.

174 Contentious points surfacing in legal and policy debates in connection with that jurisprudence, covering issues as diverse as the recognition of a minority group, the ramifications of non-discrimination or the right to life, personal law regimes or the right to self-determination, the role of external standards or evidential matters, are very much part of this discursive exercise.

Between Universalism and Justice

In many ways, the interplay of substantive and procedural elements that we have examined so far, and indeed the role of international jurisprudence more generally, can be viewed through the lens of the wider debate over the human rights narratives relating to minority groups.

The traditional and dominant account of instruments on minority protection, one which is also largely assumed by this book, is that such instruments – like all other international human rights instruments – are meant to protect universal features of what it means to be a human being (*in casu*, as they relate to ethno-cultural identity) from the exercise of sovereign power. State sovereignty thus serves as the fundamental starting point for a discussion which is presented essentially in terms of the content and limits of minority protection within the framework of international human rights law. The vocabulary of universalism frames minority issues in ways that concentrate on the legitimacy and scope of minority claims within a sovereign system whose very existence is presupposed by international law.[175] A different account of human rights provisions on minority groups, though, speaks, not only to some universal features of human identity, but also to minority protection as justifying sovereign authority within a political community where minority claims are made. On this latter account, international human rights law in general, and minority rights in particular, not only limit the exercise of state power, they may also engage, depending on the case, with the very legitimacy of asserting sovereign authority.

The case of *R. v. Van der Peet* before the Supreme Court of Canada[176] helps briefly explain these perspectives. It arose out of a sale by Ms Van der Peet, a member of the Sto:lo First Nation, of fish caught under the authority of an

[175] Hence, the traditional debates over the compatibility of minority rights with individual human rights, or the extent to which minority claims foster moral relativism in the name of cultural difference. For recent analyses from a broader perspective, see K. De Feyter & G. Pavlakos (eds.), *The Tension Between Group Rights and Human Rights* (Oxford/Portland Oregon, 2008); F. Francioni & M. Scheinin (eds.), *Cultural Human Rights* (Leiden/Boston, 2008); M. Iovane, 'The Universality of Human Rights and the International Protection of Cultural Diversity: Some Theoretical and Practical Considerations', in G. Pentassuglia (ed.), 'Reforming the UN Human Rights Machinery: What Does the Future Hold for the Protection of Minorities and Indigenous Peoples?' (2007) 14 *International Journal on Minority and Group Rights*, Special Issue, p. 231 et seq.; B. Berry, *Culture and Equality: An Egalitarian Critique of Multiculturalism* (Oxford, 2001), pp. 63–109. It goes without saying that, beyond the theoretical approach, concerns for minority issues continue to arise in the context of conflict prevention and management: W. Kymlicka, *Multicultural Odysseys: Navigating the New International Politics of Diversity* (Oxford, 2007), Chapters 6–8.

[176] [1996] 2 S.C.R. 507.

Indian food fish licence, contrary to the Federal Fisheries Act, 1970. While raising the specific question of whether there existed an aboriginal right to sell fish under the Constitution, the Court effectively discussed the constitutional position of 'aboriginal and treaty rights' vis-à-vis non-indigenous citizens. It importantly offered two basic justifications for the recognition of those rights under the Constitution. One was that indigenous communities' way of life is the expression of a 'distinctive culture' within Canadian society that needs to be adequately protected. In essence, the argument was that aboriginal people's attachment to their ancestral land and the traditional activities that have been performed for centuries on the land constitute the hallmark of a distinctive cultural affiliation that should be recognised by a democratic society which understands cultural diversity as being essential to the actual enjoyment of individual freedom. The other justification rested on the historical presence of indigenous communities on the lands which were subsequently to fall under Canadian sovereignty. Their organised existence predates the establishment of the Canadian state and for the Court, this 'simple fact' is to be reconciled with the territorial sovereignty of Canada.[177]

Both justifications have different, though not necessarily mutually exclusive rationales. The first one argues that, whatever the limits on constitutionally protected aboriginal and treaty rights as minority rights, they are meant to protect cultural features as universal traits of human identity, that is, as features that inhere in all human beings. The second one appeals to injustices produced against indigenous peoples at the time of the formation of the Canadian state which qualify them, and them alone, for unique status under the Constitution as a way of remedying those injustices.

The complex and often problematic interrelation between the vocabulary of universalism and that of (in)justice associated with history and territory, is ultimately reflected in the specific minority rights discourse generated by international law. For one thing, all international minority rights instruments are permeated by the notion that protection of minority identity is necessary to secure 'full' or 'more effective' protection of rights afforded to the majority or other members of the state population under international human rights law.[178] Whatever their actual scope,[179] such instruments are all capable of being

177 For further elaboration on these themes across the whole of Canadian jurisprudence, see e.g. P. Ochman, 'Recent Developments in Canadian Aboriginal Law: Overview of Case Law and of Certain Principles of Aboriginal Law' (2008) 10 *International Community Law Review*, p. 319 et seq.

178 See e.g. the preamble of the 1992 UNDM; the preamble and Article 2.2(a) of ILO Convention 169; the preamble and Articles 1–3 of the UNDIP.

179 For example, controversies persist over definitional terms and their implications, see *supra*, Chapter 1.

understood in universalistic terms. In this sense, at least, the vocabulary of universalism informs what Will Kymlicka terms 'generic minority rights', namely entitlements that apply to ethno-cultural minority groups by virtue of a universal right to enjoy one's own culture.[180] On the other hand, such groups have traditionally sought a measure of autonomy from the central government in areas critical to the preservation of their cultural integrity, particularly in connection with their own specific historical experiences and/or territorial settlements. For example, autonomy claims made by Eastern European minority communities, on a territorial or non-territorial basis, can be traced back to the reconfiguration of the political and territorial boundaries of Europe following World Wars I and II.[181] Indigenous claims clearly reflect the legacy of European colonialism and its concomitant history of exclusion and territorial dispossession. In *Sawhoyamaxa*, Paraguay – echoing the justice theme in *R. v. Van der Peet* – implicitly acknowledged the historical backdrop to the claims by complaining that it was being 'condemned for sins committed during the Conquest' and that accepting such claims would lead to the 'absurdity that the whole country could be returned to the indigenous peoples, since they were the first inhabitants of the territory that is now Paraguay'.[182]

International law, more 'targeted'[183] responses mostly revolve around a wider re-conceptualisation of the right to self-determination in a way that exposes multiple levels of minority protection within established state boundaries,[184] including an open recognition of the territorial dimension of ethno-cultural identity through the distinctive notion of indigenous self-government and land rights. Yet, there remains a fundamental ambivalence of international human rights law towards these aspects of protection. While minorities can and should partake in the process of internal self-determination within the state at the political, cultural and/or territorial levels, there is still no specific right to autonomy for them under positive international law.[185] While indigenous self-government and land rights have been recognised in international instruments, including the UNDIP, there is still concern – at the political and normative levels – as to their exact implications for state sovereignty;[186]

---

180 W. Kymlicka, *Multicultural Odysseys, supra* note 175, pp. 199–204.

181 It is no coincidence that cultural autonomy was partly re-introduced following the dissolution of the Soviet Union: G. Pentassuglia, *Minorities in International Law, supra* note 161, pp. 234–235.

182 Judgment of 29 March 2006, Series C No. 146, para. 125.

183 The expression is borrowed from Will Kymlicka, *Multicultural Odysseys, supra* note 175.

184 G. Pentassuglia, *Minorities in International Law, supra* note 161, pp. 166–176.

185 *Ibid.*, pp. 172–176.

186 Indeed, all autonomy/self-determination claims have typically raised – wrongly or rightly – security concerns and/or normative dilemmas as to whether and to what extent international

unsurprisingly, indigenous protection tends to be presented primarily in universalistic terms.

It is the tension between a universalistic and justice-based view of minority protection that can help explain the ambiguities surrounding the role of international human rights law in dealing with demands for robust (minority rights) regimes as a way of remedying injustices against minority groups. While the universalistic approach levels the playing field of cultural difference by appealing to universal features of human identity and bringing such difference to bear on pre-defined state boundaries and communities, the justice-based account effectively provides an additional (and alternative) rationale in that it is meant to expose the foundations of sovereign authority under international law, that is, to inquire into the extent to which specific minority rights can and should mitigate the injustices produced by the allocation and exercise of that authority within the international legal system. As Patrick Macklem explains:

> A distributive account of international human rights law...facilitates differentiation among minority claims by locating their international legal significance in relation to the legitimacy of the sovereign power that they challenge, which in turn rests on the way in which international law participates in the formation of minorities by distributing and redistributing sovereign power among states. Indigenous rights and national minority rights claims speak to different distributive injustices caused by how international law organized and continues to organise international political reality. Claims based on religious and cultural difference challenge the limits of sovereign power more than its sources. Differentiation does not resolve the contentious ethical, political and legal issues associated with international minority rights. But is clarifies why some minority rights and not others might merit international legal protection and locates their legal significance in relation to the structure and operation of the international legal order.[187]

The deeper normative tension between universalistic and justice-based readings of the field resonates with the legal significance of substantive and procedural elements underpinning the international jurisprudence on minority issues. For one thing, judicial discourse has appeared increasingly sensitive to minority needs on the basis that international human rights law can and should

---

(human rights) law should support them. Conversely, minority rights based on individual rights with a more tenuous connection with the notion of group rights is generally perceived – wrongly or rightly – as instrumental in alleviating the risk of ethnic conflict.

187 P. Macklem, 'What is International Human Rights Law? Three Applications of a Distributive Account', Bernard and Audre Rapoport Center for Human Rights and Justice, University of Texas School of Law, November 19, 2007, pp. 31–32; see also pp. 25, 29; id., 'Minority Rights in International Law' (2008) 6 *International Journal of Constitutional Law*, p. 531 et seq.

generate 'full' or 'more effective' protection for minority groups. International courts and court-like bodies resort to the vocabulary of universalism in order to link minority issues with fundamental concerns for human dignity and cultural identity. It is no coincidence that the hallmark of this progressive jurisprudence is represented by an expanded interpretation of those human rights instruments which are not per se designed to address minority issues. Indeed, it is primarily at the level of interpretation that such jurisprudence seeks to relate *general* human rights to minority claims. In this sense, the type of judicial elaboration that we discussed in Chapter 3 should be seen from a classic universalistic perspective. It aims to (more effectively) integrate the identity affiliations brought up by minority issues into the existing code of universal human needs that are enshrined in those international human rights instruments that apply within a state's jurisdiction.

Particular rationales may well help buttress the wider conceptual underpinnings of this jurisprudential line. For example, *Chapman* and *Cyprus* under the ECHR, and *Hopu and Bessert* under the First Optional Protocol to the ICCPR, suggest one such rationale, namely a connection between identity concerns and the effectiveness of general rights. As noted, in *Chapman* the EurCrtHR's majority upheld in principle the notion that the applicant's occupation of her caravan was an integral part of her ethnic identity as a Roma. More than that, it recognised that measures interfering with the applicant's stationing of her caravans did not simply impact on the right to respect for home, but 'also affect[ed] her ability to maintain her identity as a Gypsy and to lead her private and family life in accordance with that tradition'.[188] The dissent led by Judge Pastor Ridruejo disagreed with the majority's conclusions (which had ultimately reverted to the right to a home theme) by viewing Article 8 ECHR as providing for a positive duty to provide a practical and effective opportunity for Roma members to enjoy the right. For them, the lack of provision of alternative sites by the government, coupled with the practical unavailability of private residential sites, had made the majority's identity-friendly interpretation of the general right to private and family life 'theoretical or illusory' rather than 'practical and effective'.[189] They upheld a particular theme (minority identity) through the lens of the principle of effectiveness frequently relied upon by the EurCrHR in interpreting the universal rights set forth in the ECHR.[190] *Cyprus* more clearly combines these

[188] Application No. 27238/95, Judgment of 18 January 2001, para. 73.

[189] *Airey v. Ireland*, Application No. 6289/73, Judgment of 9 October 1979, Series A 32, para. 24.

[190] As noted, the dissent also referred to non-discrimination as a separate argument; on the doctrine of effectiveness, see A. Mowbray, 'The Creativity of the European Court of Human Rights', *supra* note 125. For a somewhat similar line in the context of indigenous politi-

dimensions. The EurCrHR held that secondary school education in Turkish or English-speaking schools for Greek-Cypriot pupils in Northern Cyprus was both unrealistic, having such pupils received their primary school education in Greek as a result of mother tongue education previously available, and at odds with the wishes of the community concerned. For the EurCrtHR, the consequences of the lack of provision of Greek-language secondary schooling amounted in practice to a denial of a universal right which was in principle available to Greek-Cypriot children. Similarly, in *Hopu and Bessert*, involving the construction of a hotel complex in an ancient Polynesian site, the HRC construed the notion of 'family' in Articles 17(1) and 23(1) ICCPR in connection with the identity aspect relating to the Polynesian burial ground in question, on the – at least implicit – basis that a general right may have to be interpreted in its own specific (cultural) context for it to have any meaningful impact on the (indigenous) group concerned.

A more obvious yet distinctive rationale for the universalistic approach to minority groups is provided by the negative and positive aspects of equality. As we have seen, the Inter-American organs have construed the ACHR and ADRDM around the theme of non-discrimination between indigenous and non-indigenous perspectives on such general human rights matters as political participation[191] and property. In *Saramaka*, the IACrtHR responded to Suriname's objection to indigenous land claims on non-discrimination grounds by even stating that positive protection of indigenous land rights is fully compatible with the prohibition of discrimination:

> [T]he State's argument that it would be discriminatory to pass legislation that recognizes communal forms of land ownership is also without merit. It is a well-established principle of international law that unequal treatment towards persons in unequal situations does not necessarily amount to impermissible discrimination... Legislation that recognizes said differences is therefore not necessarily discriminatory. In the context of members of indigenous and tribal peoples, this Court has already stated that special measures are necessary in order to ensure their survival in accordance with their traditions and customs... Thus, the State's arguments regarding its inability to create legislation in this area due to the alleged complexity of the issue or the possible discriminatory nature of such legislation are without merit.[192]

Whatever the particular rationale and/or legal setting, the universalistic thrust of this jurisprudence enables minority issues as direct or indirect manifestations of identity claims to gradually creep into (general) international human

cal participation, see *Yatama v. Nicaragua*, Judgment of 23 June 2005, Series C No. 127, para. 201.

[191] E.g. *Yatama v. Nicaragua*, Judgment of 23 June 2005, Series C No. 127.

[192] Judgment of 28 November 2007, Series C No. 172, para. 103.

rights law, not to better insulate them from the human rights discourse,[193] but to make such discourse genuinely sensitive to cultural differences, and thus genuinely universal.[194] It is not surprising that the most fundamental themes relating to Article 27 ICCPR – the key global treaty minority provision – are non-discrimination and non-assimilation in relation to a measure of cultural protection that must be extended to members of minority groups living within the political community.[195] Seen in this light, the substantive and procedural elements of the international jurisprudence discussed earlier on intervene separately or concurrently to uphold the cultural paradigm, but it is arguably the substantive re-conceptualisation of international human rights standards that most directly impinges on the normative relationship between universalism and minority groups.

When we shift the focus from a universalistic to a justice-based approach, jurisprudential assessments somewhat symmetrically mirror the uncertainties of international human rights law in responding to complex minority claims that in effect call for a wider and deeper re-definition of the relationship between sovereign authority and the community concerned. As noted, on a justice-based or, in Macklem's words, distributive account of international human rights law, minority rights do not necessarily determine *ipso facto* the content of any rights due to a particular group within a particular context, nor do they question the basic structure of state sovereignty under international law.[196] They do seek, though, to mitigate the adverse consequences for minority groups arising out of the allocation and exercise of sovereign authority within the international legal system. In other words, international human rights law does not exhaust the inquiry into the appropriate level of, and justification for protecting minority groups, but at least does recognise the need to attend to questions of distributive justice linked to minority claims.

For one thing, international jurisprudence reveals awareness of the justice dimension of such claims and the extent to which they may ironically come to inform an advanced understanding of universal rights. In *Lubicon Lake Band*, the HRC implicitly confirmed that Article 27 rights are not only about

193 After all, the post-1945 discourse rested on identity-blind notions of international human rights: I. L. Claude, *National Minorities: an International Problem* (Harvard, 1955), p. 211.

194 H. Arendt, 'The Perplexities of the Rights of Man', in P. Baehr (ed.), *The Portable Hannah Arendt* (London, 2000), p. 31 et seq.

195 *Sandra Lovelace v. Canada*, Comm. No. 24/1977, Views of 30 July 1981, (1981) Annual Report 166; (1983) Annual Report 248; on the mediating impact of judicial discourse on women's issues, see *supra*, Chapter 4.

196 P. Macklem, 'What is International Human Rights Law? Three Applications of a Distributive Account', *supra* note 187, p. 12.

protecting minority members against discrimination but they are also about responding (at least in part) to 'historical inequities' suffered by 'ethnic, religious or linguistic minorities' in relation to the material and spiritual base of their way of life.[197] More generally, the HRC has recognised that Article 27 may include protection of traditional lands and their resources[198] and may be interpreted in the light of the right to self-determination.[199] In its Advisory Opinion on *the United Nations Declaration on the Rights of Indigenous Peoples*, the AfrCommHPR noted that the notion of indigenous populations and communities in Africa 'tries to guarantee the equal enjoyment of the rights and freedoms on behalf of groups, which have been historically marginalized',[200] and reaffirmed internal self-determination in its multiple ramifications as a peaceful response to the inter-communal complexities of African history.[201]

But when it comes to articulating the implications of an implicitly construed justice-based view of standards, international jurisprudence – whatever substantive elements are implicated in it – stands out for its fundamentally procedural dimension. It is not simply a formal question relating to the degree to which a right to minority autonomy (or internal self-determination) can be read into international human rights law. In many ways, the uncertainties surrounding the exact ramifications of autonomy regimes (broadly understood) within a particular context from the perspective of international human rights law, effectively require international supervisory bodies to bridge the gap between the latter's ambivalence or ambiguities and the difficult task of working out domestic solutions that adequately respond to whatever injustices may have been unearthed in the particular case at issue.

As suggested by the discussion in Chapters 2–4, this is essentially done by setting out procedural guidelines that are designed to guide, facilitate and/or assess the political processes of contestation – or struggles over recognition, in Tully's words – generated by justice-based claims. Jurisprudential investigations into the edges or retrospective justifiability of autonomy regimes, as well as the pre-conditions under which such claims can be debated within society, should be regarded as exposing – directly or by implication – that

197 Comm. No. 167/1984, Views of 26 March 1990, Annual Report, vol. II, 1990, 1, para. 33.

198 HRC General Comment No. 23 (50), 1994, para. 7.

199 *Supra* note 1; as for the reporting practice, see the HRC's Concluding Observations in UN Doc. CCPR/C/79/Add. 105, 109 and 112 (Canada, Mexico, Norway), and UN Doc. E/C.12/1/Add.50, para. 10 (Russia); on the connection between 27 ICCPR, self-determination and indigenous property, see *The Saramaka People v. Suriname*, Judgment of 28 November 2007, Series C No. 172, paras. 93–95.

200 May 2007, para. 19.

201 *Ibid.*, paras. 23–24, 27; *Katangese Peoples' Congress v. Zaire*, Comm. No. 75/92 (1995).

dimension. The same applies to the several ramifications of the judicially generated process concerning the settling of indigenous land disputes in the Americas, which arguably constitute the crux of the matter of indigenous self-determination in international human rights law. Generally speaking, the jurisprudential focus is not so much on spelling out the exact form of protection,[202] or even (depending on the case) on whether any special protection at all is required under international law. Rather, the focus is on finding an appropriate procedural framework within which existing or future autonomy regimes can generate a conversation between international supervisory bodies, states and minority communities, and thus potentially vest international standards with greater normative significance within a particular setting. By so doing, judicial discourse can make (an inevitably partial, less than perfect) contribution to re-conceptualising, rebuilding or simply reinforcing a 'democratic and pluralistic society'[203] that encompasses the legal recognition of group identities vis-à-vis the state.

Reference Re Secession of Quebec can probably be seen as amplifying these more ambitious narratives within a multinational and multicultural context. On the one hand, the Supreme Court's exposition of the constitutional framework as defined by the interplay of federalism, democracy, the rule of law and minority protection, relates the position of the French-speaking community of Quebec to that of indigenous communities within Quebec, the other provinces, the federal government and the Canadian state as a whole. On the other hand, it de facto links the 'meaningful exercise'[204] of the right to internal self-determination under international law to more general constitutional conversations amongst the parties concerned over the nature of the state and the legitimacy of its authority and how that reverberates with the position of the group(s) concerned. It crucially involves the constitutional right to initiate change and the constitutional duty to listen to the other side.[205] It dynamically seeks to attend to both the universalistic ideals of human rights and participatory democracy and the contingent challenges posed by group claims associated with distinctive historical and territorial circumstances.

---

[202] As mentioned earlier, this is far from suggesting that procedural reasoning substitutes for recognition of substantive rights in jurisprudential analysis, let alone that this is in any way desirable.

[203] *Yakye Axa Indigenous Community v. Paraguay*, Judgment of 17 June 2005, Series C No. 125, para. 148.

[204] [1998] S.C.R. 2, para. 134.

[205] J. Tully, 'Introduction', *supra* note 32, p. 32.

Chapter 7

Conclusion

This book has attempted to trace the origins and basis of what we have termed the emerging fourth movement in the complex, multifaceted history of minority protection. Whereas the post-1919 League of Nations system of minority treaties and declarations formalised a minimum code of identity rights for (certain) minority groups without endorsing international human rights as such, and the immediate post-1945 period witnessed a move away from international minority rights as the universal mantra of human rights for all came to shape discussions and protection strategies, minority provisions established themselves within the frame of modern international law as a somewhat obvious consequence of wider processes embedding the international community's concern for group abuse and exclusion within states in the human rights canon.

The tensions generated by the third movement in the form of controversial standard-setting and weak monitoring mandates are being paralleled by an ever greater body of international jurisprudence on minority issues, notably under general human rights treaties, in ways that both assume yet partly transcend the *acquis* of the third movement and reflect varying degrees of interaction with domestic case law. Chapters 2–5 sought to capture the articulation of the emerging fourth movement by exposing four conceptual dimensions of judicial discourse – recognition, elaboration, mediation, and access to justice. Aside from the doctrinal aspects which inevitably underlie this typology, a fundamental attempt has been made to identify overarching themes of analysis and relate them – as discussed in Chapter 6 – to the evolving role of international jurisprudence on minority groups.

The *tour de force* generated by the comparative approach to central elements of protection as opposed to a systematic assessment of one or more particular regimes taken separately, has enabled us to precisely unearth those overarching narratives and the way in which judicial discourse becomes implicated with minority issues. The first, most immediate level of inquiry is of course defined by the specific legal and institutional setting within which such issues can be raised. There is no question that, to a greater or lesser extent, separate instruments may produce separate outcomes depending on the case, thereby projecting different levels of acknowledgment of group identity, adjustment of norms, management of complex claims, and access to the judicial space onto the wider frame of international human rights law. In most, if not all of these cases the varying degrees of judicial intervention can be traced back as much to the historical contingencies of the relevant regime as to the numerous possibilities offered by the interpretive process. As indicated in Chapter 1, the analysis offered in this book is not meant to question or dispense with this basic level of inquiry. In systemic terms, the decentralised and fragmented nature of the international human rights machinery and its supranational variations, coupled with the distinctiveness of the constitutional experience of fundamental rights protection,[1] undoubtedly preclude any attempt to identity single narratives or approaches to minority issues through courts and court-like bodies. Rather, the previous chapters sought to offer a view of the 'local' jurisprudence being developed in the context of individual (human rights) regimes that exposes the increasingly global, inevitably intertwined conceptual ramifications of judicial discourse as captured by the four above-mentioned dimensions, and what they tell us about the impact of that discourse on minority issues from a procedural and substantive perspective. The focus has not been on the empirical (undoubtedly crucial) question of national compliance with a given set of international decisions, but on the prior, more general question of how such issues are construed by international (and partly domestic) jurisprudence for purposes of human rights law.

Based on our proposed typology of judicial discourse, we have argued that minority related jurisprudence sets limits on state intervention in order to secure a fair and inclusive political process (procedural perspective), while at the same time engaging in a re-assessment of rights that are relevant to minority groups within the human rights canon (substantive perspective). By and large, procedural and substantive components create a continuum whose precise levels of intensity are a function of the complexities of the claims at issue – an interplay of process and substance that somewhat resonates with the complex relationship between universalistic and justice-based accounts of minority protection. Support for the political process comes mostly in the form of findings of obligations upon the state that are informed by the notion of group participation or inclusion, and are further reinforced by interventions over issues of recognition and access to justice, thereby exposing the role of

[1] For similarities and differences between constitutional and international protection of human rights, see S. Gardbaum, 'Human Rights as International Constitutional Rights' (2008) 19 *European Journal of International Law*, p. 749 et seq.

courts and court-like bodies as the guardians of the democratic process. More than that, both perspectives are largely driven by a process of cross-fertilisation whereby human rights standards that are internal and/or external to the regime at hand (normally a treaty) form the basis of international (and domestic) judicial conversations, reaching out to the wider legal community and the public at large.

While heated debates about multicultural and multinational societies, a growing involvement by domestic courts, a rising demand for more effective international legal regimes, as well as an ever greater 'judicialisation' of international law may go a long way towards explaining – either directly or indirectly – the rejuvenation of international jurisprudence on minority protection and how it builds upon earlier judicial experimentation with group issues, it is the shifting boundaries of this jurisprudence that arguably capture its present role on the global stage. International (and domestic) judicial discourse – i.e. the multiple narratives it produces and the dimensions those narratives represent – is increasingly of a global nature in that it inescapably moves between systems in ways that generate, implicitly or explicitly, interactions between distinctive levels of international (universal and regional) jurisprudence and between the latter and national jurisprudence.

It is this fluid milieu that seems to be shaping the conceptual (and doctrinal) link between the third and fourth movements as we see them. Indeed, while the standard-setting euphoria of the third movement is largely over, the question arises as to its long-term legacy under international human rights law. It is not simply a matter of securing implementation of existing instruments on minority protection. The tensions and uncertainties that still surround the field – at the normative or political level – effectively call for creative exercises whereby minority issues are not only the subject of institutional debates but are also comprehended as legal sites of a discourse that is capable of reinforcing and expanding the content of international human rights.

In this sense, the fourth movement holds the promise of a wider and deeper (re-)assessment of minority issues within the human rights framework. This is particularly evident in the context of regional jurisprudence under general human rights treaties. Again, consider the Inter-American jurisprudence on indigenous land rights. Despite the long and articulated process of standard-setting characterising the third movement in relation to indigenous groups – from the general layers of protection of the UN Covenants to the specialised ILO instruments and the UNDIP – the language of the resulting standards on a range of crucial issues, such as historic claims to ancestral lands, ownership of natural resources, and land demarcation and titling has proved cautious or even elusive. ILO Convention 169 embodies entitlements to the land that indigenous peoples traditionally occupy, not to lands they ever occupied and were deprived of. The UNDIP is arguably unclear as to the extent to which the history of indigenous dispossession creeps into its protective scope, just as it leaves the question of ownership of natural (sub-surface) resources essentially unresolved. On the latter issue, both instruments seem in effect to assume directly or indirectly the centrality of state ownership of sub-soil resources.[2] The UNDIP remains silent on the key aspect of demarcating the land as a fundamental pre-condition for protection, while ILO Convention 169, for its part, does set out an obligation in Article 14(2) 'to take steps as necessary to identify' the lands at issue, without spelling out the contours of such obligation.

What has been the jurisprudential response to those issues under the Inter-American system? For one thing, as discussed in Chapter 5, historical dispossessions of indigenous ancestral lands have been understood in relation to contemporary circumstances underlying the dispute in question. The past gains judicial significance because of its marked connection with the present. At the same time, *Sawhoyamaxa* does generate a framework for addressing claims that go far back in history. It importantly elaborates on the connection between the past and the present by referring to an existing material and/or spiritual attachment to the land.[3] By emphasising the diverse ties of indigenous communities to their traditional lands rather than uninterrupted material possession, the IACrtHR echoes domestic jurisprudence upholding a flexible standard of proof of indigenous title, and thus accounts for earlier involuntary disruptions of occupation.

As noted, *Saramaka* firmly establishes the notion of natural resources, including sub-soil resources, as part of indigenous property under Article 21 ACHR in the face of controversies over the scope of the UNDIP in this regard. Even though recognition of indigenous property over natural resources that are found on and within the land is in principle limited to those which are necessary for the community's survival and the sustainability of its way of life, the *Saramaka* approach appears to reduce the centrality of state ownership of sub-soil resources as reflected in ILO Convention 169 and the UNDIP.[4] The entire body of Inter-American land rights jurisprudence, starting with the ground-breaking *Mayagna* decision,[5] is built around a fundamental obligation upon the state to delimit, demarcate and title the land, as well as its accompanying process relating to the settlement of disputes arising from

[2] S. Errico, 'The Draft UN Declaration on the Rights of Indigenous Peoples: An Overview' (2007) 7 *Human Rights Law Review*, p. 754.

[3] In this sense, it clarifies the basis for some form of corrective justice which is left uncovered or unexplained in ILO Convention 169 and the UNDIP, respectively.

[4] For further implications concerning indigenous *consent* to large scale development activities affecting lands and resources, see *supra* Chapter 4.

[5] Judgment of 31 August 2001, Series C No. 79.

competing claims. While the practice of ILO supervisory bodies has emphasised demarcation and consultation under Convention 169,[6] that jurisprudence adds detail and clarity to the interpretive process.

In short, while all of these cases use or refer to ILO and UN standards, all of them somewhat conceptually transcend them in ways that deepen the role of international human rights law relative to indigenous communities.

This is far from suggesting that the standard related achievements of the third movement have lost momentum or are of limited use. Quite the reverse, specialised standards are an indispensable force in the process of articulating and recording minority claims at the universal and regional level. They are a powerful drive in framing a discourse about minority groups and soliciting responses from international law. But in order for them to acquire solid legal bite, to effectively penetrate the realm of international law, they require international and domestic jurisprudence to embrace and expound them, in synergy with other structures and global networks, in an attempt to generate a conversation between states and minority communities within particular settings, and ultimately to help shape internal policies and legislation. There are of course limits to what judicial discourse can do: individual cases may prove less progressive or convincing than others – more a 'site of betrayal', in Upendra Baxi's words,[7] than the fulfilment of a promise;[8] the reach of jurisprudential assessments, including continuing monitoring over the implementation of the decision, varies depending on the regime under which they operate;[9] those assessments alone cannot bring long-standing crises that involve intense political hand tailoring and institutional involvement to an end.

Overall, though, recent and less recent practice speaks to the capacity of judicial discourse to address minority issues in ways that account for

[6] See e.g. Representation under Article 34 of the ILO Constitution, Guatemala, GB.299/6/1, Governing Body, 299th Session, June 2007.

[7] U. Baxi, 'The Avatars of Indian Judicial Activism: Explorations in the Geographies of (In)Justice', in S. K. Verma & Kusum (eds.) *Fifty Years of the Supreme Court of India: Its Grasp and Reach* (Oxford, 2000), p. 161: 'judicial activism is at once a peril and a promise, an assurance of solidarity for the depressed classes of Indian society as well as a site of betrayal'.

[8] See also W. Sadurski, 'Promoting Rights in the Shadow of the Judiciary: Towards a Fact-Sensitive Theory of Judicial Review' (2001/14) European University Institute Working Papers LAW, p. 1 et seq.

[9] With regard to the IACrtHR's latest jurisprudence, see *supra* Chapter 6, note 168. The case may be further complicated by the lack of ratification of the relevant human rights treaty by a particular state and/or the failure by that state to accept the competence of the relevant monitoring body (see e.g. the United States in respect of the ACHR and the IACrtHR's jurisdiction), so that the impact of jurisprudence may have to be assessed in terms of either alternative human rights instruments (e.g. the ADRDM) or general international law.

developments under human rights law. Internationally, the formal legal outcome of this process has been repeatedly examined in debates over the role of soft law instruments within the wider legal order: they mainly reinforce the scope of existing treaty obligations (*in casu*, especially at the regional level), and occasionally produce new norms or principles of general international law.[10] In this sense, judicial discourse is, or can be instrumental in transcending the original (narrower) meanings of human rights provisions, or even transcending the very conventional nature of the norm by promoting global, legally binding standards.

But at a deeper level, the growing interaction between specialised instruments and international (and domestic) jurisprudence paradoxically amplifies the role of the fourth movement in its ability to diffuse minority issues within the human rights framework in a way which is relatively unconstrained by the practice and classifications of the third one. The protection of Roma identity under the ECHR,[11] the protection of 'non-native' communities on the same basis as indigenous peoples under the ACHR,[12] the expanded notion of indigenousness under the African system,[13] and more generally, the fast developing re-consideration of general human rights categories such as non-discrimination, private life, participation or property, on the basis of a direct or indirect connection with specialised instruments,[14] are all examples of how conceptually pervasive international jurisprudence can be when 'normalising' community

[10] In *Aurelio Cal et al. v. The Attorney General of Belize and the Minister of Natural Resources and Environment*, the Supreme Court of Belize went as far as to characterise the UNDIP (in relation to land rights) as embodying 'general principles of international law', Claims Nos. 171 and 172 of 2007, Judgment of 18 October 2007, paras. 131–133.

[11] *Chapman v. UK*, Application No. 27238/95, Judgment of 18 January 2001.

[12] *Moiwana Village v. Suriname*, IACrtHR, Judgment of 15 June 2005, Series C No. 124, para. 19; *The Saramaka People v. Suriname*, IACrtHR, Judgment of 28 November 2007, Series C No. 172, paras. 78–86; *Garifuna Community of Cayos Cochinos and its members v. Honduras*, Report No. 39/07 (admissibility), 24 July 2007.

[13] Advisory Opinion of the African Commission on Human and Peoples' Rights on *The United Nations Declaration on the Rights of Indigenous Peoples*, May 2007, paras. 9–13.

[14] Attempts to push the boundaries of human rights law even further are being made in relation to the impact of global warming on the human rights of indigenous groups: see *Petition to the Inter-American Commission on Human Rights Seeking Relief from Violations Resulting from Global Warming Caused by Acts and Omissions of the United States, Submitted by Sheila Watt-Cloutier with the Support of the Inuit Circumpolar Conference, on Behalf of All Inuit of the Arctic Regions of the United States and Canada*, 7 December 2005, particularly sections V. B. and V. C. In general, this re-consideration process seems to be further reinforced by the human rights reporting practice, whose analysis was beyond the scope of this book: for evidence in the context of 'minorities', see e.g. K. Henrard, 'Ever-Increasing Synergy towards a Stronger Level of Minority Protection between Minority-Specific and Non-Minority-Specific Instruments' (2003/4) 3 *European Yearbook of Minority Issues*, p. 15 et seq.

concerns within the human rights frame, between or beyond the strictures, straitjackets or ambiguities of the third movement. As the jurisprudence in the Americas, Europe, and Africa clearly reveals, general human rights regimes set out the terms of an accommodation of ethno-cultural diversity that, while drawing on specialised instruments as an explicit or implicit source of inspiration, may not resonate with their language or scope.

As the whole body of international jurisprudence indicates, the dimensions of recognition, elaboration, mediation and access to justice as well as their attendant procedural and substantive ramifications, reverberate well beyond the parameters laid down by the regime at issue, and perhaps general international law as well. Whereas specialised instruments are being used to inform the interpretation of comprehensive human rights texts and possibly act as a springboard for customary law, and such texts are expanding on the specificities of those instruments as the latter become embraced in the interpretive exercise, contemporary judicial discourse about minority groups – the emerging fourth movement in the time-honoured experience of minority protection – stands out for its conceptually 'trans-jurisdictional' outlook, that is, as a global context of ideas that resonates across universal, regional and domestic lines.

Bibliography

R. Ahdar, '*Indigenous Spiritual Concerns and the Secular State: Some New Zealand Developments*' (2003) 23 *Oxford Journal of Legal Studies*, 611.

R. Alexy, 'On Balancing and Subsumption. A Structural Comparison' (2003) 16 *Ratio Iuris*, 433.

A. Amor, 'Le Comité de Droits de l'Homme des Nations-Unies: Aux Confins d'une Jurisdiction Internationale des Droits l'Homme?', in N. Ando (ed.), *Towards Implementing Universal Human Rights: Festschrift for the Twenty-Fifth Anniversary of the Human Rights Committee* (Leiden/Boston, 2004), 41.

J. Anaya, 'The Protection of Indigenous Peoples' Rights over Lands and Natural Resources under the Inter-American Human Rights System' (2001) 14 *Harvard Human Rights Journal*, 33.

D. Armstrong, T. Farrell & H. Lambert, *International Law and International Relations* (Cambridge, 2007).

H. Arendt, 'The Perplexities of the Rights of Man', in P. Baehr (ed.), *The Portable Hannah Arendt* (London, 2000), 31.

M. A. Baderin, 'The African Commission on Human and Peoples' Rights and the Implementation of Economic, Social, and Cultural Rights in Africa', in M. A. Baderin & R. McCorquodale (eds.), *Economic, Social and Cultural Rights in Action* (Oxford, 2007), 139.

M. A. Baderin & R. McCorquodale (eds.), *Economic, Social and Cultural Rights in Action* (Oxford, 2007).

U. Baxi, 'Taking Human Suffering Seriously: Social Action Litigation Before the Supreme Court of India', in N. Tiruchelvan & R. Coomaraswamy (eds.), *The Role of the Judiciary in Plural Societies* (New York, 1987).

——, 'The Avatars of Indian Judicial Activism: Explorations in the Georaphies of (In)Justice', in S. K. Verma & Kusum (eds.), *Fifty Years of the Supreme Court of India: Its Grasp and Reach* (Oxford, 2000), 161.

K. Baynes, 'Disagreement and the Legitimacy of Legal Interpretation', in O. A. Payrow Shabani (ed.), *Multiculturalism and Law: A Critical Debate* (Cardiff, 2007), 101.

S. R. S. Bedi, *The Development of Human Rights Law by the Judges of the International Court of Justice* (Oxford/Portland Oregon, 2007).

S. Benhabib, *The Claims of Culture: Equality and Diversity in the Global Era* (Princeton, 2002).

——, *The Rights of Others: Aliens, Residents and Citizens* (Cambridge, 2004).

E. Benvenisti, 'Margin of Appreciation, Consensus and Universal Standards' (1998–1999) 31 *New York Journal of International Law and Politics*, 843.

——, 'National Courts and the International Law on Minority Rights' (1997) 2 *Austrian Review of International and European Law*, 1.

N. Berman, 'The International Law of Nationalism: Group Identity and Legal History', in D. Wippman (ed.), *International Law and Ethnic Conflict* (Ithaca/London, 1998), 25.

R. Bernhardt, 'The Convention and Domestic Law', in R. St. J. Macdonald, F. Matscher & H. Petzold (eds.), *The European System for the Protection of Human Rights* (Boston/Dordrecht, 1993), 25.

B. Berry, *Culture and Equality: An Egalitarian Critique of Multiculturalism* (Oxford, 2001).

A. Bickel, *The Least Dangerous Branch: the Supreme Court at the Bar of Politics* (Indianapolis, 1962).

D. Bilchitz, *Poverty and Fundamental Rights: The Justification and Enforcement of Socio-Economic Rights* (Oxford, 2007).

M. Boltjes (ed.), *Implementing Negotiated Agreements: The Real Challenge to Intrastate Peace* (The Hague, 2007).

B. Bowring, 'European Minority Protection: The Past and Future of a "Major Historical Achievement" ' (2008) 15 *International Journal on Minority and Group Rights*, 413.

A. Boyle & C. Chinkin, *The Making of International Law* (Oxford, 2007).

K. Boyle, 'Human Rights, Religion and Democracy: The Refah Party Case' (2004) 1 *Essex Human Rights Law Review*, 1.

A. Bröstl, 'Positive Action and the Principle of Equality: Discussing a Decision of the Constitutional Court of the Slovak Republic' (2005/6) 5 *European Yearbook of Minority Issues*, 377.

I. Brownlie, *Principles of Public International Law* (Oxford, 6th edition, 2003).

——, 'The Rights of Peoples in Modern International Law', in J. Crawford (ed.), *The Rights of Peoples* (Oxford, 1988), 1.

D. Caruso, 'Limits of the Classic Method: Positive Action in the European Union After the New Equality Directives' (2003) 44 *Harvard International Law Journal*, 331.

J. Castellino & E. Domínguez Redondo, *Minority Rights in Asia: A Comparative Legal Analysis* (Oxford, 2006).

S. Chambers, 'It is Not in Heaven! Adjudicating Hard Cases', in O. A. Payrow Shabani (ed.), *Multiculturalism and Law: A Critical Debate* (Cardiff, 2007), 115.

W. L. Cheah, '*Sagong Tasi* and Orang Asli Land Rights in Malaysia: Victory, Milestone or False Start?' (2004) 2 *Law, Social Justice & Global Development Journal*, at http://www/go.warwick.ac.uk/elj/lgd/2004_2/cheah.

S. Choudhry (ed.), *Constitutional Design for Divided Societies: Integration or Accommodation?* (Oxford, 2008).

I. L. Claude, *National Minorities: An International Problem* (Harvard, 1955).

B. Conforti, 'The Role of the Judge in International Law' (2007) 1 *European Journal of Legal Studies*, 1.

R. Cover, 'The Origins of Judicial Activism in the Protection of Minorities' (1982) 91 *Yale Law Journal*, 1287.

P. De Azcárate, *League of Nations and National Minorities: An Experiment* (New York, 1972).

K. De Feyter & G. Pavlakos (eds.), *The Tension Between Group Rights and Human Rights* (Oxford/Portland Oregon, 2008).

M.-B. Dembour, *Who Believes in Human Rights? Reflections on the European Convention* (Cambridge, 2006).

A. M. de Zayas, 'The International Judicial Protection of Peoples and Minorities', in C. Brölmann, R. Lefeber & M. Zieck (eds.), *Peoples and Minorities in International Law* (Leiden/Boston, 1993), 253.

P.-M. Dupuy, 'The Unity of Application of International Law at the Global Level and the Responsibility of Judges' (2007) 1 *European Journal of Legal Studies*, 1.

R. Dworkin, *Taking Rights Seriously* (Harvard, 1978).

——, *Law's Empire* (Harvard, 1986).

A. Eide & R. Letschert, 'Institutional Developments in the United Nations and at the Regional Level', in G. Pentassuglia (ed.), 'Reforming the UN Human Rights Machinery: What Does the Future Hold for the Protection of Minorities and Indigenous Peoples?' (2007) 14 *International Journal on Minority and Group Rights*, Special Issue, 299.

A. Eisenberg & J. Spinner-Halev (eds.), *Minorities within Minorities: Equality, Rights and Diversity* (Cambridge, 2005).

J. H. Ely, *Democracy and Distrust: A Theory of Judicial Review* (Harvard, 1980).

S. Errico, 'The Draft UN Declaration on the Rights of Indigenous Peoples: An Overview' (2007) 7 *Human Rights Law Review*, 741.

M. Evans & R. Murray, *The African Charter on Human and Peoples' Rights: The System in Practice 1986–2006* (Cambridge, 2008).

M. Fitzmaurice, 'The Dilemma of Traditional Knowledge: Indigenous Peoples and Traditional Knowledge' (2008) 10 *International Community Law Review*, 255.

C. Foster & V. Jivan, 'Public Interest Litigation and Human Rights Implementation: The Indian and Australian Experience' (2008) 3 *Asian Journal of Comparative Law*, 1.

F. Francioni & M. Scheinin (eds.), *Cultural Human Rights* (Leiden/Boston, 2008).

S. Fredman, *Human Rights Transformed: Positive Rights and Positive Duties* (Oxford, 2008).

S. Gardbaum, 'Human Rights as International Constitutional Rights' (2008) 19 *European Journal of International Law*, 749.

J. H. Gerards, 'Intensity of Judicial Review in Equal Treatment Cases' (2004) *Netherlands International Law Review*, 135.

——, *Judicial Review in Equal Treatment Cases* (Leiden/Boston, 2005).

O. Gerstenberg, 'Germany: Freedom of Conscience in Public Schools' (2005) 3 *International Journal of Constitutional Law*, 94.

J. Gilbert, *Indigenous Peoples' Land Rights under International Law: From Victims to Actors* (Ardsley, 2006).

——, 'Indigenous Rights in the Making: The United Nations Declaration on the Rights of Indigenous Peoples', in G. Pentassuglia (ed.), 'Reforming the UN Human Rights Machinery: What Does the Future Hold for the Protection of Minorities and Indigenous Peoples?' (2007) 14 *International Journal on Minority and Group Rights*, Special Issue, 207.

G. Gilbert, 'Religio-Nationalist Minorities and the Development of Minority Rights Law' (1999) 25 *Review of International Studies*, 389.

——, 'The Burgeoning Minority Rights Jurisprudence of the European Court of Human Rights' (2002) 24 *Human Rights Quarterly*, 736.

V. Gómez, 'Economic, Social, and Cultural Rights in the Inter-American system', in M. A. Baderin & R. McCorquodale (eds.), *Economic, Social and Cultural Rights in Action* (Oxford, 2007), 166.

J. Habermas, *Between Facts and Norms: Contributions to a Discourse Theory of Law and Democracy* (Cambridge/Malden 1996).

——, *The Inclusion of the Other: Studies in Political Theory* (Harvard, 1998).

H. Hannum (ed.), *Guide to International Human Rights Practice* (Philadelphia, 2nd edition, 1992).

L. R. Helfer & A.-M. Slaughter, 'Toward a Theory of Effective Supranational Adjudication' (1997) 107 *The Yale Law Journal*, 273.

L. R. Helfer, 'Redesigning the European Court of Human Rights: Embeddedness as a Deep Structural Principle of the European Human Rights Regime' (2008) 19 *European Journal of International Law*, 125.

K. Henrard, 'Ever-Increasing Synergy towards a Stronger Level of Minority Protection between Minority-Specific and Non-Minority-Specific Instruments' (2003/04) 3 *European Yearbook of Minority Issues*, 15.

——, 'The Protection of Minorities Through the Equality Provisions in the UN Human Rights Treaties: The UN Treaty Bodies', in G. Pentassuglia (ed.), 'Reforming the UN Human Rights Machinery: What Does the Future Hold for the Protection of Minorities and Indigenous Peoples?' (2007) 14 *International Journal on Minority and Group Rights*, Special Issue, 141.

P. Hilpold, 'UN Standard-Setting in the Field of Minority Rights', in G. Pentassuglia (ed.), 'Reforming the UN Human Rights Machinery: What Does the Future Hold for the Protection of Minorities and Indigenous Peoples?' (2007) 14 *International Journal on Minority and Group Rights*, Special Issue, 181.

R. Hofmann, 'National Minorities and European Community Law' (2002) 2 *Baltic Yearbook of International Law*, 159.

M. Iovane, 'La Participation de la Société Civile a l'Élaboration et a l'Application du Droit International de l'Environnement' (2008) 3 *Revue Générale* de *Droit International Public*, 465.

——, 'The Universality of Human Rights and the International Protection of Cultural Diversity: Some Theoretical and Practical Considerations', in G. Pentassuglia (ed.), 'Reforming the UN Human Rights Machinery: What Does the Future Hold for the Protection of Minorities and Indigenous Peoples?' (2007) 14 *International Journal on Minority and Group Rights*, Special Issue, 231.

M. Janis, R. S. Kay & A. W. Bradley, *European Human Rights Law: Texts and Materials* (Oxford, 3rd edition, 2008).

S. Joseph, J. Schultz & M. Castan, *The International Covenant on Civil and Political Rights: Cases, Materials, and Commentary* (Oxford, 2004).

B. Kingsbury, 'Reconciling Five Competing Conceptual Structures of Indigenous Peoples' Claims in International and Comparative Law' (2001) 34 *New York University Journal of International Law and Politics*, 189.

K. Knop, *Diversity and Self-Determination in International Law* (Cambridge, 2002).

M. Koskenniemi, *The Gentle Civilizer of Nations: The Rise and Fall of International Law 1870–1960* (Cambridge, 2001).

W. Kymlicka, *Multicultural Citizenship: A Liberal Theory of Minority Rights* (Oxford, 1995).

——, *Multicultural Odysseys: Navigating the New International Politics of Diversity* (Oxford, 2007).

T. Koivurova, 'The International Court of Justice and Peoples' (2007) 9 *International Community Law Review*, 157.

A. S. Laden & D. Owen (eds.), *Multiculturalism and Political Theory* (Cambridge, 2007).

F. Lenzerini (ed.), *Reparations for Indigenous Peoples: International and Comparative Perspectives* (Oxford, 2008).

G. Letsas, *A Theory of Interpretation of the European Convention on Human Rights* (Oxford, 2007).

R. M. Letschert, *The Impact of Minority Rights Mechanisms* (The Hague, 2005).

M. Levin & T. Tsunemoto, 'Symposium: The Indian Trust Doctrine after the 2002–2003 Supreme Court Term: A Comment on the Ainu Trusts Assets Litigation in Japan' (2003) 39 *Tulsa Law Review*, 399.

J. B. Liisberg, 'Does the EU Charter of Fundamental Rights threaten the supremacy of Community law? Article 53 of the charter: a fountain of law or just an inkblot?' (2001) 04/01 *Harvard Jean Monnet Working Papers*, 1.

P. Macklem, 'Minority Rights in International Law' (2008) 6 *International Journal of Constitutional Law*, 531.

——, 'The Wrong Vocabulary of Right: Minority Rights and the Boundaries of Political Community' (2005) *University of Toronto Legal Studies Series*, Research Paper No. XX–05, 1.

——, 'What is International Human Rights Law? Three Applications of a Distributive Account', Bernard and Audre Rapoport Center for Human Rights and Justice, University of Texas School of Law, November 19, 2007.

A. Malicka & K. Zabielska, 'Legal Status of National Minorities in Poland: The Act on National and Ethnic Minorities as well as Regional Language' (2005/6) 5 *European Yearbook of Minority Issues*, 471.

T. H. Malloy, *National Minority Rights in Europe* (Oxford, 2005).

J. Marko (Guest Editor), 'Minority Rights in an Expanding EU' (2003) 25 *Journal of European Integration*, 175.

S. Marks & A. Clapham, *International Human Rights Lexicon* (Oxford, 2005).

J. Martinez Cobo, *Study of the Problem of Discrimination against Indigenous Populations*, UN Doc. E/CN.4/Sub.2/1983/21/Add.8.

C. McCrudden, 'A Common Law of Human Rights? Transnational Judicial Conversations on Contitutional Rights', in K. O'Donovan & G. R. Rubin (eds.), *Human Rights and Legal History: Essays in Honour of Brian Simpson* (Oxford, 2000), 29.

A. Moucheboeuf, *Minority Rights Jurisprudence* (Strasbourg, 2006).

A. Mowbray, 'The Creativity of the European Court of Human Rights' (2005) 5 *Human Rights Law Review*, 57.

S. Mullally, *Gender, Culture and Human Rights: Reclaiming Universalism* (Oxford/Portland Oregon, 2006).

——, 'The UN, Minority Rights and Gender Equality: Setting Limits to Collective Claims', in G. Pentassuglia (ed.), 'Reforming the UN Human Rights Machinery: What Does the Future Hold for the Protection of Minorities and Indigenous Peoples?' (2007) 14 *International Journal on Minority and Group Rights*, Special Issue, 263.

R. Murray & S. Wheatley, 'Groups and the African Charter on Human and Peoples' Rights', (2003) 25 *Human Rights Quarterly*, 213.

G. L. Neuman, 'Import, Export, and Regional Consent in the Inter-American Court of Human Rights' (2008) 19 *European Journal of International Law*, 101.

M. Nowak, 'The Need for a World Court of Human Rights' (2007) 7 *Human Rights Law Review*, 251.

H. O'Nions, *Minority Rights Protection in International Law: The Roma of Europe* (Ashgate, 2007).

P. Ochman, 'Recent Developments in Canadian Aboriginal Law: Overview of Case Law and of Certain Principles of Aboriginal Law' (2008) 10 *International Community Law Review*, 319.

Oxford Advanced Learner's Dictionary of Current English (Oxford, 2005).

J. M. Pasqualucci, 'The Evolution of International Indigenous Rights in the Inter-American Human Rights System' (2006) 6 *Human Rights Law Review*, 281.

O. A. Payrow Shabani (ed.), *Multiculturalism and Law: A Critical Debate* (Cardiff, 2007).

G. Pentassuglia, 'On the Models of Minority Rights Supervision in Europe and How They Affect a Changing Concept of Sovereignty' (2001/2) 1 *European Yearbook of Minority Issues*, 29.

——, *Minorities in International Law: An Introductory Study* (Strasbourg, 2002).

——, 'Minority Issues as a Challenge in the European Court of Human Rights: A Comparison with the Case Law of the United Nations Human Rights Committee' (2003) 46 *German Yearbook of International Law*, 401.

——, 'Inside and Outside the European Convention: The Case of Minorities Compared' (2006) 6 *Baltic Yearbook of International Law*, 263.

——, 'International Law and Institutions', in R. Green (ed.), *The State of the World's Minorities 2006* (London, 2006), 27.

G. Pentassuglia (ed.), 'Reforming the UN Human Rights Machinery: What Does the Future Hold for the Protection of Minorities and Indigenous Peoples?' (2007) 14 *International Journal on Minority and Group Rights*, Special Issue.

M. J. Perry, *Morality, Politics, and Law* (Oxford, 1988).

——, *Toward a Theory of Human Rights: Religion, Law, Courts* (Cambridge, 2007).

I. Pogány, 'Minority Rights and the Roma of Central and Eastern Europe' (2006) 6 *Human Rights Law Review*, 1.

J. Raz, 'Disagreement in politics' (1998) 43 *American Journal of Jurisprudence*, 25.

C. Reus-Smit (ed.), *The Politics of International Law* (Cambridge, 2004).

J. Ringelheim, *Diversité Culturelle et Droits de l'Homme: L'Émergence de la Problématique des Minorités dans le Droit de la Convention Européenne des Droits de l'Homme* (Bruxelles, 2006).

J. Rivers, 'Proportionality and Discretion in International and European Law', in N. Tsagourias (ed.), *Transnational Constitutionalism: International and European Perspectives* (Cambridge, 2007), 107.

L. Rodríguez-Piñero, *Indigenous Peoples, Postcolonialism, and International Law* (Oxford, 2005).

W. Sadurski, 'Promoting Rights in the Shadow of the Judiciary: Towards a Fact-Sensitive Theory of Judicial Review' (2001/14) European University Institute Working Papers LAW, 1.

M. Scheinin, 'The Right to Enjoy a Distinct Culture: Indigenous and Competing Uses of Land', in T. S. Orlin, A. Rosas & M. Scheinin (eds.), *The Jurisprudence of Human Rights Law: A Comparative Interpretative Approach* (Turku/Åbo, 2000), 159.

——, 'What are Indigenous Peoples?', in N. Ghanea & A. Xanthaki (eds.), *Minorities, Peoples and Self-Determination* (Leiden/Boston), 3.

D. Schiek, L. Waddington & M. Bell (eds.), *Cases, Materials and Text on National, Supranational and International Non-Discrimination Law* (Oxford/Portland Oregon, 2007).

A. Shachar, *Multicultural Jurisdictions: Cultural Differences and Women's Rights* (Cambridge, 2001).

O. Schachter, *International Law in Theory and Practice* (The Hague, 1991).

A.-M. Slaughter, *A New World Order* (Princeton, 2004).

S. Spiliopoulou Akermark, 'The Framework Convention for the Protection of National Minorities and the Future of Minority Protection in Europe', paper presented at Liverpool Law School on 1 December, 2006 (on file with author).

——, 'The Limits of Pluralism – Recent Jurisprudence of the European Court of Human Rights with Regard to Minorities: Does the Prohibition of Discrimination Add Anything?' (2002) 3 *Journal on Ethnopolitics on Minority Issues in Europe*, 1.

G. Stevens, '*Ogawa v. Hokkaido (Governor)*, the Ainu Communal Property (Trusts Assets) Litigation' (2005) 4 *Indigenous Law Journal*, 1.

H. J. Steiner, 'Individual Claims in a World of Massive Violations: What Role for the Human Rights Committee?', in P. Alston & J. Crawford (eds.), *The Future of UN Human Rights Treaty Monitoring* (Cambridge, 2000).

M. Suksi, 'Personal Autonomy as Institutional Form – Focus on Europe Against the Background of Article 27 of the ICCPR' (2008) 15 *International Journal on Minority and Group Rights*, 157.

L. Thio, *Managing Babel: The International Legal Protection of Minorities in the Twentieth Century* (Leiden/Boston, 2005).

P. Thornberry, *International Law and The Rights of Minorities* (Oxford, 1991).

P. Thornberry & M. A. Martin Estébanez, *Minority Rights in Europe: A Review of the Work and Standards of the Council of Europe* (Strasbourg, 2004).

S. Tierney, *Constitutional Law and National Pluralism* (Oxford, 2004).

Toggenburg (ed.), *Minority Protection and the Enlarged European Union: The Way Forward* (Budapest, 2004).

N. Tsagourias (ed.), *Transnational Constitutionalism: International and European Perspectives* (Cambridge, 2007).

J. Tully, 'Introduction', in A. Gagnon & J. Tully (eds.), *Multinational Democracies* (Cambridge, 2001), 1.

——, 'The Practice of Law-Making and the Problem of Difference: An Introduction to the Field', in O. A. Payrow Shabani (ed.), *Multiculturalism and Law: A Critical Debate* (Cardiff, 2007), 19.

United Nations, *We the Peoples: The Role of the United Nations in the 21st Century* (New York, 2000).

A. Verstichel, A. Alen, B. De Witte, & P. Lemmens (eds.), *The Framework Convention for the Protection of National Minorities: a Useful Pan-European Instrument?* (Antwerpen/Groningen/Oxford, 2008).

A. von Bogdandy, 'The European Union as Situation, Executive, and Promoter of the International Law of Cultural Diversity' (2008) 19 *European Journal of International Law*, 241.

B. Zangl, 'The Rule of Law: Internationalization and Privatization: 4. Is There an Emerging International Rule of Law?' (2005) 13 *European Review*, 73.

C. F. Zurn, *Deliberative Democracy and the Institutions of Judicial Review* (Cambridge, 2007).

F. Viljoen, *International Human Rights Law in Africa* (Oxford, 2007).

J. Waldron, *Law and Disagreement* (Oxford, 1999).

——, 'The Case Against Judicial Review' (2006) *Yale Law Journal*, 1348.

J. Webber, 'A Judicial Ethic for a Pluralistic Age', in O. A. Payrow Shabani (ed.), *Multiculturalism and Law: A Critical Debate* (Cardiff, 2007), 67.

J. H. H. Weiler, 'The State "über alles": Demos, Telos and the German Maastricht Decision' (1995) 6 *The Jean Monnet Working Papers*, 1.

M. Weller (ed.), *The Rights of Minorities: A Commentary on the European Framework Convention for the Protection of National Minorities* (Oxford, 2005).

—— (ed.), *Universal Minority Rights: A Commentary on the Jurisprudence of International Courts and Treaty Bodies* (Oxford, 2007).

S. Wheatley, *Democracy, Minorities and International Law* (Cambridge, 2005).

——, 'Minorities under the ECHR and the Construction of a "Democratic Society"' (2007) *Public Law*, 770.

J. Woehrling, 'L'obligation d'accommodement raisonnable et l'adaptation de la société à la diversité religieuse' (1998) 43 *Revue du droit de McGill*, 325.

A. Xanthaki, *Indigenous Rights and United Nations Standards: Self-Determination, Culture and Land* (Cambridge, 2007).

Index

www.ingramcontent.com/pod-product-compliance
Lightning Source LLC
LaVergne TN
LVHW080847300926
849162LV00003B/355